A COMPLICATED MAN

A Complicated Man

The Life of Bill Clinton

as Told by Those

Who Know Him

Michael Takiff

Yale

UNIVERSITY PRESS

New Haven and London

Published with assistance from the Kingsley Trust Association Publication Fund established by the Scroll and Key Society of Yale College.

Yale University Press books may be purchased in quantity for educational, business, or promotional use. For information, please e-mail sales.press@yale.edu (U.S. office) or sales@yaleup.co.uk (U.K. office).

Printed in the United States of America by The Maple-Vail Book Mfg. Group.

Library of Congress Cataloging-in-Publication Data
Takiff, Michael, 1955–
A complicated man : the life of Bill Clinton as told by those who know him /
Michael Takiff.
p.   cm.
Includes bibliographical references and index.
ISBN 978-0-300-12130-8 (cloth : alk. paper)
1. Clinton, Bill, 1946–. 2. Presidents—United States—Biography. 3. United States—
Politics and government—1993–2001. 4. Governors—Arkansas—Biography. 5. Ex-
presidents—United States—Biography. 6. Clinton, Bill, 1946– —Friends and associates.
7. Interviews—United States. 8. Arkansas—Biography. I. Title.
E886.T35 2010
973.929092—dc22   [B]   2010019584

A catalogue record for this book is available from the British Library. This paper meets the requirements of ANSI/NISO Z39.48-1992 (Permanence of Paper).

10   9   8   7   6   5   4   3   2   1

For Amy

Contents

Part III • Stumble, 1993–1994

Part IV • Recovery, 1995–1996

Part VI • Citizen Clinton, 2001–

Illustrations follow page 240

Author's Note

Throughout the book, I refer to President Clinton by his first name, Bill.

To refer to him as "Clinton," although a more usual practice in works of history, seemed impersonal. It seemed to create distance between the subject and the reader, when the goal of the book is intimacy.

The first name is used in order to help the reader follow the life and work of an individual, not an officeholder.

No disrespect is intended toward a former president of the United States.

A COMPLICATED MAN

Introduction

An Endless Argument

A remarkable talent. A gifted leader. A genius.
An overgrown teenager. A liar. A fool.
A consummate public servant.
A consummate narcissist.
A liberal.
A conservative.
A liberal in conservative's clothing.
A conservative in liberal's clothing.
A decent man with flaws.
A flawed man with no decency.
Uhhhh . . . Will the real Bill Clinton please stand up?
Wait—*is* there a real Bill Clinton? Are there *many* real Bill Clintons?
Who is Bill Clinton?

Bill Clinton did not come to the White House empty-handed: Among the assets he brought were a dazzling intellect, unmatched people skills, a passion for good governance, an insatiable curiosity. He had been a successful and long-serving governor of Arkansas. His upbringing had left him with the ability to understand and identify with the problems of ordinary people. His campaign had succeeded in painting his chief opponent, the incumbent president, George H. W. Bush, as the candidate of yesterday and the powerful, and himself as the candidate of tomorrow and the middle class. He advertised a program of investment in the nation's people and its future, and a determination to bring about what presidents for decades had tried but failed to accomplish: universal health insurance.

A substantial array of advantages with which to start his presidency—but his presidency did not start as planned. The outgoing administration's last-minute revisions of estimated budget deficits spurred a change in economic focus, from investment in knowledge and infrastructure to reduction of federal red ink. He made costly missteps—he was outmaneuvered and embarrassed on gays in the military;

he had trouble staffing his Justice Department. Established Washington treated him with disdain.

Initial moves in foreign policy were equally disappointing. He got the cold shoulder from China for tying trade relations to human rights. Two complex and perilous situations were not of his making—his predecessor had involved America in Somalia and dodged involvement in Bosnia; nonetheless, Bill did not handle those problems well. He slept while Rwanda burned. And for his first year and a half in office, he ran a White House that reflected, and was hobbled by, his own lack of intellectual and managerial discipline.

Still, his opening months in office saw big achievements. He pushed through a budget that cut spending and raised taxes (slightly) on the well-to-do, setting in motion a process that would lead to a budget surplus by the end of his tenure in office. And whether or not his "fiscal responsibility" was the cause, the economy boomed in the 1990s as never before. Against bitter opposition from his friends on the left of his party, he won the assent of Congress to the North American Free Trade Agreement. He defied the National Rifle Association to enact two major pieces of gun-control legislation.

In foreign affairs he laid the groundwork for a fruitful relationship with Boris Yeltsin's Russia and a peaceful resolution to "the Troubles" of Northern Ireland. With help from Jimmy Carter and without a shot being fired, he reinstalled the democratically elected leader of Haiti.

Yet by the time he'd been president for nineteen months, he had met with his most heartbreaking failure: health care reform. He chose his wife to lead the enormous undertaking; she recruited other brilliant minds to team with her own; together, they came up with a plan. The effort fell apart, because the plan was too complex and not well explained, or because she had not worked closely enough with Congress, or because the forces opposing it were too well funded and too willing to scare the public, or because Bill had taken hold of too many issues at once—or just because overhauling our nation's health care system was at that time impossible.

The failures of the first two years—and one of the successes, gun control—exploited by a savvy opposition led by the cunning Newt Gingrich, produced a stunning rebuke in the midterm elections of 1994. From then to the end of his presidency, Bill would have to work with a Congress controlled, in both houses, by the opposition party. Momentarily shaken by the slapdown, Bill came back. He trimmed his sails, playing "small ball" with initiatives like school uniforms and V-chips. He responded to a terrorist attack in Oklahoma City with rare humanity and warmth. He led NATO in finally standing up to ethnic cleansing in Bosnia.

And he picked a fight with Gingrich, now speaker of the House, over the upcoming budget. Cleverly, and with help from the unappealing and overconfident Gingrich, he succeeded in casting the speaker as the face of a heartless assault on middle America's way of life and himself as that way of life's defender. Seeking reelection, he tied Gingrich around the neck of the Republican nominee, Bob Dole, and barely broke a sweat on the way to a comfortable victory in November 1996, just two years after his political obituary had been written.

He was set up for a successful second term. He was prepared to spend political capital to take on an issue long considered the most perilous in Washington, entitlement reform. But a year into that term, the world learned of his affair with an intern young enough to be his daughter.

There is always the sex. During the time I was working on this book, whenever I would meet someone new and would answer the "So what do you do?" question, that person's follow-up to me would always be, "So, what did he see in Monica anyway?" Or "Who's he sleeping with now?" Or "Is he really a sex addict?" Or "How could he have been so stupid?" Never "Gee, what a bang-up job he did on the economy." Or "What an accomplishment it was to restore fiscal sanity to the government." Or "He sure did stick it to Slobodan Milošević." Or even "Man, he really blew it on health care" or "That SOB screwed the middle class on NAFTA."

For all his accomplishments as president, Bill Clinton is stuck, fairly or unfairly, with the image of a sex-crazed dude who loves to party, an incorrigible lech who can't resist a piece of ass no matter how awkward or inappropriate or dangerous the circumstances. (In fact, the titter factor forced a change from the original subtitle of this book: An Oral Biography of Bill Clinton.) And he had to know the circumstances with Monica were dangerous. For the Lewinsky matter to become the scandal it did required not only the sex but also the lying; not only the lying, but also a press corps willing to drop all else to focus on the story; not only a press corps willing to drop all else to focus on the story, but also a Republican opposition willing to paralyze the wheels of government for a year in order to pursue the scandal to its logical, absurd conclusion. Bill should not have been surprised: The press and the opposition acted exactly as they had been acting toward him since he'd campaigned in the New Hampshire primary six years earlier.

From the Gennifer Flowers story to his draft history to the Whitewater land deal to firings in the White House Travel Office to FBI files found where they shouldn't have been found to campaign-finance irregularities, the GOP and the press had been after Bill. For all their labors, however, they had been able to make nothing stick—at least not in the eyes of anyone beyond the Republican base. But here was one more crack at him—and it was the best yet. It was as though Bill's critics and opponents had been aiming guns at him from close range and firing nonstop— except that their wide variety of bullets, while noisy, were all blanks. By giving in to temptation with Monica, Bill was saying, "Sorry to have made you waste your time so far. Here's a truckload of live ammunition."

Once impeachment started, domestic policy stalled, so Bill looked overseas. He toured Africa, solved Northern Ireland—two observers who should know say that it's not an exaggeration to credit him with the end of the Troubles—and evicted

Milošević from Kosovo. In taking on the Middle East, Bill put all his gifts to work—his intellectual capacity to assimilate endless details of land swaps and security; his empathy for the needs and feelings of others, and his ability to communicate that empathy; his powers of persuasion; his explosive temper; his optimism—and nearly achieved the impossible: a final settlement of the Israel-Palestine conflict. But Yasir Arafat said no, and Bill left office with a second grand failure added to his flameout on health care.

Bill Clinton had the luck—good or bad—to serve in a time of relative quiet. He entered office as the Cold War ended and left as the War on Terror was about to begin. He served at a time when the public was suspicious of grand schemes, when it had little interest in being called to greatness.

Considering that limitation, Bill's accomplishments were not insignificant: He steered the economy to twenty-two million new jobs, the budget to surplus, and the tax code to a bit more fairness; he signed the Family and Medical Leave Act and welfare reform; he foresaw globalization and acted to ease the nation's adjustment to it; he helped calm the Balkans and Northern Ireland; at great political risk, he took action to save Mexico from financial ruin.

But shouldn't this rare politician have been able to accomplish more? Shouldn't he have produced that one shining achievement to prod history into judging him as something other than a competent steward of the nation's business between wars?

Perhaps not—and for reasons beyond his dalliance with Monica Lewinsky. Although a time of peace and prosperity, the nineties were hardly an era of good feeling. With the rise of Newt Gingrich—who had built his career on ad hominem attacks and intemperate language—the culture of the nation's capital became one of vilification rather than respect, of obstruction, not compromise.

And it wasn't only the rise of Gingrich that made life difficult for Bill and infected the nation's politics with ill will. For all Bill's ability to make people like him, some, from the beginning of his career in Arkansas, have always despised him—not just differing with him on issues, but actively, avidly, thoroughly hating his guts. He left office with 66 percent approval, according to Gallup—one point higher than Reagan's, it is the highest outgoing mark on record. But a minority of the country—not a majority by any means, but not an insignificant number, either—finds him loathsome.

Why? He governed, essentially, from the center. That posture certainly frustrated allies on the left but was hardly enough, by itself, to generate such animus on the right.

So was the hatred cultural—was it tied up in the conflicting forces that had roiled American society since the sixties? Did this "draft-dodging, pot-smoking" graduate of fine eastern universities embody, for some, the side of that decade that seemed to have brought us affirmative action, gay rights, and abortion? Was it resentment that Bill expropriated issues that conservative Republicans had owned for years—crime, welfare, fiscal prudence? Was it that Republicans simply could not accept the fact that their most prized possession, the presidency, had been taken from them?

Or was it less the haters' worldview than Bill's own personality? Is he, in fact, what people accuse him of being: a con man, a phony, a charlatan? Too facile in his language? Is he, to use the adjective applied to him long ago in Arkansas, "slick"? Bill's defenders would have us believe that it's all sour grapes—that such perceptions of him are no more than cover stories for people who have never been able to get over his theft, as they see it, of their culture, their issues, their White House. Certainly the rabid reaction in some quarters to the presidency of Barack Obama— "I want my country back"—makes clear that a minority of Americans will react with revulsion to any Democratic president. But do sour grapes, even enhanced by a dose of psychopathology, entirely explain Clinton hatred? I'm not sure.

I interviewed 171 people for this book—people who grew up with Bill Clinton, went to school with him, worked for him, worked against him, covered him, prosecuted him, defended him, loved him, hated him. Evenings, I'd report to my wife on the day's interviews. She tells me that my opinions are strongly and stubbornly held. She was, therefore, struck that I saw merit in the views of most of the people with whom I spoke, pro–Bill Clinton and con. One interviewee would argue in a loud voice that impeachment for lying about sex was a travesty! How did that qualify as "high crimes and misdemeanors"? *Hard to disagree with that,* I'd think. Another day I'd be told that lying under oath was simply wrong. It cannot be condoned, especially on the part of the president of the United States. *You've got a point there,* I'd want to say. The process was crystallized one day when I interviewed Dick Armey in the morning and Terry McAuliffe after lunch. Dick Armey has contempt for Bill Clinton. "The most successful adolescent I've ever known," he calls him. Terry McAuliffe loves Bill Clinton. "What a guy!" he kept saying. I walked away from McAuliffe's office wondering, *Were we talking about the same person?*

All American presidents must be protean figures to a degree—if not all things to all people, then many things to many people—in order to lead this large and diverse country. But in Bill's case, the opinions people hold of him are endlessly varied and often extreme, and every one of them—well, not the stuff about drug running and murder—can be argued with solid evidence to back it up. Indeed, the conflicting data are often found within the same issue.

Friend of the poor? Look at the overdue and worthwhile reform of welfare. Betrayer of the poor? Look at the cynical and callous reform of welfare. Courageous statesman? Look at the campaign of bombing from the air, in the face of a hostile Congress, to save lives in Kosovo. Political coward? Look at the refusal to even try to muster public and legislative support for sending ground troops, who could have saved more lives in Kosovo.

Detractors point to his exorbitant flaws, boosters to his prodigious talents. But no one can point to one momentous contribution and say, "Here is what this man achieved as president of the United States. Here is his lasting effect on the well-being of his fellow Americans and fellow members of the human race." Because that one momentous contribution—that one signature accomplishment that would change the world—eluded him. And so, for all we know about Bill Clinton politically and personally (and wish we didn't), he remains an enigma.

Principled battler for the common good? You bet. Shameless opportunist? Yup. Authoritative commander in chief? Affirmative. Feckless commander in chief? Indeed. Brilliant pragmatist? Yes. Inveterate compromiser, willing to sell out millions to get a deal? Right. A man of rare empathy? Obviously. Self-interested son of a bitch? Certainly. Liberal? Conservative? Centrist? Check, check, check.

One of the smartest people on the planet? No doubt. An unbelievable dope? And how.

And so the question: Who is Bill Clinton?

This book presents the argument over this complex, compelling, confounding American.

It will not settle that argument.

PART I

Local Hero

1946–1987

1

Small Town Boy:
Hope, Arkansas

"He was supposed to come back and get her."

On the morning of May 18, 1946, Marie Baker and Maxie Fuller were on duty at the Southwestern Bell switchboard on Second Street in Hope, Arkansas, population 7,475.[1] Both women were cousins of Virginia Cassidy Blythe, the twenty-two-year-old wartime bride of William Jefferson Blythe Jr., a salesman she had met three years earlier in Shreveport, Louisiana, where she was studying nursing.[2]

Marie Baker: I answered what was an inward, public signal. This operator told me, "We want the Eldridge Cassidy residence in Hope. We have an emergency for it." I turned around to Maxie and I said, "Oh, my lord, Maxie, something has happened. I'm getting an emergency call for the Eldridge Cassidy family." The cop—I guess it was the cop on the other end, in Missouri—said, "It's a death message."[3]

Bill Blythe had set out the previous afternoon from Chicago, where, just out of the army, he had landed a job selling heavy equipment. He'd intended to drive all night to Hope to pick up his pregnant wife and bring her back up north. But three miles outside of Sikeston, Missouri, a front tire blew out, and the Buick spun out of control. Rescuers searched for the driver for two hours before finding him in a drainage ditch. He had escaped the overturned car only to drown in three feet of water.[4]

Marie Baker: We knew it was Virginia's husband because we knew that he was supposed to come back and get her.

On August 19, fatherless, William Jefferson Blythe III was born. Later he would be called Bill Clinton.

"Laughing, happy, precious."

Margaret Polk was a distant cousin to Virginia, Bill's mother. Conrad Grisham and Myra Reese were first cousins to Virginia—their father and Virginia's mother,

Edith Grisham Cassidy, were brother and sister. Like all three, Hugh Reese, Myra's husband, was a longtime resident of Hope. Grisham and Hugh Reese are now deceased.

Margaret Polk: You could tell Clinton was going to be something from the time he was born. The Lord just cut him out to be something.[5]

Conrad Grisham: Virginia went to school not long after Bill was born. That's the reason her mother, Aunt Edith, raised him for his first few years. Aunt Edith loved Bill like her own child. "Eat, Billy, eat now, eat," she'd say, with him in the high chair. It's a wonder he hadn't been overweight more than he was those first few years, because she believed in children having plenty to eat.

Just after Bill turned one, his mother left for New Orleans, where for two years she would study to be a nurse-anesthetist.[6] She returned when she could, but while she was gone she left her son in the care of her parents, Edith and Eldridge Cassidy, whom Bill knew as Mammaw and Papaw.

Myra Reese: Aunt Edith took the responsibility of teaching him. I'd be there at mealtime. As he was eating she was showing him flashcards—ABCs and 123s. In the living room of that old house was a coffee table and that's where they had their study time. She had it filled with kindergarten books and preschool books. She had him reading when he was three.

He was never hard as a child. Aunt Edith would say that he had just as soon play with a powder can and a spoon as to have a new rattler. He didn't demand things.

Margaret Polk: Laughing, happy, precious, and the best thing!

Myra Reese: Aunt Edith drove this huge Buick. On Saturday she would drop the two of us off at the movie theater. That was about the extent of the entertainment in Hope, especially for that age child—he must have been six. I babysat him for the Saturday Westerns.

Myra Reese is seven years Bill's senior.

That let Aunt Edith go do her shopping. We would stay there for hours. It was no problem. He was a very well-behaved child.

The theater isn't here anymore. It was called the Saenger.

Hugh Reese: It was in downtown Hope on Second Street, near the Frisco Railroad. It was a very elaborate theater, real fancy, with a balcony. The balcony was for so-called "colored people."

• • •

George Wright Jr. was Bill's contemporary in Hope.

George Wright Jr.: All physicians' offices had a white waiting room and a colored waiting room. And that's what they had on the door. All restaurants had a colored section and a white section.[7]

Hugh Reese: We had a black high school, grade school, grammar school. We had a white high school, grade school, grammar school. All the churches: white Methodist, black Methodist; white Baptist, black Baptist.

George Wright Jr.: That's just the way we grew up in the small-town South. They had their section and we had our section. We never did mix that much.

Hugh Reese: Hope was typical. We were just like 99 percent of the other southern towns.

Raised on a farm, with only a fifth-grade education, James Eldridge Cassidy, Bill's grandfather, made deliveries for Southern Ice.[8]

Hugh Reese: Eldridge had been an ice man before Bill was born. Then he got the grocery store.

Tom Purvis: Back at that time there were quite a few iceboxes in town—not electric refrigerators, iceboxes—and he delivered ice.[9]

Tom Purvis, a few years older than Virginia, moved to Hope in 1941. Mary Nell Turner, around the same age as Purvis, was born in Hope.

Mary Nell Turner: Icebox—open the door and put the ice in.[10]

Hugh Reese: An outgoing, friendly, sociable guy. Gregarious. Billy inherits some of his charisma from his Grandpa Eldridge, I'm sure.

Margaret Polk: He was a ladies' man. He had another man on the ice route with him and he would send him on ahead, away from his girlfriend's house.

Myra Reese: As grocery stores go today, his was very small. He had a wood-burning stove in it. And a couple or three chairs sitting around, so that people did go in and gather and talk.

He bootlegged out of that store.

Hempstead County had gone dry in 1944.[11]

That brought in a little extra income and attention.

Marie Baker: Virginia said he had something in the bottom of the apple barrel. Everybody in Hope knew that.[12]

Margaret Polk: Another thing I want to tell. Edith bootlegged. She did, because we bought whiskey from her. Right out of that house!

Hugh Reese: North Hazel Street, where Eldridge had his store, was black. He had primarily black trade. Eldridge was very popular with the blacks. He didn't make any difference between a black man and a white man as far as coming in to do business with him. I'm sure Bill was influenced by that.

Joe Purvis: His grandfather treated everybody just the same.

Joe Purvis, Tom's son, attended kindergarten with Bill.

I don't think that was unusual in itself. I think the thing that made it unusual for Bill was that his dad was not around. I don't remember anybody else who was divorced or without two parents at that time. I'm sure Mr. Cassidy had an undue influence on Bill since he was the only male adult in his life for a while.

Decades later, Bill would still point to the lesson he learned from his grandfather, "an uneducated rural southerner without a racist bone in his body."[13]

An imposing, heavyset woman, Edith Cassidy, Bill's grandmother, worked as a private-duty nurse. Whereas Eldridge was likable and easygoing, Edith was competent and industrious—and not content with the modest income her husband brought home.[14]

Myra Reese: Aunt Edith and Uncle Eldridge would have their spats. Heated arguments. Eldridge drank quite a bit, and Aunt Edith didn't, and she didn't approve of that. Aunt Edith was a very, very opinionated person. Everything had to go her way or no way. He was a meek man.

Margaret Polk: She had hellfire in her, but she was a good woman. Eldridge was just as humble as a poor little kitten. She just bossed him like he was her little boy, but he didn't seem to mind. He'd go along with everything she said and wanted him to do. Now, I wouldn't say they were mean, she and Virginia, but they had a streak of hell in them.

Hugh Reese: Edith was the most prominent nurse in town. Really talented as far as the medical aspects of it, and then a great bedside manner. She would come in, pat you on the back, and say, "You're looking great this morning. You're improving wonderfully."

Joe Purvis: A lot of the nurses back then would wear nurses' outfits, and they'd wear these capes. A cape added an air of mystery to a lady, like somebody you'd see in one of the serials on Saturday at the "picture show," as we called it. I have memories of her picking Bill up at kindergarten with that kind of a cape on.

Kindergarten was held at Miss Marie Purkins' School for Little Folks.[15]

There were two sisters who owned the kindergarten: the Purkins sisters, both of whom were old maids.

The kindergarten was in their backyard. It was built like a small schoolhouse, with a bell that you would ring. There was one big open room. There were probably anywhere from thirty to fifty kids in that school at any one time. There was no public kindergarten then.

Bill very much was a good guy. I remember on several occasions different folks would get into it, and before an actual fistfight would break out Bill would be brokering the peace, saying, "You guys don't want to be mad at each other." He was a peacemaker.

He's always had some amazing abilities.

"Had a tremendous warm smile."

Conrad Grisham: Virginia had her mind on the future, even in high school. She had her mind on that nursing degree and went to Louisiana to school. She finally went to school enough that she was a registered anesthetist. That was her trade in the nursing business.

Margaret Polk: They worked at the same hospital—Virginia worked days and Edith worked nights.

Virginia and her son still lived with her parents in their two-and-a-half-story house on Hervey Street. With the two women of the house working, the child of the house needed another caregiver.

Donna Taylor Wingfield: Of course, both Billy and I had black nannies.[16]

Donna Taylor Wingfield was also a classmate of Bill's at Miss Marie's.

Margaret Polk: That old colored woman would work for them, to stay over here in the morning after Virginia went to work, about six-thirty or seven until about eleven-thirty or noon.

Conrad Grisham: Virginia was really easygoing. I never saw her get mad.

Joe Purvis: Virginia was always a laughing and fun-loving lady. Had a tremendous warm smile. In fact, in every memory I have of Virginia from growing up she was smiling.

On the other hand . . .

Margaret Polk: You better not cross her, because she'd be as mean as hell. She'd cuss you out.

Thomas F. "Mack" McLarty III attended kindergarten with Bill. He would be Bill's first White House chief of staff.

Mack McLarty: She was a truly loving and caring mother.

Margaret Polk: She smoked and drank. But she was a good nurse.

"Roger had bought her a lot of pretty clothes."

A frequent visitor to Eldridge Cassidy's grocery store—a man who supplied some of the liquor sold under Papaw's counter—was a car dealer who had moved to Hope from Hot Springs.

Hugh Reese: Physically, Roger Clinton was of real short stature. And real nice looking. Dark curly hair. Well dressed all the time. What we'd call a high roller in his gambling. He liked to party.

His brother Raymond owned the largest Buick distributorship in Arkansas, in Hot Springs. The Buick distributorship here came open for sale, and Roger got word of it through the GM grapevine. And came and bought it. That's why he came from Hot Springs to Hope. He was very successful here in that business.

Car dealerships were highly profitable, and you drove a new car yourself all the time. Your salesmen drove a new car. It was a very lucrative business. Especially GM.

The father of Donna Taylor Wingfield worked for Clinton Buick in Hope.

Donna Taylor Wingfield: It was a good dealership, a good business—made us all a good living. We weren't rich, but we weren't poor.

Hugh Reese: Not many Arkansans had a Cadillac in those days. Buicks were high up on the hog.

Even after discovering another woman's lingerie in Roger's apartment, Virginia decided to marry him.[17]

Margaret Polk: Roger had bought her a lot of pretty clothes. He'd given her beautiful things, and Edith just tied them up in the backyard and burned them. She was just that kind of person. Edith did that, the mother of Virginia. Because she didn't want Virginia to have anything to do with Clinton.

Edith threatened to seek custody of her grandson should her daughter marry the flashy auto salesman, but the attorney Edith consulted told her she had no case. Virginia, dazzled by the man nicknamed "Dude," went ahead and married him on June 19, 1950, when Bill was almost four. Edith and Eldridge did not attend the wedding.[18]

They wouldn't have anything to do with him, but he was all right. He worked hard. He had the Buick dealership here. He did all right. She drove a beautiful car and had everything she wanted.

"He shot at her."

Bill, his mother, and his stepfather, whom he called Daddy, moved into a small white bungalow on Thirteenth Street. The Taylors and the Polks were among their neighbors.

Margaret Polk: Bill had a little tricycle. I can see him now sitting and watching the street. He'd have loved to come across the street more, but they watched him.

Donna Taylor Wingfield: He wasn't allowed to cross the street. But I could cross over to his house. We could play up and down the street. When he broke his leg in kindergarten I could go over there. Because he had a cast on his leg, we would put his leg with the cast in a little red wagon and we would run up and down the sidewalk. Bill would push with one leg and had his leg with the cast in the wagon.

Clinton was a real sweet kid, but he was almost obsessed with being included in everything that went on in the block. The Mosleys lived down the street. They had three children, and if you were down at their house, here Billy would come, but he couldn't cross the street. Something happened one day when we were playing out in his yard and we got aggravated at him for something, so the next day we weren't playing with him. He came down the street where we were playing and he told us he got a new swing set. We decided he was okay then. We weren't mad at him any more.

From the beginning, the marriage was troubled. On some of the occasions when Roger came home drunk—which he did not infrequently—he would sit quietly by himself in whatever room was unoccupied by his wife and stepson. Other times he would be verbally abusive, usually accusing his wife of infidelity.[19] One night he went beyond words.

Margaret Polk: They had that shooting over here, right across the street.

Donna Taylor Wingfield: Roger had been drinking, and he had a gun.

Virginia had readied Billy for a trip to the local hospital, where her maternal grandmother lay dying. Roger objected to their leaving. When Virginia refused to change her plans, he took out his gun.[20]

Margaret Polk: He shot at her. He missed her, but the holes are over in that house.

In fact, Roger fired only one shot. Virginia believed he was trying to scare her, not hit her.[21]

Donna Taylor Wingfield: The police came down.

Margaret Polk: He was a good-looking young man, and he was a good man. The night that he did that shooting, nobody wanted to call the police on him. No, but I had a brother who was the night clerk at the old Barlow Hotel up by the railway. He walked up and said, "I'll call the police."

Donna Taylor Wingfield: Virginia and Billy came over and stayed at our house.

Margaret Polk: They locked him up for the night, but they got back together and moved to Hot Springs.

Hugh Reese: Roger came from Hot Springs. And Hot Springs is a different culture from almost anywhere else in Arkansas.

2

A Big City (pop. 29,307): Hot Springs

"Bill Clinton and I ate matzoh-ball soup."

The young family stayed in Hope only three years. In the summer of 1953, after Billy Clinton, as he was now known, had completed first grade at the Brookwood School, Roger sold his business and relocated the household to a four hundred−acre farm just outside Hot Springs, the resort town known for its soothing waters, its sparkling nightlife, and its intoxicating gambling.[1] Roger tried his hand at farming, but the simple life—featuring a wooden outhouse as the household's only toilet—quickly lost its appeal for the husband and wife who loved a drink and a party. Soon Virginia was working long hours at the two hospitals in town. Bill also spent his days in town, at Saint John's Catholic School, preferred by his mother over the small rural school closer to the farm.

The Clintons lasted on the farm barely past the first frost. Accepting a position as parts manager at his brother Raymond's Buick dealership, Roger moved his family into town.[2]

Patty Howe Criner, a year older than Bill, attended Saint John's and then public school with him. Bill's first stepcousin Roy Clinton Jr., a dozen years older than Bill, is the son of Roger Clinton's brother Roy. Clay Farrar went through the Hot Springs school system four years behind Bill.

Patty Howe Criner: Bill Clinton would've probably never been elected president had he not grown up in Hot Springs.[3]

Roy Clinton Jr.: Hot Springs is like a big old Catholic church. There is somebody from every place in the world from Estonia to Albania to Malaysia to whatever.[4]

Patty Howe Criner: Hot Springs was exciting, eclectic, unlike any city in the state of Arkansas. Even people who live in Hot Springs now say, "Well, it's the craziest place we've ever been, but it's home and it's different." There was a huge Jewish community in Hot Springs. Bill Clinton and I ate matzoh-ball soup and knew what a blintz was.[5]

Clay Farrar: We were one of two places in the entire United States of America where you had casino gambling. You had Las Vegas and us, and it was a big deal here.[6]

Patty Howe Criner: We had met every great entertainer around the country by the time we were 12. We had seen the candelabra ring that Liberace wore. We had seen his long fur coats. We had heard great performances because Hot Springs was such a tourist attraction.[7]

Roy Clinton Jr.: There weren't whorehouses on every corner in other towns like there were in Hot Springs, trust me. Nor bars, nor slot machines in bars. Hot Springs was wide open.

Patty Howe Criner: I have friends who say, "I never met anyone from New York until I was in college," or, "I never met a Catholic until I was in high school." In Hot Springs, people from all over the world came.[8]

Lonnie Luebben and Paul Root taught Bill at Hot Springs High School.

Lonnie Luebben: The circus used to winter here, so all of a sudden the classrooms would swell with some extra students who had been all over the country with the circus.[9]

Paul Root: I don't know of any other place in Arkansas where Bill Clinton could have grown up with the attitudes he came out of Hot Springs with: a broad sense of what a lot of different kinds of people do and think and how they live.

"Hi, I'm Bill Clinton."

Roger Clinton told his wife that he'd bought the house at 1011 Park Avenue. In fact, the family's new dwelling belonged to Raymond. Roger had mismanaged the Hope dealership, and what money he did receive for its sale he gambled away. His brother was helping him get back on his feet.[10]

Bill spent two years in Catholic school, then enrolled in public elementary school.

Paul Leopoulos: I was going to a little neighborhood school called Ramble School. In the fourth grade one day on the playground this guy came up and he said, "Hi, I'm Bill Clinton." Kids didn't normally do that. We grew up together as best friends for, now, fifty-something years. When you're friends with him you are always friends with him.

Paul Leopoulos and Rose Crane went to school with Bill.*

Rose Crane: It was a classic red brick schoolhouse, and it had giant old windows that the teacher had to have a pole to pull the top down to get air. There certainly was no air-conditioning. And old wooden floors and old wooden desks.[11]

Paul Leopoulos: In those days I was a skinny little runty Greek guy and I was scared to death of school and I stuttered. He probably noticed this guy who looked lost, which he would do.

Rose Crane: He would have been the valedictorian of our sixth-grade class, except that he got a "B" in deportment for talking.[12]

Paul Leopoulos: We were at each other's house all the time in the summer. In Hot Springs there was gambling, but our growing up was just real. It was touch football and Monopoly and canasta and Elvis Presley. Small-town values. A simple, wonderful life.

One Thanksgiving I walked down to his house just to say hi. Virginia was cooking their Thanksgiving dinner and he wasn't there. A couple minutes later he comes in and he's with this kid that we didn't know. Virginia says, "Who's your friend?" Well, there was a city bus stop right at the bottom of his driveway on Park Avenue. And this boy was sitting at the bus stop and Bill had gotten to know him. Probably went up to him and said, "Hi, I'm Bill Clinton." He said to Virginia, "His mom and dad are divorced and he's not going to have Thanksgiving dinner today. Would you mind if he has Thanksgiving dinner with us?" This is at nine years old. Typical Bill Clinton. And of course she said, "No problem."

Patty Howe Criner: Bill Clinton has never met a stranger since the day he was born.[13]

Virginia's anesthesia practice flourished in Hot Springs, even if she bristled under the condescension of the town's male medical establishment. As full as her surgical schedule was, during horseracing season she managed to perform most of her duties in the morning, leaving afternoons free to cheer the thoroughbreds at Oaklawn Park.[14]

Her marriage, on the other hand, foundered. While she and Roger enjoyed the

---

*Paul Leopoulos was known during childhood by his middle name, David, and is thus referred to as David in Bill's autobiography, My Life (New York: Knopf, 2004).

town's nightlife, she grew tired of his drinking and his increasing violence toward her. Still, she and her family kept their domestic troubles private.

Rose Crane: When we were very small kids playing, sometimes Virginia would come in and she would say, "It's time for you to go home." I thought that I had done something wrong. I know now that she was getting everybody out of the house because Roger had come home having had too much to drink and she didn't know what was going to happen.[15]

Roy Clinton Jr.: Roger drank to excess. Virginia drank. They partied a lot. They would have spats. Roger was never going to change.

Bill's Clinton stepcousins liked their uncle.

Liz Clinton-Little: Uncle Roger was a hoot. He was always joking and carrying on and everything.[16]

First stepcousins Liz Clinton-Little and Dan Clinton are Roy Jr.'s younger sister and brother.

Roy Clinton Jr.: Roger was always loving, great with kids, always giving you money—"Here's a quarter, go get something"—playful.

Liz Clinton-Little: I never saw anything but the fun between the two of them. I never saw any fighting or any kind of thing like that. Uncle Roger did drink, but he was a funny drunk when he was drunk.

The problems he created for Bill notwithstanding, Roger did help his stepson develop what would be a lifelong passion.

Dan Clinton: When I was in grade school, Roger gave me a soprano saxophone that he played.[17]

Roy Clinton Jr.: He played in a band.

Dan Clinton: He was a real musician. He could sit down and play almost anything.

When I graduated to an alto sax, I gave the soprano sax back, and I think Bill used it. I'm not sure. I know they had it—I think Bill used it to start with, too.

In *My Life,* Bill reports that he "started band" in the fourth grade playing clarinet, then switched to tenor sax about a year later. He does not mention his stepfather's musical talent.[18]*

---

*Rose Crane also recalls that Bill began his musical studies with the clarinet.

"Honest injun, Bubba."

Finally, Virginia had had enough of her husband. In April 1962, before Bill's sixteenth birthday, she and her two sons—she had given birth to young Roger in 1956—moved out of the house on Park Avenue. After three weeks in a motel, she bought a newly constructed house, which boasted central heat and air conditioning, on Scully Street. She paid for it with money she'd been saving for just such an eventuality.[19]

Although Virginia promptly divorced Roger, she could not get rid of him. "He was pitiful that summer," Virginia would recall. "He would park his car across the street from our house and sit there in the long summer twilights, until finally I would break down and go get in the car with him." Some nights he slept on Virginia's concrete front porch. Roger implored his stepson to ask Virginia to take him back. Bill, however, advised the opposite: "Mother, in my opinion, that would be a mistake." But Virginia, feeling more pity than love, went ahead and remarried Roger. The divorce had lasted three months.[20]

Marie (Clinton) Bruno, daughter of Roy Clinton Jr., is Bill's first stepcousin once removed. Carolyn Staley, daughter of a Baptist minister, moved to Hot Springs in 1961, in time to attend high school with Bill. She lived next door to the Clintons on Scully Street and, like Paul Leopoulos, is one of the preeminent "Friends of Bill" (FOBs)— as are known the thousands of people Bill has come across, and not let go of, throughout his life.

Marie Bruno: Aunt Virginia was ebullient, outgoing, fun. She wasn't in the children-should-be-seen-and-not-heard category that a lot of us were being raised in. Spoke her mind, lots of laughing, smoked a lot. She was a loving, caring, giving person.

Carolyn Staley: We were just teenagers, but Virginia looked at us and said, These are people worth investing in-depth conversations in.

Paul Leopoulos: From the time we were eight, nine, ten years old, when she would come home in the summer, it was the same routine every time. She'd make her coffee. Bill and I would be standing in the kitchen with her and she would invariably be talking about some issue. Maybe a black man had died because he couldn't get health care. She was always talking about those kinds of things.

When he was younger, he would listen, listen, listen, and ask questions. The older we got—tenth, eleventh, twelfth grades—he would react to what she said and then pretty soon he would even disagree with her at times and they would have verbal back and forth, like in a college debate. It was amazing to watch. Who else did that? Who cared about those issues so fervently at that age?

Carolyn Staley: Those wheels were always turning. The idea that people have an obligation to help others was very much in Bill's heart and mind from an early stage.

Paul Leopoulos: She was black and white: There's right and there's wrong. Oh, she gambled and all that kind of stuff, but she was a lady of very high standards in terms of helping other people and making a difference in this world.

Carolyn Staley: She was passionate about her belief in Bill and his friends. She treated Bill as an adult, and he seemed older than a lot of other kids because he was responsible for young Roger, getting him after school. So Bill was generally home from the afternoon on and would do his homework, and Roger would do *his* homework. Or Bill would practice the saxophone.

It was almost like parent and child because it was such an age difference. What is it, ten years? Bill taught him ethical behavior. When Roger would say something, Bill would say, "Honest injun?"

"Honest injun, Bubba."

He called him Bubba. If Bill needed to run an errand and Virginia and Roger Sr. weren't home, Roger always went with us. Roger went with us to movies. Bill never once complained. He never saw Roger as cramping his style.

Mike Karber, another classmate, also lived on Bill's block.

Mike Karber: Billy was so protective of him. He loved that boy.

Just before big Roger's return, Bill went to the courthouse to at last change his name legally from Blythe to the name by which he'd long been known, Clinton. His brother was about to begin school; Bill wanted to make things easy for him. Perhaps, Bill later suggested, he also intended the change as a gesture of goodwill toward Daddy.[21]

Mike Karber: I can remember eating at their house one time. It seems like it was sandwiches, because she was so busy as a professional.

Clay Farrar: Before the mid-1970s, you really did not have many practicing physician anesthesiologists. So, as a result, she was the number-one—for all practical purposes—anesthesiologist in Hot Springs.

Mike Karber's wife, Laura, lived in Hot Springs, as well. She is the same age as young Roger.

Laura Karber: She was a good mom but she wasn't a big homemaker.

Carolyn Staley: Virginia had a housekeeper who came. She would make fried pies and Bill loved those. It's a circle of pie-crust dough, with fruit, sugar, and some butter put on half of it, and then you fold it over and you take a fork and crimp around the edges and you deep-fry it. That was a real treat to come home and have that. Bill's diet was terrible.

Patty Howe Criner: She would leave the house, and I've actually seen notes left on the refrigerator that would say, "I sure do love you, son. Mother." And there would be a note there later in the day that he wrote back and put on the refrigerator, to her: "I love you, too."[22]

Carolyn Staley: Because she normally had her surgeries in the morning, when I would see her in the evening she always had on her pajamas and her mule houseshoes. Or she was in the backyard in a tube top and shorts, working on her roses.

But what I remember of her at home was that she was doing her own thing and there was very little interaction between her and her husband, Roger Sr.

"I think that's a southern thing."

Readmitted to the Clinton household, Roger was chastened, and more withdrawn than before, although the violent incidents did not cease entirely.[23] And still, the Clintons guarded their secrets.

Paul Leopoulos: The troubles Bill had with his stepfather—we never knew about it. Never. I would see Roger sit on a couch, sort of docile. He never acted out when I was in there.

The first time I knew about it was, there was the first deep article written about Bill in early '92, when he first started running for president. The article told all about that. I read it and I'm going, "What?"

I think that's a southern thing. We all grew up feeling that your personal life is *your* business.

Mike Karber: Roger was quiet. I'd call him a man's man. He worked on cars. That's what he did for a living and he sometimes had grease on his hands. He and Virginia didn't seem to match. Just by her being the loud and him being the quiet, and her being a medical professional and him being an advanced mechanic. They just didn't seem to geehaw, to use a good old southern term.

Bill finally aired his family's dirty linen when he ran for president.

At the Democratic National Convention in July 1992, the party's nominee was introduced by a film, *The Man from Hope*. Bill's campaign had made the video as part of its effort to rehabilitate Bill's character in the public mind after revelations of extramarital sex, draft-dodging, and marijuana use. In the film, Bill described an incident that took place when he was fourteen. One night he heard his stepfather beating his mother behind the closed door of their bedroom. Bill picked up a golf club, opened the door, and threatened to beat Roger with the club if he didn't stop. "Never . . . *ever* . . . touch my mother again," he said, according to his mother's account. Roger did stop.[24]

The story's picture of courage and filial devotion played a key role in the successful reintroduction of the candidate to the American electorate. The Clinton side of Bill's extended family, however, found the publicity painful.

Marie Bruno: The inferences that were made on my family during the 1992 campaign really upset my grandmother, because she knew what all happened. I wasn't there. I'm not quite sure if some of the things that allegedly happened are true or not, but who am I to say?

She had a chance to confront Aunt Virginia that summer about some of the things—when Aunt Virginia was talking about the gunfire that Uncle Roger shot and all that. Aunt Virginia was in town; she had stopped in to see how my grandmother was doing. I just so happened to walk in right after Aunt Virginia left. I saw my grandmother and she was crying. Apparently, there were some very heated words said by her: "How dare you say this about our family?" And "Why are you doing this? You're destroying our name."

You don't see your grandmother cry very much, and she was in tears.

I did notice some changes after that, some backtracking. I remember an interview Aunt Virginia did, saying, "Gosh, I know I said some harsh things, but alcoholism is a disease. It wasn't understood back then like we understand it now. He was a good man." I'm convinced that conversation with my grandmother had a lot to do with that.

A lot of inferences were made that the entire Clinton family—my family—were all bad people, rednecks and all that. That upset me a lot.

If you look in any family, you'll find warts. I understand why Bill told that story, but it didn't feel good.

• • •

Carolyn Staley, Bill's next-door neighbor, holds memories of Roger at odds with the image conveyed in 1992's carefully constructed presentation of Bill's life.

Carolyn Staley: Roger was a quiet man. He worked in the parts department at the Clinton Buick business. Bill and I both had part-time summer jobs taking inventory there. If you've been in a parts shop, there were these little three-inch boxes with nuts and screws and bolts and all that. We would have to count them. I would be up on a ladder counting or Bill would be up counting—we'd take turns. And gaskets and tailpipes.

Bill went to band camp one week and I was doing it by myself. And a car came in that had been involved in a fatality. I guess I was walking past his little window—you know how parts guys would sit in a little glassed-in place with a half-moon window, kind of like a ticket booth in a movie theater. He said to me, "Carolyn"—and he never talked much, so this was something— "Carolyn, I want you to walk out there." And he pointed out to the lot where cars to be repaired were parked. "I want you to walk out there and take a look at that car." I went out and I bent down and I looked in, and there was flesh hanging from the steering column. I had never seen anything like that. I got myself together and I walked back in, and he said, "You drive carefully." A man of very few words, but he wanted to get a point across to me.

The fact that he wanted me to have that experience to make me a careful driver said, "I love you. You matter. Be careful."

Virginia was so, so sad when he died. She gave me a really pretty little gold bangle bracelet. It was inscribed something like, "To Carolyn. Love, Roger." She'd had it made—just a token of my being special in his life, his being special in mine. He thought of me in kind of a daughter way, I think.

I loved him, and I know he loved me. I never saw him drunk. I never saw the rotten side. I'm sure it's all true. It just was not my experience.

In the spring of 1967 Roger spent time at Duke University Medical Center to undergo treatment for cancer. Bill, finishing his junior year at Georgetown, drove every Friday from Washington to Durham to spend the weekend with him. In the fall, as Roger's condition worsened, Bill returned to Hot Springs, where the deathwatch was under way. The two men spoke to each other that year with more candor and affection than ever before. "We came to terms with each other," Bill remembered, "and he accepted the fact that I loved and forgave him."[25]

Roger died in November.[26]

"He walked around like he was running the place."

"High school was a great ride," Bill would recall.[27]

Paul Leopoulos: He really consumed school. In social studies class we had all kinds of debates about whatever was going on during those days—Nixon and Kennedy and all that kind of stuff. And there was Bill debating. In English, he got a B. I think that was the only B he got. And he was livid—*li-vid*.

The teachers cared about all of us and it was a close community. There were cliques, but everybody got along with everybody else. Of course, what was missing was that it was totally segregated. After a while it just sort of hit us. I remember asking my mom, "Why are there no blacks?"

Carolyn Staley shared Bill's love of music. She sang and played piano.

Carolyn Staley: There was a black high school and they had the best band and the best drum section and the best beat. We always loved to hear the Langston High School Band in the Christmas parade because they just played rings around our guys.

It was a thread that ran through our discussions at home and in the community. We knew that the Little Rock integration of Central High had been a national news item, a black eye for our state.* We knew that an integrated society was the right society and that it would take years.

As exceptional as Hot Springs was, it could also be comfortably normal.

Paul Root: It was two different towns. Downtown was cosmopolitan. The south part of town was a fairly typical conservative Arkansas town.

Paul Leopoulos: None of us drank, we didn't smoke, weren't into drugs. Bill would have dates but he didn't date all the time.

Clay Farrar: He was a total straight arrow—no alcohol at all—basically was almost shy around the coeds.

Paul Leopoulos: A weekend was going to a Trojan football game—we were the Hot Springs Trojans—and then going to Cook's Ice Cream after that, which was this drive-in. Then we'd go to his house and play hearts until one

---

*When Governor Orval Faubus defied a federal order to integrate Little Rock's Central High School in 1957, President Eisenhower sent troops of the U.S. Army to enforce the law.

in the morning. Almost every weekend that's what it was. And the band: He was always all-state everything, so he would go on band trips.

Summers, Bill would attend band camp in Fayetteville.[28]

Carolyn Staley: Kids from all over the state would come and spend a week. They were the brightest, most talented kids. By the time the week was over he had a new girlfriend.

The girls didn't bother me. We were always good friends. There was a short window where we went from friendship to dating, but it was brief. I did know that girls were attracted to him, and he seemed to have a real talent for attracting women.

That figured in my comfort zone of whether or not I wanted to pursue the relationship any further, if it had been possible. I always had been living in the world of monogamous relationships and that was my ideal. And with him I couldn't have real peace about whether that would be. I mean, even when he and I were dating, there were girls.

I always felt that he belonged to the world almost. I didn't need to be possessive.

Lonnie Luebben taught Bill in her eleventh-grade honors English class. Paul Root taught Bill tenth-grade World History.

Lonnie Luebben: Bill was a fine student. Believe it or not, he said very little. He was very quiet. He was an attentive listener who would follow the speaker with his eyes. One could imagine that he was taking it all in and remembering it.

Mike Karber: Billy knew everything about this, he knew everything about that. He acquired knowledge like a magnet gets steel. Yeah, he was an intellect.

Paul Root: He was an excellent student, and unusually easy to get along with. He read all the time.

He was interested in almost everything. He wasn't preparing to be a doctor or a lawyer or anything of that sort. He was studying the world.

Carolyn Staley: He wasn't in the geek crowd, but he competed academically at a geek level. He constantly was trying to make a better grade than the guys who were known as the calculus whiz or the physics whiz.

He's very bright so he was quick. He always did his homework, but in terms of needing to go back and drill over things, I don't think he did a lot of that.

Mike Karber: His time was taken up with his extracurricular activities because he was into and doing everything.

Lonnie Luebben: All-State Band, Student Council, Key Club, Mu Alpha Theta, Beta Club, Junior Classical League, Band Key Club, Trojan Pep Band, Starlight Dance Band, Trojan Marching Band, Junior Class President, Boys State, and Boys Nation. He was a very visible student.

Mike Karber: The sense of him around school was that he *was* somebody and would *be* somebody. He was a presence.

Clay Farrar: A lot of the kids at Hot Springs High School thought he was a member of the faculty because he would wear a coat and tie to school. He walked around like he was running the place.

Lonnie Luebben: Some teachers sensed that something special was going to happen with Bill. We sensed it was political. The assistant principal, Johnnie Mae Mackey, was a figure in the state Democratic Party. She was very interested in Bill.

Mike Karber: She was assistant principal our sophomore and junior years in charge of discipline, and could that lady swing a paddle. Billy probably doesn't know that but I do. She could raise you off the floor.

I'm sure she and Bill had times that they sat down and talked about what the future held for him.

Carolyn Staley: She encouraged him at every turn. She invited him to be a student representative to meetings of the school board and different things like that. She nurtured that kind of leadership in him.

When he went to Boys State, when he went to State Band Camp, he met everybody. He was also involved in the Masonic program DeMolay, which was a service organization for young men. They had state meetings. So you could argue that before he even left high school, he knew the leadership of the state. He knew people in every town in Arkansas. He already had quite a constituency.

Paul Root, who taught music as well as history at Hot Springs High, moved on after Bill's sophomore year.

Paul Root: A year and a half after I left the high school, I got a call from this choir director who was taking a vacation and asked me to fill in for him in his church in Hot Springs. So I went there and I saw Bill Clinton in the congregation. When church was over that night, he came up and he said, "Have you got a few minutes? Let's go talk." So we went to a little restaurant right down the street from the church, and talked for a couple of hours. He was graduating and he was planning to go to Georgetown. His eyes were big and his goals were way out above what I had thought about or expected. He talked about the things he wanted to do. He talked about the problems of Arkansas.

I don't remember if we talked about what he would do after he had gotten all of his education, but I somehow knew he was coming back to Arkansas.

I started thinking about him as a potential governor along about that time.

Robert Haness: This always sounds terrible, but my first impression of him was that he was a band nerd.[29]

Robert Haness attended junior high and high school with Bill.

Bill's saxophone was as important to him as his classwork. He and two fellow students formed a jazz trio, the 3 Kings, that entertained at various school functions. He played in the concert and marching bands, as well as in the school dance band, the Stardusters.[30]

Rose Crane: I think in younger years if someone had asked me, I'm fairly sure I would have said that he was going to be a rock-n-roll star. I remember him racing over with a 45 record—the old single records with the big centers in them—and he said, "You gotta hear this guy. He's gonna be great." It was Elvis Presley and the song was "Hound Dog."[31]

He started his music on the clarinet in grade school. I would listen to him practice, and it was pretty grim for a while.[32]

Carolyn Staley: Music was always an underpinning, whether it was the focus of why we were together—to listen to a new album, to go shopping for records—or just to have it in the background. Music was always on.

Sometimes we'd listen to symphonies. He loved Dvořák. He also loved jazz—he often had Dave Brubeck on or Stan Getz. We loved listening to the great sax players. Boots Randolph. And then there was Ray Charles—he was in a class by himself.

He was very serious about saxophone. I had the piano, so our rehearsals for his solos were at my house, and they were all business. We would run through a piece and work until we got it just right.

He was offered, unsolicited, a music scholarship to Louisiana State University. At that point he had already decided to go to Georgetown. He said later that he didn't think he was good enough to be a professional. Also, if he did go into it, he would likely go the direction of jazz and he didn't want to be up all night. He didn't want the lifestyle that went with being a jazzman.

(The countless recipients of 2 A.M. phone calls over the years might suggest that Bill kept jazzman's hours anyway.)

For the time being, however, Bill enjoyed the special prestige accorded musicians at Hot Springs High.

Paul Root: We were really good in music, and not bad in basketball. But we didn't have a good football team.

Paul Leopoulos: Our team was so bad because all the skinny guys were on the football team and all the big guys were in the band. Bill weighed probably 220 pounds in those days. Our linemen on the football team were 165, 180.

Paul Root: I think we tied one game and won one in the three years I taught there. I don't know, he might have played football if the attitude about football had been different. But he never did and we never won.

Liz Clinton-Little: Bill was never really athletic. Bill didn't even learn how to ride a bicycle until after he was out of high school.

"He knew."

The American Legion sponsored Boys State and Girls State, each one a week-long citizenship program run in every state for high school students. During the summer of 1963, after their junior year, Bill and his next-door neighbor both attended.

Carolyn Staley: We went two different weeks: Boys State was first and Girls State came next. That really was a turning point.

The teachers nominated the students who would go—maybe a dozen boys, a dozen girls, from our school. We went to Camp Robinson, which was a World War II base here in North Little Rock. There were probably five or six hundred kids there, maybe more, from all over the state.

The students slept in the camp's barracks.

It was a week of learning how state government and state elections work. You started the very first night, divided into two parties, the Federalists and the Nationalists, and positioned in cities. If you wanted to run for mayor or for dogcatcher, you had to muster the votes, and there was balloting the first night. It was a system of party caucuses, then elections, culminating in running for senator, governor, lieutenant governor, secretary of state, and on down the line. Each state in the United States sent two senators to Boys Nation and to Girls Nation.

Bill knew that winning a Senate seat meant a trip to the nation's capital. He arrived politicking.

Joe Purvis: I have a mental picture of him standing there in one of the ugliest pairs of shorts I ever saw that looked like they were made out of material somebody's grandmother would make drapes out of. He's standing there talking to somebody, shaking his hand with one hand and had the other hand on the guy's shoulder. It's the same thing you'll see in him now. He'll shake hands with you and it's more than just the simple shaking of the hand. The other hand will be on your arm, your shoulder, somewhere, and he gives you that intense gaze right into your eyes so that it seems like you've been talking for quite a while and it may only be ten or fifteen seconds. You've got his undivided attention.

The Clinton magic worked; he was bound for Washington.

Housed in dormitories at the University of Maryland in nearby College Park, the boys of Boys Nation were given the red-carpet treatment by the city's potentates. Bill lunched with Arkansas's two barons of the Senate, J. William Fulbright and John McClellan, but the highlight of the week was the visit of all the boys to the Rose Garden to meet President John F. Kennedy. After his remarks, JFK approached the boys. Bill stepped forward. "I made sure I'd get to shake his hand," he would recall, "even if he shook only two or three."[33] Twenty-nine years later, as Bill campaigned for the keys to the same Rose Garden, Americans would see the photograph and film footage of the historic handshake.

Carolyn Staley: Having access to members of Congress, being in the halls of the Capitol, riding on the underground train system—that was heady for us. The spoken and unspoken message of that entire week was, "Government's a good thing, public service needs you. It's a high calling."

When Bill applied to college, he had only one school on his list: the Georgetown University School of Foreign Service. Mrs. Irons, our guidance counselor, was hysterical that he had applied to only one school. It was assumed that you'd apply to two or three at least, so you had safe schools.

He got in.

He was positioning himself. From his trip to Boys State and then Boys Nation, from that point on, he knew: Yeah, it's politics, it's service.

3

Positive, Positive, Positive, Positive:
Georgetown

"He was testing himself."

Melanne Verveer: I have these mental snapshots of him sitting on a stoop on campus and having lots of people surrounding him.

Melanne Verveer and her husband, Phil, attended Georgetown two years ahead of Bill, she in the Institute of Languages and Linguistics, he in the School of Foreign Service. Melanne Verveer would be First Lady Hillary Clinton's chief of staff.

Here he was a Protestant from a southern state coming up to Washington to a Catholic university, where there were a lot of foreign students. It was a place where he was introduced to the world in many ways. I think he really got into it and kept growing as a result of it.

Phil Verveer: It would be fair to say that he had a very, very successful time of it at Georgetown.

Georgetown in 1964 harbored two distinct identities. The undergraduate college of arts and sciences, called the Yard, was 96 percent Catholic and 100 percent male. But a few blocks away was the East Campus, containing schools of business and languages in addition to the School of Foreign Service, and attracting a more eclectic student body—including even women.[1]

Christopher Hyland: The School of Foreign Service was not just Catholic.

Christopher Hyland attended the School of Foreign Service in the class two years behind Bill's.

There were Buddhists and Hindus and Jews and Protestants and others. Nonetheless, it was still basically a white, affluent world. The number of Southern Baptists would have been very few.

Phil Verveer: The orientation of the student body was strongly Northeast. His being southern was a quality I think he was able to play up, to suggest: "I'm just a fellow who fell off the turnip truck. I'm not as sophisticated as the rest of you."

He has intellectual qualities that are absolutely unusual. He played those down at Georgetown. He may have played them down much of his life. I suspect it's because of an instinct that people might not like him if they thought he was so much smarter than they were. Consciously or subconsciously, there was a tendency not to want to let people know that he was literally a genius.

Phil Verveer: Shortly after freshman students arrived, there would be an election for the president of the class.

Once again, Bill wasted no time before launching his campaign. He sized up the competition, enlisted friends to help him distribute mimeographed fliers throughout the East Campus, and shook every hand he could find.[2]

He won that election.

Tommy Caplan: That was an unusual thing for a guy who had not gone to a Catholic school.

Thomas Caplan, now a novelist, lived a few doors away from Bill on the second floor of Loyola Hall.

It wasn't a question of your religion, it was a question of the number of people you already had as friends. If you came from Xavier High School in New York, you came with a whole batch of friends. There were three or four of those schools that fed Georgetown. He'd come from a different world and was still elected president of the class. That meant that he was testing himself. I think he was discovering, first, that his gifts were adequate, and then, that they were more than that.

"To hell with Plato!"

Among the professors with the most influence on Bill was the one teaching Development of Civilizations, a course required of all freshmen.

Tommy Caplan: Carroll Quigley was a great teacher. He was able to make huge concepts real to kids, and he was a captivating performer. It was a class you didn't want to miss.

Christopher Hyland: There were ideas flowing out of him like a machine gun: "To hell with Plato! Plato represents Nazism and fascism. Forget this worshiping of Plato you learned in your high schools."

Phil Verveer: He was a man given to large ideas and large movements in history. One of his propositions was that the key to Western civilization was the notion of deferred gratification: We sacrifice today for the sake of a better tomorrow.

Christopher Hyland: He was positive about the aspirations of what we as human beings can be. Positive, positive, positive, positive. Tomorrow will always be better than today.

There's no one who could have gone to that class who did not for the rest of their lives measure their actions against what Quigley professed. There's no way that Clinton could not have been heavily influenced by Quigley. At Bill's first National Democratic Convention, the night he accepted the nomination, they had this song, "Don't Stop Thinking About Tomorrow." That was pure Quigley.

Tommy Caplan: Sophomore year we had Giles, who taught a course called U.S. Constitution and Law. You went through basically the entire Supreme Court history picking salient cases.

We both loved it. I think that course was one of the things that confirmed in him a love of public policy. It took law away from minutiae—the history of ambulance chasing—into really big themes.

Like the Giles course, working for Senator Fulbright increased his reverence and appetite for public service. He was now in the government, getting close to something that was very central.

During the summer following his sophomore year, Bill worked in the Arkansas gubernatorial campaign of Frank Holt, a former state attorney general.[3] Holt lost, but Bill's work bore fruit immediately when Holt recommended him to Lee Williams, a staffer in the office of William Fulbright, the brilliant chairman of the Senate Foreign Relations Committee who was just beginning his stand as one of Lyndon Johnson's most nettlesome adversaries on the Vietnam War. Bill had previously written to the office asking for a job, with no luck. Now, Williams offered Bill a position.[4]

David Pryor, a Democrat from Arkansas, served in the House of Representatives from 1966 to 1973. He would later serve as the state's governor (1975–1979), then represent it in the United States Senate (1979–1997).

David Pryor: I would see Bill Clinton fairly often. He would come by the office from time to time in the afternoon, sit around, and visit with staff or myself. He loved to talk policy. He was over in Senator Fulbright's office, in the mail room.

He read a lot of the letters about Vietnam, pro and con—during those hearings they came in by the huge mail sacks. Bill Clinton would devour those letters, and I have a sense that while he was reading them, he was mentally saying, "I've got to remember this name, Mrs. Bill Sharp, in Magnolia. That's someone I need to know." He would cultivate these lists. He was a consummate people person, always staying in touch. You'd hear from people, "Oh, I just heard from Bill Clinton. He dropped me a postcard," or "He called me up on my birthday," or "My mother broke her ankle and Bill Clinton called her." He was constantly massaging people. That's Bill Clinton.

I don't think he played any golf at that time. He wasn't an athlete. Didn't play tennis. Politics was his sport, that was his hobby, that was his passion. If he's ever gone fishing I don't think I ever heard of it.

"He wanted to walk and breathe and feel."

Carolyn Staley, Bill's friend from Hot Springs, was studying music at Indiana University.

Carolyn Staley: In '68, he invited me to come see him at Georgetown over my spring break. Martin Luther King was killed on April 4, the day before I arrived. Flying into D.C., I could see smoke coming from the burning blocks in town. I remember when he met me at the airport: just the pale face. It wasn't the big hug and welcome. It was a grave Bill Clinton.

He had taken a chance even to drive to the airport to pick me up. Students at Georgetown had been told to stay on campus. The National Guard was guarding the perimeter.

He said, "We have a job to do," and we went straight from the airport. He had volunteered with the Red Cross. He had driven his white Buick convertible to Georgetown for his senior year—they put a red cross on the car.

We pulled up to this building that was the office of the Red Cross, and a guy came out with boxes of supplies. Whether it was food or medicine or water I'm not real sure, but it was things needed by people who, because of the rioting, were staying in the basement of a church near Florida Avenue. The guy who came out to the car told me that we needed to let as little of our face show as possible. He said, "Put a hat on, Bill," and he told me to put on a scarf.

It was so that people wouldn't see our white skin. We were to follow another car. We didn't stop at any stoplights, we just barreled through. Bill would be saying, "Go, go, go, go," to the car in front. This was a city under siege.

After we dropped the stuff off, that wasn't enough for Bill. So we parked the car. There was glass everywhere, bricks in the middle of the street and the sidewalks, bashed-in windows where looting had taken place, some buildings completely burned to the ground. We were the only souls—it was like there had been a nuclear explosion and we were the only two people left on earth. It was eerily quiet. We got out. He wanted to walk and breathe and feel and have firsthand knowledge.

We were walking quietly, and there was nobody within sight. We turned a corner and saw a group of four or five young black men, walking abreast down the middle of the street. We both knew we needed to get out of there. We didn't run, we just turned and made our way quickly back to the car, got in, and left.

4

Man of the World: Oxford and Yale

"He was a raconteur."

Bill would later say he'd been interested in a Rhodes Scholarship since high school, but as the end of his Georgetown career approached, he was further motivated by the example and urging of his boss, William Fulbright, a Rhodes Scholar during the 1920s.

The process for selecting 1968's thirty-two American Rhodes Scholars covered the entire nation. After candidates were winnowed in each state, eight regional committees selected four young men each—women did not become Rhodes Scholars until 1977—to spend two years at Oxford.[1]

Bill made the cut. He graduated from Georgetown in June, and in October he sailed to England on the SS *United States*.

Tom Williamson, a lawyer in Washington, served during the Clinton administration as solicitor of labor. Robert Reich, a scholar of public policy and a frequent media commentator, served as Bill's first secretary of labor. Both 1968 Rhodes Scholars, they got to know Bill at Oxford.

Tom Williamson: He was very interested in sports, he was interested in music—jazz, R&B. We were very interested in talking about politics, the issues of our day. The big issues were the civil rights movement and the war in Vietnam.

Robert Reich: In those days, he wasn't an intellectual. He was a raconteur. I thought he was very funny and he had scores—in fact, he seemed to have an infinite storehouse—of political stories. He liked nothing better than to hold forth for hours at a time, usually on political or politically related subjects.

He was very popular. He had a kind of southern good ol' boy quality about him that was charming and funny and gave him license to tell stories that seemed to have no beginning and no end.

Tom Williamson: Bill wasn't a bad basketball player back then. The Oxford basketball team was composed of, I think, fifteen Americans and one Englishman. In those days the English were terrible at basketball.

Robert Reich: I have a picture in my head of him telling us stories and laughing—a great, great laughter and joie de vivre. A huge capacity for enjoying himself.

Robert Reich: Rhodes Scholars don't have to do much academically if they don't want to. Some of us took our studies more seriously than others. Bill did not take them terribly seriously.

And the holidays at Oxford were very generous.

Tom Williamson: You'd go to school for eight weeks and then have a six-week break; then eight weeks of school, six-week break; then eight weeks of school.

Robert Reich: We all spent our holidays traveling. He was enormously excited by the world that he was seeing. Bill had a ravenous appetite for facts, ideas, new perspectives, new points of view. He seemed to relish all of that.

Tom Williamson: You're young guys, you don't have a job, you don't have an official role. You just have license to explore and apply your energy to meet new people, learn about new cultures. Bill was probably better at that than anyone else in the group, because he has an inexhaustible supply of energy for engaging with people of all sorts.

He is a special person, because his spirit, his soul, is fueled by connecting with others. Other people get tired of reaching out and reaching out. He's energized by it.

Tom Williamson: We also would travel around the U.K. together. It was very common for students in those days to hitchhike. We would put our thumbs out and hitchhike across Wales. Sometimes we would go into London to hang out and explore the town.

Williamson, who is African American, remembered engaging in some playacting with Bill.

A lot of times, hitchhiking is pretty boring—you're just waiting for a ride. One of the things we used to do to entertain ourselves was a kind of role-reversal where, when somebody would stop to pick us up, I would say, "Boy, get in the back of the car!" and he would say, "Yassuh. Yassuh. Yassuh." We knew, or we suspected, that people had stereotypes about black folks and white folks, and it amused us to see if we might unsettle them a bit.

We were just young guys trying to have a good time.

"He was agonizing."

Reality, however, in the form of America's war in Southeast Asia, intruded on the fun.

Robert Reich: Most of the time at Oxford we Americans were worried about the war. We were worried about being drafted.

Rhodes Scholar Strobe Talbott, now president of the Brookings Institution, became Bill's deputy secretary of state.

Strobe Talbott: As the world knows he had some issues with the draft.

During his undergraduate years at Georgetown, 1964–1968, Bill had been protected from the draft by a student deferment. But after changes made by Congress in 1967, such deferments did not apply to young men enrolled in most forms of graduate school—and a Rhodes Scholar's adventure at Oxford was not one of the exceptions.[2]

Tom Williamson: He was agonizing over how he should deal with the prospect of an induction notice. Bill was among the most knowledgeable and thoughtful of us about how wrong the American effort in Vietnam was, because he had worked in Senator Fulbright's office. And because he came from a southern state, where there was a fair amount of poverty, he was more aware than most that one consequence of so many middle-class college kids being exempt was that children of poor black, white, and Hispanic families were the ones who were dying in this war.

Robert Reich: I recall one demonstration in London most of us attended.

Tom Williamson: There was a huge antiwar demonstration in London. We participated as monitors, where you would stand at a certain place to ask people who were involved in the march to walk in a way that was going to be orderly. It was, "If you want to be a monitor, show up at this time and wear an armband." You had the incidental benefit that you got to see a lot of the American students who were at this demonstration, including a lot of the women students.

As Bill wrestled with the issue that would determine his immediate future, the draft, he also considered his long-term future.

Tom Williamson: Not a lot, but some people thought they might be interested in electoral politics. What differentiated Bill is that early on it was evident that he was prepared to go back to his home state of Arkansas and build the foundation for his political career there.

Bill clearly loved Arkansas and was dedicated to the idea that he would return home. Well, when you thought about it for a moment, you realized he might have a much better chance of achieving his national ambitions that way, because he's going back to a fairly small state, where he already knew quite a few people and understood the political and business network. Now, if you're going back to California or New York or Massachusetts, with big, cosmopolitan cities, there are already a whole bunch of people who have Ivy League degrees. It may be a stimulating environment for you, but you are not going to be that special.

Robert Reich: I remember talking to him when he was trying to decide between the University of Arkansas Law School and Yale Law School: In political terms, which would be more advantageous? On the one side, going back to the University of Arkansas Law School would put him right back in Arkansas. He reasoned it would give him an opportunity to make a lot of connections down there and would legitimize him in the eyes of voters. Voters might look askance at Yale, at the Ivy League.

But the Yale Law School education, he felt, might be a bit better. I urged him to go to Yale. I thought he'd get much more out of it.

Bill had another, more urgent, reason for considering law school in Arkansas.

In the spring of 1969, while at Oxford, Bill received notice from Arkansas that he had been drafted. The rules allowed him to finish the academic term that had just begun, but he was scheduled to be in uniform by the end of July. Bill's classmates didn't expect to see him at Oxford in October when they would begin their second and final year there.[3]

At home after the spring term ended, however, Bill decided to explore his options.

His uncle Raymond Clinton and his new stepfather, Jeff Dwire—Virginia had remarried in January—investigated nearby reserve and National Guard outfits, but all were full.[4] Bill looked into becoming an air force pilot but found that a minor defect in vision disqualified him; he took a physical for a naval officer-training program but flunked due to defective hearing.[5] With help from Bill Fulbright's Senate office and elsewhere, however, he landed a spot in an ROTC program at the University of Arkansas, in Fayetteville, provided he attended law school there. Bill's draft board—like draft boards around the country, indulgent toward local academic stars—withdrew his induction notice.[6]

Bill's original deal with Colonel Eugene Holmes, the commander of the university's ROTC program, called for his enrollment in the program and at the law school during the upcoming fall term, but he managed to put off his commitment by a year. In October he returned to Oxford.[7]

By then, Bill had misgivings about the arrangement. In September, Richard Nixon had begun drawing down U.S. forces in Vietnam and slowing the rate of conscription. And he called for a lottery system to determine, by date of birth, the order in which young men would be taken. Wagering on the luck of the upcoming draw, as well as the anticipated reduction in the number of draftees, Bill, in October, gave up his 1-D ROTC deferment and was reclassified 1-A—"Registrant available for military service."[8] On December 1, when the Selective Service held a lottery for men born 1944–1950—the nation's first draft lottery since 1942—Bill's bet paid off: August 19 came up 311th out of 366.[9] With the number in his pocket he wrote to Holmes, thanking the colonel "for saving me from the draft" and noting a desire "to maintain my political viability within the system." The letter would become famous in 1992.

As events played out, there were no surprises. The annual number of draftees dropped by almost half from 1969 to 1970, with steep reductions continuing until the draft ended in 1973.[10] The highest number called from the 1969 lottery was 195.[11]

No doubt out of self-interest, but no doubt also out of principled opposition to a controversial war, Bill had managed to dodge military service. He was not alone. Avoiding Vietnam—by pulling strings, concocting medical excuses, joining the National Guard, or conducting subterfuge of the draft system in countless other ways—was the rule, not the exception, among the better-educated, better-heeled, better-connected young men who were Bill's contemporaries. But two decades later, his

hardly remarkable history nearly cost him the White House, and certainly complicated his role as commander in chief of the nation's armed forces.

Meanwhile, Bill was free to attend law school wherever he wanted.

"Of course, there was no dynasty."

Bill barely showed up for class the first couple of months he was enrolled at Yale
Law, in the fall of 1970. Instead, he worked on the campaign of Joe Duffey to
represent Connecticut in the U.S. Senate. Bill labored to sell the antiwar ethics
professor in the working-class precincts of New Haven and surrounding towns, but
with little success. The seat went to the Republican, Lowell Weicker.[12]

Robert Reich: Yale Law School in the early '70s, like Oxford, was the kind of
place that once you were there you could get by without doing much work.
If you wanted to do very well, you had to work very hard. But they were not
going to flunk people out.

You went there if you wanted to be exposed to some of the best legal
minds in the country, and if you wanted to have classmates who were likely
not to go into corporate law but to do a lot of other interesting things.

Two years later, Bill cut most of his pre–Election Day classes for another cam-
paign—he spent his time in Texas, as one of three state coordinators for the 1972
Democratic presidential nominee, Senator George McGovern. As futile as Bill's
efforts were on behalf of the hapless candidate—Nixon thrashed McGovern in
Texas, 67 percent to 33 percent, on his way to a forty-nine-state humiliation of the
South Dakotan—Bill's experience was not wasted, for he made the acquaintance of
Betsey Wright, who would be his indispensable organizer and enforcer for the
dozen years leading to his entering the White House.[13]

Robert Reich: There are some people who come to politics naturally and
who love it and who breathe it. Bill was one of those from a very early age.

He was immersed in American politics right from the get-go at Yale. I
wouldn't go so far as to say he learned a lot of law, but, of course, if you go to
law school some of that rubs off on you as well.

*Bruce Morrison served in the House of Representatives (D-CT) from 1983 to 1991.
He attended Yale Law with Bill.*

Bruce Morrison: He never said, "I'm Bill Clinton. I'm going to run for
governor of Arkansas." It was just that people would say, "Yeah, Bill—he's
going to go back to Arkansas and run for governor." This was Yale Law
School, where everybody thinks they're going to be president or something,
but most people didn't have a plan that was that extensive.

His political plan made you think that he was part of a political family in Arkansas. The way you computed it was, there are lots of people who go to a place like Yale Law School who are the son of a congressman or a senator. If they were going back to Arkansas, they would be going back to an expectation: "Oh, that's the son of Congressman So-and-So; he's going to be somebody in politics." The impression was that he came from a dynasty. Of course, there was no dynasty. He'd worked for Fulbright, but he was just a bright kid from the wrong side of the tracks who had made his own way.

What was really audacious was that Bill thought that on the pure strength of his talent he was going to go back there and parlay it, which he did. He graduated from law school in '73. He lost the race for Congress in '74. He was elected attorney general in '76. Then was elected governor in '78.

So hey, audacious, right?

5

On the Move:
An Arkansas Politician

"The hit of the evening."

Audacious, indeed. In the spring of 1973, before receiving his diploma from Yale, Bill wrote to the University of Arkansas Law School in Fayetteville seeking a job on the faculty. After telling a professor involved in the selection process, "I have no plans at this time to run for public office," he was hired.[1] (Perhaps by "no plans at this time" Bill meant "no absolutely final decision at this immediate moment on exactly which race to enter exactly when." Fortunately, he did not have to defend the truth of his words before a grand jury.)

In three years as a law professor, 1973–1976, Bill would teach antitrust, admiralty, and constitutional law, among other subjects.

One of Bill's students recalled the new instructor's first year at the law school.

Mac Norton: Bill was a good teacher. Everybody liked him and respected him because the intellectual capacity was evident and was enormous.

N. M. "Mac" Norton is an attorney in Little Rock.

Bill could've been more demanding of his students. That maybe is one criticism of him as a teacher.

I'd frequently drop in to his office to talk politics. It was well known that he was thinking of running for Congress—he made no secret. And when he began to run, his classroom attendance fell off. I had to teach class some days because he wasn't there.

Bill's relocation to Fayetteville was not coincidental. Only twenty-seven years old, he decided to run in 1974 for a House seat held by a longtime Republican incumbent, John Paul Hammerschmidt. The Third Congressional District, situated in the northwest corner of the state, included Fayetteville.

David Pryor: When the state ticket closes in April, the first rally of the season to kick off the primaries and to celebrate the Democratic candidates is in Russellville. The Pope County Democratic women hold a big dinner.

It's a must performance for all politicians whether they are in that district or not.

Ernest Dumas: It's a big rally and they have hot dogs and Cokes, and people pack in there.

Ernest Dumas, often called the dean of Arkansas political journalists, now writes for the Arkansas Times.

It's a cattle show where all of the local candidates get up, and they've got one minute if they're running for justice of the peace or county clerk. They herd them across the stage and everybody is out talking and eating hot dogs. And then they get up to the statewide candidates, who get two minutes.

David Pryor: I spoke, Robert C. Byrd* came down and spoke for Bill Fulbright, Dale Bumpers spoke—Fulbright and Bumpers were running against each other and that was a bloodbath. And so the evening went on and on and on, candidates for sheriff spoke—all in this big dining hall at Arkansas Tech University. At the end the master of ceremonies says, "Well, folks, it's eleven o'clock now, and everybody's tired. Good night and go work for the Democrats."

Someone said, "Wait a minute. We haven't heard from this guy Bill Clinton. He's running against Hammerschmidt."

"Oh, excuse me. Okay, we'll give you two minutes."

*U.S. senator (D-WV) from 1959 until his death in 2010.

Ernest Dumas: So Clinton walks up and, of course, he's good-looking, twenty-seven, tall and erect, and he moves with this easy grace across the stage, and he starts speaking in a very soft, conversational tone. Within seconds you could hear the noise die down and people stop, so that a minute into his speech, everybody's listening. And he makes this elegant little talk. Says nothing. It doesn't mean anything. I began to take some notes on it and then I looked at my pad: I don't have anything here.

David Pryor: He said something like, "If we're not careful, we as Democrats are going to lose our way. We can't be Republicans, we've got to be Democrats. Let's be proud of it. Let's not run away from our base."

Ernest Dumas: He finishes, and receives this big ovation.

He was the hit of the evening. Nobody there knew who he was, but he had this kind of magical presence—his voice and his rhythm, the cadence of his sentences, or something. It had that magical effect, and he really didn't say a damn thing. He just had that effect on people.

Dale Bumpers: Bill Clinton delivered one of the most beautiful speeches I ever heard.

Dale Bumpers served as governor of Arkansas from 1971 to 1975. After defeating William Fulbright in the 1974 Democratic primary, he entered the U.S. Senate, where he remained until 1999.

You talk to any of the two, three, four hundred people that were there that night, and every one of them will remember it.

Ernest Dumas: Later that night I went to have dinner at this old restaurant, and David Pryor comes in and we sit and talk. He says, "Who's this guy Clinton? I was at the stage before he spoke and he pulled out an envelope and started writing on it, scribbling something down as he was waiting. I had this impulse to tap this young man, this neophyte, on the shoulder and tell him, 'Look, don't write anything down. Just get up and tell them who you are, why you're running. Just be at ease.' Hell, this guy gets up there and the whole place is mesmerized. I'm glad I didn't make a fool of myself by trying to give him some advice, because he was the slickest guy there."

Bill received a plurality in the three-man Democratic primary, then won the runoff easily.

With the Solid South only beginning to crumble due to the Democratic Party's identification with the civil rights movement, the Democratic primary remained the only meaningful competition for most offices in Arkansas. Moreover, since Richard Nixon would resign in August, November 1974 would be a good time to be a Democrat in most of the country. The Third District, however, presented Bill with an uphill fight.

David Terrell: It's traditionally a Republican area up in that corner. Plus, Hammerschmidt was not just a Republican, he was a long-term incumbent with a fair amount of clout and a lot of history of pork.

David Terrell covered Bill Clinton as a reporter for the Arkansas Democrat *and the* Arkansas Gazette.*

Hammerschmidt seemed to feel secure in all the advantages of incumbency. He would drive into some little town and talk to the banker and leave. That was pretty much his manner of campaigning.

Clinton, on the other hand, ran a vigorous, flashy campaign. Lots of personal meet-and-greets, lots of speeches to small groups, which is where he has always been at his best.

Patty Howe Criner: He was willing to work endlessly. He's not an early riser, but once he was up he would work until after midnight, meeting people in all twenty-one counties, asking about their families, going to their houses, not just their businesses. "Take me home for dinner. Show me where you live. Tell me what you deal with every day."[2]

Marie Bruno: He made a point to go everywhere, to talk to everyone. I never saw him hesitate. It didn't matter what people looked like, it didn't matter how dirty they were.

Martha Whetstone is another Friend of Bill. An Arkansas native, she met Bill around this time.

Martha Whetstone: The issue was the energy crisis, and we'd be driving and he'd stop in gas stations and talk to these independent owners. This guy is twenty-seven talking to these codgers, and he would look at their books to see whether they were getting screwed by the oil companies. It wasn't just about going and making speeches.

If Bill's signature talent at connecting with ordinary voters was evident in 1974, so was a signature shortcoming.

The two papers merged in 1991, creating today's Arkansas Democrat-Gazette.

He was constantly late then, too—it was not just a presidential phenomenon. It drove people nuts. He'd think almost that it's rude to leave—he's always talking a person to death, he's always blabbing.

If you have to say what his worst fault is, it's that he's doesn't feel bad enough when he's late. He doesn't have guilty feelings about it. You say, "Mr. President, you've been keeping these people waiting for two hours," and you don't think it registers.

A longtime writer for the Arkansas Gazette, *Max Brantley is now editor of the* Arkansas Times.

Max Brantley: One of the things about charisma is an ability of a person to connect with other people, and Bill Clinton can do that. He does it quickly, serially, and effectively.

He gets close to you, he touches, he establishes a physical connection—arm on a shoulder, a handshake. He looks you in your eye, and for a short period of time makes you think that you're the only person in the room. And he quickly finds the common foundation—hometown, knows your cousin, knows somebody who went to the school you went to, knows your boss. And then the other thing he can do, which is the real trick, is file it away and have near total recall of it at some point way in the future.

I've known politicians who can do some of these things but they do it in a way where it seems palpably a parlor trick. But Bill Clinton really is interested that much in people—some of it is just genuine. He has a deep and abiding empathy for human beings, and people can tell it.

People can tell a phony. In terms of his interest in human beings, he's not necessarily constant, but he's not a phony. At that moment, he's definitely in love with you.

Mac Norton recalls another element of Bill's campaigning that would later become familiar to a national audience—albeit in improved form.

Mac Norton: One of Bill's political standby tactics was evident even in 1974, and that's when you're attacked, answer, hit back, and do so right away. I think he still believes that his failure to do so in the 1980 campaign—his departure from what comes naturally for him—is why he lost.* Well, in 1974 Hamerschmidt had a radio commercial running, which said something to

*In 1980, seeking reelection after his first term as governor, Bill lost to Frank White, a Republican bank executive.

the effect of, "Bill Clinton receives over 50 percent of his campaign contributions from organized labor." In the Third District that wasn't such a great idea. Clinton's on the radio within two or three days: "John Paul Hamerschmidt said I receive over 50 percent of my campaign contributions from organized labor. Ladies and gentlemen, that's a lie. I receive only 48 percent of my total contributions from organized labor."

We're thinking, "Jesus, Bill."

"She wore granny dresses."

As Bill was introducing himself to Arkansas voters, he was introducing someone else, an acquaintance from Yale, to his friends and family.

Marie Bruno: He had told my parents he had this girlfriend from Chicago. I didn't have a sense of how serious it was. I'd heard, "Oh, they're not serious" —little snippets from these southern girls who were in college and came over to volunteer for the cute guy running for Congress. There were a lot of college volunteers, a lot of women. He's very attractive.

I was really anxious to see who this lady was.

Martha Whetstone: When he told me the very first time about Hillary, he said, "I can't wait for you to meet her."

Marie Bruno: But when she came in the door she was unlike what girls looked like in the South.

Hillary Rodham arrived in August after finishing work for the House Judiciary Committee on impeachment proceedings against Richard Nixon.[3]

Martha Whetstone: I was floored. It couldn't have been a bigger surprise if she had been a Martian in a spacesuit. She had brown crinkled hair, no makeup, glasses that were six inches thick, she wore granny dresses—we call it "frumpy" in the South, to put it mildly. And her shoes and everything.

Marie Bruno: Big wooden shoes.

Martha Whetstone: We were in shock. *This* is Bill's girlfriend? That from the southern perspective of one who at the time looked like Dolly Parton. We all looked like Dolly Parton and Loretta Lynn, with no disrespect to Dolly Parton and Loretta Lynn. But we were big-old-hair girls, and we thought that Hillary should aspire to be like us. Little did we know that she had better self-esteem and perspective than we did. She was a shock to the Arkansas system. It was not what your typical southern boy brings home to mother.

Marie Bruno: It was real interesting to watch the dynamics in the campaign change, which they did very suddenly. She said, "This needs to be done, that needs to be done. Have you made these phone calls yet?" Not that people were slacking off, but she had a different dynamic that she brought in—a Yankee, I'll come right out and say that. Not meaning to be abrupt, but very abrupt with how she talked to people. It was definitely noticed.

David Terrell: He had a young, energetic staff, with a lot of volunteers from the university, but things were a damned mess. Nobody knew what the hell was going on until this woman showed up named Hillary Rodham. She took over his love life, and she took over the organization of that campaign, and certainly it took on a lot of discipline and organization and force that it hadn't had up to that time.

Hillary turned a lot of people off, in terms of her public persona, and personally, as well. Somehow, she seemed to come off to a lot of people as cold, maybe even aloof, protective, closed, maybe rigid. This was never my impression of her. To the extent that I did get to know her, I liked her. I thought she had a blazing intelligence, much more than he, in fact, in ways that were important to me.

Marie Bruno: She was a woman with a strong personality. In the South in those days you didn't see a whole lot of that. Men and women alike were thinking, "Who does she think she is?"

Hillary joined Bill on the law school faculty in the fall of 1974, but she was still uncertain about marrying him and making her life in Arkansas. The following summer, she would leave Fayetteville to visit friends and potential employers in Chicago and on the East Coast. As Bill was driving her to the airport, they passed a red brick house marked with a "for sale" sign. She told Bill she thought the house was "sweet-looking"; by the time she returned, Bill had bought it. "Now you'd better marry me," he told her, "because I can't live in it by myself."[4]
The wedding took place on October 11, 1975.

On Election Day 1974, Hammerschmidt drew 52 percent of the vote to Bill's 48.[5]

David Terrell: He lost the election because it was not winnable. Clinton came very close indeed. And because he had, he set himself up for the attorney general's race. Coming close was good enough.

David Pryor: It was not, "Man, you lost that race, you should have won it." It was, "You almost did win this race, young man, and you'll have another chance some day."

Ernest Dumas: Everybody acknowledged that whatever he ran for next, he was going to be elected. And of course, two years later he ran for attorney general and got elected easily.

"I am so mad."

Gene Lyons: Everybody who was involved in Arkansas politics, or around Arkansas politics, thought of him as the next big thing.

Gene Lyons is an Arkansas journalist and coauthor with Joe Conason of The Hunting of the President *(St. Martin's, 2000). Ellen Brantley, Max's wife, is a judge in Little Rock. She taught at the law school in Fayetteville for the 1975–1976 academic year—Bill's last as a professor.*

Ellen Brantley: It was clear he was going to run for something else. As I recall, the bumper stickers that were printed up that year when I was in Fayetteville just said "Clinton" on them. They didn't say what he was running for, the idea being that he was going to find the best thing he could run for.

He ran for state attorney general in 1976 because that was a good open slot.

Bill defeated two opponents in the May primary to take the nomination without a runoff. With the general election only a formality—no Republican was on the ballot —he devoted much of his energy that fall to running the Arkansas campaign of Jimmy Carter, the Democratic nominee for president.[6]

Bill took office in January 1977.

The late Kent J. Rubens, a lawyer from West Memphis, Arkansas, served as a Democratic member of the Arkansas State House of Representatives, 1975–1981.

Kent Rubens: The last thing Clinton wants to be is a lawyer. It's just a means for him to run for elected office. He skillfully used the attorney general's office as a consumer-protection-type office that got him around the state.

Fayetteville friends Mac Norton and Ellen Brantley took jobs under the new attorney general.

Mac Norton: We had a really good team in that office, a bunch of fine lawyers. Recognizing, I think, his own limitations as a practicing lawyer, Bill left the practice of law to us. He didn't get involved in the details of cases, but he stayed up with what was going on in the docket all the time.

Max Brantley: Rate cases—electric rate cases, gas rate cases—were publicly contested, and they were large political news.

Ellen Brantley: It was a period when there was a tremendous amount of increase in utility rates.

Mac Norton: The attorney general's role in those cases, as a practical matter, is usually secondary to that of the Public Service Commission. But it was a good opportunity for the attorney general to have an impact—and be seen having an impact—on an issue that's important to everybody, because everybody gets an electric bill.

Max Brantley: My wife would talk about working on a rate case, spending weeks and months gathering information. Then before the public hearing, where Bill would be the front man, the staff would brief him for an hour. And then he'd go in and put the case together in a way that was more persuasive than they'd have been able to do—as if he'd been the one who had done all the research.

Ellen Brantley: He got a lot of good publicity out of it—that was clearly part of it. But I would say we had a fair amount of success. Definitely.

Paul Leopoulos: One Christmas I got home and I walked into his office. He was screaming on the phone: "I don't care. You don't need a rate increase for these telephones." AT&T was trying to raise pay phones from a dime to a quarter. Screaming and yelling: "Poor people can't afford to do anything. So, now we're going to almost triple this cost?" And boy, I mean he slammed the receiver down.

I started laughing. He said, "I am so mad."

They did not get that rate increase.

Julie Baldridge headed Bill's consumer-affairs department and, because the office of attorney general lacked a separate press office, acted as his de facto press secretary.

Julie Baldridge: He always was good for a quote. He knew quite a bit about everything. With the legislature in session and different policies taking place —and there'd be train wrecks with chemical spills—it got to be common for the press to gravitate over to him, and not just on the attorney general issues. David Pryor was the governor, and he was so wonderful and so good at what he did, but far more self-effacing in a way and quieter—I guess a more subdued person compared to Clinton.

Clinton came in with low name recognition. By the time he ran for governor, his name recognition was up close to 80. It was all free press.[7]

Steve Smith managed Bill's campaign for attorney general, then became his chief of staff when Bill took office.

Steve Smith: He was AG just a little over a year before he started running for governor.[8]

Max Brantley: The attorney general's post has been viewed as a stepping stone here, and he used the office to its maximum. He was in the paper a lot and it was a good platform for his skills as a smart lawyer who was genial and engaging at the same time. He was a guy who was going to go far fast. It made his election as governor almost a given.

Politicians like Bill Clinton don't come along very often. I can't think of a person who's met him, even those who don't like him—and there are a lot of people who don't like him—who immediately and instinctively doesn't recognize a towering political force.

6

Too Much, Too Soon, Too Bad:
Rookie Governor

Bill faced four opponents in the 1978 Democratic primary for governor, but none approaching him in prominence. "I just had to run hard, avoid mistakes, and go on doing a good job as attorney general," he recalled. He did all three to win 60 percent of the vote, then took the statehouse with 63 percent in November.[1]

Under Arkansas's constitution, the governor's term lasted two years.

"This may not be good."

Rudy Moore: Because of the token opposition, we actually started the transition—in other words, getting ready for him to be governor—long before the November election.

Rudy Moore Jr. managed Bill's 1978 campaign, then went to work as Bill's chief of staff in the governor's office.

We started looking at policy issues, legislative issues. We brought in consultants.[2]

Julie Baldridge became the new governor's press secretary. Patty Howe Criner, Bill's childhood playmate from Hot Springs, started as the new governor's scheduler; she would later serve as press secretary.

In January 1979, thirty-two-year-old Bill Clinton took office as the nation's youngest governor.

Julie Baldridge: We had a 150-bill gubernatorial legislative package ready to go on the first day of the legislative session, and actually passed it out when they were sworn in and seated.

Patty Howe Criner: There was a lot of leeriness because the old-time politicians had never had anyone come into office in January, be sworn in, and hand them a printed budget book—a paperback—of what the governor's office was interested in, what it would propose, what the dollars would cost, where they would come from. The pages were numbered, the plan was outlined, and it was put on their desk. That alone would be scary to some, who'd say, "Now wait a minute. We don't move that fast around here, young man."[3]

Marie Bruno: I didn't care for Bill's inaugural night. It was bitterly cold, and they had the party out here at Ricks Armory. I remember seeing him and he was abrupt, curt, leave-me-alone. To some of my aunts and uncles it was the same. We'd say, "Hey, congratulations." And from him it was, "Gotta go see other people. See you later," instead of the usual way he was: A hug, and "Oh, isn't this great? I'm so excited." His attitude that night was very uncharacteristic of him. "Haughty" would be a good word to describe it.

I remember thinking, "If this is the way things are gonna be, this may not be good."

As it would during his first two years as president, Bill's ambition got the better of him during his first two years as governor.

The journalist Jack Moseley was then editor of the Southwest Times Record, *a newspaper in Fort Smith, Arkansas.*

Jack Moseley: He won the governorship and promptly went about surrounding himself, in my opinion, with young intellectuals and hippies, which just did not geehaw at all with the Arkansas good ol' boys. He raised the Arkansas license tag fees, which was very, very unpopular with good ol' boys and members of the NRA. His staff looked down on, and even talked down to, the average Arkansas voter.[4]

David Terrell: Clinton hired not just a chief of staff, but a kind of triumvirate, including two old Arkies, Steve Smith and Rudy Moore. The third was a fellow named John Danner, who was from California. And golly, these people were arrogant and condescending and difficult. They did not understand how you do business in the South. You don't just start out on a phone call doing business. You ease into it from some personal chat. They had trouble with that.

Jack Moseley: Those people were about as congenial as a porcupine in a bird dog's nose.

Gene Lyons: They were perceived as out-of-state wise guys who wore beards.

Indeed, Moore, Smith, and Danner acquired a nickname: "The Three Beards."

A lot of rural people in the state, a lot of small-town people, got the impression that Clinton thought he was better than they were.

David Terrell: The interesting part of that first term was the whole atmosphere of it. Clinton looked like such a kid. The governor's office was awash in all these very young, very spirited, aggressive, splashy people. A lot of old mossbacks in the legislature had a hard time dealing with them. Man, there were a lot of young women in skirts slit up their thigh. It was quite an eye festival there for a few years.

David Pryor: It wasn't my opinion, but there was the image some people had of this easterner who had gone up there and brought back this smarter-than-the-rest-of-us wife, Hillary Rodham, who didn't bother to take his name.

Rudy Moore: Hillary Clinton going by Hillary Rodham—that rubbed people the wrong way.

"Clinton has a way of shedding allies."

The thousands of FOBs notwithstanding, David Terrell detected something ruthless in Bill's interpersonal relations.

David Terrell: There are ways in which Bill Clinton is a sorry dog, and one of them is a lack of loyalty to anybody. I'm thinking about an individual named

Paul Fray. Paul's dead. He was very devoted to Clinton, and helped him a great deal on his campaign for Congress. Paul got into some legal trouble and this and that.* Suddenly, he was shut out of Bill's life and couldn't see him. He couldn't help Clinton anymore, so he's gone. He doesn't exist. He's a non-person. That would be one example. There were others.

As governor, as he would as president, Bill sometimes found himself caught between progressive causes and political realities. His moderate impulses—or, some would argue, his fealty to corporate interests—lost him the friendship of a trusted adviser.

Rudy Moore: Bill Clinton mishandled Steve Smith.

Ernest Dumas: Steve was head of a thing called the Task Force on Timber. The big issue in all these national forests was clear-cutting. It was a big environmental issue of the time.

Steve Smith: We had a series of hearings on this around the state and brought in expert witnesses to testify, and Clinton came up with a report that was generally pretty mild, but it was critical of the timber-management practices that had been going on and recommended some things. He gave a copy of the draft of that report to the timber industry before it was released, and they were not pleased with it at all. And whereas in the past he had been in favor of doing something about it, after this meeting, he decided he didn't want to do anything on it and pretty much gutted the report, which didn't make anybody happy.

David Terrell: Steve's a great guy, a kind of a fire-eating old liberal. He doesn't have a lot of compromise in him, and he espoused some ideas that were just suicide. Oh, hell, he wanted to ban clear-cutting in Arkansas. To understand what that means, you need to know that, at the time, if you drew a line of latitude across Arkansas in the center, more than half the land below that line was owned by four large timber companies. This fellow was eager to take on some of the most powerful interests in Arkansas.

---

*Paul Fray, at whose wedding Bill acted as best man, managed the campaign for Congress in 1974. Around that time Fray lost his license to practice law after he was shown to have changed a court document to hide a client's conviction for drunken driving. Interview of Paul and Mary Fray, PBS, Frontline Online, "Once Upon a Time in Arkansas," http://www.pbs.org/wgbh/pages/frontline/shows/arkansas/interv iews/fray.html; "Fraying the Truth," CBS News (AP), http://www.cbsnews.com/ stories/2000/07/18/politics/main216489.shtml.

I don't know that Clinton ever committed on the issue. Well, eventually I guess he said no to a ban, but he let the caterwauling go on for way too long.

Ernest Dumas: Steve made the remark out in the papers that called the big timber companies like Weyerhaeuser and Georgia Pacific and Anthony—the giant timber family, the most powerful family in south Arkansas—corporate criminals. Here's Clinton's chief of staff calling all the big timber companies corporate criminals.

Rudy Moore: Bill Clinton pulled the rug out from under Steve Smith.

Steve Smith: All the environmentalists thought he'd sold out. All the timber industries still hated him and gave money to Frank White and worked against him. And that's when I decided that I had better things to do with my life.

Smith resigned in October 1980.

I remember how hard it was to get him to support a minimum-wage increase. I mean he did, but we had to drag him to it and it shouldn't have even been a question. And the timber-management thing on clear-cutting, where he just caved in and kissed their ass. Which is okay—I mean, if he was going to do it, he shouldn't have gone through the process. I wasted a lot of time trying to do what I thought was the right thing and I could have been doing something else. I think a lot of the staff people experienced that. They'd get a signal from him and take off with it and then if there was some political heat he'd back off, leave them hanging out there.

Gene Lyons: Clinton has a way of shedding allies that way, because they are more committed to their position than he is.

Steve Smith: The only issue area or concern that I think he has been entirely consistent on and right on is his commitment to racial justice. Not a single time have I ever seen him compromise or waver on that.

Gene Lyons: All of the things that people later said to his discredit were said about him right from the start: He's a little too pliable. He's a little too glib. Once you're his political ally, he takes you for granted and begins to try to win over his enemies. As with any gifted politician, there was always concern: Is he about helping Arkansas or is he about helping Bill Clinton?

David Terrell: Let me add something here. The interesting thing about him to me, always, is this: People hate his guts. A lot of people do. The right and the left hate him for the same reason. They think that's he's really about what, in fact, he's really about: They think that somewhere down in his soul, he really is a New Deal liberal. The right hates him because that's a fact. The left hates him because he won't do anything about it.

I think Clinton believes in some things, and I think he wants to see life better for people. But boy, if he learned anything in his first term as governor, it was that there are distinct limits to possibilities.

Another way Clinton's a sorry dog is, perhaps, a lack of adherence to principle. But that doesn't mean he doesn't have principles. It doesn't mean he doesn't want to do good things. I've always believed that he did—and that if he didn't, the central fact of his tenure in office wouldn't be the truth, and that is, we are better off for his having served.

"Clinton was oblivious."

Kent Rubens: I begged him to not go with those taxes.

Rudy Moore: Nothing created the downturn for Bill Clinton politically any more than did the car-tag issue. That was bred in the 1979 session of the legislature when Bill Clinton tried to up the licensing fees for trucks in order to pay for his highway program.

"Arkansas hadn't had a good road program in more than a decade," Bill wrote later, "and potholes and slow travel were costing people time and money."

Well, unfortunately, between the poultry industry and the trucking industry, they beat back that effort. So as a compromise, the Clinton administration raised the licensing fees on cars.

Rates varied according to a vehicle's weight—the fee on a heavy automobile, for example, rose from nineteen to thirty-six dollars.[5] Bill did not foresee that the modest increase in cost to drivers would come at an enormous political cost to him. Neither did many others.

Max Brantley: It caught me blind. It turns out that small things like paying their car tags really mattered to a lot of people. It was a sign that he wasn't in tune with the average guy.

Rudy Moore: It wasn't the money as much as it was the symbolism of, "Hey, the economy is not good. I'm having a hard time earning a living and now you're kicking me in the teeth by making me pay more for my license fees."

David Terrell: It was a stupid way to raise revenue, because it hit different people in different months. I go in and pay a much-increased car tag, and the next month you go and pay it. And I'm all pissed off about it and I talk to you and catch you pissed off.

Julie Baldridge: People were mad, really mad.

Rudy Moore: The car tags were his biggest political issue, but there were others. We had managed to alienate doctors with a rural health program. We had alienated the utilities because of some regulatory issues. We had alienated the timber industry over clear-cutting issues. We had alienated the poultry and the trucking industry over the licensing issues. So all of a sudden, there were all of these strong interest groups that were mad at Bill Clinton and the administration.

Julie Baldridge: We needed the money for the roads. I know we needed it. There were potholes all over Arkansas.

Gene Lyons: Clinton was oblivious, which was funny for him being from here and not being from moneyed people. The car tags became symptomatic to a lot of people that Clinton thought he was too good for Arkansas. His opponent in 1980, Frank White, made it a big issue, and it really hurt.

Julie Baldridge: They beat us to death with it.

"If somebody has to die, it'd better be a Cuban."

The other issue that sank Bill in 1980 originated in Cuba.

Responding to domestic unrest, Fidel Castro announced in April that anyone who wished to leave the island could do so. Over the next five months, the Mariel Boatlift brought some 125 thousand Cubans from the port of Mariel across the Florida Straits, most via small seacraft dispatched to Mariel by Cuban-Americans. To add to the headache he was causing his *yanqui* neighbor, Castro included in the exodus a number of mental patients and convicts.[6]

The Carter administration was already reeling over its failure to resolve the crisis created the previous November, when Iranian students took hostages at the American embassy in Tehran. Now it had to deal with the Mariel Cubans.

Walter Mondale: We had to find a place to keep them till we figured out what we could do.

Walter "Fritz" Mondale served as Jimmy Carter's vice president, 1977–1981.

Some of them were very difficult to deal with. So we decided to put them in military bases. One of them was in Arkansas.*

---

*Others were in Wisconsin and Pennsylvania. Robert Pear, "Behind the Prison Riots: Precautions Not Taken," *New York Times*, December 6, 1987.

By late May, some twenty thousand Cubans were living at Fort Chaffee, a mostly inactive military base in northwest Arkansas.[7]

David Pryor: A lot of people said, Why would Jimmy Carter, Bill Clinton's big friend, send all those Cubans out of the insane asylums and prisons and everything else up here to pollute our state?

Walter Mondale: Clinton believed that that was really rough on him. He was very angry about it.

Rudy Moore: The next thing we know, we're starting to have all these riots because these people are not happy.

Frequent disturbances erupted among the refugees, who came to America seeking freedom, not confinement. Their passions were further enflamed by the sight of Ku Klux Klan members demonstrating, in robes and hoods, outside the fort's front gate. Tempers ran high in nearby Barling, too. There local citizens marched through the streets, guns in hand, to protest the presence of the refugees, many of whom were dark-skinned.[8]

On May 26 the disorder leaked from the fort as a small number of Cubans escaped its bounds. Bill called in sixty-five National Guardsmen to restore order. Six days later, however, as Bill would recall, "all hell broke loose."[9]

Jack Moseley: On June 1, 1980, the Cubans rioted. They stormed past American soldiers, who stood at parade rest with empty rifles and did nothing to stop them, out onto U.S. Highway 22 outside of Barling. State police and sheriff's deputies and local police actually grabbed Cubans and physically threw them over the fence back into Fort Chaffee. This was a terribly dangerous situation. If they had gotten to the city limits of Barling, which was about a half a mile up the road, some 300 Arkansas good ol' boys, some of them with loaded guns, some of them liquored up on beer and whiskey and wanting to kill themselves a Cuban, would've met those people and it would've been a massacre. The police stopped the Cubans on that side of the fort, but the Cubans on the other side of the fort rampaged out. Meanwhile, they burned a couple of buildings and several guard shacks at Fort Chaffee.

Rudy Moore: Bill Clinton was assured by the White House that security would be handled by the military. The military said, "No. That's not our job."

Jack Moseley: Meanwhile, our police radio was blaring with the fact that the state police and the deputies of Sheriff Bill Cauthron of Sebastian County were herding hundreds of Cubans off U.S. Highway 71 from the community of Jenny Lind where they had rampaged, speaking a foreign language, leaping on cars and front porches. By some miracle, people had simply locked themselves in their houses and had not killed, or wounded even, a single Cuban.

Rudy Moore: Bill Clinton goes to the scene, he gets the National Guard to help, he gets the state police to help.

Jack Moseley: I was informed that he would arrive by helicopter from Little Rock. And so I met him at a helipad on the edge of town and there was an old grizzled National Guard colonel who, I'm sure, had been through World War II as a regular army solider. He was loading live .45 caliber bullets into a clip and putting them into his .45 caliber Army pistol. A state police car was there to carry the governor. Clinton, because of my support of him, invited me to go with him.

The first place we went was an IHOP, International House of Pancakes, on Rogers Avenue in Fort Smith, where we met with a gentleman named Causey, who was the head of the local state police troop; Sheriff Bill Cauthron of Sebastian County; Ron Fields, the prosecuting attorney; and myself. There may have been one or two other people there. We had some pancakes and coffee and that is where I saw Bill Clinton firsthand demonstrate leadership. He looked at the lawmen and said, "I don't want any of our people killed. If somebody has to die, it'd better be a Cuban. And unless there is a senseless act of violence against the Cubans, I don't want to see anybody charged with a crime. Do I make myself clear?" And he looked straight at Ron Fields, the prosecuting attorney, and Ron nodded slightly as if to say, "Governor, I understand what you are saying."

Moseley then went with Bill to the fort, where the young governor met with General James "Bulldog" Drummond, the base commander. Bill demanded that federal troops quell the rioting and keep the Cubans inside the fort, as the White House had promised him they would. Drummond, however, citing orders from his commanding officer in Texas, refused.[10]

This general began saying, "Posse comitatus, gentlemen.* We're only innkeepers. These people are civilians. This is America. They have the right to roam free as they choose. We cannot keep them here at Fort Chaffee. That's not the American way of doing it. The military has no responsibility whatsoever in this." Finally, one voice spoke up and said, "General, I understand

---

*The Posse Comitatus Act of 1878 restricts the use of the federal armed forces for law enforcement.

you can't even keep the ones in the stockade in the stockade." Another voice spoke up and said, "Sir, that was the not military's fault. The maintenance people left the bolt cutters in the stockade"—the Cubans had used them to escape. That same old Army colonel I had met putting live ammunition in his pistol walked up to me and he knew who I was. And he had a coffee cup in his hand and he was headed for the coffee pot. And he looked at me and said, "Moseley, you know all my life I've heard about a monkey trying to fuck a football. I never believed it was possible, but that's been going on out here." That was probably the most accurate description of the confusion and backside covering that had gone on that day.

That was the situation into which young Governor Bill Clinton walked. He stood up, and he stood up for the people of Arkansas. And he demanded assurances that the military would do whatever was necessary to prevent another mass riot and rampage outside the fort and into the territory of the people of Sebastian County. He had a terrible time. There was one telephone call after another to the Department of Defense, which maintained they had no responsibility whatsoever, that it was a civilian matter, that they were just providing a place for the Cubans to sleep. Clinton stood his ground.

Bill refused to leave the fort without a resolution of his problem.

He did not win his fight until after two in the morning. Again and again, the federal and military officials said, "This has gone on long enough. We can take this up tomorrow." Clinton said, "No. This meeting will not end until I have assurances."

Finally, the White House ordered the Department of Defense to order the commanding general at Fort Chaffee to do whatever was necessary to keep the Cubans on the military reservation.

With the military now actively engaged, the uprising ended. Fort Chaffee would be quiet the rest of the summer.[11]

I thought Clinton handled himself with remarkable restraint, maturity, and decisiveness. I believe to this day that this was his first real test in a crisis situation. I think he handled it well.

While Bill had made the best of a bad situation, he could see the peril the Cubans presented in an election year. He shared his concerns with Washington.

Peter Bourne worked in the Carter White House.

Peter Bourne: Clinton extracted a commitment from the White House that there would be no further refugees sent to Fort Chaffee. He said, "It's killing me politically here in Arkansas," and the commitment was made in Carter's name. Subsequently, more people were sent to Arkansas.

In August, Carter called Bill with the bad news. Because the facilities in Pennsylvania and Wisconsin housing the rest of the Cubans were not insulated against the coming cold weather, the president told the governor, he was transferring those refugees southward, to Fort Chaffee.[12]

Clinton later said that this is what cost him the governorship.

Rudy Moore: Frank White started running these ads saying Bill Clinton wouldn't stand up to Jimmy Carter. Jimmy Carter wasn't very popular in 1980.

Steve Smith: The way that was used against him primarily was as a racial issue. The same way that Hispanics are still discriminated against by legislators who want to yell and scream about race.

Marie Bruno: He handled it as best he could, but he just wasn't going to recover from that.

There were no more disturbances by Cubans before Election Day, but that tranquility did not erase Bill's electoral problem. He was desperate to limit the damage.

Jack Moseley: He called me and said, "Jack, I need your help. I need an editorial that says I did everything right with the Cubans."

I said, "Governor, you are welcome to use and reprint the editorials I wrote at the time. But I cannot write an editorial like that. I feel that you politicized a lot of the situation during the current campaign."

He paused and said, "You're going to endorse that son of a bitch, aren't you?"

That was Frank White, his Republican opponent. I said, "Governor, you need to wait and see what the paper says on Sunday."

He then went into absolute rage and began cussing and told me that he was tired of "taking shit" from a "total asshole" like me, and he wasn't going to stand for it. He wanted to talk to the people who ran the company, who owned the newspaper. He wanted me to get in touch with them and have them call him immediately.

And then all of a sudden, he said, "Oh, my gosh."

I said, "What happened?"

He said "It's the baby. She just rolled off the bed."

Chelsea Clinton had arrived on February 27, 1980. Unlike his father, Bill had lived to see his child.

He had called me from the bedroom in the governor's mansion in Little Rock. Hillary was out shopping and he was babysitting with his daughter. The baby had rolled off the bed and I heard the baby crying. Then I heard him cooing and talking to the baby and whatnot.

He came back and I said, "What happened?"

He said "Oh, it's a thick carpet. The baby's okay. Now, where was I?"

I said, "Well, you had just said so-and-so."

"Yes, and you son of a bitch, I want to say this, this, this and this. And god dang it, get your bosses on the phone. I'm not gonna take it." So I went and contacted my boss and informed him of what the governor's message had been. He said, "He's gonna have a long goddamn wait for any of us to call him. We never liked him in the first place. You're the one who's his buddy."

The following Sunday, I endorsed his opponent.

"Arkansans were in a bad mood."

Rudy Moore: You have to remember that this was not that long after Vietnam and, particularly, Watergate. It was the year of the Olympic boycott, the Iranian hostage crisis.* We had double-digit inflation in 1980. The economy was clearly in the dumps, we had interest rates of twenty percent and more on bank loans. It was a hard time. And by the way, those are things Clinton didn't have any control over. In Arkansas there were things he didn't have any control over. There was a gasoline shortage in 1980. It affected farmers, it affected truckers, it affected consumers. There was a heat wave in the summer of 1980. There were water restrictions. There were areas in southeast Arkansas that were disaster areas because of the drought. All those things contributed to a bad economy in Arkansas.

Arkansans were in a bad mood in 1980.

Marie Bruno: And then the missile silo blew up.

Patty Howe Criner: In Damascus, Arkansas, we had a warhead that was loose on the ground someplace. We didn't know whether to evacuate the neighborhood around. There was a wrench that was dropped by a workman in the silo where the Titan missile was.[13]

---

*Jimmy Carter had the United States boycott the 1980 Summer Olympics in Moscow to protest the Soviet Union's 1979 invasion of Afghanistan.

The wrench that fell into the Titan II missile silo on September 19 broke open a fuel tank, setting off a fire and explosion that not only killed the mechanic, injured twenty people, and destroyed the missile, but also sent the missile's nuclear warhead flying into the surrounding cow pasture. Strategic Air Command assured the governor that the warhead was in no danger of detonating or releasing radiation. Nonetheless, Bill could not help feeling that a final insult had been added to an already multifaceted injury.

"I was beginning to feel snakebit," he would recall.[14]

Marie Bruno: Bill was in Hot Springs at the Democratic Party's state meeting. I could see the reaction on his face.

"I'm going to send old Bill a message."

The Democratic primary had taken place in late May, just as the Cuban situation was deteriorating.

David Pryor: In the primary he had a turkey farmer named Monroe Schwarzlose, who was really an old Nestor, an old character. He was close to eighty. I never will forget the first returns that came in. I was the commentator that night on TV on one of the Fort Smith stations, and somebody came into the newsroom and says, "You know this Monroe Schwarzlose is getting about 30-something percent of the vote." I said, "Oh no, that's not right." And then sure enough he was. People then sensed that Bill Clinton was in trouble.

Schwarzlose ended with 31 percent of the tally. Two years earlier, he'd received 1 percent.[15]

Rudy Moore: We didn't think about that hard enough.

Julie Baldridge: It was a lack of comprehension. And not to be disrespectful to Governor White, because I'm sure he was a decent, honorable person, but he just didn't seem like the kind of guy who could beat Bill Clinton.

Max Brantley: A whole lot of people voted against Bill Clinton in 1980 not expecting he would lose, not viewing Frank White as a candidate who was going to win, but saying, "I'm going to send old Bill a message." And boy, they woke up the next morning: "Damn, he won." There were a lot of people who would have taken their votes back.

Bill had won 63 percent of Arkansas voters two years earlier. This time he took only 48.[16] It was a bad year to be a Democrat: The GOP increased its share of America's governorships and of both houses of Congress, while Ronald Reagan trounced Jimmy Carter to win the White House.

Rudy Moore: He never blamed anybody else. He accepted the responsibility. He didn't whine about it. In fact, it was within days, we were trying to figure out what we could do to improve his political life after that.

7

Out of the Woodshed:
Exile and Return

"Bored stiff."

Max Brantley: The guy was like a death in the family. He was really destroyed after losing that election.

Soon after he left office in January 1981, Bill went to work for Wright, Lindsey and Jennings, a large law firm in Little Rock.

Ellen Brantley: I don't think he did much legal work. I think he stayed in his office and was calling all his political contacts.

Carolyn Staley: Bored stiff. Lost. At sea. He didn't want to be there. He thought a hundred dollars an hour—whatever it was—was outrageous to be making as a lawyer, even as a former governor.

Carolyn Staley: The good news about a two-year term is that it's not that long that you have to sit out. Betsey Wright came on board, and she began taking his scrap-paper people list and making a database for him for reelection.

Kent Rubens: Bill Clinton depends upon the public attention. There was no doubt in my mind that he was going to run again.

"It would be fair to say he was gloating."

His first move was to confess and repent. Working with his political guru (and evil twin), New York political consultant Dick Morris, he recorded a television commercial in which he begged Arkansas's pardon and announced his intention to seek the statehouse again. It began running in February 1982.

Max Brantley: The apologies. Yeah, that was the first step, the ad that said, "I'm guilty of doing too much but I've learned a lesson and I've been to the woodshed and I'm going to listen to you more." It was very effective.

He promised to do better this time, stating, "my daddy never had to whip me twice for the same thing."[1]

Max Brantley: Concurrent with Bill Clinton apologizing for his mistakes, his wife made it public that she was going to adopt his name and not be Hillary Rodham any longer; she was going to be Hillary Clinton. I think that was her way of saying, "Okay, I'm apologizing, too." That had to be hard for her but she didn't let it show.

I don't think Hillary ever quit, and Betsey Wright came in and started bucking him up. Somewhere along the way he got the fire to run again.

In May, Bill won 42 percent in a three-way Democratic primary; two weeks later he won the runoff with 54 percent, setting up a rematch with White in November.[2]

Frank White was an amiable sort of guy but he was not much of a leader and didn't establish much of a record and was pretty well a tool of the electric company and a few other special interests. He was easy work for Clinton the second go-round. The black vote was astonishing. It was enormous, enthusiastic, and universal. When I saw the weather was good that day and I saw the lines of people at black voting precincts I thought, Bill Clinton wins.

He clobbered Frank White.

On November 2, 1982, Bill won back the governor's mansion with 55 percent of the vote. He carried fifty-six of the state's seventy-five counties.[3]

Ellen Brantley: When he beat Frank White, he was always gracious in public. But I saw him somewhere, and it would be fair to say he was gloating. He knows enough to say the right thing, but it was a payback kind of deal in his mind.

That was fine; I was gloating, too. Everybody liked Frank White, but, I mean, he was a dope.

8

Busy, Busy, Busy:
Governor Again

"He led us to expect miracles."

Kent Rubens: When Frank White defeated him, I think he took a paralyzed oath that he'd never again be for something that 51 percent of the folks were against.

You see in Clinton a view that getting elected is more important than a principle. He has some clear exceptions. Women's rights is probably the biggest one that comes to my mind—he's been stalwart there. But in terms of seeking compromise, he always does it. And makes no pretense about it.

Martha Whetstone: He learned that good ideas aren't enough. And you can't ignore the values of the state.

I asked him, "Are you going to keep those people you had?"

"Well, I guess I can't really do that, can I?"

Bill's staff was older now, and all-Arkansas. The Three Beards, the high-powered operators who had tried to push the state faster than it wanted to go, were gone.

Ernest Dumas: The lesson he learned was that he had tackled too much and made too many enemies and so he couldn't get anything done. So he would come back and he would tackle things one at a time. And so he did education, and then he did some economic development. He never really took on the energy industries or any of those interests.

All those years Clinton was governor, I was an editorial writer at the *Gazette,* and all those years we always endorsed him warmly, saying, "He's still got a lot of promise. One more term and he's going do it right."

He raised some taxes and there were some significant improvements in education. He did a very modest highway program, and toward the end, in his last session of the legislature—maybe his best—he got a bit more done.

But it was a very modest, modestly progressive regime. I would not rank him, nor would most historians or political scientists rank him, at the top among Arkansas governors as far as progressive reform. Ranks down third or fourth, fifth, and that ain't a good crowd—I mean, among Arkansas governors the competition is not tough. But he was good for Arkansas—a better governor than the vast majority of our governors or other southern governors generally.

Yet he was so smart, with so much talent, such rare political gifts. That was always it. There was so much promise and he didn't deliver. He led us to expect miracles and all we got was modest good works. That's true of him as president as well.

Of course, part of the failures as president was because of Whitewater. If the Republicans had not taken over Congress in '94, and if Whitewater hadn't been there, we might have a national health care system, and he might have done a great deal more. I still think he was a pretty good president, but that's it: pretty good. Maybe a little above fair, but that's all.

You look back all across his career and you see so much waste. So much promise unfulfilled.

"He's truly due credit."

Whatever the emphasis of his administration at any given time, Bill was always, on paper at least, ambitious.

Max Brantley: He always had monumental legislative programs that covered a range of issues from crime and punishment to roads to what have you. But the abiding concern over the years was education.

Arkansas was behind in every category that you could name, from teacher pay to school district size to student achievement. It's always been so. So the bigger challenge—and this was a place where he's truly due credit—was to change the mindset about education.

Ernest Dumas: The central problem in Arkansas was that people really didn't value education. Kids needed to learn to read and write, but a higher education wasn't important. In fact, there was a fear of education, that if kids got educated they'd go someplace else.

That's all he talked about for years, was education.

• • •

Bill recruited Paul Root, his high school history teacher, to work on the issue.

Paul Root: Now, a lot of people before had talked about all the things that were needed in education, but everything that needed to be changed needed money to change it. The general understanding was, if you vote for a tax, you won't be here next time. But during Clinton's second term, people were saying he made it more dangerous to vote *against* education than to vote *for* taxes. I thought that when Clinton was gone, all that would be gone. But there are other leaders now who are keeping that thing alive. It goes back to him and his courage.

I was with him several nights when he was explaining to people what was happening in the worldwide economy—what would happen to these people who worked in a shoe factory or a shirt factory. He was warning them that all these jobs are going to go to Asia, and here are things we've got to do.

He would ask a question at the end of each session: "How many of you would lower your standard of living in order to ensure that your children never have to face this?" He would take a vote. He'd get 80 percent, asking people to be for raising their own taxes. It was like that night after night. He covered the state. There weren't many people he didn't talk to.

My question, when he was running for governor, was, "Can personality overcome philosophy?" I said, "Clinton is way ahead of us, but his personality will cause people to vote for him." It's been his personality, pushing good programs, that has made the difference.

Besides calling for a tax increase, Bill's administration recommended a package of education reforms, including universal kindergarten and added instruction in science. But it was another proposal that raised the ire of a powerful Democratic constituency.[1]

Kent Rubens: When Clinton wanted to get money for education, which was sorely needed and a praiseworthy project, what did he do? He coupled it with testing teachers. That made Joe Six-Pack happy. The idea that them thar' perfessors were going to be tested made the passage of the taxes palatable. Even though it was a gratuitous insult and even though the test was meaningless.

Max Brantley: It was hugely unpopular with teachers—the veterans had to take a test to be eligible to do the job they'd been doing for decades. It left a bitter, bitter taste with the teachers' union, the Arkansas Education Association, one that took years for them to work out.

Paul Root: It was the AEA who had helped to elect him in the first place, so they felt like he owed them some allegiance.

Max Brantley: There's the old saying around here: Bill Clinton will walk past a hundred friends to shake hands with an enemy. It's because of his understanding of the landscape. Are friends going to vote for a right-wing Republican? No, they're not. Now, the teachers' union in Arkansas, they might have supported a Democratic primary opponent against him, but ultimately they had nowhere else to go. He counted on that.

By contrast, if you win over an enemy, then you've really gained ground.

Bill got his education program, including the tax increase and the teacher testing.

Max Brantley: I don't think we can look back at what he did and look at where Arkansas is today and say that we made any quantum leap forward in product. But you can say that we've reached a point in Arkansas where more people think education is where our future lies. That in a state that had long said, "If it was good enough for my grandpap, it's good enough for me." That has to count as an improvement.

Kathy Van Laningham: I was going to Monticello one evening and driving down through the pinewoods of southeast Arkansas.

Kathy Van Laningham also worked on education issues as a member of the governor's staff.

It was election time, so there were all these ads on the radio, and there was a guy who was running for county judge. He came on the radio and said, "My highest priority is education." I thought, "As county judge you have nothing whatsoever to do with education."

But you couldn't run for anything in this state during that time without saying something about education.

I thought, Bill Clinton really put that issue in the forefront for the entire state and it paid off.[2]

"Do you know what those farmers are thinking over there?"

In 1982 Bob Nash was working on economic development for the Rockefeller Foundation after dealing with the issue as a state appointee of Dale Bumpers and David Pryor. An African American, he helped lead the outreach to Arkansas's black community during Bill's 1982 campaign.

Bob Nash: He called me at home, about 11:30 P.M., after the elections and said, "Thank you for helping me get reelected. I appreciate it." And then he said, "I want you to come to work for me. I want you to be my economic adviser."[3]

At first, Nash declined.

I decided that I was not going to do Bill Clinton's minority economic development work and I went to see him the next day to tell him that. When I got there and he started asking me questions about economic policy in the state and what was wrong with it, it suddenly hit me that he was not talking about minority economic development. He was talking about economic development for everybody everywhere all over the state.

The conversation got around to the substance of the job.

He said, "What is wrong with economic development policy in the state of Arkansas?" He knew the answer. He knew what was wrong.

Bob Nash worked as Bill's top adviser on economic development from 1983 to 1989. From 1989 through 1992 he headed the Arkansas Development Finance Authority.

He knew that the Arkansas workforce had to be better skilled, better educated, and better trained to compete in the national and international economy. That's more true today than it's ever been before, but he saw it two decades ago.

One day, Nash and Bill were driving to Pine Bluff for a conference with a group of bankers. This time, at least, Bill had good reason to be late.

Bob Nash: On the way to the meeting, he saw some people standing under a shed, talking. He said, "Let's stop and talk to those farmers over there."

I said, "Governor, we're going to be late for the bankers' meeting in Pine Bluff."

"Well, do you know what I'm gonna say to the bankers?"

"Yeah."

"Do you know what they're gonna say to me?"

"Oh, yeah. The lobbyists have been up to the capitol already."

"Do you know what those farmers are thinking over there?"

"No."

"That's why we're stopping over there."

"I get it."

We stopped over there with those folks and we spent about twenty-five or thirty minutes. He learned more about the issues of agriculture from those folks that was important for him to know. We were late for the bankers' meeting, but it didn't matter. They knew what we were going to say. We knew what they were going to say. That's the kind of instinct that has driven this man to where it's just amazing.

"He just did not want me to be upset with him."

Kent Rubens: What is it about Clinton? The answer's real simple: If you put him in War Memorial Stadium, Texas-Arkansas game (assuming it was still played), after two minutes you would have everyone in the stadium swearing that he or she met with Clinton for a full hour. That Clinton listened to what he or she had to say. And that Clinton convinced those folks that he had learned something from them that would save the world and he'd never thought of it.

Clinton is a hell of a listener. If you watch most politicians when they're talking, they're talking about themselves, their programs. Clinton, whether it's real or not, causes people to believe that he listened to everything they had to say. That is one hell of a trait.

David Pryor: He was a very effective governor. He lobbied one on one. He knew every legislator. He knew their strengths, their weaknesses, their wives' names, their husbands' names, their children, their dogs, their parakeets. He stayed in touch with them. He'd call them up at night. If they had a rodeo parade on Saturday morning, he was there and he was praising them. He won a lot of converts by doing this.

Kent Rubens: Bill Clinton wants to be liked.

Ernest Dumas: He hates disagreement and strife. He'd occasionally scream at his staff, but he didn't want anybody to be unhappy, to be mad at him, to be disappointed with him.

At a reception out at the art center one night for some French artist, in the reception line going through he got my hand and started chewing at me. He wouldn't turn loose my hand, and he got red-faced about some editorial or column I'd written in which I had criticized him as caving in to the big power interests. With people standing around and waiting, he just chewed me out. Of course, I was livid as well. My wife, who was standing beside me, was in a rage about it.

A while later, he sought me out and spent a good forty-five minutes talking about some things he knew I'd want to talk about—Ronald Reagan or something. He didn't apologize. He just shifted gears and got mellow and asked my advice about things. Obviously, he didn't care about my advice. He just did not want me to be upset with him. There are thousands of stories like that.

He did not want me to leave there that night upset with him. I think that's his whole life, it's everything he's ever done.

Numerous observers have described a remarkable Clintonian phenomenon. Here are four of them—with four different explanations of the phenomenon's cause.

Ernest Dumas: People would go to his office and they'd leave thinking, "Yeah. He's with us on this." Another group would come, on the other side of an issue, and they would leave feeling that he was siding with *them*. He didn't want anybody to leave his office unhappy.

Kent Rubens: You've got to listen to everything he says. Because you can walk away thinking you've convinced him and he's going to do something. And he can look you square in the eye later on and say, "I didn't promise that."

Gene Lyons: I've felt that his political genius consisted of: He can pick your brain on whatever your particular passion is, and by the time he's drained you of everything you know about the subject, he not only knows how you feel about it, he can also explain it back to you better than you explained it to him. Also, he understands intuitively the connection between what you think and how you feel, and who you are and what you espouse. So people think he agrees with them because he can explain their point of view to him better than they explained it to him, and they feel this empathy that he can give out. He's the smartest person I've ever met who actually seems to care about other people.

Max Brantley: I think what his process is, to understand your issue he'll repeat what you've said: "So what you're saying is X, Y, and Z." I think people hear that and they say, "Yeah he's getting it. He's with us." I don't think it's by design meant to mislead. I think it's part of his evaluation process.

Kent Rubens: You've talked to him. He sounded so understanding. But he doesn't do what you thought he committed to do, and you look foolish.

Then again, that's because most southerners don't ask direct questions. There are all sorts of understandings and winks. You never get to the point of saying, "Well are you for me or against me?"

Gene Lyons: What was that old thing we learned in sophomore philosophy? You can never step in the same river twice. That's Clinton politically. The river's always moving, and he's always moving with it, trying to keep his canoe in the middle of the stream, understanding that it's a river and he's not in control of it. For that reason I think people would get these intense crushes on him and then they would get their hearts broke, as they say in country songs. But always, when election time came around, he seemed the better of the alternatives.

This process is somewhat seductive. It's certainly like the process a person might use when he or she is trying to get laid: Tell me about yourself. Tell me what you think. . . . Well, that's amazing. Tell me more.

Maybe that person didn't want to fall in love. Maybe he or she just wanted to use you. I think that's a thing he did. Politics is always partly a process of seduction, isn't it?

"He starts eating these stupid things."

Joan Duffy: He eats like a pig, and he'd eat anything. I remember one time at the coon supper. I tasted raccoon; Clinton loved it.

Jimmie Lou Fisher: In Arkansas we're famous—not famous, infamous maybe—for the Gillett Coon Supper.

Joan Duffy covered Bill for the Arkansas Democrat *and the Memphis* Commercial Appeal. *Jimmie Lou Fisher was appointed state auditor by Bill in 1979. In 1980 she won election as state treasurer.*

It started years ago as a fund-raiser for the athletic program at the small school district there. Everybody that's anybody goes to the Gillett Coon Supper, and you're expected to eat the barbecued raccoon. It's very greasy and not very tasty, but there are folks who really enjoy it.

Joan Duffy: It's in Gillett, the hometown of Marion Berry, the local congressman. It's in January, and it's the start of the political season before the primaries. There are the pie suppers and the chicken dinners—the coon supper's the first one.

Jimmie Lou Fisher: The local gymnasium is where the coon supper is held. Marion Berry and his wife always opened their home to those of us who came from out of town—a place to stop and have a drink and hors d'oeuvres before and after you went to the supper.

Joan Duffy: I was in Marion Berry's house after the supper—there was a telephone jack in the kitchen and I was trying to use that to file a story. And Clinton is rooting through the cabinets looking to get something to eat. I guess he didn't have enough coon. He finds a can of Vienna sausage and he goes, "Oh, man," and he pops the lid and he starts eating these stupid things. I said, "You are such a pig. Do you say hello? Do you ask? I mean, you're rooting through this woman's cabinets eating her Vienna sausage."

"Oh, she won't mind."

He would do things that were so real that I never saw politicians do, because he didn't care about appearances—like licking his fingers at a dinner. I was like, "I can't believe you're sitting here and you got all these people and you're licking your fingers like a yahoo."

"Well, it was good. I liked it."

It was as though he didn't have time for those niceties of life. He had more important things to think about than table manners. Appearances were not all that important to him.

One time I was in the car with him and he was eating a McDonald's fish sandwich, and he's glomming it down, and I'm trying to get my notes together and he burps. The mother in me thinks, "Excuse me?" I think I stopped myself before I told him to excuse himself.

"You have to compromise."

Ron Fournier: He would tack and ebb as the politics changed or the situation changed. Some people say that's good, smart politics and the sign of an open, facile mind.

Ron Fournier covered Bill for the Associated Press in Arkansas, then in Washington.

Clinton is a guy who has never closed his mind to an opinion or a thought, who's always looking for another way to see something. That kind of open-mindedness got him in trouble when he couldn't close his mind on a decision and would change his mind, and then have to go out and explain it. That earned him the Slick Willie moniker.

Max Brantley: Charitably, you could say consensus building contributed to that perception. Uncharitably, you could say his attempt to try and please everybody led him to make formulations that were misleading, perhaps intentionally so. In trying to keep everybody happy, he ended up making nobody happy.

Dale Bumpers: I suppose all politicians can be fairly accused of that at some time or other in their career. I know I've changed my mind on issues. But it seemed with Bill Clinton that it was always some issue that was extremely visible, and people hated or loved it. I've heard so many stories about how he would change his mind about things. You show me a politician who doesn't change his mind sometimes for political reasons, and I'll show you a guy who doesn't know what he's doing.

Judy Gaddy: The thing that he taught me, especially in trying to get legislative packages and bills through, is that you have to compromise.

Judy Gaddy worked in the governor's office as Bill's scheduler and as a special assistant for constituent affairs.

You don't get everything you want the first time. You begin to get the reform, the changes that need to be made, and you get a little bit this time and then next time you get a little bit more. And people that fight you teeth and toenail—you may be with them next week.[4]

Paul Greenberg: I would say that there is a good case to be made for political expediency if you're doing it in pursuit of some principle.

The Arkansas journalist Paul Greenberg, now a columnist for the Arkansas Democrat-Gazette, *has been a caustic critic of Bill's for thirty years.*

I was never able to find the single principle that he would not compromise on, that he would not chip away at in order to keep people happy, which meant that they would vote for him the next time.

Max Brantley: Those who say Bill Clinton doesn't have a core—doesn't have a center, polls everything, goes whichever way the wind blows—don't fully understand Bill Clinton. There are issues throughout his career that are not negotiable with him. One of them is racial equity. He has been resolute on abortion rights. Another issue was the NRA. He stood up repeatedly to legislation offered by the National Rifle Association in Arkansas.

The NRA came around the country with cookie-cutter legislation that would prevent municipalities from passing gun-control laws. This was big in Arkansas. They ultimately passed it, but Clinton wouldn't go along with it. And they hated him for it.

Now, he did the requisite things that a southern politician will do. He was careful to be photographed out hunting—preferably with some dead ducks in his hand, coming out of the field, that sort of thing. He was not antihunter by any means. But Clinton himself still believes that the NRA cost Gore Arkansas in the 2000 election. They are a force.

So there are places beyond which he won't go, but he is a politician, and he's looking for solutions. And he believes solutions are more important than suicidal stalemates where nobody advances.

"Governor, get back in the house."

Kathy Van Laningham: I had a Ph.D. so I knew I wasn't dumb, I knew I could learn. But I will tell you, it is very intimidating to be around a man as smart as Bill Clinton.

Gene Lyons: The only thing I found out by getting into good classes and good schools was: There's smart, and then there's Clinton.

Kathy Van Laningham: To watch him and his grasp of all of the issues that come through the governor's office: Health Department issues, Medicaid, Medicare issues, prison issues. It was this array of very complicated things, and he had a grasp on every one of them.

Judy Gaddy: He wants to cram at least thirty hours' worth of work and events into every twenty-four hours' space. He's sure there's a way to do it.

He has a boundless energy—I've never seen anyone like him. He'll say, "I'm gonna rest for a minute," he'll put his head down or put it back and take a little cat nap, and I'll be doggone if he's not ready to go for another four or five hours. It's amazing. I think the energy comes from all the things he wants to get done and all the ideas he has. He's never still.

One time he was having terrible allergies while I was at the state house and we were trying to get him to rest. He wouldn't rest, and finally I marked a day off and I said, "I want you to stay at the mansion. You can't come here, we don't want you here, stay there. Stay in the air-conditioning and try to get your allergies under control." Not only did he call me 15 times, but also one of the times he called me I said "What are you doing?" and he said, "I'm outside sitting under a tree watching some of the yard people." I said, "Governor, get back in the house. Number one, you're supposed to be in air-conditioning. Number two, you don't need to be out there while they're pruning and cutting and raking and all that." I also learned the bad part about giving him free time is that he just sits there and dreams up things. Every time he called me he had a new idea of people we needed to get in touch with: "Get them in here, I want to meet with them. We could do so-

and-so and so-and-so." Finally we said we need to keep this boy busy because if we don't he's gonna drive us all crazy. So we brought him back and put him back to work.

Bob Nash: The National Governors Association has a summer meeting and a winter meeting each year. The governors would be there and key staff folks would be there. First of all, Bill Clinton was one of the few governors who had African American staff members with him at those meetings. That's one point I'll make.

When the formal meetings were over, the staff members would all go to the bar and talk about what was going on in their states and new programs.

Most governors would go off to these big, highfalutin parties—go where other governors were. Bill Clinton, over half the time, after the big formal meetings were over, would be at the bar with staff members from seven or eight different states picking their brains, listening to them about new things that they were doing in their states. He sat there for an hour with us. Other staff members would say, "God, I wish I worked with a governor like that."

"No, no, no, they were all my roommates."

Although Paul Fray and Steve Smith may have perceived betrayal by the man they considered their friend, a legion of FOBs have always considered him supremely loyal.

Martha Whetstone: He is addicted to human beings. It's like a drug for him. He can be with heads of state one minute and have a wonderful time and love all that, and the very next minute walk into the next room and play cards with somebody like me, and I know he loves that minute every bit as much as the other.

He's a people prostitute. He has to have people around him. He needs that. He can't be isolated.

Beginning in 1985, Craig Smith worked for Bill in a variety of political and policy positions. He would go with Bill to Washington, eventually becoming White House political director.

Craig Smith: I always used to make a joke with him that he went around and collected people. When he started to run for president, people would call from all over the country and say, "I'll coordinate the activities here in Dearborn, I used to be Bill Clinton's college roommate." Well, after you get about the seventieth call of somebody saying, "I'm Bill Clinton's roommate,"

I would go to him and I'd say, "This person called from Poughkeepsie and they said they were your college roommate."

"Oh yeah, that's right, that's right."

"And the Mayor of Portland, Maine, says he was your roommate in college."

"Oh, absolutely."

At one point I said, "What did you live in, a Quonset hut? How many roommates did you have?"

He said, "No, no, no, they were all my roommates."

His whole life—everything he did, everywhere he went—everybody he met stayed as a piece of his life.

That's why the whole FOB thing, when he ran for president, was such a big phenomenon. Because he had collected all of these people over the course of his life, and he knew folks everywhere. And it's because he cared about everybody and their stories.

Martha Whetsone: I've described him to people as a leech—but in a good way. Once he's determined that you're his friend, you can't shake him. People say, "Why do you people walk through fire for him? Don't you see his weaknesses, his faults?" Yeah, sure, but there is no one who does what he does to keep up a friendship. He doesn't trade you in, he doesn't trade you up, he always has time.

Paul Leopoulos: At the moment in time that he meets you, he looks you straight in the eyes and he knows who you are, and he remembers you.

An example of that was when my daughter, Thea, took some friends of hers to the airport to meet him. This was a couple or three years before she died. So he gets off the plane and there's four high school kids standing down there. And Thea introduced him to her friends. One of them was named Josh. And they take a picture and then he goes on.

At her funeral, Josh was there, and the president looked up and he said, "Hey, Josh."

Where does that come from? It's because he focuses. Every individual is important to him. Every life is important to him. People say, "Oh it's a trick." Well, no. Sincerity is not a trick. Sincerity is how you do things.

9

Comfort Level:
Bill and Black Arkansas

"It got played out in front of the country."

If its school board had had its way, Little Rock would have desegregated its public schools with much more ease, and much less infamy, than many other cities in the South. Only a year after the Supreme Court struck down segregated public education in *Brown v. Board of Education* in 1954, the Little Rock board unanimously endorsed a plan to gradually integrate the town's schools, beginning with the 1957–1958 academic year. But Governor Orval Faubus saw opportunity in the situation—opportunity to win white votes by inflaming white passions. And so, when nine African American students walked through a rabid mob toward the entrance of all-white Central High School on September 4, 1957, they found their way barred by troops of the Arkansas National Guard, acting at the order of Faubus.

A federal court order eventually forced Faubus to withdraw the Guard, but the police who took the place of the soldiers were unable to control the angry crowds that gathered daily outside the school. And so on September 24, President Dwight Eisenhower dispatched troops from the 101st Airborne Division. The following day, the nine children started their school year. "Mob rule," Eisenhower declared, "cannot be allowed to override the decisions of our courts."

Orval Faubus would win reelection four more times before finally leaving office in 1967. The city's school system would not be fully integrated until 1973. To Arkansans above a certain age, the words *nineteen fifty-seven* alone evoke a deep feeling of shame.[1]

Ernest Green: The black eye for Arkansans came because they saw themselves as not a Deep South state. They thought they had fairly progressive attitudes about race compared to Mississippi and Alabama and Georgia.

Ernest Green, now an executive in the financial-services industry, was one of the Little Rock Nine—the group of African American youngsters who enrolled that fall in the formerly all-white school.

If it had not been for the emergence of television, this would've been a local story that few people saw. But it got played out in front of the country. It was the imagery—mobs in the street, the nine of us simply pursuing a better education—that helped move President Eisenhower to say, "Enough is enough."

From my discussions with President Clinton, I know that as a boy—he had to be in fifth or sixth grade—he followed these events closely. His reaction at the time was he was disgusted by it. He thought it was not the way adults should act.

The imagery affected Arkansas's ability to grow. Faubus left a legacy of limited economic development, few job opportunities.

Lottie Shackelford served as Little Rock's mayor, 1987–1991. She was the second African American to hold that position.

Lottie Shackelford: When Bill Clinton was governor, he spoke of how '57 forced people to take a look at themselves.

"He believed in pushing the buttons."

Bob Nash: Bill Clinton was hell-bent on making sure that the people in the state government looked like Arkansas—women and people of color.

Max Brantley: He didn't fall back on the tried-and-true liberal cliché of "I really would like to hire blacks but I can't find blacks who are qualified." He found them. He put a black man, Mahlon Martin, in charge of the state Department of Finance and Administration, the biggest job in state government by some reckoning. And he was not a token. He was a guy who was qualified for the job and was one of the great figures in the early Clinton administration.

If one action Bill took as governor displays the scope of his imagination on the matter of race, it is the Martin appointment. He appointed this African American not to run an antipoverty program, not to be a liaison to minority communities, but to be in charge of the state's money. Such an appointment may seem unremarkable now; it didn't then.

Rodney Slater: I remember when it was done it was like, "Did he do that?"

Rodney Slater, a prominent African American aide to Bill in Arkansas, would serve as director of the Federal Highway Administration and secretary of transportation during Bill's presidency.

It was a signal at the very outset that "I see talent everywhere and I'm going to bring the full talent of the state to bear."

Ernest Green: He brought in talented young African Americans in nontraditional areas: Mahlon Martin; Rodney Slater, an aide to him who eventually ended up on the Highway Commission. Nobody black had ever been put on the Game and Fish Commission, the State Police. One of the campaign commitments that he made in '82 was to put African Americans into every state bureaucracy. He really lived up to that commitment. People like Richard Mays and Les Hollingsworth served on the Supreme Court.

Richard Mays: I had a big afro. I was a part of an integrated law firm that was activist in the area of civil rights, school desegregation, police brutality, employment discrimination.

Richard Mays, a lawyer in Little Rock, was appointed by Bill to serve out an unfinished term on the state Supreme Court.

Lottie Shackelford: A more cautious person would have tried to get someone who was a little more mainstream than Richard Mays. But Clinton was not that kind. He believed in pushing the buttons.

Richard Mays: He was effective because he could communicate differently about those issues—saying "diversity" as opposed to "integration": "Our strength is in our diversity. We want to be stronger as a community, so we can't leave talent isolated." He was saying it in a way that the white community felt less threatened, and the black community totally understood it. When whites hear "integration," they think about forced social interaction. When they hear "diversity," it's entirely different.

Bob Nash: For us, particularly African Americans and people who have been shut out, to have a guy like this to bring you inside was something that you wouldn't have dreamed would happen in your life.

Dale Charles, the longtime head of the Arkansas chapter of the NAACP, has been one of the Bill's few persistent critics among the state's African Americans.

Dale Charles: Bill Clinton made some strides to address equality, but I think he kind of gauged the climate and saw it wasn't wise to do an awful lot, because the people were just not ready. The African American community was not ready for great change. They wanted just a little bit. A little bit was one person appointed to these boards and commissions.

He put some into his cabinet who had never served before, which symbolically made a great difference. But he could've done more.

Paul Greenberg raises another issue.

Paul Greenberg: He was much more comfortable appointing prominent black folks to his administration than he was in actually changing the law. We did not get a standard civil rights act until Jim Guy Tucker, his successor. I think he didn't want to offend the business community.

His popularity in the black community is a great testament to his personal charm. He's given some very good speeches in black churches.

He practiced a kind of patronage civil rights that brought black votes to his administration. But he never actually risked anything for the cause of civil rights.

Lottie Shackelford: I was on a radio talk show in 1992 in Illinois, and a councilwoman called and blasted me for asking folk to support this southern white man, and then says, "I wouldn't live in a state that didn't have a civil rights law." To which I said, "Bill Clinton has done more for civil rights even without a law than Illinois has done with a law." Bill Clinton named a black guy director of the Department of Finance and Administration. You still can't find that much these days.

"He attended funerals."

Richard Mays: I remember an event when he was attorney general—a party at the home of a young lady he had working for him. Clinton was the only white there, and you could not tell in any way that there was discomfort. I was impressed with that. Blacks frequently find themselves in an event where they are a significant minority. Whites usually don't, unless they're traveling abroad. Clinton had a comfort level that allowed him to connect to people.

Max Brantley: He's got rhythm. He goes to a black church and he sings and claps along with the hymns. He does not seem out of place there, as a lot of politicians might.

Craig Smith: You never hear him use racial epithets in private. Clinton doesn't think of blacks or gays or any minority as a minority. He thinks of them as human beings. And that is not an act.

Ernest Green: People thought that here was a white person who spent time really trying to understand what was going on in the African American community. And he knew individuals. He invited people into his house. He attended weddings. He attended funerals. He didn't just find the black community during campaign time. He had relationships that went beyond that. He could talk to you about what your kids are doing and did you mow your lawn last week—the kinds of discussion that real people have. That's not something that most whites, whether they were politicians or not, were able to do. Clinton felt comfortable around black folks, so black folks felt comfortable around Clinton.

We were on a trip once, and he said that he was one of the few white people who knew all three verses to the Negro National Anthem, "Lift Every Voice and Sing." I said, "Mr. President, I beg to differ. One of the few *people* who know all three verses."

10

Not Bad, But . . .
Potential Unfulfilled

Two Arkansas journalists assessed Bill's tenure as governor.

Max Brantley: I don't think you achieve anything by losing, by rolling a bunch of stuff out and then getting beat on. But sometimes you get something hammered into such a consensus that it doesn't accomplish a whole lot. I was wondering the other day if somebody ever had the time and energy to go through point by point these dozens and dozens of pieces of legislation he used to introduce at every legislative session, and look at which ones passed—most of them did—and then what, if anything, came as a result of them. I'm guessing for a lot of them the answer would be: Not much. But it seemed like he was doing something. He was always busy.

Ron Fournier: There was a sense that if he had used all his political capital and all of his skills, and really tried to do some big things and taken some chances and been a little bit bolder; if he'd made sure some things got finished off and actually got implemented, and not just the bill being signed and claiming credit for it; if he'd used all the skills and advantages he had, he could have pushed the state even further. This goes back to the "slick" thing. He was a guy who very carefully calibrated what he was going to do. When you're that careful and that cautious, you don't reach as high as you would otherwise.

When you look at it, the state did improve, but it didn't make any leaps. It didn't leap in education standards. Its students still have among the lowest test scores. Its economy improved, but still was nowhere near the middle or top tier in the country. Its judicial system improved, but still had severe problems. The health care system improved, but nowhere near where other states have improved. You can't put the blame on Clinton, but the state is still in the bottom tier of most national rankings, and that's after he was governor for twelve years.

I don't think he lived up to his potential. And part of that's because he had enormous potential.

I remember writing in '92—and to me, it's the best way to sum it up—that the state was better off than when he started as governor, but not as good as it would have been if he'd lived up to his potential. It's the same thing as president. A lot of people will say, "The country was better off after he left. But he didn't live up to his potential."

I think his heart was in the right place. He tried to—and did—make the state better. But when someone is that talented and has that many advantages going for him, you always wonder, "What if?"

Part II

Rising Star
1987–1992

11

National Democrat:
Moving Toward the White House

"Let's go to Clinton."

Bill kept running for reelection and kept winning—to another two-year term, in 1984, and to four-year terms, in accordance with an amendment to the state constitution, in 1986 and 1990.[1] The longer he served, the better known he became nationally—if not among the general public, then certainly among the political class.

John Breaux: His reputation always preceded him. He was always being introduced as the next new leader.

John Breaux, a Democrat, represented Louisiana in the House of Representatives from 1972 to 1987 and in the Senate from 1987 to 2005. Tom Brokaw is a reporter for NBC News.

Tom Brokaw: I had been tracking him early on, from the time he first ran for attorney general.

I'm a junkie, I'm like the guys who follow the college football recruiting classes. That's what I do with politics. I've got my ear to the ground—Who's out here? Who's interesting? Who's good? And Clinton was this hot, young guy. When I was doing the *Today* show in the eighties, I would use Clinton and guys like Bob Kerrey, who was governor of Nebraska at the time, as my little repertory company. Got a story about housing, we want to hear from the rest of the country—let's go to Clinton. Clinton was a rock star. Whatever the subject—"I know something about that." And he did.

"There were always rumors."

Of course, a national reputation as a thoughtful policy wonk was not an end in itself for Bill—the pot of gold at the end of the rainbow lay at 1600 Pennsylvania Avenue. So in 1987, at age forty, he had a decision to make: Was 1988 the year to make his run for the White House? The decision rested, in part, on his estimation of his readiness for the campaign and for the office. But there were other considerations.

Max Brantley: There's no doubt he was wrestling with personal issues—he knew there was a possibility they would arise. We were out watching our kids play softball in a city park one day, and we stayed long after the game, sitting on a picnic table. He talked to me for a long time, this not very specific discussion about, Is there a time at which youthful indiscretions are no longer asked about? Or are they doomed to follow you the rest of your life?

Turned out he had this discussion with any number of people. Gary Hart had become an issue. I think that had brought it into focus for him.

In May 1987 Senator Gary Hart of Colorado, the leading contender for the 1988 Democratic presidential nomination, was linked romantically by the *Miami Herald* to a woman not his wife. Hart lasted only days before dropping out of the race.

I didn't know what he was getting at. I guessed it was a drug question— smoking marijuana or something. Who knows what he really meant at that point? We can guess there'd been some marital indiscretions, if half the stories out there are true. Some of them must be true.

But understand, that was not a big issue with the press here at that time. It was commonly mentioned by a lot of people, but it never once, to my knowledge, had made it in any form into any medium—radio, TV, or newspaper. Of course, that was before the Internet, where anybody can say anything and publish it. I'm sure I heard it said, but I had no knowledge, even thirdhand, that it was so. Was he a flirt? Yeah. But what does that mean?

Anyway, when he made the decision not to run in 1988, he used Chelsea as an excuse.

Craig Smith: Came very close to running. Scheduled an event in Little Rock in the summer of 1987. At the last minute it came down to Chelsea, who was seven then.

I used to travel with him. He'd say, "We're going to Pine Bluff tomorrow. Meet me at the mansion, we'll leave from there." And I get there in the morning and the first thing we would do is drop Chelsea off at school. He took Chelsea to school every day. He said, "Let me give you a piece of advice if you're going to have a life in politics. Take your kids to school in the morning, because you never know what time you're going to get home at night."

We had a little lunch set up—about ten or twelve of us at the governor's mansion, talking about it—and he said, "Look, I'm not going to do it. I'm young, there will be other times in my life. I was with Chelsea last night, and she looked at me and she said, 'If you're going to go do this, Dad, does that mean I'm not going to get to see you anymore?' And the answer is yes, she is."

Richard Mays: We'd been meeting regularly as he was deciding whether he was going to run—we'd had maybe eight or ten meetings. It looked like he was going to run.

The biggest issue circulating was the womanizing. Some people who were a part of that process were saying, "If he runs, they're gonna go and find every bimbo this side of the Mississippi River. And that's gonna be a big number." But even with those questions, everybody around him thought, "Look, this is your time. Even if you don't win, you need to establish your presence. You need to run." Well, I didn't know he wasn't going to run until he made the statement at the luncheon. He'd had consultants come down for the luncheon—people who were going to work on his campaign.

When he said, "I'm not gonna run because of my daughter and my family," in my mind I said that whatever the reason he's chosen not to run, I still see him as a viable candidate.

Nobody questioned his talents.

Joan Duffy: Everybody knew that Clinton had the eye for women, and there were always rumors. I think there was probably some infidelity going on, but I don't think it was with the people we know.

Here's the deal with Bill Clinton: He loves the attention. He loves to be the star of the show. He's got an ego like most men do, but he's got more ego, super über ego, because he's a politician and he loves to talk and he has that charisma and women are attracted to politicians for some godforsaken reason. Does he love his wife? Yeah, he loves his wife, and they're committed to each other, and they have a connection, an intellectual connection, that no Gennifer Flowers or Paula Jones is going to take away.* A lot of it is just that women are hoping to get a little time with him, and he'd be sitting there talking about policy. He can be a goober.

Ron Fournier: As we got closer to the '92 election, probably starting in '90–'91, we realized, "We're covering someone who may be a national figure."

---

*Gennifer Flowers is the Arkansas lounge singer whose tale of an affair with Bill surfaced in early 1992. Paula Jones is the Arkansas state employee whose sexual-harassment case against Bill led to his impeachment.

We started reporting on the rumors. We ran them all to the ground. My bureau chief secured an affidavit from Gennifer Flowers saying she had not had sex with the governor. She repudiated it a year or two later.

We weren't able to verify the rumors or we would have done something with them. None of the accusations that came out after the election surprised me, but I still don't know which ones are true and which aren't.

How do you know? We all heard his denials on Gennifer Flowers. There were a lot of other names floating out there. A couple of the women I actually knew, and I'm convinced those rumors weren't true. There were other rumors out there that haven't been disproven.

You'd have people tell you stuff as if they knew about it, but they weren't willing to put it on the record, which always made me wonder how much they really knew.*

Gene Lyons: There are two kinds of womanizers: the ones who like women and the ones who don't. He's one of the ones who does. I knew the women who worked for him. He didn't put his hands on them. He treated women with respect.

Most people find my wife attractive. She never got a flutter. All of her buddies are attractive women roughly Clinton's age. They've all been around him, one of them worked for him. He never got out of line, so none of them knew how to take those stories. Probably, in hindsight, the way he operates is like a lot of ballplayers or celebrities: The girl has to make the first move. If she does, well, let's go.

"It was crushing for him to bomb before the world."

Harris Wofford: The Democratic Convention of '88 was where he laid an egg by his nominating speech.

Harris Wofford, who was JFK's White House adviser on civil rights, represented Pennsylvania as a Democratic U.S. senator from 1991 to 1995.

Bill's first big national moment came in Atlanta on July 20, 1988, when he gave the speech nominating Massachusetts Governor Michael Dukakis, the victor in that year's round of presidential primaries, at the Democratic National Convention. Far from making Bill's career, the speech nearly consigned it to an early grave.

The only positive reaction from the delegates came after he said, "In closing . . ." Bill later called the speech "thirty-two minutes of total disaster."[2]

---

*This author's experience exactly.

David Pryor: The expectation level was so high for him. It was crushing for him to bomb before the world.

After that speech was the lowest point I've ever seen him—he'd been laughed at, booed, hissed at. The national press were ridiculing him—jokes, editorial cartoons. He did not want to get up and come out of his hotel room the next day, he was so embarrassed. Bruce Lindsey* got him to come out. Bruce says, "You're going to face the world." Within about a week he was on the Johnny Carson show. He used humor, and he pulled it off.

Hollywood producers Harry and Linda Bloodworth Thomason, FOBs from Arkansas, arranged for Bill to appear on *The Tonight Show,* whose host, Johnny Carson, had been taking great delight in Bill's oratorical misfire. (Bill's speech, Carson cracked, had as much popular appeal as "the Velcro condom.") Carson's first question for Bill was, "How are you?" and before Bill could begin his answer, Johnny took out a large hourglass to time it. Although aching inside, Bill tossed off a few self-deprecating one-liners, making the best of the humiliating situation. Before he left he sat in on sax, for George Gershwin's "Summertime," with Doc Severinsen and the band.[3]

Jimmie Lou Fisher: He came on *The Tonight Show* with his saxophone and made light of the fact that he talked too long. We all breathed a sigh of relief.

"That was what Bill Clinton learned from 1988."

During the summer of 1988 Vice President George H. W. Bush, the Republican presidential nominee, under the ruthless guidance of the political guru Lee Atwater, launched a set of withering character attacks on Michael Dukakis, impugning his patriotism, his record, and his decency. The most inflammatory charge was that he favored the well-being of criminals—especially criminals with dark skin—over that of their victims: Dukakis had approved a weekend prison furlough program in Massachusetts that saw Willie Horton, an African American murderer sentenced to life without possibility of parole, fail to return to prison until after he'd committed rape and armed robbery in Maryland. The charges added up to one thing: Dukakis was a "liberal." While liberalism had fallen out of favor in the age of Reagan, the word *liberal* wasn't a slur until the 1992 Bush campaign made it one—a label to be avoided by any politician aspiring to broad appeal.

Craig Smith: Clinton and another prominent Democrat went to Dukakis and said, "You've got to respond to these charges." Dukakis's answer was,

---

*A Little Rock attorney who, from Arkansas to Washington to the postpresidency, has been one of Bill's closest confidants.

"These charges are so ridiculous, I'm not going to dignify them with a response." Clinton was like, "Look, if you don't respond, people are going to assume the charges are true, because they assume that if they weren't you'd say so." Dukakis would have no part of it.

Michael Dukakis served as governor of Massachusetts from 1974 to 1979, then 1983 to 1991.

Michael Dukakis: There had been a lot of polarization under Reagan—I thought people were tired of that stuff. I said, "I'm not going to respond." It turned out to be a huge mistake.

By the time Dukakis recognized the need to respond forcefully to the allegations, it was too late—the image of him that Bush and Atwater had painted in the public mind was indelible. Bush coasted to an easy victory in November.

The lesson was not lost on the next Democratic nominee.

Bush's attack campaign on Clinton in 1992 was even worse. Nobody remembers that now because Clinton organized and equipped himself and his campaign to deal with it. And they did, very effectively.

Craig Smith: Every attack gets responded to. That was what Bill Clinton learned from 1988—it's a direct correlation. No matter what they say, you've got to respond. Because if you don't respond, voters are going to assume it's true, a hundred percent.

"He was trying to find language."

Dukakis's tactical blunders notwithstanding, the central lesson many Democrats took from 1988 was that the Massachusetts governor had been their party's second consecutive losing presidential nominee with a liberal pedigree and a northern address. Indeed, former Vice President Walter Mondale's futile effort to unseat Ronald Reagan in 1984 had already triggered a movement among some Democrats to shift the party's center of gravity away from its northern liberal orientation and its image as a servant of so-called "special interest" groups, such as labor and minorities.

Bill would make the most of the organization that resulted.

Al From left his job as a congressional staffer to become president of the Democratic Leadership Council (DLC), which he would head for twenty-four years.

Al From: The Democratic Leadership Council was formed in the early part of 1985 after the 1984 presidential debacle when we lost forty-nine states.

There were a lot of us who thought that if we didn't do something to modernize the Democratic Party, to reconnect it with voters who had been straying, this great party that had been the source of so much of the economic and social progress in the twentieth century was going to cease being a national party.

We had lost touch with middle-class voters. We were a party that in the 1980 platform spent three times as much space talking about police brutality as public safety.

Walter Mondale: The DLC was started as a reaction against what I was doing and people like me were doing. They decided that we were too liberal, that the image that we were projecting couldn't resonate in the South and maybe in the West. That's what the DLC tried to shape. But unlike some of the others in the DLC, Clinton tried to remain close and within reach of the old constituencies in the North. He was not seen as an alien force coming North at all.

Clinton came up with these wonderful formulations about having a different kind of Democratic Party—a lot of what I thought were very good ways of emitting the signal of freshness, of differentness, without alienating a lot of people who felt strongly about things like Social Security and education. It's one of Clinton's geniuses that he never let that line get hard. Some of the DLC leaders just hacked away at northern Democrats, and I didn't like that at all. That was never Bill Clinton's way.

Al From: He started coming to meetings regularly in 1987. People would talk about him for days or weeks afterward.

In April of '89 I went down to Little Rock and I said to Clinton, "If you become chairman of the DLC, we'll pay for your travel around the country. We'll work together with you on an agenda for the country that our party needs in order to have a chance at winning the presidency again. And you'll be president someday and we'll both be important."

He said, "I'll take it."

While Al From ran the organization as its president, its chairmanship rotated among prominent elected officials, including Chuck Robb (1986–1988) and John Breaux (1991–1993). Bill held the position from 1990 to 1991.

John Breaux: As chairman he was able to take what we had done in the DLC, what he had done, and use it to do editorial boards and give speeches all over the country.

Charles Robb: Bill Clinton was already a darling inside Washington. His greatest value to us was that he was accepted as a legitimate national Democrat. And he had an ability to communicate that was simply superior to anybody else on the political scene at that time. He was a cut above.

Charles Robb, governor of Virginia, 1982–1986, and U.S. senator from that state, 1989–2001, was a founding member of the Democratic Leadership Council.

He was not eloquent in the sense of some of the great orators of our time. If you stop and think about it, there are not that many phrases or speeches that you remember. But everybody remembers being in his presence, and boy, did he make sense: He uncomplicated a complicated issue, and he was talking only to me. It isn't so much the specific words he crafts, it's the way he crafts them that makes the recipient feel as if they're crafted because he knows me, he understands me, he's talking to me. And then had the intellect to back it all up. You have people with one or the other, but you don't very often find somebody with gifts like he has, combined in the same person.

Henry Cisneros: He steers away from the language of the traditional left and away from couching things in divisive ways and finds the broadest common ground. I'd say it's one of his major gifts: the gift of language that is embracing, that is inclusive.

From 1981 to 1989, Henry Cisneros was mayor of San Antonio, Texas. He would serve in the Clinton administration as secretary of housing and urban development.

The language became well known—"ending welfare as we know it," education strategies that focus on accountability and performance, job strategies that are not just about economic development but about decent wages and economic justice in the workplace.

He was trying to find language that would appeal to the whole country. If you come from a state like Massachusetts, for example, you never have to find that bridging language. But Bill Clinton, being from Arkansas and a progressive, a Democrat, had to find language that would relate to the more conservative elements of Arkansas.

"He's somebody who's very careful with words."

Bill's facility with the English language had another, less appealing, aspect.

Paul Greenberg: When he would take a position, there was always a Clinton clause snuck in, a *sotto voce* reservation that would give him a loophole to get out of it in case he wanted to change his mind.

Max Brantley: As events would later prove and as we in Arkansas learned a long time ago, he's somebody who's very careful with words. He doesn't speak as most of us speak, in fumbling, inarticulate ways. He speaks nearly always in complete sentences, and the choice of words is intended.

Throughout his career and through his time in the presidency, his very careful way of parsing things, as the phrase came to be, got him in trouble. What the definition of *is* is; the marijuana thing, very famous: I never broke the laws of my country. Answers that, when you look back at them, were clearly evasive, but accurate to the letter of his saying them. The world at large has decided that he has lied in the course of testimony on Paula Jones, but as he has made the case, the intention was to leave a dishonest impression about some things without actually lying. His relationship with Monica Lewinsky—was it a sex act or not? That's the sort of thing that he's famous for.

As he was preparing to run for president, Bill staked out firm positions on domestic issues. On a preeminent issue of national security, however, George H. W. Bush's 1991 war to reverse Saddam Hussein's August 1990 invasion of Kuwait, he waited to see which way the wind blew—how Desert Storm, as the war was called, turned out and how the Democratic Party's primary electorate and the U.S. public at large came to view it.

Jim Hoagland: I remember meeting him for the first time at a New Year's Renaissance Weekend at Hilton Head, South Carolina, December 1990–January 1991.*

Jim Hoagland is the foreign affairs columnist for the Washington Post.

It was a month before Operation Desert Storm and we had an hourlong casual conversation, at the end of which I could not tell you what his attitude about Iraq really was.

That's the fascinating thing about the man, who is one of the most intelligent people I've ever met in any country. He was interesting, he was responsive, but when you sat down and really thought about what he'd told you, you realized that it was capable of being construed in several different, and at times even contradictory, ways. His verbal dexterity is phenomenal. I think it reflected an unwillingness to commit to a specific stand on an issue that could come back to bite him.

---

*Renaissance Weekends bring together movers and shakers from a variety of fields for a few off-the-record days of outdoor recreation interspersed with policy wonkery, power networking, and therapeutic confessional. Bill and Hillary first attended at the end of 1983, and attended regularly thereafter.

Lawrence Korb attended the same gathering.

Lawrence Korb: We had a panel on the lead-up to the war. I was on the dais looking out on him—we couldn't get him to go one way or the other.

The Reagan administration Defense Department official Lawrence Korb is a defense analyst with the Center for American Progress.

Paul Greenberg: In September of 1991, shortly after the Gulf War, I was attending a press conference at the governor's mansion, and he really lit into me for criticizing a commission he'd appointed. Then, almost as a throwaway line, perhaps in response to a question from someone else, he said, "Oh yes. I was definitely in favor of giving the president the power to go to war. I was definitely in favor of that war."

At the time, Paul Greenberg wrote for the *Pine Bluff* (Arkansas) *Commercial.*

I remember driving back to Pine Bluff, the sweat beading on my forehead. I was going to have to run one heck of a correction. I went back to our old files and looked up the Associated Press story, and our headline was, "Clinton Waffles on War," which was slightly different from our saying he had opposed it.

What he had said was that he agreed with the arguments of those who did not want to give the president authority at this point to go to war, but he wouldn't say how he would have voted if he'd been in the Senate. That was a typical Clinton clause. He left the door open so that he could say later at the governor's mansion, "Oh, yeah. I would have voted to go to war."

Bill, June 2004, fifteen months after the younger President Bush had launched his invasion of Iraq to finish what his father had started:

I supported the Iraq thing.[4]

Bill, November 2007, as his wife was seeking the support of an antiwar Democratic primary electorate:

I approved of Afghanistan and opposed Iraq from the beginning.[5]

"The whole place just exploded in sound."

Craig Smith: The two best speeches I ever saw him give prepresidency—one was in New Orleans, at the DLC in 1990, when he was installed as chairman. People were captivated. Sometimes when politicians speak, they speak really loud. At this speech he spoke very softly. You could have heard a pin drop.

Bill, New Orleans, March 1990:

In closing, let me ask you to remember what it's all about. I never get anybody asking me a question about the people that really count in this business. About four or five weeks ago, one of my favorite relatives, an 81-year-old aunt, died. And we took her down to the family cemetery 11 miles out down a country highway and three miles out on a dirt road to a beautiful old wooden church built in the late 1800s. And while I was there, I knelt by the grave of my great-grandfather and great-grandmother who were born in 1872 and 1873, and helped raise me when I was a little boy because my mother was widowed. I've got a picture of my great-grandfather holding my hand when I had my leg broken when I was five in my office, and he looks like a figure out of American Gothic, you know, with his overalls. And I look at that picture every day because it roots me. It gives meaning and organization and richness to my life.

And I was there in that churchyard thinking about the experience I'd had the first of last October when I went to Los Angeles. . . .

Bill went on to tell of a ninety-minute visit he and Hillary had had with a dozen inner-city eleven-year-olds, who told him of the gang violence that afflicted their daily lives.

And I asked these children to tell me about their families. And there was one child there not living with either parent, was a foster child, and she basically acknowledged that her parents were both drug abusers.

And then I asked these children if they thought they should turn in their parents if they were addicted to drugs if they knew their parents would not be put in jail for the first time, but would be given the opportunity for treatment. And all but two of those kids raised their hands. Now, it's a long way from a kid who can remember holding his great-grandfather's hand to a child who will never have a picture of a grandparent in the house and thinks that he or she ought to turn their parents in because they can't fulfill the most basic responsibilities.

That's what we're fighting for.[6]

Craig Smith: He finished speaking. Dead silence. I was thinking, This is falling flat. Then everybody leapt out of their seats. They were sitting on metal folding chairs on a hard floor—everybody jumped up so fast, a lot of the chairs collapsed. So there was this roar from the crowd and then you had all these metal chairs falling. The whole place just exploded in sound.

The second of the two best speeches recalled by Craig Smith took place in Illinois.

Craig Smith: It was at the J-J dinner,* in probably the spring of 1991, right before he decided to run. It was held in Carbondale.

We flew up there in this little twin-engine plane. We got there and we did the prereceptions and took a hundred photos. His speech built off what he said in New Orleans. And it was just stunning. At this time I've basically heard this guy give a speech five hundred times. So I was pretty much over the awe. But it was an incredible speech. After it was over the place exploded in applause and basically everybody got out of their chair and ran to the dais to shake his hand. He stood there, shook hands, and signed autographs for an hour and a half. Everybody was saying, "If you run for president I'll do whatever I can to help you."

After it was over we got in the car and we went back to the little Carbondale airport. And we got in this little twin-engine plane, and it was just me and him and the security guard. We sat down in the back seat, and the plane goes down the runway and takes off. We both felt that something unusual had happened that night. I didn't really know what to say. Finally, he looked at me and he said, "So what do you think?"

I said, "I think I'm sitting next to the next president of the United States."
We flew the rest of the way home in silence.

"What's a centrist these days?"

Did President Bill Clinton, with his embrace of the DLC's reexamination of Democratic verities, revive the Democratic Party or betray it? Did he modernize the New Deal or terminate it?

Did he save liberalism or kill it? Did he reverse or even slow the conservatism that had dominated national politics since the election of Ronald Reagan in 1980, or did he surrender to it?

Al From: We at the DLC looked at Andrew Jackson's credo of opportunity for all; Kennedy's ethic of civic responsibility; Truman's tough-minded internationalism, which we also got away from as we were traumatized by Vietnam; Roosevelt's thirst for innovation.

And so what I saw us doing was saying, Here are the first principles of our party. What are ways that we further them in today's world? How can we use activist government—which is part of the Democratic Party's DNA—in a way that is in tune with the times? Big bureaucratic government doesn't work. One of the hallmarks of the Clinton administration was, we used

*Jefferson-Jackson Day dinners are a tradition among state Democratic parties.

market forces to encourage progressive social ends. That was an important modernization: how you use government in a different era.

It's not right versus left, it's new versus old.

Michael Dukakis: When people talk to me about Clinton being a centrist, I've got to laugh. That's a big joke.

What's a centrist these days? I don't know, but he was very much a progressive guy. Okay, we disagree on the death penalty. Abortion's an issue, gay marriage is an issue, this kind of stuff. But in my judgment they're not at the top of the priority list. I'm talking about these fundamental domestic issues.

What he really did was get back to where this party ought to be and where it now is. What are we for? We've always been for a decent minimum wage. Basic health coverage for all working people and their families. Good schools. I could go on and on and on. That's where the Democratic Party has always been and should be.

Look at that first budget. Totally repealed the "Reagan Revolution." Gone in six months. Poof. People don't understand this. The so-called Reagan Revolution was repealed lock, stock, and barrel by the Clinton budget.

This stuff about Clinton in the mushy middle is absolute foolishness.

Douglas Brinkley: I was with President Clinton once at Hyde Park.*

Douglas Brinkley teaches American History at Rice University.

I got to talk to him a little bit about Franklin Roosevelt, and how much Roosevelt meant to him. He had read virtually every biography of FDR. He knew every cabinet member, knew the day of each bit of New Deal legislation. Talking with him in the library where FDR used to live, one felt that he considered himself a Rooseveltian, that his hero was FDR and his wife's hero was Eleanor Roosevelt.

That was the impression, but when you look at the record, it's very hard to see. He seems to be the end of the New Deal tradition. The Clinton years were a time when Bill Clinton was saying that he was a "New Democrat," meaning, "I'm not an FDR liberal. I'm not a Kennedy. I'm a new breed of Democrat, which is much more centrist, which repudiates a lot of liberalism. I'm closer to being a Rockefeller Republican† than I am to being a Roosevelt New Dealer."

---

*Birthplace of Franklin Delano Roosevelt, and the location of his presidential library and museum.

†Nelson Rockefeller, governor of New York, 1959–1973, and vice president, 1974–1977, was the most prominent of the relatively liberal Republicans of the 1950s and 1960s.

He made liberalism shameful—you didn't want to be caught with the "L" tattooed on your chest or you'd lose elections. That might be true, but a great Democratic leader would have embraced the liberal tradition: "If being liberal means caring about the poor, then I'm a liberal. If being a liberal means Social Security, then I'm a liberal. If being a liberal means education, then I'm a liberal." A real leader would've been able to grab hold of liberalism, because it's the great, noble tradition of the Democratic Party, and you can run on it. He never did that after his health care effort sunk in 1993.

David Kusnet was Bill's chief speechwriter during the 1992 general election campaign and for the first two years of the Clinton administration.

David Kusnet: A central part of Clinton's appeal was his ability to understand what was going on in the world. He understood sooner than most what the imperatives of the global economy were, that if you were going to get paid decently, you had to offer employers and investors something in return. You had to improve the skills of the people. He understood that, and he understood it from the perspective of someone who believed in the New Deal tradition, not somebody who thought that states running around chasing smokestacks and offering tax breaks and low wages was the way things ought to be.

The idea that you had to have active effort to sustain and maintain the social fabric and what he called "normal life"—that was something new. That you had to have more than material comfort for people, that there had to be some kind of community support to have structure and order and discipline in people's lives. Also, for all that we think of the New Deal as a liberal force in American life, it did very little about racism. Clinton was very much a product of and a believer in diversity. A thread in his life was this interest in people different from himself. You'd have his childhood friends coming up to visit him in the White House and work for him and you'd think he grew up in Brooklyn. There'd be David Leopoulos, who's Greek, and Vincent Foster, a Catholic, and there'd be some Jewish guy. He seems to gravitate toward the outsider.

Clintonism goes beyond the New Deal.

12

Going for It:
Candidate

"He's ready."

As 1992 approached, Bill had no doubt: It was time to run for president. First, though, during the summer of 1991, he had some business to attend to.

Gene Lyons: He went through this absurd charade of asking people's permission to run for president.

Max Brantley: He'd gotten cornered in a TV debate during the 1990 campaign for governor and pretty well directly said that if he were elected he would serve out his term. Then came the opportunity to run. He went on this listening tour around the state, supposedly to see if people would release him from his promise. Surprise! They did.

I can't believe anybody really believed that, given the opportunity, he wasn't going to run. Anybody who'd ever met Bill Clinton—particularly once he'd achieved the governor's office—knew immediately that this was a guy who was going to run for president someday. That was an inevitability.

Joan Duffy: On Fourth of July weekend it's traditional that politicians go to all the parades and picnics in eastern Arkansas, and he was flying around to them. He was using this trip to visit with people to see if they would mind if he broke his promise.

After one event, we were waiting to go back to the airport and there was a kid hanging back, a twenty-year-old grease monkey–looking kid with a ponytail. He was obviously waiting to talk to Clinton. Clinton shook his hand and the kid started to talk, and all of a sudden Clinton put his arm around him and moved with him away from the crowd, from the reporters, from the security. He had this long conversation with the kid, patting him on his back. He told me afterward that this kid had a horrible academic record and was getting ready to drop out of school. As we were walking to the car, Clinton was crying. Tears were rolling down his face. He said, "This is why I don't want to leave this job."

On October 3, 1991, standing in front of the Old State House, an antebellum landmark in downtown Little Rock, Bill announced his candidacy for the White House.

Carolyn Staley: The city was transformed. There were satellite dishes. There were bleachers for the press. The streets were blocked off.

Max Brantley: Huge crowd in front of the Old State House.

Carolyn Staley: There was a festival feeling. The expectation had been building from when he didn't run in '87. So now: He's ready, Hillary's ready, they think Chelsea's in a good place. It was an ain't-no-stopping-us-now kind of a feeling.

Craig Smith: I told him, "You're fixing to get on an airplane, you're not going to spend much time in Arkansas. We're going to get the biggest ballroom we have. We're going to invite everybody in the state to a fund-raiser. Minimum ticket price is five dollars, the legal maximum is a thousand. Anybody who wants to can come, stand in line, make a contribution. I need you and Hillary to stand there and shake every hand." He said, "How many do you think it will be?"

I said, "It could be a lot of hands."

We announced in front of the Old State House at noon, then went next door to the Excelsior Hotel for this event. It turned out to be three or four thousand people. He'd been governor so long, he knew every single one of them. He and Hillary stood there nearly three hours.

It was a way for the people of the state to say, "Look, we're for you. Go out there and do good." It was also his way of saying, "I won't forget you."

"I told him he was crazy."

Max Brantley: At that point it was almost a lark. I don't mean to say that people here didn't think Bill Clinton had what it took to be president. But after all, run against George Bush, winner of the war in Iraq? Governor of a small, southern state?

James Baker: Everybody opted out.

In August 1992 James Baker left his post as secretary of state to become White House chief of staff and from that position manage the reelection campaign of his fellow Texan, George Bush.

Lloyd Bentsen* decided not to run. All these other people said they weren't going to be the sacrificial lamb against a president who had a 90 percent approval rating.

In March 1991, following the successful prosecution of the Gulf War, Gallup measured George Bush's approval rating at 89 percent. In addition to Bentsen, other heavyweights who let the opportunity pass included Senator Al Gore of Tennessee, Representative Dick Gephardt of Missouri, and, most formidable of all, Governor Mario Cuomo of New York.

Max Brantley: I think the one person who thought he could win was Hillary. I think she saw where Bush's weaknesses lay.

John Breaux: I told him he was crazy to think about running against President Bush. I said he ought to wait until the next time. Bill Clinton said, "He's vulnerable on a lot of issues. The economy is one of them."

He was very right. I was very wrong.

Stan Greenberg: The general presumption was that given Bush's success in the Persian Gulf War, national security issues would trump other issues.

Bill hired Stan Greenberg to be his pollster in the 1992 campaign.

But I argued that the Iraq glow wouldn't hold up. In surveys we would test lines of attack on President Bush—almost all of them centered on the recession and the performance of the economy. People found the attacks credible.

It was also Bush's qualities as a person—they fit his role as a strong foreign policy president but reinforced the idea that he was out of touch with the economic distress people were feeling.

I was telling Clinton that this race was doable.

"He wanted to be president."

One of Bill's most successful decisions as he set his campaign in motion was hiring, in November, the political-consulting team of James Carville and Paul Begala. The pair had just scored a victory in a special election in Pennsylvania that

---

*Democratic senator from Texas, on the ticket with Dukakis in 1988; later Bill's secretary of the treasury.

allowed Harris Wofford to keep the Senate seat to which he had been appointed after the death of Senator John Heinz.

James Carville and Paul Begala both now provide political analysis for CNN.

James Carville: After the Wofford election, Clinton was talking to us and his people were calling us. The Bob Kerrey people were calling us and we talked to the Harkin people—everybody who was running at the time, I think, but Jerry Brown. We went to work for Clinton.

Bill's opponents in the primaries would be a former governor, Jerry Brown of California; two senators, Tom Harkin of Iowa and Bob Kerrey of Nebraska; and a former senator, Paul Tsongas of Massachusetts.

It wasn't a hard decision. It was obvious that he was playing at a different level than everybody else.

If you sit down and talk politics with him, he knows it. He was so far ahead of where somebody else would be. It's like a baseball scout watches five pitchers and sees Sandy Koufax. If you say "How did you know?"—you just knew.

Paul Begala: We met at a hotel in D.C. and fell in love with him. He was the first presidential candidate I ever talked to who didn't talk to me like a strategist. He didn't say, "I think I can win New Hampshire because of this reason," or "My wife's from the Midwest so I'll do better in the Illinois primary." He talked about his daughter and what he wanted the world to look like after eight years of a Clinton presidency. He had a strong sense that the economy was faltering and socially we were coming apart. It was very much what he wound up running on.

In most cases when you get a candidate, even one with some talent, you think, "He's a bit of an empty vessel into which we've got to pour some content." Clinton was already overflowing, so we were trying to think, "How do we reduce the content to bring some focus?"

It's like the emperor says in *Amadeus,* "Too many notes." You can't talk about fifty issues.

Dee Dee Myers was Bill's spokeswoman for the campaign and would be his first White House press secretary.

Dee Dee Myers: My first impression of him was, he had all the gifts you can't teach. He loved the grip-and-grin part of the business—a lot of politicians get tired of it, but he clearly reveled in it. And on a substantive level, he was talking about things Democrats needed to talk about.

Friends thought I was crazy. "Who is this governor of Arkansas? Haven't you worked on enough losing campaigns?" I'd worked for Mondale and I'd worked for Dukakis. For Democrats, the eighties were all about losing campaigns.

Even though my friends thought I was crazy, the national press was quite interested in Clinton. Joe Klein wrote a cover story in *New York* magazine. And Clinton gave a series of speeches at Georgetown. He was laying out his vision on domestic policy, economic policy, and national security policy. You might not agree with his positions, but I never heard anybody who had spent any time with him say, "This guy's a mile wide and an inch deep." He was a mile wide and a mile deep.

During the fall of 1991, Bill, looking to impress the chattering classes with the seriousness of his vision, delivered three speeches at Georgetown, in which he called for a "New Covenant" between the nation and its government.

"We need a new covenant," he stated in the first address, which laid out the concept,

> a solemn agreement between the people and their government to provide opportunity for everybody, inspire responsibility throughout our society and restore a sense of community to our great nation.[1]

Anthony Lake, a foreign policy veteran of the Kennedy, Johnson, Nixon, and Carter administrations, advised Bill during the campaign. He would be Bill's first national security adviser.

Anthony Lake: I flew down to Little Rock in the fall of 1991 to go over the speech on foreign policy a few of us had drafted for him to give at Georgetown.

After a second speech that dealt with economic issues, the third detailed Bill's approach to foreign policy.

Please note that no other Democratic candidate was talking about foreign policy, because Bush was unpopular for spending too much time on it. But Clinton did, which impressed me.

Emphasizing trade, Bill framed foreign policy in a way advantageous to a governor basing his campaign on bread-and-butter issues:

> Now we must understand, as we never have before, that our national security is largely economic. The success of our engagement in the world

depends not on the headlines it brings to Washington politicians, but on the benefits it brings to hardworking middle-class Americans.

Bill concluded that passage with one of his signature formulations: "Our 'foreign' policies are not really foreign at all."[2]

Anthony Lake: I don't even pretend to think that it was my phrase. I'm sure it was his. Of course, it would have been good politics to blur the distinction between foreign and domestic policy, so that you could keep drawing it back to the domestic. But that's not what he was doing. It really was more how you think about the "foreign."

Anyway, flying down to Little Rock, I changed planes at Memphis. On the plane from Memphis to Little Rock, a woman sitting next to me could see me working over the draft of this speech and it said "Governor Clinton" on top. She said, "Oh, you're going to see the governor?" I said, "Yes, I am." And she went off, for ten minutes, abusing him about everything. It was my first encounter with Clinton hatred. I said, "Oh, that's very interesting."

At the end of the day in Little Rock, I said, "By the way, Governor, I met a woman on the plane down here who was not a fan of yours." Guess what his answer was: "What's her name?" Because he was going to go out and convince her she was wrong.

Dee Dee Myers: The biggest issue in those first weeks was whether Mario Cuomo would run.

Richard Mays: Cuomo was perceived as the big honcho. And then he was from New York. Does he take the Arkansas governor's calls?

Mike McCurry: Cuomo, most likely the strongest Democratic candidate, waited till very late in the process to announce that he was not running.

Mike McCurry, a veteran Democratic press operative, worked as press secretary to the presidential campaign of Nebraska Senator Bob Kerrey and later filled the same role in Bill's White House. The columnist Michael Kinsley was from 1989 to 1995 the "from the left" cohost of CNN's Crossfire.

Michael Kinsley: Cuomo's a good example of how you can turn indecisiveness into a reputation for statesmanship and thoughtfulness.

Clinton went for it when everyone thought the Democratic nomination to be worthless because George Sr. had won the Gulf War. That showed real character. One of the many silly myths in American politics is that if you actually want to be president, that's a disqualification. You have to reluctantly agree to serve because it's so patriotic. Clinton didn't horse around with that; he wanted to be president and he went for it. That's admirable.

James Carville: In late November, early December I was more afraid of Douglas Wilder being in the race than Cuomo. Clinton and I thought that southern African Americans were the key.

Douglas Wilder, the African American governor of Virginia, entered the contest in September, then withdrew in January.

Any nonlobotomized person could watch Bill Clinton with any audience and see he was something else. And watch him with a black audience—he knew the tones, he knew the rhythms. Once we hit the South, you had high numbers of blacks voting.

We spent an inordinate amount of time in the South—no one was going to challenge us there.

No other candidate had that kind of connection, not even close. Clinton and I always thought that Wilder getting out was a big deal.

The New Hampshire primary would take place February 18.

Mickey Kantor: Iowa was not a factor because Tom Harkin was running; that was a terrific boon to us because we didn't have the resources to fight Iowa and New Hampshire.

Mickey Kantor, an attorney from Los Angeles, was chairman of Bill's campaign. During the Clinton administration, he would serve first as trade representative, then as secretary of commerce.

The more Bill Clinton campaigned in New Hampshire, the more he began to gather adherents. By January, he jumped to the top of the polls in New Hampshire. Not by a lot but by some. He held that position until the Gennifer issue hit a few weeks before the primary.

13

Near-Death Experience:
New Hampshire, 1992

"There was an article in a supermarket tabloid."

Dave McCurdy, a founding member of the DLC, represented Oklahoma in the House of Representatives from 1981 to 1995.

Dave McCurdy: In 1991, we both looked at running for president; I finally decided not to run. The next day, Bill Clinton calls and says, "I want to come see you."

"Great. When?"

"Tomorrow."

He flew up from Arkansas and met with me in my office in the House office building with his legal counsel, Bruce Lindsey.

He said that he knew how disappointed I was, but that my decision made him the happiest person in the world. He wanted my support.

And so we had a conversation, very direct, about philosophy and ideas and the campaign. I did end up supporting him.

In the conversation, I said, "Governor, I've been out on the campaign trail. There are some rumors. Before I can support you, I want to know that we share family values. We've talked about this in the past, but I wouldn't do either of us justice if I didn't raise it."

He looked me directly in the eye, in his very persuasive way, and said, "Dave, there's nothing to it. There's nothing you would ever have to worry about."

End of conversation.

Steve Kroft: Clinton was emerging as a force to be contended with. He was on the cover of *Time* magazine, and it was a very favorable story, saying he might be the most attractive and electable Democratic candidate.

Steve Kroft is a reporter for 60 Minutes *on CBS.*

That same week, there was an article in a supermarket tabloid, the *Star,* in which Gennifer Flowers, this former television reporter and lounge singer from Little Rock, told the paper that she had had a long relationship with Clinton. Twelve years, she said.

The news of the story broke in late January.

Jack Moseley: As frequently happens in scandal cases where one or the other person wants to kiss and tell all the details to the tabloids for a price, things get exaggerated. Now, the story about Gennifer Flowers and Bill Clinton, if I remember correctly, indicated that they had made passionate love on the top floor of the Excelsior Hotel in downtown Little Rock at a particular time and sipped wine. This didn't ring real true since at the time they were supposed to be copulating, that hotel was under construction and didn't have any windows in it. Also, the sipping wine didn't seem very realistic since Bill Clinton is allergic to wine and breaks out in hives anytime he drinks wine.

Gene Lyons: He may have given Gennifer Flowers a tumble or two, but she overplayed it.

It didn't take the local media much time to figure out that she was not a credible person.

Mickey Kantor: I remember that initial phone call. He called me from somewhere in a car driving between two towns in New Hampshire to tell me what was going on. He wasn't angry. He was focused on trying to walk through what she had said, what the implications were, how we should handle this. He knew he was going to have to face the press on it.

"It was tough medicine."

Steve Kroft: The mainstream press didn't report it the first night, but it was too irresistible to ignore. People started asking Clinton about it, and it got to a point where it was the only thing the press wanted to know about.

Bill & Co. were looking for the right forum in which to address the womanizing issue, so the campaign approached *60 Minutes,* normally broadcast every Sunday evening. On the upcoming Sunday, however, no show was planned, because CBS was carrying the Super Bowl. Kroft raised the possibility of a special shortened edition of the program immediately after the game.

Steve Kroft: That definitely got their interest up.

There were some discussions about what we would talk about, and I told them that the only thing we were interested in talking to them about was Gennifer Flowers; that we weren't going to give them time after the Super Bowl to talk about policy. Otherwise, there was no reason to do it.

It became clear to me that the Clinton campaign's goal was to address it, and address it only once. They were looking for a big forum so they could say, "We talked about this on *60 Minutes* and we're not going to talk about it again."

James Carville: We were trying to establish that they were a real couple and that there was another side to the story. And we weren't oblivious to the fact that there were piles of rumors around. We didn't want it to fester.

Bill and Hillary sat down in Boston with Steve Kroft for about an hour on Sunday morning, January 26, 1992. The interview, condensed to nine minutes, aired after the Washington Redskins defeated the Buffalo Bills, 37–24, in Super Bowl XXVI.

Steve Kroft: My aim was to get him on the record—I wanted to push him as hard as I could. I asked the same question like six different ways to try and get a denial or an acknowledgment: Are you denying you've ever had an affair with her? Do you deny you ever had a relationship with her? That was my whole point in doing it.

From the interview transcript:

Kroft: You've said that your marriage has had problems, that you've had difficulties.... What does that mean? Is that some kind of—help us break the code. I mean, does that mean you were separated? Does that mean that you had communication problems? Does that mean you contemplated divorce? Does it mean adultery?
Bill Clinton: I think the American people, at least people that have been married for a long time, know what it means and know the whole range of things that it can mean.[1]

Steve Kroft: That wasn't going to cut it. If he wanted this to be the one interview that he did, that wasn't gonna cut it.

I did pin him down on one question. I think people came away with the impression that he denied ever having a relationship with Gennifer Flowers.

Kroft: I'm assuming from your answer that you are categorically denying that you've ever had an affair with Gennifer Flowers.
Bill Clinton: I've said that before. And so has she.

Another "Clinton clause": Clearly, Bill is trying to convey the impression that he and Flowers never had an affair. Just as clearly, if the words are read carefully, he is not "categorically denying" a thing. (Six years later, under oath in the Paula Jones case, Bill would admit to sex with Flowers—in 1977 and only one time, he claimed.)[2]

Steve Kroft: I didn't really buy it. It's hard to separate now because of Monica Lewinsky, but I came away from it with the idea that yes, he probably had some kind of a sexual relationship with Gennifer Flowers and that he wasn't going to talk about it.

> Kroft: I think most Americans would agree that it's very admirable that you've stayed together, that you've worked your problems out, that you seem to have reached some sort of understanding and an arrangement—
> Bill Clinton: Wait a minute, wait a minute, wait a minute. You're looking at two people who love each other. This is not an arrangement or an understanding. This is a marriage. That's a very different thing.

That was the strongest point of the interview for them. He was obviously taking issue with that word and was very sensitive to the notion that some people considered their marriage to be an "arrangement."

> Hillary Clinton: You know, I'm not sitting here—some little woman standing by my man like Tammy Wynette. I'm sitting here because I love him, and I respect him, and I honor what he's been through and what we've been through together. And you know, if that's not enough for people, then heck, don't vote for him.

The fact that Hillary was there was, to me, the most important thing of the whole interview. She carried the day for him—the fact that they were able to say, "Look, we're in this together, we're working on this marriage. It's a real marriage." She was very strong and very impressive. She saved his bacon.

Gene Lyons: The amazing thing to me was that Gennifer Flowers actually helped him in the short run. It made him a nationally known figure. He said something that, to my knowledge, no American politician had said in the TV era: "Yes, I've caused pain in my marriage and everybody out there knows what I'm talking about"—and yeah, we do.

Steve Kroft: It was tough medicine. I think it was very difficult for the two of them to sit down and discuss their marriage on national television. That's not something anybody would want to do. They did it only because they had to. Like chemo, they survived it.

And it was very revealing. It was a crucial step in the Clinton political DNA. In a way, it defined both of them.

"He's not a cruel person at all."

In 1981 Ricky Ray Rector committed two murders in Conway, Arkansas. After dispatching his second victim, Rector pointed his gun at his own head and fired. The bullet did not kill him; it did inflict severe brain damage. After he'd spent a decade on death row, his execution by lethal injection was scheduled for January 24, 1992, two days before Bill and Hillary would appear on *60 Minutes*. Bill flew home from New Hampshire to preside. Rector, an African American, was put to death that evening.

To his critics, Bill's return to Arkansas for the execution—of a man who barely understood his plight—represented a cold-blooded move to burnish his crime-fighting bona fides. Four years earlier, Michael Dukakis had been tripped up by his opposition to capital punishment and his alleged liability for the crimes of another African American convict, Willie Horton. Bill, critics argue, was determined not to suffer the same fate. In addition, some say, the execution provided a handy distraction to a press corps preoccupied with his sex life.

Others defend Bill's actions. Here three Arkansans discuss the matter.

Kent Rubens: I am utterly convinced that he came back to the state of Arkansas during the 1992 campaign to make sure Ricky Ray Rector was put to death because it was good politics.

Max Brantley: Most people thought it was terrible that he would take a break just to come home and preside over an execution—that it was bloodthirsty, that it was gruesome. It was generally viewed uncharitably, as a politically calculated thing to do. Particularly because the guy they executed was mentally deficient.

But that may be unfair. Perhaps the charitable view is to say, Why pass to another person the responsibility to hear the final pardon request? He was elected to do it. He was going to be there to do it.

Maybe that's the fairest way to look at it.

Ernest Dumas: He's not a cruel person at all, I think he really is a deeply compassionate person, I think he does feel people's pain. My hunch is he grieved a little bit about that execution. I like to think he did.

"Much more damaging."

Mickey Kantor: The Gennifer situation, and then the draft thing. It was like getting hit twice in the face.

Stan Greenberg: If you look at what happened in New Hampshire, Flowers did not bring him down. It was the *Wall Street Journal* story on the draft that brought him down. The military side was much more important and would have been fatal in a different decade or even four years earlier.

On February 6 the *Wall Street Journal* published a story detailing Bill's draft history.

Paul Begala: Much more damaging, because it was more relevant. It hurt a lot.

Some of it was tactical mistakes we made. We had about a two- or three-day period where he was sick and he flew back to Little Rock. That turned out to be a big mistake. He needed to be out there answering it again and again.

Mike McCurry: Reading the *Wall Street Journal* story on the draft, I thought to myself, "Boy, there's no way this guy will survive this." Tad Devine, who was the campaign manager for Senator Kerrey, said, "I think Clinton's toast. We better get ready for the fact that he'll be out of this race within a matter of hours." He had successfully negotiated himself out from underneath the Gennifer Flowers story with the *60 Minutes* appearance. But, I thought, you can't sustain two of those.

James Carville: I would describe the feeling as a gut-shot Confederate soldier leaning against a tree ready to die. We flew back to Little Rock—like eight of us jammed in on one of these small jets. And then we got there, and got the polling. The bottom fell out. It was pretty gloomy.

Stan Greenberg: When I called the mansion my first word was *meltdown*. Then I gave them the numbers. A 15-point drop—from 45 to 30. But he was not dead. Thirty percent in a multicandidate field—he was not gone.

James Carville: We flew back to New Hampshire. We had eight days to go. When we got on the ground, Jim Wooten of ABC News meets us at the airport and says, "There's this letter where you talk about your 'political viability.' " And that's when I said, "Fuck this, we're going to publish the letter in the newspapers, and get out front."

Jonathan Alter: I was in New Hampshire with Clinton the day the letter—"Thank you for saving me from the draft"—was released.

Jonathan Alter is a columnist for Newsweek.

A health care forum was to be held at a hotel near Nashua. We get there, and Clinton is mobbed at the door. People are firing questions at him about Vietnam and the draft.

Inside, when it's his turn to speak, he passes by me and gives me a wink.

Totally self-assured, confident, the-bastards-aren't-going-to-get-me-down wink. And then he goes up on stage and he homers. Even though Kerrey has by far the better health care plan, and Clinton has been winging it and playing catch-up on health care, he's just fantastic.

I realized that this guy can take a punch.

Bill had written to Colonel Eugene Holmes on December 3, 1969, two days after his birthday came up 311 in the draft lottery. No longer at risk of an all-expenses-paid visit to Vietnam, and thus in no further need of the colonel's good offices, Bill was free to unburden himself.

The letter is a *cri de coeur,* to be sure, the passionate statement of an eloquent young man who considers his country's conduct immoral. It's also a vivid illustration of Bill's need to be liked—in this case, by a man he has deceived.

Bill begins by thanking the general "not just for saving me from the draft, but for being so kind and decent to me last summer, when I was as low as I have ever been."

He goes on to call Vietnam "a war I opposed and despised with a depth of feeling I had reserved solely for racism in America before Vietnam."

Some friends at Oxford became draft resisters, Bill continues. In the section of the letter that became the most controversial, Bill explains why he did not follow their example:

> The decision not to be a resister and the related subsequent decisions were the most difficult of my life. I decided to accept the draft in spite of my beliefs for one reason: *to maintain my political viability within the system.* For years I have worked to prepare myself for a political life characterized by both practical political ability and concern for rapid social progress. It is a life I still feel compelled to try to lead.[3]

Bill had taken the ROTC slot, he says, because "ROTC was the one way left in which I could possibly, but not positively, avoid both Vietnam and resistance." However:

> After I signed the ROTC letter of intent I began to wonder whether the compromise I had made with myself was not more objectionable than the draft would have been, because I had no interest in the ROTC program in itself and all I seemed to have done was to protect myself from physical harm. Also, I began to think I had deceived you, not by lies—there were none—but by failing to tell you all the things I'm writing now.

Bill says that he had earlier written a letter to his draft board asking to surrender his deferment and be drafted immediately, but never mailed it, because I didn't see, in the end, how my going in the Army and maybe going to Vietnam would achieve anything except a feeling that I had punished myself and gotten what I deserved. So I came back to England to try to make something of this second year of my Rhodes scholarship.

And that is where I am now, writing to you because you have been good to me and have a right to know what I think and feel. I am writing too in the hope that my telling this one story will help you to understand more clearly how so many fine people have come to find themselves still loving their country but loathing the military, to which you and other good men have devoted years, lifetimes, of the best service you could give. To many of us, it is no longer clear what is service and what is disservice, or if it is clear, the conclusion is likely to be illegal. Forgive the length of this letter. There was much to say. There is still a lot to be said, but it can wait. Please say hello to Colonel Jones for me. Merry Christmas.

Sincerely,
Bill Clinton

Stan Greenberg: James said, "This letter is your friend."

Paul Begala: The leak of that letter helped enormously.

People saw that he was like a whole lot of people in his generation. You read that letter and it's a heartfelt plea for his country. He loved his country. He'd grown up on John Wayne movies. About the only thing he knew about his father was that he'd served in a war. At Georgetown, he'd interned for Fulbright, so he knew more about the war than most people. He knew it was wrong. He didn't want to serve. I think you see all of that in there. He wasn't comfortable with the furthest extremes of the antiwar movement. There are these legends that he was burning his draft card. That's preposterous. It's not in his character. That letter was an extraordinary statement for a young man.

Stan Greenberg: That phrase, "maintain my political viability," was a problem, but the totality of it was not, and in the end we controlled the interpretation. If it was just an opportunistic letter to get out of the draft, he wouldn't have been the "comeback kid."*

Paul Greenberg: He writes a letter from Oxford to Colonel Holmes. It's not only a confession that the colonel had gotten him out of the draft, but there's a self-satisfaction there that this young man had fooled the colonel: "Am I not

---

*Bill's description of himself on primary night.

clever?" It's like he's still in front of the Rhodes Scholars committee showing how bright he is. And it's as if he expects the colonel to admire him for this.

If Bill did expect to make Colonel Holmes an admirer, he failed. In the fall of 1992 Holmes said, in part:

> I was not "saving" him from serving his country, as he erroneously thanked me for in his letter from England (dated December 3, 1969). I was making it possible for a Rhodes Scholar to serve in the military as an officer. In retrospect I see that Mr. Clinton had no intention of following through with his agreement to join the Army ROTC program at the University of Arkansas or to attend the University of Arkansas Law School. . . . I believe that he purposely deceived me.[4]

When the letter was made public, Bill's fellow Rhodes Scholars recalled the discussions they'd had at Oxford.

Robert Reich: He and I and others talked about the options, everything from conscientious objection all the way through various possible deferments and then obviously the option of serving.

He expressed moral indignation about the war, but his position was complicated by political considerations. Bill clearly had his eye on a political future. He had already talked about going back home and running for office. I think by that time he'd mentioned governor of Arkansas.

His political future was only one of many considerations. I don't think that it was the major one. He was, as I recall, genuinely and deeply perplexed about what to do in light of what we all considered to be the immorality of that war. To separate out one motive from the others is very difficult.

Plus, I don't think that when he wrote about "political viability" he thought of it in quite the cynical way the term might now be seen. All of us had a very idealistic view of what we could do with our lives. Politics was not a dirty sport, it was a matter of giving to the country. Viability, for Bill and for the rest of us, was about what we could do with our democracy not to help ourselves, but to help the country. It sounds corny saying it from where we are now, but that was very much the mood of 1968.

Bill, on ABC's *Nightline*, February 12, 1992, six days before the balloting in New Hampshire would take place:

> For three weeks, of course I've had some problems in the polls. All I've been asked about by the press is a woman I didn't sleep with and a draft I didn't dodge.[5]

Dee Dee Myers: What became a challenge dealing with Bill Clinton was his past, and that started pretty early. There were certain reporters who were disinclined to ever believe anything he said after that whole draft situation.

Bill told reporters that he'd given up his ROTC deferment

> under circumstances that any reasonable person would have thought made it virtually 100 percent lock down certain that I would be drafted.[6]

Of course, this is nonsense. At Oxford, Bill and his friends discussed the war and the draft obsessively, so he well knew at the time that draft quotas had been slashed and that a lottery was in the works, and that those developments much improved the odds that a young man might avoid the draft. And even after surrendering the deferment, he was still preserving an out should his birthday come up early in the lottery. The proof is that although his status changed to 1-A on October 30, he did not write to Holmes until December 3, two days after the lottery assigned him number 311. Only then did he burn his bridge to the now superfluous escape route offered by the ROTC program.[7]

Dee Dee Myers: After that, there was always a challenge for me to unravel Clinton's artfully worded answers. He learned to be careful about what he said. In the campaign we all got careful with how we interpreted what he said.

As time went on, with issues like Whitewater, you'd always find out there was more to the story. It wasn't that what he told you wasn't true, it just wasn't the whole story. And the facts as he laid them out and the facts as he left them out led to conclusions that weren't necessarily true. That was hard for everybody.

My view is that intentionally creating a perception that's false is the same as lying. I was no longer working for him when he said, of Monica Lewinsky, "There *is* no sexual relationship," and a lot of reporters said, "So he's saying it's over." And I was like, "No. Even he wouldn't do that." But that's exactly what he was doing. That all led to "what the meaning of the word *is* is."

The whole country was introduced to that in its earliest relationship with him, and it didn't change. I say that as someone who has continued to have great affection for him and respect for his skills and what he wanted to do. And yet, this was a facet of his personality, and a not unimportant one. It undermined his credibility and was counterproductive to what he wanted to accomplish.

"He was still standing."

Jonathan Alter: In the middle of this, Mario Cuomo gives a speech at Harvard. Cuomo had earlier decided not to run, but now that it looked like Clinton was collapsing there was suddenly intense interest in him: Would he get in?

Most of the press corps that was up in New Hampshire went to see him. I decided not to. Instead, I drove to Dover, New Hampshire, where Clinton was giving a speech at the Elks Lodge.

There were a lot of people there and they were people who had seen better days. Clinton gave a speech where he said, "I'll be there for you until the last dog dies." Even for people who weren't there, it entered political lore. Years later people would say, "You were at the 'last dog dies' speech?"

It took place only hours before Bill's appearance on *Nightline*.
Bill, February 12, 1992:

I'll tell you what I think the character issue is: Who really cares about you? Who's really trying to say what he would do specifically if he were elected President? Who has a demonstrated record of doing what they're talking about? And who is determined to change your life rather than to just get or keep power? . . .

I'll tell you something. I'm going to give you this election back, and if you'll give it to me, I won't be like George Bush. I'll never forget who gave me a second chance, and I'll be there for you 'til the last dog dies.[8]

Jonathan Alter: There was a quality of grit and personal determination that was a positive dimension to his character. Those of us who saw it felt it was neglected. I always wanted to make the character issue more complex rather than more simple. What happened was, it just became shorthand for bimbos.

He had taken two shots to the solar plexus, over a couple weeks, that would have knocked anybody else out of politics. And he was still standing. It wasn't clear that he was going to win, but you knew he wasn't done.

The campaign needed to change the subject.

Stan Greenberg: We bought all the TV that could be bought—it was wall-to-wall Bill Clinton. We paid to televise our own town meeting.

Mickey Kantor: Harry Thomason told Stan Greenberg, "Go out and find people who are trying to make up their mind. We don't want Bill Clinton adherents in this audience. We want the toughest questions we can find." Harry's view was that television exposed dishonesty. You had to make this as open, and even as raw, as possible.

We bought a half-hour of television time in New Hampshire for the first one. We had maybe twelve people in chairs in front of him.

As it was on we realized, "This is something special." His ability to talk to people—we should have known; it was the way he talked to us—could come through on television. You really got who he was and what he was. And what was also stunning, in a half-hour not one question about Gennifer Flowers, not one. I don't think there was a question about the draft.

All they wanted to know is what he would do as president.

Paul Begala: It helped enormously. It was a way to refocus the debate and to shame the press. We could go back to the press and say, Now wait a minute. You've just asked seven questions in a row about some tabloid story. That's not what your readers or viewers want to hear about.

Mickey Kantor: It turned out to be successful way beyond what we thought.

James Carville: We said, "Shit, this is it. Yeah, this is it."

Paul Begala: He loved them. He was so smart about so many things but also could connect. The whole thing about biting his lip—that was coached. Because he would answer so fast. We'd say, "Take a beat. Pretend you're thinking about it. Pretend you haven't already got an answer." It was a studied thing to give himself a second to force himself to slow down.

Mickey Kantor: After it ended we went into the station and said we want to buy another half-hour tomorrow night.

But then something else happened. He stood around I bet for an hour afterwards talking to the people in the audience. Now, every politician will stand around and say thank you to people, but he was engaged in real substantive conversation with them. He didn't want to leave.

"Even today it seems a little bit of magic."

Dave McCurdy: Election eve in New Hampshire, past midnight, Bill Clinton and I are at a bowling alley in Manchester.

We rode in the van, looking for the last people at the last hour who were sober enough to be persuaded to vote for him.

Mickey Kantor: On Monday night, my wife, Heidi, and I went to dinner with David Broder, Dan Balz,* and another reporter or two. They were telling us about all the polls that showed Clinton still dropping like a rock.

So we go back to the Days Inn, and Greenberg, Carville, and Stephanopoulos† come to me and say, "We need to go through this with Clinton." So we sat

---

*Broder and Balz wrote for the *Washington Post*.

†During the campaign, George Stephanopoulos was Bill's top communications aide.

down with him in Heidi's and my room. It's 1 or 1:30 in the morning. Hillary went to bed. She didn't want to engage in a meeting that was downbeat.

It was a typical motel room. Two double beds, one desk. You almost couldn't walk between the desk and the beds.

There we were, six or seven people in there, sitting on beds and sitting on the floor, and Stan goes through all these polls that were just devastating. And to Clinton's credit, he went through a couple of them, blaming himself. Then he said, "Look, we're going to do two things. One, I'm going to go out tomorrow morning. I'm going to campaign all day and all night, and we're going to do the best we can. And then we're going south.

"We're not getting out of this campaign. We can withstand this. We can overcome it."

We're breaking up, and everybody's impressed with the fact that he's hanging in there, but everybody's thinking, "I hope he sees reality here. This is going to be difficult. New Hampshire has always had a huge impact."

Stan says, "There's one thing, by the way, that's an anomaly. USA Today is coming out tomorrow morning showing you're going up." And I looked at Stan like, Oh, he's trying to make us feel better.

Well, the next morning when the first exit polls came out, suddenly Bill Clinton not only was coming back, Bill Clinton was in first place. In the second rollup he was in first place; in the third rollup he was in first place. It looks like a political miracle has occurred.

At 4 or 5 in the afternoon Joe Grandmaison, a great New Hampshire politician, calls me and says, "Mickey, he has got to go on television immediately when the nets come up and declare victory."

I said, "What do you mean?"

"McGovern did that in 1972. It doesn't make any difference what the votes actually show by then. If he declares victory, that's what people will remember."

So I called Clinton and he agreed that would be the thing to do. We told the networks we're going on right at 9 o'clock, if I'm not mistaken.

We're all in our hotel suite, and Paul Begala is off in the corner tapping out what turns out to be the "comeback kid" remarks—Begala came up with that language. Clinton is doing his usual, he's multitasking. He's talking to Paul, he's talking to other people about another issue, and the time is getting closer and closer. Finally, Heidi grabs him and says, "You have got to get down there or you're going to blow this." Grabs him—literally, physically. He wasn't president then. You could grab him and say, "Come on." So he went down.

Great speech. I mean, a great speech.

James Carville: We lost New Hampshire to Tsongas by a few points.

But we came from behind and we came out early. It was a kind of win. It was much better than we thought we were going do.

Bill: "I think we know enough to say with some certainty that New Hampshire tonight has made Bill Clinton the comeback kid."[9]

Indeed it had, even though, when the final tallies came in, Tsongas won with 33 percent of the vote to Bill's 25, with Kerrey, Harkin, and Brown clustered far behind.[10]

Mickey Kantor: At that point all everyone knew is that the exit polls showed him winning. It didn't make any difference that Clinton came in second. The myth had been struck.

James Carville: I have never seen a human being perform like he performed that week in New Hampshire. It was stunning. It was more like an athlete than it was a political candidate. I mean, event after event, every interview, every town hall meeting.

Mickey Kantor: Even today it seems a little bit of magic. One reason was that there is no harder worker you'll ever find than Bill Clinton, particularly when his back is against the wall. He believes he can work his way through any problem. You and I know that's probably not true, but in many cases he's been able to do it.

In New Hampshire, the end of the primary, he's at a home for the elderly, and they're talking about the price of pharmaceuticals, and people were talking about how they didn't have enough money. Remember, drugs weren't covered by Medicare at that point. And a woman in the front row, after asking questions, starts crying. He just walks up, and he kneels down in front of this woman and hugs her.

Dee Dee Myers: There is a certain shamelessness that comes from thinking you should be the most powerful person in the world, and they all have it. He won by connecting with people on a personal and important level. People voted for him because they really believed, after seeing him, that he got their problems and cared about them, that when push came to shove—despite Gennifer Flowers—he would act on their behalf.

That's why his approval rating when he left office was 60-plus percent. People had to voice some disgust with his behavior, yet his job approval stayed so high because they thought that he was for them. There was this remarkable dual track that people, I'm particularly thinking of reporters, were proceeding along: How could this guy be such a shit and be so compelling at the same time?

14

All Roads Lead to Madison Square Garden: Nominee

"New York was a roller coaster."

After Kerrey took South Dakota on February 26, seven states voted on March 3. Bill took only one, Georgia, but Kerrey came up empty and promptly withdrew from the race. Bill's victory in South Carolina four days later chased out Harkin. Brown remained, but the press never took "Governor Moonbeam" seriously. Only Paul Tsongas stood between Bill and the nomination.

Mike McCurry: When you get through New Hampshire, campaigns very quickly become binary events, because the press needs a point-counterpoint. The press has a hard time accommodating a multicandidate field after New Hampshire.

The press took the traditional model and made it Tsongas versus Clinton.

Tsongas ran as the cold-shower candidate, urging stringent measures to reduce the federal deficit. Calling Bill "cynical" and "unprincipled," labeling Bill's proposed middle-class tax cut "economic nonsense," the New Englander took to holding up a stuffed teddy bear to illustrate his point that the smooth-talking governor of Arkansas was a "pander bear."[1]

Dee Dee Myers: Tsongas was the darling of the reformist do-gooders, the Volvo drivers. The people who want politicians to talk about taking your medicine. Clinton always opposed that. He was always like, "Yeah, they want you to tell these hard truths and lose so that the Republicans get to run the federal government for another forty years. I ain't playing that game. We're not here to let Republicans continue to drive the country over a cliff."

Bob Kerrey: The two scandals would have sunk Bill Clinton were it not for a number of things. One was his own talent and Hillary's talent. Second, Tsongas was not prepared to win the New Hampshire primary.

Before representing Nebraska in the U.S. Senate from 1989 to 2001, Democrat Bob Kerrey served as Nebraska's governor from 1983 to 1987.

Tsongas went to Florida. No infrastructure coming out of his victory, none, whereas Bill Clinton had a national organization. So Clinton goes down to Florida. He's campaigned in Florida. He's been there before as a governor. Tsongas shows up in the condos down there and is completely unprepared for the questions, as if his campaign just began. So he runs out of steam. He was not as prepared as Bill Clinton was to go the distance.

Florida voted on Super Tuesday, March 10. Bill swept the southern contests on the way to winning eight of the day's eleven states.

March 17: Michigan and Illinois. March 24: Connecticut.
April 7: New York.

Mickey Kantor: We won Michigan and Illinois on the same day. Big, huge. Stumbled and got beat by one point in Connecticut by Jerry Brown, which was a shock to us. Went into New York with Jerry Brown having some momentum.

Dee Dee Myers: We were in Little Rock for a couple days' break between primaries and we were heading up to Connecticut. John King, from the AP, called the governor's residence and said, "Tsongas has dropped out." Clinton flipped out. He knew instinctively that the liberal reformist wing of the party would blame him for driving Saint Paul Tsongas out of the race. And he would be left to run against Jerry Brown and the ghost of Paul Tsongas in New York. We got on the plane, and he was just a wreck.

There was no one left in the race except Jerry Brown, who wasn't a real candidate. He was someone you had to debate and he obviously had some real skills as a politician, but he was never going to be the Democratic nominee. So, how could New York have become such a test?

Paul Begala: A lot of politics is not so much ideological as it's cultural. Do you get it? Are you one of us? New York is the hardest place to be "one of us" if you're a small-town boy from Arkansas.

Mickey Kantor: The first week in New York did not go very well. Day after day we were hit on the draft—remember, the second draft letter came out.

Only days before the voting in New York, the Associated Press released the induction letter, received by Bill in England in the spring of 1969, that had spurred him to make his commitment to ROTC. During all the uproar over his draft history before February's New Hampshire primary, Bill had neglected to mention that he had, in fact, been drafted. He now defended his earlier statements, asserting that the facts he'd related in New Hampshire constituted his "best memory at the time." His receipt of the induction notice, he said with a straight face, was not "relevant to the story."[2]

Harold Ickes,* God love him, came to see me at 4 o'clock one morning and said, "This isn't working. You cannot campaign in New York the way you campaign everywhere else. New York is divided ethnically. It is old-style politics. He's going to have to go group to group, synagogue to Catholic diocese, the Irish community, Latinos, and so on, and he's going to have to talk to them, or you're not going to get anywhere in New York." Clinton got it immediately, and he was a better New York politician by the end than any New York politician. Of course, we won four primaries the night of the New York primary.

The others were Kansas, Minnesota, and Wisconsin.

Paul Begala: New York was a roller coaster. You had to surrender to it and enjoy it and ride it. It was completely wild. But he loved it. He wasn't intimidated by it.

On March 26, speaking in a Manhattan nightclub, Bill was confronted by Bob Rafsky, a member of Act Up, an organization of AIDS activists. After Rafsky told Bill that AIDS patients were "not dying of AIDS as much as we are from eleven years of Government neglect," Bill promised to implement policy recommendations already made to President Bush by the National Commission on AIDS.

Rafsky was not satisfied. He continued to heckle Bill.

From the *New York Times,* March 28, 1992:

> Clinton: Would you just calm down?
> Rafsky: You're dying of [unintelligible]. . . .
> Clinton: Let me tell you something. If I were dying of ambition, I wouldn't have stood up here and put up with all this crap I've put up with for the last six months. I'm fighting to change this country. . . .
> I feel your pain, I feel your pain, but if you want to attack me personally you're no better than Jerry Brown and all the rest of these people who say whatever sounds good at the moment. . . . If you don't agree with me, go support somebody else for President but quit talking to me like that. . . .
> I'm sick and tired of all these people who don't know me, know nothing

---

*A Democratic political operative from New York.

about my life, know nothing about the battles that I've fought, know nothing about the life I've lived, making snotty-nose remarks about how I haven't done anything in my life and it's all driven ambition. That's bull, and I'm tired of it.[3]

Paul Begala: "I feel your pain" became a famous Clinton phrase. As smart as he is, I think that's his greatest gift. My conservative friends never understood it. Still to this day they make fun of that—"I feel your pain." Empathy is the most important characteristic we can have in a president.

Clinton has so much empathy. In New York he was able to project that.

On March 29, Bill took part in a debate, on a New York City television station, with Jerry Brown, who was participating by satellite from Green Bay, Wisconsin. At one point, the reporter Marcia Kramer asked about possible past marijuana use. "I've never broken a state law," Bill responded. "But when I was in England I experimented with marijuana a time or two, and I didn't like it. I didn't inhale it, and never tried it again."[4]

Three words of Bill's answer—"I didn't inhale"—attained instant notoriety.

Paul Begala: I almost fainted.

It was my fault. I had prepared him exactly the worst way. I had been really annoyed by his answer before this, which was, "I've never violated the drug laws of my country." Which would lead someone to believe he'd never used illegal drugs. But what it really meant was, I tried it in England where it didn't violate America's drug laws. That was way too cute for me. I rode around the plane with him and I went back to it again and again. I tried to persuade him, "It's not a killer, if you just tell the truth about it." He said, "I was never a pothead or anything. I tried it once or twice, didn't like it." And I said, "Say that."

He never said "I didn't inhale" to me; it just came out.

Dee Dee Myers: We were in a conference room and they had the monitor on. James Carville was there, Harold Ickes was there. Everybody was there. We were sitting around the table watching it and it was like, "You have to be kidding me."

Stan Greenberg: He came out and said, "See, it's no problem." He thought it was a home run.

Dee Dee Myers: It was a head-slapping moment. We knew we were going to have to try and fix this—it was too good for the press not to roll out, especially in New York. It was obvious that this was going to feed right into what had already been the rap against him: He's admitting that he smoked pot, but not really. He's trying to have it both ways.

The saddest part about it was, it was probably true. Ever seen somebody try to smoke pot who had never smoked pot and didn't really want to smoke pot but didn't want to be the kid who wouldn't smoke pot?

There's a nerdy quality to him. He probably took a joint or a bong, whatever it was, and he probably didn't like it and didn't really want to do it and maybe coughed and then got on with his life. He's not somebody who drinks. That's not his thing.

Paul Begala: He always chews cigars; he doesn't smoke them. He was kind of a band geek. He has real sensitive lungs. He's forever fighting allergies. I'm sure he coughed and sputtered and choked and literally did not inhale.

What was funny is he didn't get in trouble for the answer I thought was so misleading. He got in trouble for what actually was the truth.

What sent it over the top was Billy Crystal. He stood at the Oscars the next day. In front of one billion people. And that's all he said: "Didn't inhale?" And the place fell apart.

It was one of the most truthful things the guy ever said, but it stands as one of the great lies of American politics.

Bill won New York with 41 percent of the vote. Brown, with 26, finished behind Tsongas, who was still on the ballot and received 29.[5] The strong showing by Tsongas fed speculation that he would reenter the race. Two days later, however, he put a stop to the discussion, saying he did not wish to play "the role of spoiler" in the face of Bill's commanding delegate lead.[6] The nomination battle had, effectively, ended.

"Watch this."

Paul Begala: We still had the California primary. By then we were desperately worried about the general.

California, where not only Brown but also his father had been governor, concluded the primary season with its vote on June 2. Bill won with 47 percent of the vote to Brown's 40.[7]

That night he stayed up and did interview after interview back east with the networks. Dan Rather—the only questions he asked him were about Ross Perot.

Ross Perot, the Texas billionaire, had announced his self-financed run for the presidency in February on CNN's *Larry King Live*. A Gallup poll taken just after the

California primary had him leading the national race at 39 percent, with Bush at 31 and Bill at a mere 25.[8]

Then we read a front-page story that suggested the convention might still somehow be brokered; that Clinton might fall below 25 percent in the polls and lose federal matching funds, and actually end the existence of the oldest political party on earth. It was that dire.

Clinton was furious. No one had ever beaten a Brown in a California primary; he got zero credit for it. Oh my God, it was the angriest he was in the whole campaign. He pounded his leg and pounded this glass table in his hotel room—so much that the Secret Service agents came in. They thought there was a fight going on. It was like, "What do I have to do?"

What he had to do was shape public perceptions. Just days after the California primary a golden opportunity fell in his lap.

Stan Greenberg: On national security—on China and other issues—he staked out tougher positions than Bush. We tried to be assertive about American national interests.

This may seem unrelated, but when he stood up to Jesse Jackson with Sister Souljah, when he stood up to Jerry Brown in not letting him speak at the convention,* what that said to people is: This is a strong leader. He's able to control his own party. Our standing as a "strong leader" moved up in the polls. Even though it's not a foreign policy issue, people perceive as strong someone who leads a united party and can dominate their own party.

In May, the rap artist Sister Souljah, referring to the recent riots after a jury acquitted four Los Angeles Police Department officers in the Rodney King case, said, "If black people kill black people every day, why not have a week and kill white people?"[9] On June 12 she addressed a convention of Jesse Jackson's Rainbow Coalition. Bill spoke there a day later. In his remarks, he discussed his antipoverty agenda but also took a moment to chide the gathering for including the rapper on its program: "If you took the words 'white' and 'black' and reversed them, you might think David Duke† was giving that speech.... We have an obligation, all of us, to call attention to prejudice whenever we see it."[10] To people suspicious of Bill's centrist

---

*Because Brown by then had not yet formally withdrawn from the race and endorsed Bill, he was allotted only twenty minutes at the podium, out of prime time, to second his own nomination.

†White supremacist state legislator from Louisiana who ran numerous times for higher office.

positioning, the criticism represented a calculated attempt to win over white swing voters by publicly insulting Jackson, a man those voters detested.

Thus the "Sister Souljah Moment" was born—thereafter defined as an instance when an office seeker criticizes a supposed ally to demonstrate his or her political independence.

Tom Brokaw: Sister Souljah was a bold move. It helped him, it really did. He walked into Jesse Jackson's den and popped him on the snoot and walked out. No one had done that before. I always thought that was an undercurrent in this country, especially in the blue-collar, working-class crowd: How much is someone going to be hostage to Jesse or to that culture? I'm not talking about African American culture in general; I'm talking about a subset of the African American culture that, to some, can get away with anything. That was a page out of the "silent majority"* handbook: Watch this.

Lottie Shackelford: I was there that day. We didn't hear anything. It was after the fact—maybe a couple of days—that it started to brew: "Can you believe Bill Clinton chastised somebody in his own house?"

The interesting thing about Bill Clinton and Jesse Jackson was that neither feared the other. The thing is—and most white politicians don't have this—Clinton had his own relationships with black folk across the spectrum: the religious community, the business community, the working community. These people know who you are.

In Jesse's world, so many white politicians feared him. I don't think Clinton feared him.

"People had to know who he was."

On July 9 Bill would announce his running mate: Al Gore. Three days later the 1992 Democratic National Convention, where Bill would be anointed his party's standard bearer, was to begin in New York's Madison Square Garden.

The gathering would provide Bill his best—and perhaps last—chance to change the way people thought of him.

David Kusnet: He had not really closed the deal with the Democratic Party electorate, much less the American electorate, by the time he'd cinched the nomination.

---

*Richard Nixon's phrase to describe Americans who did not protest the war in Vietnam and did not approve of those who did.

Stan Greenberg: After every primary, the networks would pose the question through the exit polls: Does Clinton have the honesty and character to be president? The numbers were always awful, and got worse and worse.

When we came out of the New York primary, James and I went to Mickey Kantor and proposed that a group of us pull out: We have the nomination. What we really need now is a plan for how we rebuild his character.

The idea was to get us out of the day-to-day of the campaign and focus on the longer-term problem. We created a group, which we called the Manhattan Project.

James Carville: The name came about because it was actually conceived in Manhattan. We also liked making it akin to the Manhattan Project in New Mexico.

Stan Greenberg: The simple answer to the problem was biography.

Paul Begala: They looked hard at what people thought of Clinton. This is what people knew: Yale, Georgetown, Oxford, dodged the draft, smoked pot, cheated on his wife. And because we reason by inference, they stitched all those things together and they came up with: rich, spoiled, never had a hard day in his life, driving his father's Alfa Romeo around the Ivy League campus. That's where the "Man from Hope" came from.

Stan Greenberg: In focus groups we discovered that simply knowing he was a poor kid from Arkansas would change everything, which is why Hope became so central to the campaign.

Bill's speech accepting the nomination detailed his background and emphasized his place of birth—Bill ended it, memorably, with "I still believe in a place called Hope." But perhaps even more important than the speech in reframing Bill's life story was the seventeen-minute film, *The Man from Hope,* that preceded it. The centerpiece of the film was the incident in Hot Springs when Bill protected his mother from the attack of his stepfather.

Paul Begala: Clinton struck some people as the quintessential compromiser, and he is. But even he knew that there's a time when you have to stand up and say, "No more." And so he told that story.

He was resistant to getting into all of that; he loved his stepfather. But he understood that people had to know who he was and where he came from.

James Carville: We did a lot of research on this then and during his presidency. And the thing that we always walked away with—and the thing that saved him throughout his political career—was, I've seen voters disgusted with him, turned off by him, mad at him, disappointed, but I never saw them give up.

Even in '94, even through Lewinsky, through everything. I was always waiting for a phone call from people doing research that would say, "This thing is changing out there. People are cashing in on us." We never got that. Believe me, we were always looking for it.

The Man from Hope gave him something so that, if you wanted to be for him, you'd say, "That guy's had an interesting life, he grew up different, had a single mother." You had the sense that people wanted to be for him and this gave them a validating reason.

Here was a guy who had the courage to stand with his mother and stand up to his stepfather. Very few people, if you know them or talk to them long enough, don't have something complicated about their lives. This story told people, "I know the kind of life you have. I've faced that, too."

And it contrasted very well with Bush. People said, "He's the guy who was rich and who's out of touch. I can't trust him to understand my life. He'd rather be dealing with foreign leaders than be dealing with me."

Paul Begala: There are a lot of aspects to "character." Marital fidelity is one of them. Serving your country when called is one of them. But also being true to your values, to a set of principles. Overcoming adversity.

Unlike a lot of people who have overcome adversity, he grew in empathy. People go one way or the other. I know people who have had tragedies in their lives and it hardens their hearts and they're unable to feel anyone else's pain. Because there's a part of them that says, "You think that's pain, buddy? You don't know from pain." I can understand that and I don't judge it. Much more admirable, though, is for somebody to go through what he went through and to emerge more open to other people's pain.

That's character.

15

A Bubba, Not a Bozo:
President-Elect

"Our analysis was, he was out of it."

James Baker: There were three reasons we lost. The first one was that we'd been there twelve years. President Bush had been an incumbent vice president for two terms under Reagan, and then he'd been president for a full term. There were a lot of people who were tired of us.

The second is that we had Ross Perot running.

Leading Democrats do not share this view of Perot's impact. (See Chapter 19.)

The third problem was of our own making. In January of '92, when President Bush had a stratospheric approval rating after Desert Storm, we didn't go up to the Congress and put on the table a domestic economic program. By not doing that, we didn't have an economic or domestic program around which to coalesce the campaign.

Those were the three main reasons. Another obvious reason was our opponent, who was an extraordinarily good candidate.

Paul Begala: Clinton's attitude toward Bush was: Give him a gold watch. He's a good man but doesn't have the slightest sense of how to use power to help people, has no elemental populism about him, no activism about him. Clinton thought we needed to be much more activist and much more on the side of the middle class.

The Gulf War worked against Bush terribly—Clinton made it work against him. He basically said, "Look, this guy's capable of activism." I don't think Clinton ever said this, but it was my shorthand: "He moves heaven and earth when the Emir of Kuwait loses his job but does nothing when you lose yours."

And he called Clinton "Bozo" and Gore "Ozone Man." That really helped to discredit him. Poor guy. Our analysis was, he was out of it. The more he said stuff like that the more he looked out of touch. I mean, Clinton's a lot of things but he ain't a Bozo. He ain't stupid. There's a lot of ways to attack him, but that ain't the smartest.

We didn't answer in kind. In the convention speech Clinton compared Bush to General McClellan. Lincoln said to McClellan, "If you don't want to use the Army I should like to borrow it for awhile." Clinton said to Bush, "If you won't use your power to help America, step aside. I will." That was the indictment, that he was passive and elitist. Not that he was evil. It worked because it was true.

An incident earlier in the year had helped the Clinton campaign make its case that the incumbent was not only elitist, but also a man of the past.

David Barram is a Silicon Valley executive who during the Clinton administration served in the Commerce Department and as head of the General Services Administration.

David Barram: I thought Bush got a bum rap on the supermarket scanners—there were a lot of people who didn't know about scanners, a lot of guys who didn't shop.

On February 4, 1992, while Bill was laboring to salvage his campaign in New Hampshire, Bush toured exhibits at a convention of the National Grocers Association in Orlando. There he encountered, apparently for the first time, a supermarket price scanner. "Amazed by some of the technology," he (sans first-person pronoun) told the grocers afterward. Unbeknownst to him, this amazing technology had been a feature of ordinary Americans' daily lives for years.[1]

Maybe the reason it worked against him was that it showed his lack of interest in technology. What I felt is that George Bush and George Bush the Younger don't have much curiosity. Out here, we wake up in the morning and say, What hundred things can I learn today? We looked at George Bush and he wasn't asking that at all.

Bill Clinton might not have been as interested in the technology as I would have been, but he would have been interested in the clerk. He'd ask the person, "How does this work? Do people like it?"

At a fund-raiser in Woodside, it was late and everybody else was gone, and the rich guy who owned the house had a maid who was cleaning up. Clinton started asking her about her life: "Do you have children? How do you make it around here?" It was like 10 o'clock at night and the rest of us are "Hey, let's go."

We're with people who think they deserve all the money they have, that they have it because of what they did instead of being at the right place at the right time. But this lady—I recall her being an immigrant—he really wanted to know who she was.

James Baker: Clinton did a fine job of moving to the center. He was not seen to be anywhere near as liberal as most Democratic nominees. He was a governor of a southern state. He was a Bubba, if you will.

We tried to make character an issue. We were unsuccessful in doing so. You had that same phenomenon during the impeachment debate. The argument was made that we elect our leaders not so much on the basis of character but on the basis of ability—their ability to do the job, to get things done for the country.

Dee Dee Myers: The character issue was, if not the main thrust of the Bush campaign, certainly one of the pillars. I remember Mary Matalin* saying he's a "philandering, pot-smoking draft dodger." They wanted to keep the focus on that. Clinton had been very successful in New Hampshire saying, "They want this to be about *my past.* I want it to be about *your future.*"

The Clinton campaign argued, with some success, that there is such a thing as political character. It's not about whether Clinton committed some sins in his past; he acknowledged that he did. The question was, Who's the best person to lead the country forward and who will make decisions based on what's best for the most Americans?

People say, "Oh he's a chameleon. He changes." But he really does think about the issues. Clinton really was up late at night talking about how can we retrain workers to be competitive in the changing global economy. It wasn't just a line. He's on the phone at one A.M. talking to some policy wonk in L.A. about some new program that they started, because he really is interested in it. You can't take that away from him, as much as people tried to.

Paul Begala: It wasn't ever personal from our side. People every day were throwing things to us over the transom: Bush cheated on his wife too; you should say that. It wasn't true—at least, I'm persuaded it wasn't. And who cares? We weren't going to win that contest.

So as these things go, we had a high-road campaign by Clinton, despite the

---

*A highly partisan Republican operative, then a high-ranking official in the Bush campaign. She is married to her opposite number on the Democratic side, James Carville.

fact that Bush was out there saying Clinton had spied for the KGB on a student backpacking trip, and all that nonsense.

Bush was referring to Bill's five days in Moscow as a wandering Rhodes Scholar in 1969.[2]

Clinton never rose to the bait.

It was hard not to answer in kind. It took iron will. What upset him the most were the attacks on the Arkansas record. He loves that state. It was hardest to restrain him when they said he's the "failed governor of a small state."

John Sununu: That was an accurate statement, if you look at where Arkansas ranked on education and on social services.

John Sununu, the Republican governor of New Hampshire from 1983 to 1989, served as George H. W. Bush's White House chief of staff from 1989 to 1991.

It was a weak forty-ninth, close to fiftieth, and he made it a strong forty-ninth, close to forty-eighth.

James Carville: It was a problem: "the failed governor of a small state." That gave people some pause. It wasn't a bullshit charge, there was something to it.

Paul Begala: He said, "We're a poor state, struggling through tough times with remarkable people. We're doing pretty good."

Jonathan Alter: I felt strongly at the time that character was much broader than what happened in your private life, that it was a combination of the personal qualities and your public commitment to addressing problems in a way that put you at some risk.

I defended him through a lot of the problems in his personal life. I thought at the time that he would probably not keep most of his campaign promises, that he would be weaker politically but stronger and more disciplined personally. History proved me exactly wrong. He turned out to be weaker personally than I anticipated and stronger and more disciplined politically.

At the time I couldn't believe that he wouldn't zipper up for the duration. I underestimated the personal pathologies and the personal weaknesses and what I think of as addictions.

ISSUE: "The economy, stupid"

Of the three campaign themes listed on the sign James Carville hung on the wall at campaign headquarters—"1. Change vs. more of the same. 2. The economy, stupid. 3. And don't forget health care."—the second was first among equals.

Roger Altman: It's a factual matter that in 1992 the economy was weak. Job creation had slowed to a crawl, growth was anemic, we had recessionary conditions.

After advising candidate Clinton, the investment banker Roger Altman became President Clinton's deputy secretary of the treasury.

I know what Republicans say. They say that the economy began to recover in the fall of '92, and by the time Bill Clinton came into office it was already in recovery. That may be correct. But when people went into the voting booth on November 3, 1992, their view was: This economy is in a slump.

James Baker: I've always believed that, generally speaking, voters vote their pocketbooks.

ISSUE: "Are the Democrats willing and able to use force?"

George Bush's strong suit was his experience and presumed expertise in foreign affairs. The nation's mind, however, was elsewhere.

Stan Greenberg: The timing of the election was after the fall of the Berlin Wall and of communism. We had not had an election before that like the one we would have in '92, nor have we had one since. National security issues were very much on the back burner.

Anthony Lake: Yes, the campaign was "the economy, stupid," and it was primarily on domestic issues. But if you go back and look, Clinton did quite a bit on foreign policy.

We had to take some issues and take them to Bush, as if this was a boxing match and we were getting a little jab in his face, because otherwise, since he did have more foreign policy experience, he could get off an uppercut.

Nancy Soderberg was the foreign policy director of Bill's campaign. She would be the third-ranking official on the National Security Council for Bill's first term.

Nancy Soderberg: Clinton took on Bush in three areas of foreign policy during the campaign: Bosnia, Haiti, and China.

On Bosnia, Clinton understood instinctively that stability in the Balkans and across Europe was in the United States' interest. James Baker, secretary of state, said we don't have a dog in that fight. It was pretty clear to us that we couldn't just leave it to the Europeans. We challenged the Bush administration on the need for more active U.S. diplomacy, and potentially some use of military force, against the Serbs' aggression in Bosnia.

Anthony Lake: Character emerges from the clarity with which you are taking positions, and Clinton was very clear on what we ought to be doing about Bosnia, Haiti, et cetera.

Once in office, Bill would have to do some backtracking.

It did turn out that the position we took on Haiti we couldn't live with. Within Haiti, there was increasing repression by the Cédras military after they staged a coup that almost killed Aristide, the legitimately elected president.* This helped to create a huge outflow of refugees from Haiti, who were being denied access to the United States.

It was not a happy thing, but in January we had to change the policy.

Nancy Soderberg: On China, we basically took a tougher human rights stance and linked trade to human rights.

U.S. policy toward China had been jolted by the Tiananmen Square massacre of June 4, 1989, when tanks and troops of the People's Liberation Army rolled through the plaza to put a stop to the pro-democracy demonstrations that had filled the space for weeks. Hundreds, if not thousands, of demonstrators were killed in the action.[3]

While President Bush publicly deplored the crackdown during its immediate aftermath, he muted his criticism of the Chinese regime in the months that followed, saying, "I hope, in a quiet way, to find steps that can be taken—perhaps on both sides—to see this relation move back toward more normalization."[4]

Anthony Lake: After Tiananmen Square there was real disagreement between the Bush administration and Congress, with both parties in Congress largely saying that we were too cozy with these tyrants. I'm afraid we referred to them in one campaign speech as the "butchers of Beijing." A little over the top. But mostly we argued that with the end of the Cold War, we had less need to cozy up to Beijing as a way of getting at the Soviet Union. So now we could deal with Beijing in different terms.

Nancy Soderberg: We did that for the first year in office, and then had to walk it back.

Anthony Lake: Are the Democrats willing and able to use force in our national interest? You have to demonstrate that you're prepared to. I do not

---

*On September 30, 1991, Lieutenant General Raoul Cédras led a military coup that ousted the Reverend Jean-Bertrand Aristide, who that February had taken office as the first democratically elected president in Haiti's history.

believe you do it by pointing at yourself and saying, "Look how tough I am," or by staging events in tanks or even by showing that you actually have served in combat. You do it by taking positions that are clear and forthright, even occasionally unpopular, so that people will trust that you are confident in your views, that those views make sense, and that they are backed up by a willingness to use force.

I don't think the Bush campaign believed that we could mount a serious challenge on foreign policy. But our point wasn't to win on foreign policy, it was to neutralize it.

I think we did.

ISSUE: "He saw this interdependent world."

Henry Cisneros: He was really wrestling with where he wanted to end up on NAFTA.

Beginning in mid-1991, negotiators from Canada, Mexico, and the United States worked to draft the North American Free Trade Agreement, a pact eliminating most trade barriers among the three nations. President Bush announced the completion of NAFTA in August 1992, but to go into effect, the agreement required ratification by the three nations' legislatures. Congress, and whoever won the presidential election, would take up the issue in 1993.

Brian Mulroney: I had negotiated NAFTA with President Bush and President Salinas.

Brian Mulroney was prime minister of Canada, 1984–1993.

Given the traditional ties of the trade unions to the Democratic Party, I could see that Governor Clinton had to maneuver his way past a number of obstacles, and finesse a number of others, because of the protectionist instincts that exist particularly in some areas of the Democratic Party, although not exclusively there.

I had the sense that he was a free trader when he was governor of Arkansas; he used to go on trade missions, and I had followed him for a long time. During the campaign I felt that he was in favor of the deal but couldn't say much at the time.

Mickey Kantor: He saw this interdependent world that was not only globalized but multipolar and that the only way to deal with it was to engage it. He gave a brilliant speech, that he wrote and rewrote, and was an hour and a half late for, at North Carolina State on October 4, 1992. He said, "NAFTA, yes but"—NAFTA with labor and environmental side agreements. He gets criticized for not showing courage or always trying to split the difference. Here he believed that there was no way for him to move forward and build a North American economy without NAFTA.

Owen Bieber was president of the United Auto Workers from 1983 to 1995.

Owen Bieber: I had conversations with Clinton, he knew what our problems were.

I was wishing he could stay tougher on the trade agreement with Mexico. I worked very hard on behalf of Bill Clinton—not only in Michigan but in other states.

He was candid with me when he made the decision to come out in support of NAFTA. The governor told me people were accusing him of waffling on it: "I'm getting beat up on this and if I don't take a position George Bush may win the election."

ISSUE: "It also sent a political signal."

Elaine Kamarck: Welfare was key because it was about values.

Elaine Kamarck helped found the Progressive Policy Institute, the DLC's in-house think tank. During the Clinton administration she would run Vice President Al Gore's National Performance Review, aka "reinventing government."

The Democratic Party looked out of step with most Americans on the value of work. Here you had a lot of Americans—working poor people—working hard, and they resented the culture of welfare and the culture of dependency.

Stan Greenberg: The key was, he was able to address it in an optimistic way; it didn't feel like a punitive way, because he also seemed serious about opportunity.

Brilliantly, Bill summarized his proposal to reform welfare in six simple words: He wanted to "end welfare as we know it."

That said we were not amending it, it said we were not changing it. It said that we are done with this whole concept of welfare. The phrase was a big surprise from a Democrat. This was not something tested before he said it, but I watched people in focus groups, and it was a stopper. That said to them, It's real. We're coming up with a different concept for addressing poverty and unemployment.

Elaine Kamarck: Clinton campaigned on turning welfare into a work system. Believe me, at the time the issue had a dual purpose. It had a policy centrality but it also sent a political signal and the political signal was that he was different, he got it.

Stan Greenberg: Welfare reform was seen to be racist. Nixon and Reagan used it as central to their attack on the Democrats. The implicit and explicit use of race made it something Democrats couldn't address.

But Clinton, as a southern governor, had done welfare reform. More than that, he had strong support among African Americans.

Elaine Kamarck: One of the great geniuses of Bill Clinton is that he went into black churches and sold welfare reform. One of the things we never publicized, because we were a bunch of white people, is that we focus-grouped welfare reform with black audiences. And when you had black discussion leaders leading a discussion about welfare with black working-class and middle-class people, what you discovered was, they sounded just like white racists. They were mad as hell about the welfare system.

Stan Greenberg: The fact that he came out of the South and had the support he did with black clergy meant that he could raise these issues in ways that others couldn't. And he was brave enough to do it.

"He used the phrase 'normal life' a lot."

Al From: Opportunity, responsibility, community. That was our message. It worked on welfare, it worked on national service, it worked on the economy, it worked on crime.

David Kusnet: In the campaign and in the presidency he was concerned about crime, and not just crime as politics. He was clearly torn up about it.

Clinton gave a speech somewhere, completely extemporaneous, claiming victory one night in a primary. He went through all the usual stuff you say after you've won a primary, and then he said, "Today, little Joey Méndez"— I'm making up that name—"was killed in the playground of his junior high school. Tonight, in the quiet moments before you go to sleep, say a prayer for Joey Méndez. Say a prayer for his family, who lost this lovely child. And say a prayer even for the kid who killed him." This is an incredibly moving thing: "Say a prayer." It's not the way politicians talk.

My notion about this—and this is a great leap of speculation—is if you look at people who have become president or have been in a position to contend for being president, some of them, like the elder Bush and the younger Bush, are children of privilege. Some are from small towns, but they're from the leading family in the small town. Lyndon Johnson was from a place called Johnson City. Even those who come from poverty or working-class backgrounds—they're usually like Mario Cuomo: intact, churchgoing, hardworking family.

Clinton may have come from no more impoverished, and maybe even less impoverished, circumstances—his stepfather was an auto dealer. But he probably came closest to the edge, emotionally, of anybody who's run for president. He came from a broken home, with almost mystical aspects to it. I mean, his biological father is driving from Chicago to Hope to pick up his pregnant wife, and he dies in this freak auto accident. If somehow time had stopped and an angel had come down from heaven as he's dying, never in a million years would he have believed that his son-to-be was going to become president of the United States. This is incredible. And so he grows up with a single mother and a stepfather. He tells the story about having to stand up and threaten to slug his stepfather because he was drunk and beating up his mother. For a couple of years his mother's away in New Orleans learning how to become a nurse-anesthetist, and Clinton's raised by his grandparents, who run a small store in a black neighborhood.

Close to the edge. He comes from where presidents don't come from, and it's no secret that at times he's had a messy life of his own making. So he thinks a lot about, What does it take to have an orderly, successful, disciplined life? What kinds of social supports do you need for a kid growing up without two parents under the same roof, with a stepparent who's a substance abuser, and so on? He thinks about that not as some problem he studied in graduate school, but as something he lived.

He used the phrase "normal life" a lot: What does it take for someone to live a normal life? He realized, as most presidents and most successful professionals in this country do not realize, that to have a normal life is a great accomplishment. A lot of people think of a normal life as a baseline—it's what you have if you're not a success. The kind of person who works for presidents or comments on presidents almost thinks, if I hadn't gotten a lucky break and become a columnist for the *Washington Post,* I'd have to be some nameless, faceless person doing nothing more than living a normal life. A normal life is something you rise above.

Clinton understood it's something you aspire to. He would talk about it as something good and honorable, something that society should help you attain.

Welfare reform with him certainly wasn't the desire to punish poor people. That was absolutely the last thing in the world he would ever want to do.

What Clinton was thinking was that having a job gives structure to your life. If you're a kid growing up with a single mom, your mother now having a job, even if it means she spends less time with you, means when someone asks you, "What does your mother do?" you can tell them.

I have no idea what it would feel like—you're a small child and your mother is moving out of the house for two years to go study to be a skilled hospital worker. But he has certainly reconciled in his own mind that losing his mother for that time was well worth her coming back with a skill and a job and some structure in their lives.

"Everybody's saying, 'Go! Go! Go!' "

Craig Smith: Bush didn't want to debate. There was an unemployed guy in Michigan who got a chicken costume and started going around Michigan saying, "Where's Chicken George? How come he won't debate?" Local TV picked up on it.

Our state director says, "I've got to find this guy." So she hunts him down, and she says, "Look, Bush is coming into the state. Will you show up at the event?" And he's like, "Sure I'd love to." We sent a local news package to all the national reporters: "Here's Chicken George, he'll be at the event." So he gets there, they all find him, they all take footage of Chicken George, Chicken George shows up on the national news.

We then take that and say, "Okay, Chicken George is now in every state." We instructed all our staff, "Go out and rent a chicken suit. When George Bush comes into your state, you're going to have the chicken man at every event, no matter where he goes." It made Bush crazy, to the point that in Ohio, later on in the campaign, Bush is speaking off the back of a train, there's the chicken costume, and Bush speaks to the chicken.

At that point we knew we had won. If Bush is out there talking to a guy in a chicken suit, our message got across. And then he crumbled and decided to debate.

Dee Dee Myers: It was the cheapest stunt, so high school, and yet it was successful because it got under Bush's skin. We got him off message, sometimes spectacularly, just by sending this guy in a chicken suit. Of course, the campaign loved to do it. For the staffers, it was a huge cult: "What's Chicken George doing today?"

In July, Ross Perot abruptly withdrew from the race. His stated reason had to do with his shrinking poll numbers, but shortly before Election Day he offered a different—really different—explanation: The Bush campaign had threatened to sabotage his daughter's summer wedding by releasing doctored photographs showing her in sexually compromising situations.[5]

Whatever his reason for leaving the contest, he reentered on October 1, in time to be included, ten days later, in the first of three candidates' debates.

James Carville: We knew Perot was going to do well. We did prep in Kansas City. Mike Synar, a congressman from Oklahoma, played Perot, and Bob Barnett* played Bush. The way I liked to do it was have a run-through without any prep—actually, you prep the opponents. And twenty minutes into it we're sitting there: "Shit, Perot's going to do good."

Mickey Kantor: The first evening we gave Bob and Mike the questions ahead of time, because we thought Clinton was a little too sure of his ability to debate. So he comes in, just off the campaign trail, we explain the setup to him, and he says, "Let's get going." There were only about six or seven people in the room. Begala and Heidi, my wife, were playing the reporters.

They started asking questions. Bob and Mike had their answers ready. They tore him limb from limb. After about twenty minutes of this, he got angry. He didn't realize that he had been set up. Michael Sheehan wanted him to be undressed and then have to be built back up again to make him realize he's going to have to work at this. That's exactly what happened. Of course, Bill Clinton going to work is like no other person going to work. After a day and a half, he was tearing them apart.

Mickey Kantor: Before the debate you go over to the hall. You look at it. You walk around. You see where you're going to walk in. You stand under the lights. You do all those things. Perot didn't show up for this stuff—I didn't know it at the time. I learned that subsequently.

Maybe twenty minutes before the debate there's a knock, knock, knock on Clinton's dressing-room door. There are two or three of us sitting in there with Clinton. I go over to the door and open it and it's Ross Perot. Ross says, "Mickey"—we had talked to each other in August in New York, trying to negotiate his coming out for Clinton—"I'd like to see Bill."

I said, "Ross, he's getting made up. This is not the time." I closed the door behind me, and Heidi and I walked out into the hallway with him. We wanted to keep him away from Clinton. That's the last thing you want at that point.

*A Washington lawyer and literary agent.

He says, "You're going to know this: Where do I walk in?" I swear to God. "Where do I walk in?" And so we said, "You're over on the other side."

He says, "How long does this thing last?" I swear to God. I walked him through some of the things, and then he went off. It was as if he had been asked over to a cocktail party, that's how loose he was. It showed in the debate because he was just Ross Perot. He wasn't overly prepared. We may have overly prepared Clinton. Perot was terrific. He won that debate.

What a piece of work, Ross Perot.

The second debate proved to be the decisive one. The encounter, in town hall format, took place on October 15, in Richmond, Virginia.

Mickey Kantor: The one searing incident was when Bill Clinton walks up to the woman and says, "When people lose their jobs in Arkansas, I tend to know them." He understood her question. President Bush didn't understand it.

That was not spontaneous.

James Carville and George Stephanopoulos and Paul Begala—they get the credit for this—had told him during debate prep, "There's going to come a time in this debate when you can walk up and really talk to somebody like a human being, really talk to them about their lives. Take advantage. It's going to happen, you just have to know when the time comes."

So we're back in the green room, and President Bush says, "I don't quite understand that." And everybody's saying, "Go! Go! Go!" knowing Clinton can not only deal with that question easily but ought to walk up to this woman. And when he did, there was cheering. Of course, no one can hear us.

Michael Sheehan is a media trainer and speech coach who has worked extensively with Bill.

Michael Sheehan: The woman asked the question in a slightly awkward way. She said, "What effect does the deficit have on you?" So Bush starts arguing with her.

When Bush had trouble with the question, the moderator, Carole Simpson of ABC News, rephrased it around the troubled economy. The clarification didn't help him.

My favorite line from that is, "Are you saying because I don't have cancer, I don't know what it's like to have cancer?"

And then Clinton goes down. It's the first thing out of his mouth: "Do you know someone who's lost their job? I'm the governor of a small state."

... In my state, when people lose their jobs there's a good chance I'll know them by their names. When a factory closes, I know the people who ran it. When the businesses go bankrupt, I know them.[6]

Mickey Kantor: If you had written this in a script for Hollywood, somebody would say, "This is silly. This is ridiculous. This would never happen." Remember the picture of President Bush looking at his watch right over Clinton's shoulder? It was the most telling moment of the entire campaign. At that moment, the campaign was over.

"There were bands playing."

Dee Dee Myers: We did a thirty-hour fly-around the last day of the campaign. On the plane in the middle of the night we were playing hearts and watching reruns of *Saturday Night Live*. It was obvious that we were going to win. I asked him, "Did you ever really think you'd be here?"

He looked at me like I was crazy. He said, "I wouldn't have run if I didn't think I could win. I always knew what the winning campaign was." He didn't snap at me exactly, but he was a little offended that I asked him.

Win he did. Bill finished with 370 electoral votes to 168 for Bush and none for Perot. Bill won the popular vote, too, with 43 percent to 37 for Bush and 19 for Perot.

Early on Election Day, the campaign plane arrived in Little Rock. The town was preparing to celebrate Bill's election in the same place he had announced his candidacy a year before.

Carolyn Staley: There were bands playing, because we had crowds thronging into the Old State House grounds from early in the afternoon and we had to keep them entertained.

It was everything from his announcement a year before, magnified to the nth degree. All the hotels had big satellite dishes on them, and the lights—it was like something out of *E.T.* There was a choir that he loves, from Lone Oak, Arkansas, the Pentecostals. It was a chilly fall night, a huge crowd. Joy. Anticipation.

Paul Leopoulos: I didn't see him until after his speech. Within twenty minutes everybody was gone. It was eerie quiet. It was frigid cold. It was pitch black. Then this side door of the State House opens and this Secret Service guy yells out, "Is David Leopoulos out here?"

"Yeah, that's me."

"Would you please come in here?"

So our little group came in, and the guy said, "The president-elect wants to see you."

Part III

Stumble
1993–1994

16

Not an Admiral:
Transition

The disarray that nearly overwhelmed Bill's administration at its inception was fore-shadowed in the weeks leading up to his taking office.

James Woolsey: I was not part of Clinton's inner circle.

James Woolsey served in national security posts in the Carter, Reagan, and Bush 41 administrations before becoming Bill's first director of central intelligence.

I'd met him just twice and had no expectation of being in the Clinton administration. I got a call from Warren Christopher on a Friday morning in late December '92.

Warren Christopher, who would serve as secretary of state for the first term of the Clinton administration, led Bill's transition board. He reached Woolsey at his Washington-area home.

I was packing with my family because we were flying that afternoon to California for Christmas with my wife's parents. Chris said, "Jim, do you suppose you could come down to Little Rock and talk to the president-elect about the CIA job?" I thought he meant talk to Clinton about who ought to have the CIA job. So I said, "I'd be glad to, Chris, but I'm flying to California with my family this afternoon for Christmas. Do I need to come between Christmas and New Year's or is after New Year's okay?"

"Actually, you'd better come today."

I sent my family off, and I went to National Airport and bought a ticket to Little Rock. Was met there by a staffer, who said, "The governor has a fund-raising dinner tonight. He won't be able to see you until about 11:30."

Went to the hotel. About 11, 11:15, they picked me up, I went over, and he was late. It was midnight or a little after, and I then had an interview with him. It was the only time I was ever—ever, ever—with him alone.

He's five years younger than I am. He grew up in Arkansas, I grew up in Oklahoma. We talked about fishing in the Ozarks, we talked about University of Arkansas and University of Oklahoma football. We talked about the CIA a bit. He said, "I don't really think the CIA director ought to make policy recommendations, do you?" I said, "No, I think he ought to just present intelligence." There were one or two things like that, but certainly not for more than a couple of minutes out of nearly an hour. He said, "Thank you very much," and I went back to the hotel, went to sleep.

Next morning, after breakfast, I get a call from a staffer saying, "We need to do a conflict-of-interest check. Would you go down to the Rose Law Firm and ask for Webb Hubbell?"* So I went down. Webb Hubbell asked me who my law clients were, what my investments were. He said, "I don't think any of that creates any problems, do you?" I said, "No, I guess not." And I went back to the hotel. I then got a call from another staffer, and she says, "The press conference is at 12:30. We'll pick you up at 12."

By now it's 11:30. I called campaign headquarters and asked for Warren Christopher. They said, "He's busy." I said, "Interrupt him. This is important." So Chris comes to the phone.

"Jim, what is it?"

"Chris, they're picking me up in half an hour for a press conference. By any chance, does the president-elect want me to be director of central intelligence?"

"Sure, that's what he wants."

"But he never asked and I never answered."

"Come on over to the press conference. We'll get it all sorted out."

"Chris, I'd like to know before I come to the press conference."

"Okay." He went away for a minute, then came back on the line and said, "I just stuck my head in his office. That's what he wants."

"Well, okay. I guess."

"Now it's about a quarter of 12. So they pick me up, and I go over to the governor's mansion, and there's the president-elect and Hillary, the Gores, Tony Lake, Sandy Berger, Les Aspin, Madeleine Albright, Warren Christopher, Dee Dee Myers, and George Stephanopoulos.† As I come in everybody says, "Hi, Jim, glad you're going to be with us."

*Webster Hubbell, a Little Rock attorney, began the administration as associate attorney general.

†At the start of Bill's presidency, Anthony Lake would be national security adviser, with Samuel "Sandy" Berger as his assistant; Les Aspin would be secretary of defense, Madeleine Albright ambassador to the United Nations, George Stephanopoulos director of communications, Dee Dee Myers White House press secretary.

Dee Dee and George are in the middle of doing what they often did, as I learned later, before a press conference, which is gaming it. "Suppose they ask this. What would we say?" One says, "Suppose they ask, 'Isn't this just a bunch of Carter administration retreads?'" And since we *were* Carter administration retreads, there was this silence. I said, "Governor, you could say that Woolsey also served in the Bush administration." Clinton grins, and Dee Dee Myers says, "Admiral, I never knew you served in the Bush administration." By now it's about 12:15, fifteen minutes before the press conference. I said, "Dee Dee, I'm not an admiral. I never got above captain in the army." She said, "Oops! We'd better change the press release."

And that's how I sort of got asked to be director of central intelligence.

17

Bedlam at Birth:
Getting Started

Tom Brokaw: I think it's a bigger job than he realized.

On Saturday, January 16, 1993, at Little Rock National Airport, Bill addressed the several hundred Arkansans gathered to see him off.[1]

My friends—No one not in my situation can appreciate my feeling of sadness at this parting. To this place, and the kindness of these people, I owe everything.[2]

The Clintons flew to Virginia. At the home of Thomas Jefferson they and the Gores boarded a bus to take them the 120 miles to the nation's capital.[3]

Tom Brokaw: I rode with him on the bus from Monticello to Washington for the inauguration. One of the things they were talking about was Bosnia. Al was pretty hard about "We've got to order air strikes," Clinton was not making any commitment to it. Hillary was asking all the right questions.

I had this disquieting feeling at the end of the bus ride: "Oh my God, this is like a dorm seminar"—more that than somebody who was two days away from raising his hand and taking the oath.

I got off the bus at the other end and said to a couple of my friends, "Maybe it's generational, because this is the first president who's younger than I am, but I wonder how well prepared they are for what they're about to take on."

On January 20 Bill raised his right hand as Chief Justice William Rehnquist administered the oath. Bill was now America's forty-second chief executive.

Dave McCurdy: The first two years, the administration was flawed. It started off on the wrong foot and it barely recovered.

18

Bill Asks, Colin Tells:
The President, the Gays, the Military

"He had this awful political situation."

Michael Dukakis: He's walking around the capitol building in Arkansas with a cup of coffee in his hand for the annual Veterans Day ceremonies. And Tom Friedman of the *New York Times* says, "What about gays in the military?" Clinton gives him the same answer he had given during the campaign a thousand times: "I don't think people ought to be discriminated against on the basis of sexual orientation." "Including the military?" "Including the military."

Ping! All of a sudden, front page, *New York Times:* Clinton thinks gays ought to be in the military.

Bill, November 11, 1992, discussing the lifting of the ban:

> How to do it, the mechanics of doing it, I want to consult with military leaders about that. . . . My position is we need everybody in America that's got a contribution to make that's willing to obey the law and work hard and play by the rules.

As commander in chief, Bill had the power to change the policy by executive order, as Harry Truman had ended racial segregation in the armed forces in 1948. Here, though, as the *New York Times* pointed out, he "seemed to acknowledge a need to negotiate the method and pace of the change with General Powell and his colleagues* to gain their support."[1]

---

*The *Times* was referring to Colin Powell, chairman of the joint chiefs of staff, 1989-1993, and the chiefs of each of the armed services.

Dave McCurdy: Maybe this issue could be addressed sometime, but it's not your opening play. They didn't sit down and say, "Our opening gambit's going to be this." It's that during the transition, not having the discipline and not thinking it through, he allowed others to frame the issue. And then they didn't jump on it immediately or have a way to resolve it.

Bill had more than two months, from Veterans Day to Inauguration Day, to devise a solution.

Jonathan Alter: He had this awful political situation, which he knew was awful, but he didn't know enough at that point to know how to defuse it.

Lawrence Korb: The issue was at the top of the agenda of the military leaders in the interregnum. Eisenhower called what they did "legalized insubordination," because they were out speaking, answering questions about it, when they shouldn't have been saying anything. Powell was at the Naval Academy and the subject came up.

Speaking at Annapolis only nine days before Bill was to take office, Colin Powell said that if the new president ended the ban, "We must conform to that policy. The debate will be over." But while discussing the issue with midshipmen he added, as one press outlet reported his remarks,

> that he believes the presence of acknowledged homosexuals would be detrimental to the military.
>
> "Homosexuality is not a benign behavioral characteristic such as skin color," said the general, who is black. "It goes to the core of the most fundamental aspect of human behavior."[2]

You had Carl Mundy, the marine commandant, talking about the problems it would cause. Since Dick Cheney was on his way out as defense secretary, he wasn't stopping them from speaking.

So the stage was set.

General Merrill A. "Tony" McPeak, now retired, served as chief of staff of the United States Air Force from 1990 to 1994.

Merrill McPeak: Awful mistake on the president's part. To single out the gays-in-the-military thing as the number-one problem on his national security agenda was a misjudgment. He just blew it, and I'm sure he would agree. He got taken to the cleaners, and it wasn't a nice scene to watch.

The first meeting we had with Clinton was in the White House, a few days after the inaugural, and it was on this subject. It was supposed to kick off at 4:30 in the Roosevelt Room—it started at 6:30. Aspin was with us, and the six guys in uniform—the chairman, the vice chairman, and the four service chiefs. We were all on time and got to cool our heels for two hours. It was maddening. I had things to do.

Anyway, we were called in for this meeting. We talked about nothing but gays in the military. Let's just say it was a frank exchange of views. We leveled with the president, said, "This is not going to work."

I spoke last. I gave some rationale. Unit cohesion was the problem. We know there are gays in the military, there have been since the Revolutionary War. As long as they act discreetly and we act discreetly, we're all big people, we can live with this. I even used the words, "Let's have a don't ask, don't tell policy." We said we were willing to do that, we recommended it. We could make his political day easy. At the time, to enter the armed forces, there was a form you had to sign at the recruiting station, and one question was, "Are you a homosexual?" We said, "We'll stop asking the question."

Afterwards, he came around the table and grabbed me by the shoulders. He said, "Tony, you should have been a lawyer"—I guess thinking that was a compliment, which it isn't. But I came out of there feeling ten feet tall, like you always do with Clinton. The guy's so charming, you fall in love. It isn't until the next morning you realize you had too much chocolate.

But the next day the media reported the chiefs were in revolt, this was a redo of Truman-MacArthur: Is the commander in chief in charge? Which was the exact opposite of what happened. We were asked for our opinions and we gave them. Chiefs are supposed to give honest military advice. It wasn't in the mode of defying him or challenging his authority, just saying, "This is not going to work, and here's why." We left on great terms. Every guy on our side of the table came out of there thinking, "This is a great guy. Good ol' boy from Arkansas. Hell yes, he understands. He's our kind of guy."

And the next day we get kicked in the face publicly.

National Public Radio, January 26, 1993:

> White House aides say the controversy is no longer just an issue about discrimination, it's become a test of Clinton's resolve and his toughness as a leader. . . . White House aides say they're . . . angry over what they call insubordination by the Joint Chiefs of Staff. As one put it, the Joint Chiefs took advantage of Mr. Clinton's lack of military service and the confusion of the transition in their effort to maintain the status quo.[3]

Merrill McPeak: Somebody had briefed the press, trying to wall the president off from criticism by saying, "The chiefs are fighting us and they shouldn't; they should roll over, cooperate." In the end, I don't think it was our opposition that was decisive on this issue. It was Sam Nunn and others in Congress who eventually stopped it in its tracks. But not before a lot of dumb things happened. And at the end the president got exactly what he was offered during that first conversation: Don't Ask, Don't Tell.

Al From: The Republicans pounced.

Craig Smith: After Clinton got elected, Dole put in legislation to prohibit gays serving in the military. We had campaigned on economics. And the first thing we were forced to deal with was this legislation. We had a huge head of steam going in and we stumbled at the front door.

Bill had been president only six days when Senate minority leader Bob Dole announced his intention to tack onto the Family and Medical Leave Act an amendment that would make the ban on gays a matter of congressional statute, not simply executive-branch regulation. Bill and his allies in Congress hoped for quick enactment of FMLA, which would entitle workers to a period of unpaid leave for important personal and family reasons, as a symbol of Bill's commitment to the concerns of ordinary people. Dole and his allies were now gumming up the bill's passage with an issue they intended as a symbol of Bill's commitment to the concerns of coastal elites.[4]

Dole's threat produced results in just three days: Bill agreed to leave the ban in place another six months while the Pentagon came up with a new policy. A week later Congress approved FMLA without the amendment.[5]

Craig Smith: Dole forced us to deal with an issue that wasn't popular with the American public.

Bob Dole represented Kansas in the Senate from 1969 to 1996, serving as Republican leader for the last eleven of those years.

Bob Dole: No, I don't think I forced it. We met as a Republican conference on it. It was a big issue at the time. What do they mean, "forced"?

Indeed, the most forceful congressional opponent of removing the ban was not a Republican but the Democratic chairman of the Senate Armed Services Committee, Sam Nunn of Georgia. Chuck Robb also served on the committee.

Charles Robb: Sam Nunn and I parted company on that one. He reflected what I would call the traditional southern conservative view.

He held some hearings of the committee down in Norfolk.

The hearings at the Norfolk Naval Base took place on May 10.

We toured the submarines. If you want to really show what for most people would be the best argument why we can't do this, a submarine's the place to do it, because there's no space anyplace. What people don't realize is that there have always been submariners who were gay.

I think Sam was just flat wrong on that issue. I know a little bit about unit cohesion. I've been in combat. I know how important it is.

Chuck Robb served two tours of duty in Vietnam as an officer in the Marine Corps.

I'm not suggesting that any element introduced into a military organization couldn't create its own dynamics, but it doesn't have to and it could certainly be dealt with.

Don't Ask, Don't Tell requires that people live a lie. It's a construct that was designed to look like it was fair, and it wasn't.

Merrill McPeak: Sam Nunn with John Warner* appeared on the evening news with these bunk beds—they're six inches apart in the submarine. The issue was, "Are we going to put gays in this sardine can?" And the White House, which never cared one way or the other if it was in print, just melted, because it was on the evening news, in vivid color and video. They started backpedaling, and very quickly the president gave a speech saying we were going to do Don't Ask, Don't Tell, which he could have had six months before and avoided all this public embarrassment.

Dave McCurdy: It was a bad way to start.

"He didn't seem to have an appreciation for the culture of the military."

Bill announced the new policy in July at the National Defense University in Washington; four months later, he signed the legislation that made it law. In theory, "Don't ask, don't tell" distinguishes between orientation and conduct, permitting gay servicemembers to serve as long as they do not act on or announce their orientation. In practice, discharges for homosexuality continued, with numbers rising in six of the seven years Bill remained in office following the law's enactment. Discharges declined after 2001—as they normally have done during time of war.[6] Nonetheless, between 2002 and 2004, the Department of Defense discharged thirty-seven gay linguists in a purge of the Defense Language Institute in California. Among them were specialists in Arabic and Korean, two languages at a premium after the terrorist attacks of September 11, 2001.[7]

*Virginia Republican on the Senate Armed Services Committee and a former secretary of the navy.

Bill intended his reform of the military's policy on homosexuality to promote tolerance. But the formalization of the policy, for the first time, in an act of Congress means that a president can no longer change the rule with the stroke of a pen, but must bring along a majority of lawmakers.

The effect of the flap on gay servicemembers is debatable. The effect on Bill is not: Added to his draft history it complicated his relations with the uniformed military as he embarked on his presidency.

Merrill McPeak: I don't like to take on the president and win. He's the man. As far as I'm concerned, you salute, do what he says. We have a well-understood policy of civilian control of the military. I didn't much care for some of his actions and some of his history, but he's the boss, that's it.

When he was elected he was very unliked by the rank and file. The way Clinton played dodgeball in not going to Vietnam was never going to be popular with the all-volunteer force of the nineties. I had a two-star general I had to retire early. He called the president a skirt-chasing, pot-smoking I don't know what. He stands up, in uniform, in front of an audience and does this. That was unprecedented in my opinion.

There was Clinton's famous visit to the aircraft carrier, where he was booed by the sailors.

I put a message out to all hands after that saying, "Knock it off."

Chuck Robb witnessed Bill's day at sea.

Charles Robb: I thought that because of his history with the draft, and all of the ruckus that had been raised because of gays in the military, he ought to go out of his way to show respect for the military. On his very first trip to visit a man-of-war at sea, the *Theodore Roosevelt,* he asked me if I would accompany him.

I didn't think to ask him "What are you going to wear?" or "What are you going to do?" I assumed he'd be well briefed. Of course, all of the military are in uniform. They're in working khaki or maybe the watch officers were in whites, I don't remember. Frankly, it looked to me like he had on the kind of stuff he'd have worn to a fraternity party.

I don't mean that he was disrespectful. It wasn't that he said the wrong things. It's just that he didn't seem to have an appreciation for the culture of the military that he was going to visit. It's a bit artificial, with the pomp and circumstance, but it would have been an excellent occasion to show, "Hey, I understand you guys. I respect you."

The *New York Times,* March 13, 1993:

Mr. Clinton sat in the captain's chair and rumbled about "ready rooms" and "snipes in the hole." But when the flight deck he was standing on dropped 50 feet in five seconds so he could tour the hangar below, the President looked more like a teen-ager on a roller coaster than a top gun.

"I'm afraid he has contempt for the military," said one crew member quoted in the paper.[8]

Anthony Lake: I think at first he saw the military the way you ought to see the bureaucracy generally, that is, as another constituency that has to be won over. You can't simply order the bureaucracy to do things, because it will find ways to drag its heels. You have to lead them in a political sense.

Not the same with the military. The military wants to be commanded. If you encourage them to say what they think, and then you order them to do something, even if they hadn't agreed with it, they will carry it out better than any other institution in the government. It took a while for Clinton to do the commander bit, which is to say issuing orders crisply. It's in the little things. The way you handle yourself.

It took Clinton, I'd say, a year, year and a half to get comfortable as commander in chief.

Lawrence Korb: If Bob Kerrey had won in '92, he'd have signed gays in the military as a Medal of Honor recipient. They wouldn't have come near him.

You talked to people in the Pentagon about Clinton: Given the way this man lived his life, he did not deserve to be president—that was their bottom line.

It's not that he wasn't smart enough, it wasn't the policy positions. It was the person who played games the way he did with the draft, who messed around on his wife. What the military was saying was "Look, you want to live your life like that, that's fine, but you cannot then be commander in chief."

That was the feeling among the military: We're not going to fight and die for this guy.

"I want to see them."

Hugh Shelton: Gays in the military, marijuana, the draft, Oxford—all of that was used by his opponents to paint a picture of a man not fit to be commander in chief. What I saw was 180 out from that.

Army General Hugh Shelton, now retired, was appointed chairman of the joint chiefs of staff by Bill in 1997. He remained in that post until 2001.

I never found President Clinton, from the day I met him until our last meeting in the White House the day before he left office, to be anything other than very much appreciative of the military, the capabilities it provided him as commander in chief, the quality of the men and women in uniform, and what they're dedicated to. He was a great commander in chief to work for.

The first time I met President Clinton was in 1994. I'm commander of 18th Airborne Corps at Fort Bragg, and we had a terrible accident. An F-16 from Pope Air Force Base, which is contiguous to Fort Bragg, collided with a C-130 transport plane that was landing. The fireball that ensued went right through two buildings where I had 180 paratroopers preparing to go on an airborne operation. We had 19 killed instantaneously; 123 others were injured very badly.*

Early that evening I got a phone call: "President Clinton will be landing at Fort Bragg tonight. He's coming to visit the troops in the hospital." When a president's coming to visit an installation, you really jump to it. Then, at about 8 o'clock that night, we got the call that said, "No, he's not coming."

But the next morning we got another call saying, "President Clinton will arrive at Pope at noontime."

I rode him over to the hospital. He visited every single troop there. We were getting ready to leave and he turned to me and he says, "Is that all?"

I said, "Mr. President, there are three more up on the top floor in the critical care unit. None of them will live. They were in such bad shape that we couldn't even move them to the burn center in San Antonio or to Duke or Chapel Hill. There are no families up there right now or anything."

"I want to see them."

So the hospital commander and I got into the elevator with him and we went up to the top floor. Because of the shape they were in, you had to wear a surgical gown, and you had to change it as you went from cubicle to cubicle to visit with each one of them. He did that three times: went in, went over, put his hand down next to them, prayed for them, came back out, changed clothes, went into the next one.

After we drove back over to the plane, Air Force One, we walked out to the ramp. I said, "Mr. President, I can't tell you how much this means to those men and to their families for you to take the time to come visit them."

He said, "I had to do it. I wanted to do it last night. They told me, 'You can't do that. We've got a lot of stuff lined up for tomorrow.' They talked me out of

---

*The accident occurred on March 23. The eventual death toll was twenty-four. "History of Fort Bragg: 1990s," Office of the Command Historian, Fort Bragg, http://www.bragg.army.mil/History/HistoryPage/History%20of%20Fort%20Bragg/FortBragginthe1990s.htm.

it. But about two this morning I woke up and I said, 'I should've gone last night. That was the right thing to do.' So I waited until six and called downstairs and said, 'Get the plane ready. We're going to Fort Bragg.' You know how handlers are. Immediately, they started giving me fifteen reasons why I couldn't come today: I've got this head of state in town, I've got these comments to make. Finally, I said, 'Read my lips. We're going to Fort Bragg.'"

And so he came.

19

New Kid in Town:
Permanent Washington Greets the Clintons

"In some quarters of Washington there was condescension."

"Welcome to Washington," *Washington Post* columnist Sally Quinn greeted the new First Family just after Bill's election, "But Play by Our Rules." A leading arbiter of social customs in the nation's capital, Quinn further instructed her unschooled charges to remember this: "When the Clinton administration is gone and forgotten, the Congress, the media and the establishment will remain."[1]

Much of permanent Washington—reporters, pundits, tenured legislators, lawyers, lobbyists, Georgetown hostesses—greeted Bill and Hillary with the condescension of people who just know better. Early press coverage reflected this attitude.

Gene Lyons: It seems like a lot of the worst aspects of the high school experience are concentrated in the Washington press corps. The cliquishness, the almost insane fascination with order and degree. There's this obsession with who's in, who's out, who's up, who's down, who's in what group, and who belongs where. It reminds me of the old Eagles tune, "New Kid in Town." He's the new kid in town and we don't like him. And we don't think he deserves to be prom king. And as for that bitch he brought with him . . .

To me, looking from a distance, it was, "Grow up. He's not my best friend either, but for gosh sake, he wanted to be governor and he did a pretty good job of it, so give him a chance."

But there was this immediate need to humiliate him.

At the end of January, the *Boston Globe* groused that "barely 10 days into his presidency, Clinton appears to have lost control of the political agenda."[2]

The humorist Art Buchwald lampooned the snap judgment of his more serious colleagues:

A TV reporter shoved a microphone into my face last week and asked, "How do you think President Clinton is doing in his first eight days?" I was reluctant to reply because I always write an in-depth piece on a president's first eight days. So I just said that his administration was an utter failure and President Clinton should resign and turn over the running of our country to the able Al Gore.[3]

Gene Lyons: I got the impression they were stunned and amazed by the hostile coverage in D.C. Part of it was that the right, by that time, had invented and perfected this right-wing noise machine—there was a group of journalists who were prepared to do everything they could to make life hell for a Democratic president, no matter who he was or where he came from. I don't think the Clintons were as aware as they ought to have been of the existence and the strength of that movement.

They weren't ready for the ideological hostility, they weren't ready for the character assassination.

Sam Donaldson: In some quarters of Washington there was condescension.

Sam Donaldson is a reporter for ABC News.

Here were southerners who had come to town. He was a minority president from the standpoint of the election, so he wasn't an 800-pound gorilla for whom you had to put your feelings aside. There was a lot of looking down people's noses at him.

Craig Smith: My sense is, they didn't take us really serious. They were like, "These are people from Arkansas. From *Arkansas.*" And of course we came up here as Arkansans. We wore our cowboy boots and we wore our blue jeans. My sense is people were rolling their eyes behind our back.

Bill didn't exactly help matters when he told workers at a Louisiana truck plant that during the 1970s he'd owned an El Camino, a cross between a car and a small pickup, and had covered the vehicle's truck bed with Astroturf. "It was a real sort of Southern deal," he told the workers, explaining, "You don't want to know why, but I did." The admission, according to one observer, provoked "gales of laughter from the auto workers—and gaping mouths from his aides."[4]

Ron Fournier: They were king of the hill in Arkansas and were considered—with their educations—the top of the heap. They weren't used to being looked down upon and they didn't like it.

Remember, too, they came to Washington feeling pretty bruised because they'd been through Gennifer Flowers. They thought the press was out to get them. So the first thing he did was keep the press corps away.

In its attempt to control coverage, the White House engaged in some interior redesign.

Dee Dee Myers: We said, "You can no longer walk out of the lower press office into the press secretary's suite in the West Wing." We created opportunities for the press to be pissed.

Ron Fournier: They put up walls, both literally and figuratively, and the White House press corps reaction was, "You can't do that to us. We hold the final say."

Dee Dee Myers: It was a bad decision. After that, reporters had to make an appointment or they had to call one of the assistants up in the press secretary's suite to come down and escort them up. It was like, "What? Are you kidding me? I've been working here for ten years"—twenty years in some cases—"and I can no longer walk up to ask the press secretary a question?"

Helen Thomas, long a correspondent for United Press International and recently retired as a columnist for Hearst Newspapers, covered the White House for nearly half a century.

Helen Thomas: That was the attitude. "The hell with the press. We won the election. It's our White House."

Ron Fournier: It was, "We have a mandate. We're gonna change the world and if you don't like it, we'll go around you." They really thought they could go around the White House press corps.

Helen Thomas: Plus wiping out the Travel Office.

In May 1993 Mack McLarty, Bill's chief of staff, summarily fired all seven employees of the White House Travel Office. The housecleaning may have been well deserved—McLarty had learned of bookkeeping irregularities in the unit—but the administration opened itself to charges of cronyism by moves made behind the scenes to steer business to a charter airline partly owned by top-drawer FOB Harry Thomason, as well as by other steps taken to favor friends and family of Bill. Within a week, McLarty rescinded the firings, eventually offering five of the fired employees jobs elsewhere in the government while the former director and his deputy retired.[5]

In other words, Bill canned a group of people who served "at the pleasure of the president" and replaced them with pals. Clumsily done, but not a hanging offense—or so it would seem. But because the office handled travel for the White House press corps, which, as one column noted, had grown used to being "pampered by the plush level of accommodations" the shop arranged, the firings aroused anger in the media well out of proportion to the crime.[6]

Helen Thomas: The Clintons had a chip on their shoulder.

Rumors spread that the Arkansas arrivistes were rude to their White House servants—unlike the Bushes, old-money and well bred, who were accustomed to the presence of attendants as they went about their daily lives.

Jonathan Alter: Now, of course, they love him in the drawing rooms of Georgetown, but we forget the kinds of things Sally Quinn wrote. I couldn't understand why they didn't just grit their teeth and kiss Sally Quinn's ass. For people who are as good at politics as the Clintons are, they really blew that.

They would try once in a while. They'd have people over to the White House or they'd invite them to things, but their hearts were not in it. One of Clinton's less attractive qualities is that he can be self-pitying. So he would say, "I went over there, I kissed their fat asses, and what do I get from it?" Really, it was a mark that he wasn't more skillful at making the jump from Little Rock. In so many other ways he could seamlessly adapt to the big leagues, but he couldn't do it every time.

Dee Dee Myers: I don't think it would have taken very much to win over some of the opinion makers in the social-political establishment of Washington, but the Clintons didn't think it was necessary and they didn't do it.

"His heart and his mind were in two different places."

Bill's frustrations notwithstanding, there was more to the friction between him and permanent Washington than his insufficient care and feeding of them or their innate sense of superiority to him.

Sam Donaldson: One of the seminal moments was when his nominee for assistant attorney general in charge of civil rights came under fire from the *Wall Street Journal,* and Bill Clinton blinked instead of supporting her.

Adding to the image of an incompetent new administration was Bill's difficulty in finding an attorney general: His first two nominees were derailed over irregularities in their employment of household help before Janet Reno finally got the job in March. Nonetheless, his nomination of Lani Guinier to head the Justice Department's civil rights division seemed to make perfect sense. A seasoned civil rights attorney, the University of Pennsylvania law professor in 1984 had helped file a voting registration lawsuit against her friend from law school, the governor of Arkansas.[7] But as the nomination moved toward the Senate for confirmation, senators began to squirm. In a number of law-review pieces she had suggested modification of voting laws and procedures to enhance the power of minority voters. Her views, together with her skin color—she is the daughter of a Jewish mother and a Jamaican father—made it easy for Bill's opponents to label her a "Quota Queen."[8]

Harris Wofford: Part of what makes people feel that they've been let down by Clinton—people like Lani Guinier, or maybe the Edelmans, Marion Wright and Peter—is related to the fact that he's engaged and out on a limb on so many things that he has to trim somewhere.

Marion Wright Edelman and her husband, Peter, had been friends of the Clintons since the young Hillary, just out of law school, worked for her at the Children's Defense Fund.

He has to neglect something. But part of it is they have such high expectations about him. He's theirs.

The administration asked Wofford, a senator from Pennsylvania, to advocate for the nomination. Wofford met with Guinier.

I cheerfully said, "Yeah, I'll be your defender." Then I read her writings and I said, "Oh, my God! This is going to be a really hard battle."

At a certain point, Biden* said to me, "There is no way she is going to be confirmed by this committee. I'm going to tell the president that if he wants us to hold hearings he can insist on it. But he's going to lose more and more if he doesn't withdraw it."

Richard Mays was in Mack McLarty's office, where he'd come to lobby the chief of staff in favor of Guinier's nomination, when Bill asked him to join a meeting on the subject.

Richard Mays: He had maybe fifteen to twenty of his key aides. Vernon Jordan† became the aggressor in terms of pushing to withdraw her name. And Clinton asked Maggie,‡ "Is your advice the same today as it was yesterday?" which was apparently to withdraw her from consideration. So the first two people to speak were two blacks, Vernon Jordan and Maggie Williams,

*At the time Joe Biden (D-DE) chaired the Senate Judiciary Committee.

†A classic Washington "fixer," Jordan held no title in the Clinton administration aside from "first friend."

‡Maggie Williams was Hillary's chief of staff.

which politically structured that meeting in the context of, "Let's remove race from this."

You could see Bill Clinton politically wanting to withdraw her name—although I think his gut said, "Why?"

That was the only instance where I have seen Bill Clinton totally uncomfortable with himself politically. I think his heart and his mind were in two different places. And you could feel both pulling. Ultimately, his mind won out.

Five weeks after Bill nominated her, Guinier visited him in the Oval Office. She refused Bill's request that she withdraw on her own. "Then I will have to pull you down," Bill replied. Guinier argued that she deserved the opportunity to defend her tainted reputation; no, Bill told her, among civil rights activists the episode would enhance her reputation: "I'll be the asshole and you can be the hero."[9]

The job went to Deval Patrick, who would later become governor of Massachusetts. The episode ended Bill's friendship with Guinier.[10]

Sam Donaldson: He withdrew the nomination. That shows weakness. When a president sticks by his people—sometimes, you'd say, unwisely—it shows the kind of loyalty and dedication to purpose that says, "This is a strong person." But when he blinks because the *Wall Street Journal* on its editorial page opposes one of his nominees, that stamps him as an easy mark: "We can take this guy. He doesn't stand for anything."

"He slumped in his chair."

Paul Begala: I'm at a loss to explain the snobbery of permanent Washington, because the Clintons weren't unfamiliar with the eastern establishment and its ways. Maybe it was that he was in so many worlds simultaneously. It's his great gift and, I think, why the elites hated him. They didn't think he was authentic. Clinton is an authentic southern white boy who was always liberal on race. At the same time, he's an authentic scholar of the elite northeastern academy. At the same time, he's a brass-knuckles politician. At the same time he's a policy wonk. He's all of those things.

If you were northeastern elite and he sat with you at a dinner party at Sally Quinn's house, he was on your wavelength. And then you turn on the television and see him in Louisiana making jokes about having an El Camino with Astroturf in the back, and you think, "That phony." Or if you saw him in an African American church. But all of those slices of him are authentic.

During the campaign in '92 Clinton read a biography of FDR. He said FDR was Slick Franklin.

Roosevelt was five times slicker than Clinton ever was. Lincoln was Slick Abe. It's always the challenge in a huge, diverse country with two great parties: To succeed in this business in our country you have to keep your foot on a bunch of different ice floes moving at different speeds, sometimes in different directions. A Republican has to hold together libertarians with social conservatives. Reagan was able to hold them together by being all things to all people. Clinton did the same on the Democratic side. You don't lead a great nation from one tiny extreme.

Journalists and Georgetown hostesses weren't the only people in Washington with little regard for Bill. Leaders in Congress—beginning with members of Bill's own party—were also unimpressed.

Michael Waldman: President Clinton identified campaign reform as one of his priorities early on.

Michael Waldman served first as a policy aide in the Clinton White House, then as its director of speechwriting.

The first meeting the new president had with the leaders of Congress, who were Democrats, took place in the Cabinet Room, two days into his term. President Clinton talked about how important campaign reform was, how the voters had spoken, what a priority it was. George Mitchell, the Senate majority leader, was enthusiastic about it.

Then Speaker Foley,* who was sitting right across the big table from President Clinton, spoke. "Mr. President, we're strongly committed to doing this. The only thing is Danny Rostenkowski.† He's going to have to whip this through his committee. It's going to be tough for him to whip this and the tax bill at the same time. But we are going to get it done, and we are totally for it."

I'd seen enough gangster movies to know what he was really saying: "Listen, kid, if you dare to push campaign finance reform on us, just watch what we do to your tax bill—your number-one priority." Clinton looked depressed; he slumped in his chair.

The House Democrats were very slow in getting it done. By the time the Republicans got around to filibustering it at the end of the session, the body was already long dead.

*Tom Foley (D-WA).

†Dan Rostenkowski (D-IL), chairman of the House Ways and Means Committee.

• • •

If Democrats were dismissive, Republicans were scornful.

Sam Donaldson: Bill Clinton never had a honeymoon. Most presidents are given at least a month or two of goodwill before they're savaged by the opposition; not him. The idea that a president is illegitimate from the standpoint of his election was really something new, but many Republicans took that view.

Paul Begala: There was an ongoing effort to delegitimize Clinton. Some on the right refused to call him "President Clinton." Called him "Mr. Clinton." Dick Armey, who later became the House majority leader, said on the House floor, "That's *your* president." It was deeply unpatriotic.

Michael Kinsley: In 1992 there was a feeling among Republicans of manifest destiny, that they were supposed to rule forever. At that point they had been in power since 1980, and, basically, conservatism had been dominant since the 1978 congressional elections. They thought it should go on forever. That is the reason they were so resentful of Clinton.

How could he have won? Their only explanation is he must have done something terrible. He must have cheated, because he wasn't supposed to win.

Douglas Brinkley: Keep in mind, Republicans were furious in '92 that this weird usurper from Texas, Ross Perot, took 19 percent of the vote—they believed that Bush would have won minus the Perot factor.

Paul Begala: There's this huge myth that Perot delivered the presidency to Clinton. That's not true. There's nothing in the data that says Bush wins but for Perot. Nothing. It's a complete myth.

John Sununu: With all due respect to Bill Clinton, it was not he who beat George Bush, it was Ross Perot who beat George Bush. Bill Clinton got only 43 percent of the vote. His campaign was not that effective.

James Carville: Every piece of research said Perot took equally from both. No one has ever been able to come up with any research to prove otherwise. They just say it.*

---

*Although history cannot be replayed with Perot not a candidate at all, the research supports Carville and Begala on this point. One such analysis appears in E. J. Dionne Jr., "Perot Seen Not Affecting Vote Outcome: Analysis Finds Shift in One State Likely," *Washington Post*, November 8, 1992.

Republicans, including the GOP leader in the Senate, were not about to let Bill forget the election's arithmetic: "Fifty-seven percent of the Americans who voted in the presidential election voted against Bill Clinton," said Bob Dole the day after the balloting, "and I intend to represent that majority on the floor of the U.S. Senate."[11]

Bob Dole: We weren't going to adopt all of his programs, so we wanted to put a marker out there that he didn't get a mandate. He got elected, but it was by 43 percent of the voters, and that gave us some responsibility. It's a two-party system, you know.

Nothing personal. It wasn't anything personal.

"It was the cross he had to bear."

But for a sizable group of Americans, their feelings toward Bill Clinton were, and are, personal, indeed.

Harold Ickes: There's no question that there's a group of people in the country who hate the Clintons, just fucking hate them, and I don't know why.

Harold Ickes is a veteran political operative with roots in New York and in the left flank of the Democratic Party. He would serve as deputy chief of staff in Bill's White House. Fred Barnes is a journalist for Fox News and the Weekly Standard.

Fred Barnes: He was such a polarizing figure—it's odd. Clinton is the single most charming person I have ever met in my entire life. You have heard this a thousand times, and you have heard it because it's true. He is just unbelievably charming.

Craig Smith: It's been one of the most perplexing things about the Clintons. I did Bill Clinton's politics for fifteen, twenty years. I've never really been able to figure out this visceral hatred of the man.

Dan Glickman: It was cultural as much as anything else. It was generational.

Dan Glickman represented Kansas in the House from 1977 to 1995 before serving as Bill's secretary of agriculture from 1995 to 2001.

He liked modern music. He loved movies. He was a playful sort of guy. He was handsome, and he liked movie stars. The old-line conservative forces in America didn't know what to make of him. I think the real answer is that this is the first president who reflected the social changes that had occurred in America.

The dislike of him was not because of his policies.

Mike McCurry: Remember, at the heart of the conservative movement are people who endured an enormous amount of liberal arrogance through the 1960s. For a lot of them, this was the revenge that comes with saying, "You weren't so smart after all, were you?"

He was in the antiwar movement, Hillary did the Watergate thing. They were those culturally elite liberals who looked down on us, and we're going to put them in their place.

Despite such sentiments on the right, Bill, from his adolescence intent on a career inside the system not outside, was hardly a counterculture figure during the 1960s.

Peter King is a Republican congressman from Long Island, New York.

Peter King: Psychiatrists or psychohistorians would do great trying to figure this out: How the great culture clash of the 1990s was about a guy from the 1950s who was supposed to symbolize the 1960s, but really didn't.

John Sununu traces conservatives' dislike of Bill to their distrust of Bill.

John Sununu: Bill Clinton's talent is glibness. He really is able to take on whatever topic you want and make it sound like he understands it. A lot of folks on the conservative side resent him when he uses that glibness to appear to be a centrist and a conservative when, in fact, he was governing with extremely liberal policies. That's why some folks have such an intense dislike.

Even after '94, what he did was be the most liberal he could with a Republican Congress. It's not that he became conservative. It's that the possibilities were confined to an envelope that was much more conservative than he was.

Yet the left wing of the Democratic Party hardly considered Bill one of their own.

Peter King: While the Republican base would never consider Bill Clinton to be a moderate, Democratic liberals were always yelling privately about his welfare reform and budget cutting. And they didn't like Bob Rubin—Rubin was a Wall Street guy.*

Leon Panetta: Clinton talked about the hatred a lot, and he didn't have any answers for why it was there, other than it was the cross he had to bear in his political life.

---

*Robert Rubin left Goldman Sachs, where he was cochairman, to become a key member of Bill's economic team.

Leon Panetta left his job as a Democratic congressman from California to serve in the Clinton administration, first as director of the Office of Management and Budget, then as White House chief of staff.

He knew that there were people who just did not like him, and they were going after him. It wasn't just political opposition, it was visceral hatred.

There are people who look at Bill Clinton, who's very bright and very able, and they don't think he deserves it, that somehow he's just this kid from Hope, Arkansas, and hasn't really earned it. I used to compare Bill Clinton to the kid who never studies during a course and then crams the night before the test and gets an A. Those who study and have to do all the hard work think, "What the hell's that all about?"

Which, in fact, is how Bill got through high school, Georgetown, Oxford, and Yale Law.

It's not only the way he went to school. My first experience with it was on the State of the Union address when he was making changes in the damn thing in the car going up to the Capitol. We stopped in front of the Capitol and here he has the speaker and the leadership all waiting to greet him, and he's still writing the speech.

Melanne Verveer: I don't know. Clinton taps into something or touches something in some people that they clearly don't like.

Harold Ickes: I don't know if anybody has an answer for it.

20

Debt on Arrival:
Recharting an Economic Course

"Economies are about confidence."

It was "the economy, stupid." But how?

Robert Rubin: I would say that he inherited a real economic morass.

Robert Rubin began the Clinton administration as head of the National Economic Council, then served as secretary of the treasury, 1995–1999.

Long-term interest rates were over 7 percent, unemployment over 7 percent. You'd had a recession. You now had a year of some growth, but nevertheless there was a high level of anxiety and concern.

During the campaign Bill had laid out an ambitious program to revive the economy, centered on a "middle-class tax cut" and large-scale investment in America's economic infrastructure and human resources. In addition, influenced in no small measure by Ross Perot's focus on the issue, he called for aggressive reduction of the federal budget deficit.

The plan was predicated on Bush administration numbers showing that the deficit had already started to shrink. But only two weeks before Bill took office, he received some unexpected news.

Robert Rubin: The outgoing Office of Management and Budget dramatically revised upward projected deficits looking forward, so he faced the prospect of very high deficits as far out as you could see.

According to the new estimates, the annual deficit would not decrease but rise, topping $300 billion in five years.[1]

In light of the revised numbers, Bill had to revise his thinking. Robert Reich headed the economic transition team that would help him make the adjustment.

Robert Reich: When the transition team reported to the president-elect on the extent of the deficit problem, we expected he'd be frustrated and upset because it would delay his investment plans. He was just the opposite. He smiled, his face brightened. He said, "Now we have a real challenge on our hands."

Leon Panetta has a different recollection of Bill's reaction.

Leon Panetta: He was angry, no question. He was angry because he was in a deeper hole than he had anticipated, and the decisions that would have to be made would be that much more unpopular. He thought that the Bush administration had not been honest about how bad the problem was, and he would have to reap the consequences.

He felt he'd been sandbagged.

On January 7 Bill and his economic team, eyes now wide open, met at the governor's mansion in Little Rock to devise their plan.[2]

Lawrence Summers: By the end of the meeting the president-elect had come down on the side of deficit reduction as an important priority for the administration.

Lawrence Summers served first as undersecretary of the treasury for international affairs, then as deputy secretary, and finally, after Robert Rubin left the administration, as secretary from 1999 to 2001.

Robert Rubin: The president cared enormously about public investment, and throughout his whole eight years there, he continued to pursue different dimensions of it. But he said at the very beginning that we've got to get the fiscal house back in order—that's our threshold issue.

Alice Rivlin: He figured out that he couldn't do the things he wanted to do unless he got the deficit under control.

Alice Rivlin served first as deputy director, then as director, of the Office of Management and Budget. The Nobel Prize–winning economist Joseph Stiglitz began Bill's administration as a member of the Council of Economic Advisers, then served as the group's chairman from 1995 to 1997.

Joseph Stiglitz: It was clearly one of the president's disappointments that the more aggressive agenda he would have liked—on a whole range of issues, not just investment—was put aside or at least diminished. Another example was reforming welfare. We realized that effective reform of welfare required more investments, more expenditures to move people from welfare to work. We had to train people. And what we wanted to do we couldn't do, because of the lack of money.

Leon Panetta: There was always that tension of how, as president, can I deal with the needs that have to be addressed in this country, and at the same time reduce the deficit? In addition to that, any time you talk about spending restraints, you run smack dab into constituencies out there that are going to scream. The president and the political people around the president started saying, "Holy cow, if we do this we're going to pay a political price." That's right, but it's also what leadership is all about.

Vigorous deficit reduction while the nation was emerging from a recession represented a departure from standard Keynesian practice.

Joseph Stiglitz: The most immediate conflicting problems were that the government had a very large deficit, almost 5 percent of GDP, and the economy was growing very slowly. Typically, macroeconomic advice for accelerating growth when there is high unemployment is to have larger deficits—to stimulate the economy. So solving one problem would have exacerbated another.

The way the circle was squared was a strategy of backloaded deficit reduction. Taxes were increased on the richest Americans, the upper 2 percent, for whom the increase would not lead to much of a reduction in consumption because they were so well off. So that wouldn't have much of a negative effect on the economy. And there was a commitment to cut back expenditures in a year or two when the economy was stronger.

Roger Altman: The idea was that if you reduced the deficit, you'd lower interest rates, and that in turn would be the biggest stimulus you could provide to the economy. That turned out to be correct.

If you lower interest rates, that affects people buying cars, buying homes, farm equipment, doing construction—every single credit-sensitive activity there is in the economy. Anything that has to do with borrowing money.

Robert Rubin: The deficit had come to symbolize in people's minds something much larger: an inability to manage our economic affairs. Once people felt that there had been a reestablishment of a sound fiscal path, it not only dealt more narrowly with interest rates but also—very importantly—increased business confidence and consumer confidence more generally. And then you wound up with growth, and the growth increased federal revenues. A virtuous circle.

There's a real piece to this—with a more disciplined fiscal policy, you reduce the federal government's demand for money, and you bring interest rates down—but also a psychological piece. Economies are about confidence.

Roger Altman: Clinton balanced the budget, he ran surpluses, he paid down the national debt. No president in my lifetime had a record like that. More important than that, though, the record on growth, job creation, lifting people out of poverty, income growth across the board, every sector, was unsurpassed, unprecedented. He had an extraordinary overall economic record.

"I thought it was a mistake."

If Robert Rubin and Roger Altman were, and remain, among the most ardent proponents of the primacy given deficit reduction during Bill's presidency, Joseph Stiglitz and Robert Reich were, and remain, among its most ardent critics. To them, what is often mentioned as Bill's signature accomplishment, the restoration of "fiscal responsibility" to the federal government, is not such an accomplishment after all.

Robert Reich: The decision to reduce the deficit first was made not only because it was so large, but also because Alan Greenspan* made it clear that

*Chairman of the Federal Reserve throughout Bill's tenure.

unless the deficit were reduced he would not reduce short-term interest rates, saying inflation would loom as a threat.

Joseph Stiglitz: I thought it was a mistake to frame the issue as deficit reduction. What matters is how you're spending the money. Every firm has deficits: it's borrowing to make investments. You look at the cost of capital and you look at the return.

One of the studies we did at the Council of Economic Advisers found that returns on public research-and-development expenditures were 20, 30, 40, 50, 60, even 70 percent. To say that we ought to cut back on those when we could borrow at 3 percent or 4 percent, 5 percent, was bad business. But the deficit-cutting view held sway in the administration, even though there was no strong intellectual basis—it was bad economics—and even though I think President Clinton emotionally never was on that side. I think he became convinced it was necessary as practical politics.

Robert Reich: In those first years we cut wherever we could, trying not to cut education or job training or child health or important infrastructure; cutting everything else. And even trying to put whatever money we could into these investment areas so that at least we'd end up with a beginning foundation for public investment when the economy turned up again.

We didn't anticipate the Republicans would take over Congress in January of 1995. After 1995 it was a different ballgame altogether. The Republicans were demanding that we get on a path toward a zero deficit. Completely absurd in economic terms. The president felt he had no other choice.

A balanced budget means nothing. It's a symbol. There was a surplus by the end of the Clinton administration. That surplus could have been, should have been, used for investments in public education, in early childhood education and access to college and affordable health care. All the things the country still lacks.

All of the language, all of the framework, all of the understandings that we had created in 1992—the original Bill Clinton message that this economy is nothing but its people—which I think were absolutely correct and are still correct, vanished from Democratic rhetoric. They're still gone.

Joseph Stiglitz: It was very much in the mindset at the beginning of the administration that we wanted to get to the investment agenda later. But in retrospect, what we were doing was putting aside money that was then squandered by the Bush administration, first in a tax cut for very rich Americans and then in a war in Iraq.

You might say this investment in deficit reduction was a very risky one. It did yield short-term returns. It turned out not to yield long-term returns.

21

A Casino for Jesus: The Budget Bill

"Goddammit, I am not a prime minister."

The most contentious legislative battle of Bill's first year in the White House took place over the federal budget, as the new president sought to put into effect the economic policies he and his team had settled upon.

As unveiled by Bill in an address to a joint session of Congress on February 17, his budget would slice $140 billion off the annual deficit by 1997, with a cumulative total of nearly $500 billion over four years. About half the reduction would be achieved by budget cuts, including $60 billion from Medicare and Medicaid, the other half by raising taxes on wealthy individuals and large businesses and by imposing a broad new tax on energy. The plan featured only a modest program of investment—an economic stimulus proposal totaling $30 billion.

Keeping a campaign vow, Bill offered the working poor an expansion of the Earned Income Tax Credit, the program, begun in 1975, designed to reduce the taxes and supplement the income of low-wage earners. Breaking a campaign vow, he promised middle-class Americans that their income taxes would not rise—not, as he had pledged in 1992, that they would fall.[1]

Dan Glickman: I remember thinking that the president had found the right formula to get the economy going again. There were an awful lot of Democrats afraid of taxes. It may have been one of the reasons we lost the House in '94. But it struck me that this legislation was the first example of strong leadership by the White House.

Lawrence O'Donnell: In terms of the unfolding of the administration, the number-one thing was the budget bill. If we couldn't get the budget bill passed, then nothing else was going to happen.

In 1993 Lawrence O'Donnell, now a political analyst for MSNBC, served as chief of staff of the Senate Finance Committee, which was chaired by Daniel Patrick Moynihan (D-NY).

It had the biggest tax increase in history, and the president had run as a tax cutter.

Roger Altman: Remember, it passed by two votes in the House and a tie vote in the Senate.

Vice President Al Gore cast the tiebreaking vote in the Senate.

It never attracted a single Republican vote. In either chamber.

Since Republicans in Congress wanted nothing to do with legislation that involved a tax increase, Bill had to rely on the members of his own party. Theoretically, the votes were there: Democrats held comfortable majorities in both the House and Senate. But Bill would discover that congressional Democrats were an unruly bunch, lacking in obedience to the new chief executive despite their common partisan affiliation.

Alice Rivlin: Democrats were for deficit reduction in principle, but very resistant regarding particular programs.

Elaine Kamarck: In the '92 campaign, he never allowed himself to be seen with the speaker of the Democratic House, Tom Foley. Because in 1992 the speaker of the Democratic House was a very unpopular person, a symbol of an old regime that was kind of corrupt and yesterday.

Clinton knew that. But the minute he got into the White House he lost that sense and he started listening to what Democrats in the House wanted to do. At one meeting the topic of a balanced budget amendment came up. He never supported it, but he was supportive of trying to move toward a balanced budget—which at the time was rhetoric that the Democrats did not want to hear. We were discussing this and Clinton lost his temper, finally saying, "Goddammit, I am not a prime minister." In other words, he was sick of having to coddle this party of his in the House of Representatives when he had been elected as a different kind of Democrat.

The first term was a constant struggle between the two halves of the party and the two halves of Clinton.

Michael Waldman: There was very little deference to a Democratic president among Democratic lawmakers. People like Bob Kerrey, or Moynihan, got praise from the media and from their peers only if they stood up to Clinton. When you think of how Bob Kerrey made the White House sweat for his one measly vote on the budget bill . . .

Bob Kerrey: This was a big tax increase. And I had voted against his stimulus plan, because I thought it was way too weak.

Facing resistance in the Senate, Bill reduced his stimulus plan to $16 billion, but the change didn't improve prospects for passage. Viewing the relatively inconsequential measure as an impediment to enactment of the larger plan, he dropped it.[2]

What the president faced was that he couldn't get the liberal Democrats, particularly in the House, to support the budget if it had too much in cuts.

Hank Brown and I in the Senate, Tim Penny and John Kasich* in the House, put together a list of $100 billion of additional cuts. The administration opposed it, and it lost in the Senate and in the House. So now I'm in this position: What do I do? It was a very, very tough vote.

The day before the vote was to take place, Kerrey spoke to Bill by telephone.

He said, "If I don't win this, I just might go back to Arkansas."

I said, "That's an option. I wouldn't recommend it, but that is an option you'll have if this doesn't pass."

He said, "Go fuck yourself."

Leon Panetta: When you're dealing with the Congress, there's a percentage of members who will do it based on the substance of the issue and what they think is right, there are those who don't pay that much attention to the substance but will do it out of loyalty to the party or loyalty to the president, and then there's always a group that's for sale. It's, What price are you willing to pay?

There was a congresswoman from Detroit. We couldn't get her vote and I kept saying, "She ought to support the budget. What's the problem?"

She asked to meet with me. I went up to the Hill and she said, "I had a dream last night and I talked to Jesus."

I said, "What did Jesus tell you?"

"Jesus told me I should support the president on the budget."

"Well, that's good."

"Jesus also said that I should get the casino I want in Detroit."

"I want to do everything possible to help Jesus."

"It was betrayal."

Even more than increased income taxes or decreased spending, Bill's proposed tax on energy turned out to be the biggest stumbling block to the bill's passage. The

---

*Senator Hank Brown (R-CO) and Representatives Tim Penny (D-MN) and John Kasich (R-OH).

measure was designed to tax various types of fuel according to how much energy the fuel produced, measured in BTUs (British thermal units).

Members of Congress from energy-producing states found the "BTU tax" particularly troubling. John Breaux represented Louisiana in the Senate.

John Breaux: I told them that I thought it would never work. I told them that back in my state, the BTU tax meant "Breaux Taxes You."

Billy Tauzin did not plan on supporting the budget bill as the House version moved toward the floor.

Billy Tauzin: I had announced against the bill.

Billy Tauzin represented Louisiana in the House from 1980 to 1995 as a Democrat, then from 1995 to 2005 as a Republican.

The economy in Louisiana was energy. My district was one of the biggest oil-and-gas districts. From our view, the BTU tax was a direct assault on our economy.

We said no throughout these negotiations, until right at the end, when I guess the president realized he might lose and he made the offer to strip the BTU tax out. That is, if enough of us agreed to vote for the bill, with the BTU tax in it, his commitment was to hold a press conference afterward and announce that the BTU tax would come out before the Senate voted for it.

The last conversation we had was on a speakerphone. It was about eighteen or twenty conservative Democrats in the room. He said, "I'll have that press conference if you guys will take me at my word and vote for the bill."

But the press conference didn't happen. And it was worse: When he did speak to the press, he said he was going to fight to keep the BTU tax alive.

It was betrayal. Absolute betrayal. It was one of the worst moments I ever had in thirty-five years of public life.

I felt that my vote had been stolen.

"To me, that was a great presidential moment."

Robert Rubin: One time just the two of us were in the Oval Office. He was frustrated. We'd put out this economic plan. It was serious and multifaceted, but we were not getting traction politically. He said, "I figured this out.

"We think the world is complicated. It is. We put out this complicated plan, with taxes and the deficit stuff and all that. But the American people want John Wayne to ride up on a white horse with a simple answer. There are no simple answers.

"We don't have a white horse. We're not John Wayne."

Bill realized that whatever the merits of the BTU tax, it had to go.

Lawrence O'Donnell: When the ultimate, difficult presidential decision had to be made, the president made it in a snap. We'd gone up to the Oval Office to tell him that we didn't have the votes for the BTU tax, that we'd have to do a gasoline tax.

Senator Moynihan brought it up gingerly, tentatively, because he knew the president had been opposed to a gasoline tax during the presidential campaign. As soon as the president understood that Senator Moynihan was talking about a gasoline tax, he interrupted him and said, "I wasn't against a gasoline tax in the campaign. I was against Perot's gasoline tax."

I was sitting at the side of the room thinking, "This is great. This guy is figuring out how he's going to spin being in favor of a gasoline tax now."

To me, that was a great presidential moment. He's got a very important piece of legislation in front of him, and the problem in getting it done is what he said as a candidate. He took on the burden of fixing that.

On August 6, 1993, Congress enacted the Omnibus Budget Reconciliation Act of 1993. To win approval from conservative Democrats, Bill agreed to slightly higher Medicare cuts than he'd proposed and he replaced the BTU tax with a hike of 4.3 cents in the tax on a gallon of gas. But for the most part, Bill got the legislation he'd proposed: He got his increase in upper-income tax rates, his expansion of the Earned Income Tax Credit, and his five-year tally of $250 billion in spending cuts contributing to overall deficit reduction of around $500 billion.

Bill had his first major legislative triumph as president, and it was a big one.

Senator Phil Gramm of Texas spoke for many of his fellow Republicans when he forecast a bleak future:

> I believe this program is going to make the economy weak. I believe hundreds of thousands of people are going to lose their jobs. I believe Bill Clinton will be one of those people.[3]

Gramm and the Republicans had it wrong. Whether or not Bill's reintroduction of federal fiscal discipline made the difference, he would preside over the longest peacetime economic expansion in American history. And, although few might have predicted it during his first two years in office, in 1996 he would get to keep his job.

22

The Yanks Are Coming:
Navigating a Post–Cold War World

"We stumbled, badly."

The day after Election Day, Bill vowed that during the opening six months of his presidency he would "focus like a laser beam on this economy."[1]

Within hours of his inauguration, however, gays in the military emerged as the first diversion of the laser beam; from beyond American shores, others soon arose. In foreign affairs, Bill's initial efforts were not auspicious.

Merrill McPeak: When he came to town, if you asked him a question about health care, you'd better sit down because it's going to be an hour before he's done. Or if you asked him about education issues, if you asked him about Social Security—the guy was awesome in his grasp of detail. You asked him about what to do in Bosnia, where Muslims were being slaughtered by the Serbians in large numbers, you got tap dancing.

Samuel Berger: We came into office as the dust was settling on the fall of the Berlin Wall.

Samuel "Sandy" Berger served during Bill's first term as deputy national security adviser, then as national security adviser during the second term.

For four decades following the end of World War II, the Cold War between the United States and the Soviet Union had seemed the framework in which major-power geopolitics would forever be conducted. Now, suddenly—with the fall of the Berlin Wall in 1989 and the dissolution of the Soviet Union two years later—it was over. The end of the Cold War and the collapse of the Soviet empire had occurred on the watch of Bill's two immediate predecessors. Bill's job would be to manage what came next.

Merrill McPeak: As the glaciers receded from the Cold War, they exposed all this detritus that had been frozen in place, like Yugoslavia. Like Somalia, which had been the subject of a great-power competition. The new situation of us being an unparalleled single power, the only one of any consequence in the world, meant that when this series of old problems exposed itself, we were the only people capable of handling it. And we weren't ready for it.

In '89, with the fall of the Berlin Wall, we had finally won World War II. Now we had to win World War I. Nobody had thought about "What are we going to do about all those problems that started with anarchists killing Archduke Franz Ferdinand in Sarajevo?" And especially a guy like Clinton, who had it in spades if it was health care but who didn't understand the set of international forces at work.

Intellectually, conceptually, nobody had prepared for a situation in which we would be calling all the shots, and simultaneously all these old ancient problems would be exposed to the atmosphere for the first time in many years. So we stumbled, badly.

I left after Clinton had been there a year and a half. At that point, he was still in the penalty box as far as I was concerned; he hadn't learned enough to be effective internationally. It was after I left that I thought he did a number of things that were pretty smart: the air campaign into Bosnia, a subsequent campaign in Kosovo—they were well enough done that we settled both of those cases, and Yugoslavia was not an easy case to deal with.

President Clinton was inept at the beginning and rather skilled at the end. The guy was there for eight years and he didn't sleep much of the time. He kept his eyes open in the meetings. He learned a hell of a lot.

Despite Bill's inexperience, his orientation toward economics did confer advantages as he and his team set out to reconfigure America's relation to the world.

Dave McCurdy: The big message was, "What is the role of America in the world?"

A lot of people think the toughest thing in the world is predicting the future. I think it's understanding the moment, really understanding where you are. Clinton understood pretty well, better than George W. Bush and certainly better than Bush 41.

Jim Hoagland: In terms of his intellectual involvement, he was outstanding. We were much more involved in the important big ideas of our time, the transformative ideas in world politics and world economy, than under other administrations.

Anthony Lake: He had an unbelievable ability to see the shape of things. He was way ahead of anybody else in understanding what, five years later or so, started being called globalization.

We would always give him background on issues and do the points, but he had this extraordinary ability to then put them together in his own words, in his own way, and make it better. There was one time, in a press conference early on, when he didn't make it better. He had gotten some technical detail wrong and as we were walking out of the briefing room, he put his arm around my shoulders and said, "I really screwed that one up, didn't I?" I thought to myself, This is really impressive because he has the confidence to understand when he is getting it wrong, and to be critical, so he'll get it right the next time. The most talented man I'd ever met.

Or a freak of nature. Which is also a weakness in a sense.

Many charge him with being merely a triangulator,* finding the politically savvy way winding between various points of view. Yes, he could do that, because he's a very smart politician, but I don't think it's as simple as that. I have never worked with anybody who believed in *more* things. He more than believed in—he was passionate about—restoring the American dream for the middle class. He would be passionate about Haiti. The problem with his presidency, at least my disappointment in it, was that he had trouble saying, "Okay, it will be all of this and none of that." Rather than "I'll have some of this, and some of this, and some of this." The result was that his presidency is not remembered for education reform or welfare reform or health care reform or x, y, or z in foreign policy, that one flag he would nail to his mast whether the ship went down or not. He hated to give up even a little of any of them. I think this was reflected in his personal life as well, because he'd always succeeded in having it all.

Among the first foreign policy challenges Bill faced was the savagery engulfing the city in which Archduke Franz Ferdinand had been murdered in 1914, Sarajevo, and the land of which it was the capital.

"Powell prevailed."

The multiethnic communist state of Yugoslavia survived intact from 1946 through 1980, when its founder, the charismatic strongman Josip Broz Tito, died. But in the decade that followed, the nationalist resentments Tito had managed to suppress began to tear the country apart. In 1989 Slobodan Milošević, the "colourless Com-

---

*Triangulation was the name given to Bill's positioning himself apart from not only congressional Republicans but also congressional Democrats in 1995–1996 as he recovered from the drubbing he suffered in the 1994 midterm elections.

munist apparatchik," as the BBC called him, who had remade himself as "a firebrand of Serbian nationalism," emerged as the president of Yugoslavia's largest
constituent republic, Serbia.[2] The federation was on its way to disintegration.

Between June 1991 and March 1992, the republics of Croatia, Slovenia, and
Bosnia-Herzegovina all declared their independence from Yugoslavia. But ethnic
Serbs within Bosnia declared their own independent state, refusing to accept
minority status in a Muslim-plurality entity.[3]* With men and matériel from the pre-
dominantly Serb Yugoslav National Army, Bosnian Serbs took up arms against the
republic's Muslims and, in April 1992, laid siege to Sarajevo. Soon, a new term
entered the modern vocabulary, as Bosnian Serbs practiced "ethnic cleansing" of
Muslims in their midst—by slaughter, by forcible eviction from homes and towns, by
mass rape. In August televised images of emaciated Bosnian Muslim men in Serb
concentration camps evoked comparisons to the treatment of Jews by the Nazis.
Genocide, it seemed, had returned to the heart of Europe.

The administration of George H. W. Bush had recognized the newly declared
state of Bosnia-Herzegovina in 1992 but had done little else on behalf of its defense-
less Muslims.

Richard Holbrooke: The Bush administration had taken a position that was
very specifically noninterventionist.

*The foreign policy veteran Richard Holbrooke's first job in the Clinton administration
was as U.S. ambassador to Germany.*

Baker said, "We don't have a dog in this fight." That was the situation
President Clinton faced on his first day in office.

During the '92 campaign, Bill had pledged to end the Bush administration's policy
of determined noninvolvement, crystallized in Secretary of State James Baker's
1991 comment.[4] Once Bill took office, his foreign policy team devised a strategy to
translate that pledge into action. Called Lift and Strike, the plan called for the United
States to lift its arms embargo on the region, thus enabling the Bosnia Muslims to
arm themselves, then to strike at the Serbs if they attacked while the Muslims were
preparing their defense.

America's European allies, however, had no interest in ending the embargo:
Unlike the United States, they had troops in Bosnia as part of a small U.N. force
dispatched there in 1992, and they didn't want those troops exposed to a new influx

---

*The population of Bosnia-Herzegovina at the time was 44 percent Muslim, 31
percent Serb, and 17 percent Croat. "The Referendum on Independence in Bosnia-
Herzegovina: February 29–March 1, 1992," Report for the Commission on Security
and Cooperation in Europe; Power, *"A Problem from Hell,"* 247, gives the percentages as
43 Muslim, 35 Serb, and 18 Croat.

of weapons. Secretary of State Warren Christopher traveled to Europe in May 1993 to seek European approval of the plan. He didn't get it.

Bill's Bosnia policy lay in shambles.

The Europeans weren't the only obstacle to Bill's maneuvering on Bosnia.

Before his inauguration, Bill's encounters with the Selective Service had served him well: His youthful evasions had kept him out of Vietnam; his incomplete recounting of those evasions had helped him get elected. Once he was in office, however, his draft history, combined with his mishandling of the gays-in-the-military issue, exacted a price as he went about formulating policy on Bosnia.

Indeed, his discomfort as commander in chief led to a near-inversion of the constitutionally mandated relationship between him and his senior uniformed adviser.

Merrill McPeak: I always thought Colin Powell was too political. He was willing to tell the president, "This is a bad idea." I think you can say, "This is a bad idea, but if you have to do it, here's four options that range from bad to worse. Pick one and sign me up for it. And remember, I said this is a bad idea." Colin was more of a "This is a bad idea and the hell with you, I'm not going do it" kind of a guy. And he was extremely effective: He prevented our intervention in Bosnia. I was an active advocate of trying to stop the ethnic cleansing in Bosnia, saying we could do it with little risk, just do it with air power. He was saying, "Everywhere I go all over this town, all I hear about is 'a little precision, surgical bombing,' and it's bullshit."

Jim Hoagland: I think Clinton felt, "These generals want to make me pay for the past." I think he felt quite defensive about the Pentagon. Powell thwarted him on Bosnia, saying, "We don't do mountains."

Richard Holbrooke: The gays-in-the-military thing was a body blow.

Powell's outlook had been forged while commanding infantrymen in the war Bill had skipped.

Nancy Soderberg: Powell basically said, "We fell in love with the air power in Vietnam, and it's my generation's duty to make sure that doesn't happen again. Don't talk about surgical air strikes, it won't work. If you're going to do this you have to be prepared to put 200,000 troops on the ground."

Merrill McPeak: Powell prevailed until Shalikashvili came in to replace him.

Colin Powell retired from the army on September 30, 1993. After an acting chairman of the joint chiefs served for a few weeks, Bill's appointee, General John Shalikashvili, took over the office.

Shali was a much more open, good-soldier kind of a guy, and so he eventually did a little old fifteen-day air campaign, and Milošević showed up in Dayton to negotiate.* We could have done that a long time before and saved literally thousands of lives and protected our reputation in a way that was tarnished by that whole Bosnia episode.

As chairman, Colin Powell not only commanded troops. He also commanded the nation's attention.

Lawrence Korb: Colin was not just a general. He could have been president if he wanted to be.

Richard Holbrooke: In 1993 when this new team came in, Colin Powell was a towering figure.

Merrill McPeak: I remember Colin Powell saying that he had given Clinton a copy of *Balkan Ghosts*, the book about how these guys have been killing each other for a thousand years, nothing we can do about it.†

Lawrence Korb: You've got to understand Powell. He didn't want to throw Saddam out of Kuwait. Cheney had to say, "That's not your job." So it was not out of character for him to be opposed to Bosnia. But it's the president's job to say, "General, thank you very much, but I make that decision. You tell me how."

That's what Clinton should have said: "General, thank you very much."

"This was a bad period."

On May 6, 1993, as Warren Christopher was wrapping up his unsuccessful attempt to sell Lift and Strike to America's European allies, the United Nations Security Council designated as "safe areas" six Bosnian cities with large Muslim populations.[5] But neither the Americans nor the Europeans acted to actually make the areas safe. Their inhabitants remained at risk, stuck, as Bill put it, in "shooting galleries."[6] The Clinton administration did, essentially, nothing more about Bosnia for the next two years.

In September 1994 Richard Holbrooke left his post in Germany to become assistant secretary of state for European and Canadian affairs, with responsibility for Bosnia.

---

*The Dayton Accords ended the war in Bosnia.

†Robert D. Kaplan, *Balkan Ghosts: A Journey Through History* (St. Martin's, 1993). According to McPeak, "The author has since claimed that he never meant it that way."

Richard Holbrooke: The administration had no policy on Bosnia, but they thought they did. They were just trying to get through crisis after crisis and they had these long meetings at the White House.

In October of 1993 one of the really big events of the Clinton administration had taken place, the disaster in Mogadishu, now known as "Black Hawk Down." In April 1994, Rwanda exploded, but there was no energy in the international system to respond. Meanwhile, all hell was breaking loose in Bosnia.

This was a bad period.

While Europe had resisted American intervention, by mid-1995 a deteriorating situation in Bosnia, as well as a new president of France, Jacques Chirac, had brought about a shift of opinion.

Lawrence Korb: The Europeans were looking for us to mobilize and to do it, because they were very concerned.

In the summer of '95, I was in Paris for a meeting and Chirac gave a speech. He said the post of world leader is vacant.

23

Trade War:
Passing NAFTA

"He was a free trader through and through."

After Congress approved his budget in August 1993, Bill geared up for his next major legislative goal. The budget had passed with no Republican votes. NAFTA wouldn't.

James Baker: When Clinton was president, he asked me to come be one of four speakers—he, Jimmy Carter, Henry Kissinger, and myself—in the East Room to support NAFTA, which was, of course, a Republican initiative, and passed with Republican votes.

President Clinton was a really stand-up guy on that, because it was an initiative that was very important to the economic well-being of the United States, but was thoroughly detested by a lot of the core constituency of the Democratic Party, particularly labor.

Representing Michigan in the House of Representatives from 1977 to 2003, Demo-crat David Bonior naturally enjoyed strong ties to labor. He was the Democratic whip from 1991 to 2002.

David Bonior: It was clearly a buy-and-sell operation for the multinational corporate elite that was advanced by Prime Minister Mulroney and President Salinas, and Clinton bought into it hook, line, and sinker. While he may think of this as one of his great achievements, it is one of the great disasters in modern economics.

On December 17, 1992, as Bill was preparing to take office, President Bush, Canada's prime minister, Brian Mulroney, and Mexico's president, Carlos Salinas de Gortari, met in San Antonio to sign the finalized North American Free Trade Agreement. The next step was ratification by each nation's legislature.

To Bill, free trade in general, and NAFTA in particular, represented a necessary adaptation to a new global economic order. But as Bill's effort to secure U.S. ratification of the agreement began in earnest in September 1993, he faced furious opposition from organized labor and its allies in Congress.

Douglas Brinkley: When Bill Clinton's presidency started, email was something remote. It was the beginning of the technological revolution, and the Clinton White House was receptive to it. I think he did a fine job of getting the country used to this change in culture. The State Department had trade officers in every country.

You could not have had a greater avatar of NAFTA than Bill Clinton. He was a free trader through and through. One can argue that free trade has hurt Democratic constituents, that it's hurt American unions, it's hurt cities. You've got a state like the one I'm from, Ohio—the whole industrial infrastructure is crumbling because all the jobs have been outsourced to India and China. He captured the spirit of the age with his vociferous endorsement of globalization, but some of the shortcomings of globalization are coming home to roost in the first decade of the twenty-first century that he was building the bridge to.*

"He certainly is not listening."

Charlene Barshefsky: In a policy sense, he was far ahead of other world leaders. Look, he has an intellectual capacity that's breathtaking.

*"A bridge to the twenty-first century" was a catchphrase of Bill's 1996 reelection campaign.

Charlene Barshefsky began Bill's administration as deputy United States trade representative under Mickey Kantor. She ascended to the top post in 1996 when Kantor replaced Ron Brown, killed in a plane crash while on a trade mission in Croatia, as secretary of commerce.

And he has something else that so many people lack. All of those skills—his breadth, his depth, his ability to integrate information—would be interesting but not used nearly to the extent they were used if not for the most important predicate to those skills: curiosity. Here is a man endlessly curious about how things work and why they work, about the world around him, about the way other people think, about the way other cultures operate. Curious about how the U.S. could help in ways different from the ways we had before. He would want to know how a particular negotiation went with the Japanese or the Europeans or the Chinese. You would sit in a meeting with him and he would say, "Did you try this? Did you try that?"

I was deputy USTR when we were negotiating the Japan Framework Agreement* in the spring and summer of 1993. There was a team of us in Tokyo; he was having a summit meeting with Prime Minister Miyazawa. Of course, we'd all been working around the clock. It was 1:30 in the morning and I was going to make two decisions, but I thought we probably ought to make sure the president's okay with them. So Warren Christopher, Mickey, and I went to the president's suite.

Here's what I saw: A guy wearing a rumpled madras-looking shirt. He's sitting at the dining room table in his suite, there's a newspaper that he's reading, on the left side there's a crossword puzzle with a pen, on the right side a book, open, face down.

We walk in and Warren Christopher says, "Mr. President." The newspaper comes down and the president's wearing his half-glasses. "Hey, Chris."

"Mr. President, Charlene Barshefsky is here."

"Hey, Charlene. Mickey, good to see you. Sit down, sit down."

But the newspaper is still there, all of it is still there. Chris says, "Mr. President, Charlene thought we should brief you.

"Okay, Char, go ahead." Newspaper goes back up. Then, all of a sudden he leans the paper sideways so part of it flaps on his shoulder. The hand comes out and he's writing a word in the crossword puzzle. I'm thinking, There's no way. This is ridiculous. I looked at Chris and he does a motion with his hand as though to say, "Go ahead."

*Aimed at opening Japanese markets to American autos, insurance, and other products.

So I start. "Mr. President, here's where we are, here's the situation, here's the recommendation." I can't tell what's going on behind this newspaper but he certainly is not listening. So I thought.

Mickey Kantor: I could see the color rising in her neck.

Charlene Barshefsky: I finish doing the briefing. Newspaper comes down. He takes off his glasses. He says, "But I thought when you and I met in the Oval, the situation was like this." I had, three weeks before, done a lengthy briefing in the Oval Office. And he recounted exactly part of the previous briefing. This was not the same issue I had just briefed him on, but the two went together. "Now, I gotta know how this is going to fit into that, because from what you just told me, I'm afraid we're going to run into a conflict between the two issues."

I was flabbergasted. He was making a very subtle point, which if you were negotiating the agreement you would know—not if you had been briefed on it from a distance. "Mr. President, you're absolutely right. Here is how I would look at the two issues together and why under this new approach they would dovetail quite nicely." And then we launched into a broader discussion of the agreement.

I walked out of there and Chris looked at me, laughing almost, and said, "He fooled you, didn't he?"

"He was running head-on into the Democratic caucus."

Charlene Barshefsky: The question for the president was, What is the cost to the U.S. of repudiating Mexico? We push Mexico: "Do NAFTA. Do NAFTA." Mexico finally does it, signing the basic agreement under George Bush Sr., and after they finally say yes to the U.S., we turn around and say no? How can we?

Lawrence Summers: I think he found the notion of going to Mexico and saying that the United States was now going to renounce this agreement to be almost unthinkable.

Charlene Barshefsky: Even though he knew he was running head-on into the Democratic caucus.

Head-on.

Owen Bieber: Part of the argument was that this Mexican trade agreement is going to open up the Mexican market to our cars. I remember what some

General Motors executives said: We'll be able to sell Cadillacs in Mexico. We did some surveys of our own that showed at the very best there wasn't more than 10 percent of the Mexican citizenry that could afford to buy a Cadillac. You could open all the doors you wanted. It wasn't going to help.

David Bonior: I objected to the whole notion that you could put together a trade regime and protect intellectual property and physical property, and forget the worker side of the equation. I saw this as a lose-lose for workers in all three countries. NAFTA undermined all the progressive legislation that it took a whole century to put together.

When I was growing up, the largest corporation in the world was General Motors. They had a philosophy, and that philosophy was that you should be able to afford to buy the product you're making. So they paid decent wages. Today the largest corporation in the world is Walmart and they have the opposite philosophy: If you pay people $8.50 an hour, the only place they'll be able to shop is at Walmart. It's a complete reversal. It's really ravaged working people.

Charlene Barshefsky: It got nasty. The president went headlong against the unions, at one point saying they were engaging in "roughshod, muscle-bound tactics." This is your base, right?

The president took it all on and prevailed. He took, I always felt, an absolutely principled stand. Politically, there was nothing to be gained, there was everything to lose. It was the right thing to do, much as the Mexico bailout was the right thing to do. I thought that was a great, great moment for him.

The fight for ratification of NAFTA taxed all of Bill's powers of persuasion—both his unique personal skills and the inherent weight of his office.

Michael Waldman: NAFTA was the first time he stood up to the Democrats in a significant way and mounted a public campaign that was not hand-in-glove with the leaders in Congress. It was interesting, because his position wasn't necessarily that popular, but people liked the fact that he was doing it. His poll numbers went up markedly after he won it.

David Bonior: I was the leader of the opposition forces to NAFTA, and I also was the majority whip at that time.

I started this campaign months and months ahead of time. We had a good fifteen-, twenty-vote lead up until the last two weeks. Then word got out on the House floor: You could get a road, you could get a bridge, you could get a visit into your district by the president, you could get a fund-raiser. Day by day I watched the vote shrink.

Michael Waldman: There was horse trading, but in the end it was a public argument that had to be made. I got to watch Clinton in action. I would sit in the back as he met with members of Congress, and he was masterful.

Mickey Kantor: He didn't need notes, he didn't need talking points. He not only knew NAFTA, he knew each member, their districts, and their political problems. I don't care what district, wherever in the country. He could explain their politics as well as they could explain it. It was stunning to watch.

The House ratified NAFTA on November 17, 1993; three days later, the Senate followed suit. The treaty took effect on January 1, 1994.

NAFTA's impact remains controversial.

John Sweeney: We've lost three million jobs over the past five years in manufacturing.* These are good, middle-income jobs with good benefits.

In 1993 John Sweeney was president of the Service Employees International Union. He served as president of the AFL-CIO, 1995–2009.

Many of the jobs that went to Mexico have now gone to China. It may have improved the situation in Mexico for a while, but there is high unemployment there now, and the wage situation is poor. NAFTA, we think, was a failure.

Charlene Barshefsky: NAFTA has been quite successful; certainly trade between the two countries increased substantially, which was one of the goals.

The irony is that probably 80 percent of job loss in the U.S. is technology driven, not trade driven. But you can't be against technology, right? Then you're part of the flat-Earth society. So trade's the whipping post.

Vicente Fox said that he could never have been elected as a non-PRI president but for NAFTA.† He said it forced a transparency in the country, a democratization that would never have happened without it.

I don't call that failure.

---

*Sweeney was speaking in 2007.

†Vicente Fox, in office 2000–2006, was the first president of Mexico from outside the Institutional Revolutionary Party (PRI) in more than seventy years.

Joseph Stiglitz: I took the view that NAFTA wasn't going to make much difference for the United States. Our tariffs were already very low, Mexico's tariffs were already very low.

From the perspective of Mexico, NAFTA was not a success—certainly not the success that was hoped. In the first ten years, the gap between Mexico and the United States increased, when the intent was to reduce that gap.

In the U.S. we lost a few jobs but we created more jobs. It just was not a big deal.

24

Heroic Measures:
The Fight to Reform Health Care

"It was not a question of 'whether.'"

Accepting his party's nomination at Madison Square Garden in August 1992, Bill promised

> an America in which health care is a right, not a privilege. In which we say to all our people: Your government has the courage, finally, to take on the health care profiteers and make health care affordable for every family.[1]

In early 1993 he set out to make it happen.

Chris Jennings served as Bill's senior White House adviser on health care through all eight years of the Clinton administration. Judy Feder held a high-level position in the Department of Health and Human Services. Both played key roles in Bill's health care initiative.

Jennings and Feder described the state of American health care as Bill took office.

Judy Feder: A million more people without health insurance every year. People who have it afraid of losing it. A big burden for business, particularly for small employers or for employers with substantial union commitments, the auto industry being the prime example. State governments worried about the demands of Medicaid. Concerns about a growing elderly population.

Chris Jennings: After twelve years of Republican administration where health care really wasn't a priority, there was a lot of pent-up demand for action.

People had a sense that something meaningful and comprehensive was going to happen. It was not a question of "whether," it was "when" and exactly "what."

Alan Simpson, a Republican, represented Wyoming in the Senate from 1979 to 1997.

Alan Simpson: I worked with Hillary on her health care for a while, and there were parts of it that were very good.

Then, of course, it got so complex and they made fun of it. And that was the end of that.

"I got my marching orders."

Bill, January 25, 1993:

> I am grateful that Hillary has agreed to chair this task force. . . . She's better at organizing and leading people from a complex beginning to a certain end than anybody I've ever worked with in my life. And that's what I want done here.[2]

Hillary's task force had its plan ready by September.

Judy Feder: Under the plan, everybody was guaranteed a set of benefits that were as good as or better than what was offered by Fortune 500 companies. All the health plans would have to take all comers and charge them the same rate.

The plan we ultimately designed relied on almost no taxes. It was based on aggressive cost containment.

Alice Rivlin: The group that Hillary set up was somewhat at loggerheads with the economic team. We warned them, "This is going to be more expensive than you think." They weren't listening.

C. Everett Koop agreed with Rivlin.

C. Everett Koop: There was one thing Bill Clinton understood, and it was admirable, and he bragged about it and he used it politically, and that was that it couldn't be a health care plan worthy of America if it didn't have universal coverage.

C. Everett Koop served as U.S. surgeon general from 1982 to 1989. At Bill's request, Koop traveled with Hillary to act as moderator of forums she held with groups of doctors.

What he didn't say to the public, and maybe he never really understood it himself, was that the cost of universality would have been those thirty-seven million uninsured people times $6,600 each—more money than we could retrieve from taxes on people who were not terribly interested in other people's health care coverage.

The most chilling conversation I ever had with President Clinton was at the end of a day when I was looking at the bill. He'd called and said, "Could you stop down about 5 o'clock and chat a little bit?" I went, and he said to me, "I have one big problem. How"—this is the only time he ever mentioned this to me—"How are we ever going to pay for health care?"

I said, "I've thought about that, and the only thing I can think of is that you can get away with sin tax after sin tax after sin tax, because people want the things that we call sin. They want tobacco. They want alcohol. They want gambling."

He said, "Yeah, but I can't. I got my marching orders." Those were the words he used. He said that the tobacco world said, "You can raise taxes on cigarettes, but not more than ninety-nine cents a pack. Don't go above it." He said when it came to talking with people in the alcohol business, their message was "Don't touch it at all."

"So I can't," he said.

Who can impose upon the president of the United States? I'll tell you who can do it: the cigarette people, the alcohol manufacturers.

In March 1993, as the health care task force was beginning its work, advisers to Bill floated the idea of raising the federal tax on a pack of cigarettes from twenty-four cents to two dollars.[3] That trial balloon was shot down, however, so when Bill and Hillary presented their health care plan in September, it called for an increase of just seventy-five cents. The total would be ninety-nine cents a pack, in line with the conversation Koop reports.

Bill would eventually lock horns with Big Tobacco, initiating anticigarette litigation and supporting efforts to bring tobacco under the control of the Food and Drug Administration. In other ways, however, he did Big Tobacco's bidding. His trade negotiators insisted that China further open its markets to U.S. tobacco products, and he backed a 2000 bill that granted the industry tax breaks worth $100 million a year to facilitate its exports.[4]

"The call never came."

If the Clintons saw in the health care initiative a path to solving a crisis, a band of conservative Republicans saw a path to power.

In 1994 Scott Reed was executive director of the Republican National Committee.

Scott Reed: Health care was the first time since the '92 election that the Republicans all rose up together and said, "We're going to defeat this thing." And then when it was defeated, Republicans felt alive again. They hadn't felt alive in years.

House Republicans did not trust Senate Republicans, especially the Senate Republican leader, whom they accused of fraternizing with the enemy.

Bob Dole: We were getting a lot of heat from the House. I remember a phone call—they set up a little gang-up on Bob Dole's efforts, saying I'm too soft on Clinton and the Democrats. We took a lot of flak from some of the Republicans for even speaking to Clinton.

Chris Jennings: House Republicans, like Speaker Gingrich, were worried about Senator Dole. I think the senator was troubled by positioning himself and the party as just rejecting everything. His instinct is generally to find a way to legislate. This is why he cosponsored legislation with Senator Chafee to come up with an alternative comprehensive approach.* However, as the political environment deteriorated around the Clinton administration in 1994, it became clear to him that it would be an act of political malfeasance if he helped the president achieve a signing ceremony. Around that time he was even quoted as saying he feared he might have to vote against his own bill.

Fred Barnes: There was a dinner at the White House in March '94. Dole was there, President Clinton was there, Mrs. Clinton was there, and a few others. After the dinner, Dole expected a phone call the next day. He thought that's what the dinner was about, that they would come together on some bipartisan health care bill. He thought, "This is it. Now it's going to happen. I am going to get a phone call." If Bill Clinton was going to do a compromise, Dole was the guy to do it with.

The call never came.

Bob Dole: They dropped the ball and we didn't help them pick it up.

Bob Kerrey: All of a sudden health care's the top issue; everybody's for universal health care. What happened to President Clinton is he got trapped in the rhetoric and missed a moment. It was a phenomenal moment.

---

*Moderate Republican senator from Rhode Island, who, along with a handful of other GOP members of Congress, was working with centrist Democrats to fashion a compromise health care bill.

Bill, January 25, 1994, State of the Union Address:

> I have no special brief for any specific approach, even in our own bill, except this: If you send me legislation that does not guarantee every American private health insurance that can never be taken away, you will force me to take this pen [here Bill picked up a pen from the lectern and, holding it in his left hand, used it to punctuate the rest of this sentence], veto the legislation, and we'll come right back here and start all over again.[5]

Tom Brokaw: The big mistake was when the president raised that pen.

John Breaux: It was dramatic. But when the president threatens to veto things before they're written, Congress doesn't receive it very well.

Lawrence O'Donnell: I was chilled by it. It was not the way you get things done. It left me sitting there saying, "How do I begin the conversation with the Republicans if this veto threat's out there?"

I happened to be sitting beside Bob Packwood* in the House chamber that night. Walking out when the whole thing was over I said to him, "What did you think of the veto threat?" He said, "Oh, he doesn't mean it." Packwood was completely calm about it. That was an experienced and accomplished legislator saying, "That's an impossible thing to say: 'Give me 100 percent of what I want on a piece of social legislation or I will veto it.' " Packwood was taking Clinton to be a legislating professional.

By the time Clinton did that in January of '94 we knew that we were going to have to compromise, but we didn't think we were going to have to do a big compromise. John Chafee was at 95 percent coverage; President Clinton was at 100 percent coverage.

The other guy's at 95, you're at 100, and you can't figure out what the compromise is?

Jonathan Alter: I don't know what the explanation is. But here's a guy who 99 percent of the time knows that to get things done you compromise. Why did he not in this case?

Chris Jennings: If there was going to be a time for compromise, it was late 1993 or early 1994. But the political environment was simply not there to achieve it. The party's base, the liberals, had been pushed so hard on policies like NAFTA and the 1993 deficit-reduction law that they didn't want to compromise to the right again. In the aftermath of tough tax votes on the

*Republican senator from Oregon.

deficit reduction, including the BTU tax, and tough debates around guns and crime, the moderate Democrats were afraid to compromise and become even more politically vulnerable in their conservative districts. The Republicans and their advisers concluded that any signing ceremony—even if it was kids' coverage only or insurance reform only—would be political malpractice. So what was the compromise going to be?

Jonathan Alter: He's talked about how the plan had been totally mischaracterized. He is right about that. But he let his personal pique and self-pity in having been beaten up intrude on what should have been his cold political judgment.

"He really does want to get something done."

Opponents of the bill, especially the small-business and health insurance lobbies, mounted a massive effort to kill the legislation. Ubiquitous television commercials featured a fictional middle-aged couple, Harry and Louise, agonizing over the burdens to be imposed by the bill.[6] The Health Insurance Association of America orchestrated 450,000 contacts—letters, phone calls, visits—to members of Congress.[7] The message of the campaign was constant: "Hillarycare" (aka "Clintoncare") would diminish choice, degrade quality, and increase cost in American health care. If the facts of the legislation didn't support those assertions, what did facts have to do with it?

Chris Jennings: They wanted to make it not about the policy, but about the people, and so they demonized President Clinton, they demonized Hillary. It was cynical but masterful. Health care is complicated. Make it simple. Make it about good versus bad. Make it about a bad person trying to do something that will hurt you.

It was all baloney, but fear almost always beats hope in the public discourse. And what could be more scary than taking away your choice of doctor? What could be more scary than not being able to get the care you need when you need it? And by the way, it's brought to you by these people you don't like anymore because you've been told they're heathens, they're unchristian, they're sleazy, they're cheaters, they're mongrels.

I know this will sound canned, but I believe that the Clintons' opponents can't compete with them on ideas or intellect, so they personalize and demonize them, they make it about their values or their culture or their beliefs or their personality. It's never about their ideas, which was always frustrating to the Clintons. They have always wanted the debate to be about ideas. But they learned that in Washington it is much more about politics, process, and personalities.

What people don't understand is that Bill Clinton has never been nor ever will be about power for the pursuit of power or power for the pursuit of money. He is about power for the pursuit of policy that helps people. He really does want to be a protagonist for positive change. And she's the same way. She sees problems and wants solutions.

There are no two people who have been more torn down, yet they're still standing. They keep doing it, being called every name, and being pictured in the most unattractive, unappealing ways.

No matter what, they stay in the game. Love them or hate them, they're in the game.

Against the onslaught, Bill and his allies in Congress tried to keep the bill alive, but to no avail. In late summer 1994 they gave up the fight.

Neither house of the 103rd Congress even voted on Bill and Hillary's plan—nor on any plan prescribing comprehensive health care reform. Bill's effort to remake America's system of health care began as his most ambitious aspiration. It ended as his most spectacular failure.

25

Stand-Up Guys:
Bill, Boris, Jiang, Fidel

Meanwhile, as Bill devoted himself to his bread and butter, domestic legislation, the world continued to demand attention.

"They just plain liked each other."

While at Oxford with Bill, Strobe Talbott had translated the memoirs of Nikita Khrushchev. Now he served as Bill's top Russia hand in the State Department. Policy toward Russia centered on Boris Yeltsin, the new country's president and one of the few people Bill would ever encounter with a personality larger than his own.

Strobe Talbott: There were a range of foreign policy issues where working with Yeltsin, and cultivating a personal relationship between Yeltsin and Clinton, translated into things which were good for Russia but also very much to the advantage of America and our allies, such things as removing Russian troops from the Baltic states, Russia's acquiescence—and that's the right word; it wasn't an enthusiastic embrace—in the enlargement of NATO. All of that was possible because of the Clinton-Yeltsin relationship. So did we personalize diplomacy between the White House and the Kremlin? You bet we did, and to very good effect.

We started in on it even before Clinton became president. Clinton made a point of seeing Yeltsin while he was a candidate.

The meeting took place in June 1992.

Anthony Lake: Yeltsin was here on a state visit, and we arranged a meeting. At the White House they tried to delay Yeltsin, but he just left . . . so that he could meet with Clinton. This is one of the reasons why "Boris and Bill" got along so well thereafter, because Yeltsin was quite generous in doing that.

After the half-hour talk, Bill spoke to reporters:

> He had an interesting childhood, a pretty tough childhood, and his political obituary has been written several times. Same thing's happened to me. So I admire him. He's a guy who doesn't quit.[1]

It was the same way that Clinton and Helmut Kohl got along. Both big men, with large appetites. (Watching Kohl and Clinton eat was food for a week.) I remember Clinton and Yeltsin talking about politics in that first meeting, because Yeltsin, who was a rogue in his early days, was the face of democracy in Russia. It was a surprisingly relaxed and friendly meeting.

Strobe Talbott: I think it was twelve or thirteen meetings he had with him in the course of his presidency, and he worked the phone with him all the time.

They just plain liked each other. Clinton, who was a genius at developing personal relationships, made a point of doing so with Yeltsin.

Carolyn Staley happened to see Bill during his first visit to Russia since his student days.

Carolyn Staley: I was in Russia, singing, when Virginia died in early January of '94. I called, and we planned the funeral over the phone from Russia to Hot Springs. Bill and Hillary faxed me a letter saying, "We just ache that you're not here."

Bill's mother, suffering from cancer, died in her sleep during the early morning hours of January 6, 1994. In the White House, Bill took the call from her fourth husband, Dick Kelley—she'd married him in 1982, eight years after the death of her third husband, Jeff Dwire—at around 2 A.M.[2]

A week later Bill arrived in Moscow on a state visit.

We went to Moscow and welcomed him; I had a chance to give him a hug. I hadn't seen him since his mother died. We took a chamber orchestra, and I sang some hymns.

He had dinner at the dacha with Yeltsin that night, and that's when Russia was still thinking about closing the door to Protestant missionaries, because they were coming in droves as democracy took hold. I visited with Bill after the dacha event that night, and he told me that Yeltsin had said to him, "Your faith—you're Christian, aren't you?"

Bill said, "Yes, my faith is probably the most important thing in my life."

Yeltsin said, "I've got to stop these Christians from coming into my country. They're making converts. People are being baptized. They forget their historic church. The missionaries are destroying our culture"—because the Russian Orthodox Church was the state church.

Bill said, "You can't do that. Boris; in a democracy either you're free or you're not. You can't have it both ways."

Yeltsin did not close the door to missionaries.

"This looks like World War III."

Like Russia, China was emerging from decades under a command economy. Like Russia, it was finding its way in a new world.

Jim Hoagland: One of the key questions is, to what extent in the campaign did he say what he really believed about foreign policy and then, coming to power, was it tempered by the realities of power?

I think on China it wasn't a question of hypocrisy or campaign posturing. I always had the sense that Clinton really thought that we had gone too far in indulging the Chinese on human rights abuses. Once he got into office, it turned out to be a lot more complicated than that.

While Bill and Boris were instant buddies, Bill and the leader of China were anything but.

Mickey Kantor: The first meeting he had with President Jiang Zemin was in Seattle at the APEC* meetings in November of '93. I saw a lot of heads of

*Asia-Pacific Economic Cooperation, a trans-Pacific organization bringing together nations for economic discussions.

government meet with Clinton, and I never saw anything so bad. I was sitting next to Warren Christopher—you know how the two principals sit in chairs and then, down one row are our stooges, and down the other row are their stooges. Chris and I looked at each other, like "Oh, my God, what is going on here? This looks like World War III." But that changed. They later became friends and trusted each other.

The key decision Bill made was to link trade relations with China—China sought "most favored nation" status (later renamed "permanent normal trade relations")—to that nation's performance on human rights. But a year into the administration Bill backed off.

Warren Christopher: The president said we would continue to press for human rights improvements, but we would not use trade policy as a lever in order to improve Chinese performance in human rights.

Warren Christopher served as secretary of state for Bill's first term.

Why did he do this? I think it was because he decided that the economic side of the ledger needed to have precedence over the other aspects.

Charlene Barshefsky: The president said something along the following lines: "We have a policy that links trade with human rights to get China to do exactly what we want it to do. Take a look at Cuba. This nation is a pinprick on the map. Has the U.S. successfully deposed Fidel Castro?

"We think we're going to alter the Chinese nation because—why? Because we demand it? Because we threaten them on trade? A nation that's a fifth of the world's population, when we can't get Cuba to do what we want? What exactly are we trying to accomplish here?"

Mickey Kantor: He said that by attempting to "punish" China over human rights with trade we were stepping on our own foot.

His insight was into the inevitability of technology, economic power, the growth of industry and service around the world. There has been a revolution in China, and he saw it coming.

In November 1999 negotiations that had begun during the Reagan administration concluded with the United States and China coming to agreement on China's easing of barriers to foreign exports and investment there. For its part, the United States agreed to support China's accession to the World Trade Organization (WTO). In 2000 Congress normalized trade relations with Beijing—an essential precursor to China's entering the WTO. When China joined the body a year later, Bill had succeeded in his stated goal of "integrating China into the world economy."[3]

Jim Hoagland: Whereas in the case of Yeltsin you can cite strategic gains, with the Chinese we gained very little. They did not reciprocate either with significant democratic reform at home or by changing their foreign policy.

That's the period in which you begin to get what I think of as a commercial balance of terror, where we're getting the cheap goods and they're getting our money. I'm not sure that has served our national interest as well as the Clintonites seemed to think it would.

"Fidel Castro's a real stand-up guy."

Richard Nixon visited China and the USSR in 1972, and American policy toward the two communist giants continued to soften in the years that followed. But American policy toward the tiny communist state located ninety miles from Key West, Florida, had barely budged since John Kennedy imposed a trade embargo upon it in 1962.

Peter Bourne is chairman of Medical Education Cooperation with Cuba, an organization that fosters ties between the American and Cuban health systems.

Peter Bourne: You get a lot of invitations to book parties in Washington. I usually don't go, but my wife was out of town, and I thought, "Maybe I'll go to this one." We got there, and there were Secret Service people all over the place. I said to the guy frisking me, "This is better than your average book party."

He said, "Yes, the president's coming."

There were only about fifteen people there, and Bill and Hillary were showing up because they had worked with the book's author, Taylor Branch, in the McGovern campaign.

Pillar of Fire, the second volume in Branch's three-part history of the African American civil rights movement, was published in 1998.

I immediately took the opportunity to harangue Clinton on Cuba policy.

He went into a long thing about how I didn't understand how difficult it was dealing with Jesse Helms, and Helms was the person who was stopping him from making changes.

Jesse Helms, the ultraconservative Republican senator from North Carolina, then chaired the Senate Foreign Relations Committee.

Then he said, "But I'll tell you one thing. In my book, Fidel Castro's a real stand-up guy. Every time I've asked him through intermediaries to do something, he's honored the commitment that he made. To me that's a stand-up guy."

The next morning the phone rang, and it was Madeleine Albright,* whom I knew because we'd worked together in the Carter White House. She said, "I understand the president talked to you last night about Cuba. I want you to know that anything the president said to you was off the record and doesn't in any way represent official Clinton administration policy."

26

Action, Inaction:
Somalia and Rwanda

"Somalia is a tricky country."

In April 1992 the United Nations authorized a small relief mission aimed at heading off famine in Somalia, a land riven by the clan warfare that had toppled its government a year earlier. But armed factions prevented supplies from reaching people in need, especially in rural areas, so in August, American forces began to airlift food from Kenya to airstrips in Somalia's interior. American troops were neither distributing the food on the ground nor providing security for someone else to do it.[1]

Merrill McPeak: The gangs would capture the food and sell it. We couldn't provide a relief operation until we got control of the security of the place.

Nancy Soderberg: CNN was running pictures of starving people in Somalia, and the U.S. wanted to do something and the president wanted to do something.

After a long career in the Foreign Service, Robert Oakley was called out of retirement in December 1992 by President Bush to serve as special envoy to Somalia. He remained in that post until March 1993.

Robert Oakley: CNN was definitely a factor in what happened, both in getting us in and getting us out.

Soon after Election Day, the Bush administration offered to lead an enhanced multinational force that would enable the secure distribution of food and medical

---

*By this time secretary of state. She held that position for Bill's entire second term.

supplies. The Security Council approved the proposal on December 3. The plan called for a force of forty-five thousand troops, twenty-eight thousand of them Americans. The Bush administration called the action Operation Restore Hope.[2]

And so Bill took office with Somalia in his inbox.

Anthony Lake: The troops had gone in without much more of a mission than to put a stop to the fighting at the time so that people could harvest their crops and avert a famine. There was no definition of success. So first, we needed to figure out what the mission was.

Robert Oakley: Under President Clinton, with a new Security Council resolution in March '93, the United Nations did have the task of disarming the militias. Also the task of helping them rebuild their institutions, if you will. When Mrs. Albright at one point said, "We're going to make this failed state into a democracy," I thought it was the height of folly.

The mission became much broader, much more intrusive.

In addition to expanding the United Nations' mission, the resolution arranged for a new contingent of peacekeepers to replace most American troops.[3]

As the difficulty of the mission was going up, military strength was going down.

Disarming the militias meant confronting Somalia's most ambitious warlord, General Mohammed Farah Aidid, once army chief of staff in the now deposed government and currently leader of one of the two main factions struggling for dominance in Mogadishu.[4]

The United Nations got themselves into first a political confrontation and eventually a military confrontation with Aidid.

Responding to U.N. pressure, fighters of Aidid's Somali National Alliance (SNA) on June 5 attacked a group of Pakistani soldiers serving in the U.N. operation. They killed twenty-four Pakistanis and wounded forty-four.[5]

That's when the whole mission changed. It was no longer humanitarian; it was "Get Aidid."

Anthony Lake: You couldn't let them get away with having killed these U.N. peacekeepers without endangering peacekeepers around the world.

The day after the attack, the Security Council voted to step up its campaign against Aidid and requested additional troops and arms from U.N. member states. The United States sent four AC-130 gunships. Over the following week, the planes targeted Aidid's Radio Mogadishu and stores of his weapons.[6]

On Somalia, as on Bosnia, policy suffered because of Bill's uncertain command of the armed forces.

Robert Oakley: As you recall, in the early months of the Clinton presidency there wasn't much dialogue between the people in uniform and the administration. And the people who came in with President Clinton had been out of government for eight years or longer, so they didn't really understand what they were getting into. Somalia is a tricky country.

Anthony Lake: It wasn't until we'd established the mission and the president was very much on it that the military would come and brief him before major operations. It didn't have the priority that Bosnia did or some of the others.

Nancy Soderberg: What was clearly missing was an overall diplomatic strategy. Bush didn't have it; we didn't have it.

Anthony Lake: We started to look for that by September. In a meeting between the president and the U.N. secretary general, the president argued that we needed to get more on the political track. Then the Black Hawks went down.

At 3:30 in the afternoon on Sunday, October 3, 1993, an American contingent of 160 men, led by Rangers from Army Delta Force, left its compound at Mogadishu airport to stage an air and ground assault intended to seize two of Mohammed Aidid's top lieutenants. Within minutes, the Americans arrived in the Black Sea section of town, Aidid's stronghold, and captured the two targets plus another twenty-two SNA personnel. But by that time, the U.S. helicopters and ground convoys had begun to meet with heavy resistance. The intense urban warfare that ensued would not end until 6:30 the following morning.

Eighteen American soldiers were killed in the Battle of Mogadishu, plus two Malaysians who had been part of a U.S.-led rescue force.[7] Hundreds of Somali militiamen and civilians were killed, as well. Aidid's men held an American pilot captive for eleven days. After the fighting ended, civilians and militiamen dragged the bodies of several American dead through Mogadishu streets, in full view of television news cameras.

The incident has become known as "Black Hawk Down," after the two American MH-60 Black Hawk helicopters brought down by the Somalis.[8]

Robert Oakley: There was the feeling in the White House that this fellow, Aidid, is really in our face. The people on the ground, this Task Force Ranger, have been told, "If you have a good opportunity to get Aidid, go for it. You don't need approval from Washington." A lot of people felt this was not the right thing to do, but there was a lot of pressure from above.

"They were, I would say, mau-maued by the Congress."

After the Battle of Mogadishu, Bill reappointed Robert Oakley as special envoy to Somalia. He held the job until March 1994.

Robert Oakley: The relationship between Congress and the Clinton administration over Somalia had become venomous.

The secretary of defense and secretary of state went up to the Hill on Tuesday after the Black Hawk Down events and they were, I would say, mau-maued by the Congress, who said, "All summer we've been trying to get a clear reading from you on what you were doing in Somalia, and you haven't answered our questions. And now this."

That night I got a telephone call from Tony Lake, who said, "Would you come around and talk to us first thing in the morning about Somalia?"

There was a seven- or eight-hour, I'd call it a bull session, that took place. President Clinton was there. He had all his advisers. At the end of the day, Clinton came out with a pretty sensible approach.

Anthony Lake: Clinton concluded that we shouldn't leave right away, and that we had to get as long a period as we could to stay in Somalia. This runs contrary to the popular impression, which is: Blackhawk Down, we run. And so we negotiated with Congress a date for our getting out that was longer than what they wanted and not quite as long as what we wanted.

Troops would be withdrawn within six months.[9]

For the first year, Clinton had a tendency to literally consult with the Congress, literally look for advice, rather than the way he later came to do it, the way presidents have to if they are going to be effective: certainly to consult and to listen, but also to have a clear idea of where he wants the discussion to go. To lead as well as consult.

By mid-'94, he was doing a lot better as a leader.

Bill's improved leadership did nothing to help the residents of a small central African nation.

"Why didn't we have that meeting?"

On April 6, 1994, the presidents of two adjoining African nations, Rwanda and Burundi, died when the jet aircraft carrying them was shot down over Kigali, Rwanda's capital. The incident set off an orgy of ethnic violence that ended one hundred days later with 800,000 Rwandans—men, women, and children—murdered.

Since Rwanda's independence from Belgium in 1962, Rwanda's majority ethnic group, the Hutu, had dominated the minority Tutsi. In 1990 a Tutsi rebel army, the Rwandan Patriotic Front (RPF), invaded Rwanda from Uganda; by 1993 the RPF and the Hutu-led government had negotiated a power-sharing arrangement.

Two thousand six hundred U.N. peacekeepers arrived to assist in the pact's implementation, but the small contingent was helpless to stop the mass murder that began in April 1994. Militant Hutus had over several years been stockpiling weapons; the deaths of the two presidents provided them a pretext to commence the genocide they'd been planning. Within a day of the plane crash, the killing began in Kigali with the murder of the nation's prime minister, who was the nominal head of state after the president's death, and a number of cabinet ministers. With the militants now in firm control of the central government, the killing fever spread through the ranks of the army, to the large numbers of Hutu militiamen, to police units, and to ordinary civilians, all egged on by the government radio station to kill the Tutsi "cockroaches" and any Hutu who tried to protect them.

Bill didn't lift a finger to stop the Rwandan genocide.[10]

Robert Oakley: The impact of Somalia caused the administration to lose its nerve. It didn't want to take any chances of losing any more casualties.

After Black Hawk Down, Bill sent Oakley, accompanied by General Anthony Zinni of the Marine Corps, to Somalia to seek a political way out of the military confrontation with Aidid and to secure the release of Warrant Officer Michael Durant, the American pilot who had been captured. Rather than risk further conflict with the U.S. military, Aidid freed Durant.

After we were out there awhile, we received a copy of the mission for the U.S. force. There was an element that said, "You should reopen the main roads in Mogadishu." But then orders came from the White House saying, "Cancel that part of the mission, because we might lose people. It's too dangerous politically." Very clear instruction: "Your first priority is to take no casualties," very clear. That continued. Haiti, we had an overwhelming force, we didn't take any casualties. Kosovo, we were very careful to fly at high altitudes so that nobody would be in danger.

The Rwandans deliberately killed ten Belgian peacekeepers to remind people of Somalia.

The Belgians were murdered, and their bodies mutilated, on the first day of the killing.

They said, "You see what's going to happen if you come in here?" And the United States said, "We don't want to have any part of it. We'll provide relief for refugees as they come across into the Congo, but we will not go into Rwanda." Casualty aversion was very much in the forefront.

"I don't want any of our people killed," Bill had told lawmen fourteen years earlier, during the crisis over Mariel refugees at Fort Chaffee. "If somebody has to die, it'd better be a Cuban."

Anthony Lake: We never had a serious meeting about whether to intervene in Rwanda. It's not that we had a serious meeting and said, "No, we can't do that"—because of casualty aversion or anything else.

Why didn't we have that meeting? I've asked myself that question about five hundred times. I think it was essentially a failure of imagination, which is to say that not just after Somalia, but in general, there was an international consensus—certainly a national consensus—that we weren't going to intervene in the middle of Africa. I deeply, deeply regret that.

Robert Oakley: Recall, it wasn't just not sending in U.S. forces, we blocked a Security Council resolution to send in a U.N. force.

In mid-May the United Nations proposed dispatching fifty-five hundred African troops to Rwanda. The United States forced the number of troops to be cut by more than 80 percent.[11]

That was immoral and unnecessary. Everyone since has regretted it.

Princeton Lyman: People knew what was going on.

The veteran Foreign Service officer Princeton Lyman served as U.S. ambassador to South Africa from 1992 to 1995.

There certainly was information flowing in.

The African Bureau at the State Department was pleading for the Pentagon to bomb the hate radio stations. People had information. There was just a reluctance to do very much.

Two weeks into the killing, the International Red Cross reported that more than 100,000 had been killed. A week later, a U.N. estimate doubled that number. By mid-May major American newspapers were reporting estimates as high as half a million.[12]

The killing would go on until July, when the RPF overran government forces to capture the country.

There's some debate over whether military action would have been able to stop it: It would have taken so long to get troops there, it went so fast, et cetera. But the general feeling is, it could have been ameliorated.

Merrill McPeak: This was a case where Shali was a pretty good chairman. He didn't have his heels dug in like Powell would have, so if we had got turned on by the White House, we would have gone ahead and done something.

This is in the interior of Africa, it's not like Somalia. It's a tougher logistics problem to get troops in there and keep them there. But we could have done it without any problem. The president would just have had to tell us to do it.

27

No Way to Run a Railroad: Fixing a Dysfunctional White House

"They would debate and debate and debate."

Leon Panetta: It was pretty obvious, during the time I was director of the Office of Management and Budget, that the operations of the White House were chaotic.

Jonathan Alter: The thing about Clinton in those early years is, the process would be very messy, it was like watching sausage being made. He had a way of coming out with the right result, but the process was so transparent that the messiness would erode his credibility and reputation for competence.

The White House is always a reflection of the guy at the top, and in so many conscious and unconscious ways early on he was undisciplined, he was always musing, he was rudderless. And a lot of the White House and the government reflected that.

Leon Panetta: This was a president who was interested in grabbling hold of every issue and dealing with everything. Too often there was no clear-cut "How do we focus on specific issues?"

Ron Fournier, who had followed Bill from Arkansas to Washington, noted Bill's difficulty adjusting to life on a larger stage.

Ron Fournier: You could see yearnings for Arkansas. There were many times we'd be in the Oval Office for a photo op or at an event and he would look into this group of strangers and there'd be one face he recognized: me. For the first six months or year or so, I was like a touchstone for him. There were a couple times when there was some news from back home. I'd be walking out of the Oval Office and I would say, "Hey, did you hear So-and-so passed?"

"Thank you very much, Ron. That's very nice of you. I'll send them a note."

The one that will really stick with me was his first trip to Northern Ireland, in 1995. I'm in the back of the motorcade with the press, he's up front. We drove up the main Catholic drag, went through the Peace Wall and came up the main street on the Protestant side. The motorcade stops at this market that had been bombed about eighteen months before, and the Clintons go into it.

It was a real small place, so the White House wanted only one reporter in there—since the AP works for all the media, we're kind of a de facto pool. I walk in and the president is ten or fifteen feet away. His back is to me as he's fumbling through some bananas and oranges. He turns around and sees me, and you could see him kind of stop and take it in. First, I'm a familiar face. Second, there's no one else around me; usually I'm with a crowd of other reporters. And he says, "We're a long way from Arkansas, aren't we, Ron?"

He knew intellectually that as president of the United States, his life would change. But he had a hard time adjusting. He surrounded himself with familiar faces from home, Vince Foster,* Webb Hubbell, and the like.

Another thing he had a hard time adjusting to was, he wanted to know everything about everything he was involved in. He had the time and the luxury in Arkansas to go literally line by line and write half the legislation, do his own lobbying, write his own press releases and speeches. As president, just like the CEO of a company, you have to learn to delegate. It was a very hard thing for him to do.

Leon Panetta: When we were beginning to put the budget together, he wanted to look at every program.

The president generally pursued questions about who would be affected: What does it do, whom does it touch, what are the problems with it?

Robert Rubin: He was an outstanding decision maker. In these early meetings in the Roosevelt Room he'd have a view on something, or somebody else would express a view. He would actually look around the table and say, "Now, somebody tell me the other side." He wanted to hear every side of an issue.

He was criticized for this. I thought just the opposite: that's what decision makers should do.

Andrew Friendly: He'd have these long, drawn-out discussions where every single person gets their voice heard and they would debate and debate and debate.

---

*Vince Foster, a classmate from Miss Marie's kindergarten, began the administration as deputy White House counsel.

Andrew Friendly served as Bill's personal assistant—his body man, or, as White House staffers would say, his butt boy—for the first two years of the administration.

Lloyd Bentsen was famous for being frustrated. Here he was, the old man in the room. And yet the president would still call on the most junior National Economic Council staff person for what they thought.

Jonathan Alter: Bentsen said, "This is the meetingest bunch of people I've ever seen."

Leon Panetta: He listened to a lot of individuals at the table, but the actual decisions usually came down to a smaller group. He listened a great deal to what Bentsen had to say, what Gore had to say, what Rubin had to say, as well as myself.

Members of Congress attended some of the sessions.

John Breaux: The White House would bring us in and try to convince us. Clinton would be at all the meetings. He'd go around the table and ask you for your opinions. Then, if he didn't agree with it, he'd argue with you. "Wait a minute. That's not right. What are you talking about?" He really took you on. You had to be prepared.

I remember having meetings with him where it would go on late at night and he would still be looking at maps and everything else on Bosnia or whatever. People would say, "We know you have a busy day. We've got to leave." Clinton was "No, no. Talk some more about the . . . " He could give you the two thousand–year history of the Ottoman Empire.

He liked to meet early. He liked to meet late. He'd call late at night. My wife would pick up the phone and felt it was either one of the children who had gotten in an automobile accident or it was Bill Clinton. All the times it was Bill Clinton.

"The United States is just bigger."

At the heart of Bill's problem lay his choice for White House chief of staff, his old friend Mack McLarty, an Arkansas businessman with virtually no experience in Washington.

Roy Neel, a longtime aide to Al Gore, would serve in the White House as deputy chief of staff.

Roy Neel: Mack McLarty has been unfairly tagged for a lot of that when the fact is, the president himself had to finally get a grip on how he wanted his White House to run.

Leon Panetta: To President Clinton's credit, if he thinks something's not going right, he'll change. He'll say, "How do I fix this?"

Right away, Bill saw the need for improvement, and before his presidency was four months old, he began a bout of shuffling and reshuffling his White House staff, with five shake-ups of major positions by the end of his first year in office.[1]

Through all the changes, Mack McLarty stayed put. In May 1994 Bill said, "I am so glad Mack is making it. He came into a new job and you never know who's going to make it and who isn't."[2]

Six weeks later, after nearly a year and a half of dancing around the issue, Bill finally realized that his old friend had to go. In June 1994 he had Al Gore approach Leon Panetta about the possibility of Panetta's leaving OMB to replace McLarty. Gore asked Panetta to come to Camp David to discuss the matter.

The president said, "I'd like you to consider becoming chief of staff." I said, "Mr. President, I think I'm much more valuable to you as director of OMB. We passed your economic plan. I'm negotiating with the Appropriations Committee." I'll never forget what the president said: "Look, you can be the greatest OMB director in history, but if the White House is falling apart, nobody is going to remember you."

Panetta took the job. At last, Bill's White House became an instrument of the people's business, not an obstacle to getting it done.

Dave McCurdy: Leon knew the system and was respected. He was a good, solid guy, an adult. There weren't a lot of adults in the administration the first couple of years.

Andrew Friendly: There wasn't an enforcer. It was sort of a joke that we were all so collegial. First of all, there were all of us kids running around. And there wasn't a dress code. Nobody came in shorts and T-shirts, but there was a lot of sitting around in jeans.

There weren't restrictions on who could walk in the hall outside the Oval Office in the West Wing. Every previous administration had had that.

Paul Begala: In retrospect, what we lacked was rigorous prioritizing. He wanted to be at the hub of the wheel, have everything feed into him with very little intermediate authority. And so everybody, whether they were working on health care, welfare, crime, trade, the economic plan, they all believed that their topic was the most important. There was this massive traffic jam all the time. And the one thing we couldn't create more of was time with the president. It was exciting, but I don't think we shepherded his resources well. I think we wore him out.

Leon Panetta: My not being an old friend was an advantage because relationships that go back a long way can sometimes inhibit you from doing the things you have to do. As an example, if I had to make a decision whether somebody should go on the plane because they happened to be a friend of the president, my argument was, "If they're not needed, if they don't have a role to play in why we're going, they don't have to be on Air Force One. Period." I'm willing to say no to people.

In addition, I felt as chief of staff that if I thought something was going wrong or if he said something that I thought was a mistake, it was my duty, when I was alone with him, to tell him.

Paul Begala: He had to learn how a president makes decisions. One of the conclusions he reached was that you can't show your cards too early, which he used to do in the first term, that you can't say things even to cabinet members or congressmen that you don't want to see in the newspaper. He learned to hang back, to be the last one to speak at a meeting and then to make a decision and not look back.

Leon Panetta: He welcomed the discipline and the organization. There was no way I could do this without his willingness to have it done.

Paul Begala: He's got a greater capacity for change and growth than any other middle-aged person I know. He had a definite way of doing things that he developed in Arkansas, where he was the center of everything. Well, the United States is just bigger.

If you look at some other presidents, their organizational or character flaws were fatal because they couldn't change. Most people can't, once they get to their mid-forties, their fifties. He changed completely.

Well, maybe not completely.

Andrew Friendly: When Panetta came, we got a little bit more regimented. But still, the president's the president, Clinton's Clinton.

Sharon Farmer was a photographer in the White House during the entire Clinton administration. From 1999 to 2001 she was director of photography.

Sharon Farmer: A lot of times we were late because if you disagreed with him he wanted to know why.

He wasn't ready to go. He's the president: "I ain't ready." Okay. That's why we call it the butt boy's job. They'd go up and try to tell him and he'd go, "Uh-huh," and continue to do what he was doing until somebody else would come up and go, "Now, sir . . . "

"It was almost a badge of honor."

Another lesson Bill needed to learn was the political utility of pomp and circumstance.

Andrew Friendly: At the beginning, the president was embarrassed taking Air Force One places because it was so big and so expensive to operate. We oftentimes would cut down to smaller aircraft to save taxpayers money. But we realized that the airplane itself is a big story. The local press in every city would run the Air Force One landing live. People would stand outside the airport fence to see it come in.

On those trips, I would accompany him. My job was to make sure that he had everything he needed—his briefing books, his briefcase, his reading materials, his crossword puzzle, his glasses, his golf clubs, the right clothes for all the different things that we would do, from official clothes to jogging clothes to golf clothes. There were two Filipino valets in the residence who would take care of his clothes.

I'd sit in the staff compartment of the plane and he would sit up front. Oftentimes, we would all sit together in the conference room and watch crappy movies and play cards and joke.

There was one time we were sitting in the conference room of Air Force One watching *Dumb and Dumber,* the movie with Jim Carrey. And here's the leader of the free world at one end of the table. He was playing hearts, doing a crossword puzzle, having some discussion, and trying to follow *Dumb and Dumber.* He would constantly get up and ask for details about the plot. He loved crappy, stupid movies, action movies, and playing hearts at the same time.

He's passionate about University of Arkansas basketball. One of the thrills in the job was being able to go to the NCAA Tournament when Arkansas won. I don't know that I've ever seen him as excited.*

And then also watching how excited he got about golf, a game I don't give a shit about and have never played. But he was passionate about it, and passionate about recounting the minutiae of his games. It's well known that

---

*On April 4, 1994, at the Charlotte Coliseum, Arkansas beat Duke, 76-72, to take the men's Division I title. Bill attended and joined in the Razorback cheer: Wooooooooooo, Pig! Sooie!

he would take what we would call presidential prerogative—three or four mulligans, and extra shots.

He's an exceptional person.

Chronic lateness wasn't Bill's only self-indulgent character trait that his aides had no choice but to endure.

Joe Lockhart: He did have a temper—it's the flip side of the resiliency. He had the sense, "Why is everybody picking on me all the time?" I learned quickly, and was taught by others, that you've just got to let him blow off steam occasionally. You can't take it personally.

Joe Lockhart arrived in 1996 to become press secretary on Bill's reelection campaign. He later joined the White House staff as deputy to press secretary Mike McCurry and succeeded McCurry in the fall of 1998.

He'll never yell at somebody he doesn't think is valuable to him. If someone who messed up a policy came into the Oval Office, the president would put his arm around him and say, "Let's get 'em next time." The first time he yelled at me I'd been there a couple months. Something happened and either I had nothing to do with it but was the first person he saw or it was something I messed up, I don't remember. It wasn't the most pleasant thing in the world, but when I was walking out, another guy put his arm around me and said, "Okay, you're in."

Michael Sheehan: Matter of fact, I feel part of a very privileged circle, because he never did it with anybody he didn't like. He never did it with anybody he didn't know. So it was almost a badge of honor: Unless he yells at you, he doesn't really like you. He doesn't really trust you. So I didn't mind it at all. It was just venting. That's all. He vented for, like, three minutes, got a little red in the face.

It was never, never about you. It's like lightning. It needs a place to land. Yeah, you're the tree, but it's not like lightning is mad at the tree. The tree just happens to be there.

Joe Lockhart: At times when he crossed the line, almost every single time he found a way to let the person know that, "Yes, I did cross the line. You're important to me. I'm sorry for some of the things I said." This wasn't an everyday occurrence. This was like once every six months, when the general "I'm blowing off steam" became something more harsh.

He would always seek the person out and make sure they were okay.

28

From Humiliation to Celebration:
Haiti

Although Bill had broken his campaign promise to reverse the Bush policy of refusing asylum to Haitian refugees intercepted at sea, he quickly distinguished himself from his predecessor by inviting ousted Haitian President Jean-Bertrand Aristide to make his first visit to the White House in March 1993. In July, Aristide and General Raoul Cédras, the strongman running the country, came to an agreement ostensibly designed to reinstate Aristide, but the accord meant little as Haiti's junta continued to pursue a program of political violence intended to crush its opposition.[1]

In October, Bill sent a navy troop ship, the USS *Harlan County,* to Haiti. On board were 200 soldiers—175 U.S., 25 Canadian—set to land as part of a planned force of 1,300 peacekeepers called for by the U.N. Security Council in September.[2]

When the ship attempted to dock in Port-au-Prince, a mob staged a demonstration.

After eight years as governor of Florida, Democrat Bob Graham represented the state in the U.S. Senate from 1987 to 2005.

Graham happened to be in Port-au-Prince that day.

Bob Graham: We had all those marines on board, and the junta had some of its stooges go down and posture that they were going to keep the marines from landing. We kept our boat out in the middle of the harbor until finally it turned around and left. It was a disgrace.

"Can anyone explain to me why Washington has just done this?" a Canadian diplomat asked the press. "We learned of it on CNN, and just about everyone is shocked."[3]

I don't know how much of it was President Clinton and how much of it was others, but there was a reluctance to be confrontational. The *Harlan* was a prime example of that.

Hugh Shelton: There was a feeling that America had not covered itself with glory in either Somalia or Haiti.

For a year, the situation continued to worsen. Bill and the United Nations imposed tighter sanctions, but Cédras refused to budge. In September 1994, with the blessing of the United Nations, Bill ordered the invasion of Haiti by a multinational force led by U.S. personnel. Nevertheless, in one last attempt to convince Cédras to leave in peace, Bill agreed to Jimmy Carter's suggestion that the former president, accompanied by Colin Powell and Sam Nunn, be dispatched to meet with the Haitian leader.[4]

Two days of talks did nothing to persuade Cédras as the deadline for the talks to end, and the military operation to begin, approached. Twice Carter asked Bill for more time, and got it; still, Cédras would not yield. Finally, with U.S. paratroopers in the air, half an hour from their scheduled drop onto Haiti, Bill ordered the delegation to leave immediately. The three envoys made one last entreaty to the Haitian leadership, and this time, Cédras relented.

Bill ordered the planes back to their base in North Carolina. The next day, September 19, General Hugh Shelton and the troops under his command met no opposition as they set foot in Port-au-Prince.[5]

Bob Graham: The policy was slow starting, but once President Clinton made the decision to act, he acted decisively. Then, after a period in which we'd made some representations as to what we were going to do to try to stabilize Haiti and assist in rebuilding institutions, we lost interest and left. The situation today* is not any better than it was right after our invasion.

John Conyers: President Clinton played a huge part in Haiti. It all came about because the Congressional Black Caucus had been pressing the president to do something.

Democrat John Conyers has represented Michigan in the House since 1965.

The president and a congressional delegation flew in with Aristide for his reinstallation as president, and here we were in this huge field. They had stands, like a stadium. Around the outside they had this wire fence with all these Haitians standing behind it. The president spoke, and then he jumped up from where we were on a platform and he walked around shaking hands through the wire fence with these Haitians who were clamoring, hollering, and screaming.

The Secret Service went ballistic. It was an extremely dangerous setting;

*Graham was speaking well before the 2010 earthquake.

nobody knew who was in this crowd. He walked all around the perimeter for twenty minutes or more shaking hands with people—mostly people of low or no income. Of course, everybody was applauding, but it was so dangerous. Everybody was holding their breath.

Boy, when he finally got back, everybody breathed a sigh of relief.

29

Picturing Peace:
The Oslo Signing

"I want to do that."

In August 1992 Yitzhak Rabin, recently elected prime minister of Israel, was in the United States for talks with George Bush at the Bush family home in Maine. Also on the Israeli's schedule was a meeting in Washington with the presidential nominee of the Democratic Party.

Martin Indyk advised Bill on Middle Eastern affairs during the 1992 campaign and, later, from posts at the State Department and National Security Council. He served two stints as U.S. ambassador to Israel, 1995–1997 and 2000–2001.

Martin Indyk: I went down to Miami, to the Doral Country Club, to brief Clinton. I said to him, "Those Arab states that have relied on the Soviet Union to fuel their war with Israel no longer have any option but to make peace with Israel, because the Soviet Union is gone. And with the eviction of Saddam Hussein from Kuwait and the destruction of his army, there is no military option for the Arabs anymore. This combination has created a strategic environment that is uniquely positive for peacemaking.

"All the Arab states neighboring Israel, and the Palestinians, are now engaged in direct negotiations with Israel. And Rabin has been elected with a mandate to make peace. The stars are aligned in the right way."

I explained all this to him, and I said, "If you're president you have a good chance of not one but four peace agreements in your first term"—with the Palestinians, the Jordanians, the Lebanese, and the Syrians. He was busy eating at the time, but he looked up at me and fixed me with that stare of his and said, "I want to do that."

It's as simple as that. He made a commitment to be the peacemaker in the Middle East, and it was something he lived up to the full eight years of his administration, when his policy advisers were trying to keep him focused on the economy, stupid. He made numerous visits to the Middle East, and right up to his last day in office he was pursuing those agreements.

He made it a priority.

"I'm telling you he wants to come."

Dennis Ross: In the first year, Clinton had too much of a tendency to listen to foreign policy experts, and when his experts disagreed he was uncertain as to what to do.

Dennis Ross served as chief Middle East negotiator during the Bush 41 and Clinton administrations.

He didn't change until he began to meet with foreign leaders. Then he began to say "Hell, I can see who they are. I can be effective in dealing with him."

In Bosnia and Haiti he was confronted with hard choices that involved military force. On the Middle East he wasn't confronted with a hard choice. Here he was presented with an opportunity.

In January 1993 representatives of Israel and of the Palestine Liberation Organization began a series of secret meetings in Oslo, Norway, that culminated with the signing, on August 20, of the Oslo Accords. The Accords established arrangements that, after a five-year interim, were to lead to a final settlement of the Israel-Palestine conflict. For now, Israel was to withdraw its forces from Gaza and from parts of the West Bank. Discussion of the most difficult issues—in particular Jerusalem, Palestinian refugees, Israeli settlements, borders, and security measures—were postponed to the planned permanent-status negotiations.[1]

Martin Indyk: We didn't negotiate the Oslo agreement. It was all done behind Clinton's back. For all their friendship and partnership, Rabin never told him that he was off dealing with Arafat.

We were working with Rabin on a Syrian deal. Rabin and Assad* had agreed that their secret negotiations would begin in Washington, after the summer, so we went off on vacation. Suddenly, while Dennis and Warren Christopher are out in California, they get a call that Peres† wants to meet them, and then he shows them this agreement.

---

*Hafez al-Assad, president of Syria 1971–2000.

†The longtime Israeli politician Shimon Peres, at the time his country's foreign minister.

The parties to the agreement realized that for it to work, it needed the imprimatur of the United States. Bill offered to host a ceremony at which leaders for each side would sign the document. But who would do the signing? Would Yitzhak Rabin appear next to Yasir Arafat?

The critical role Clinton played was in getting Arafat and Rabin to the White House lawn.

Tony Lake and I went in to see the president. At the time, U.S. officials, by law, could not meet with PLO officials. Tony and I were determined that Arafat was not going to come into the White House: "Arafat is a terrorist. The American people aren't ready for this." I told Clinton that Rabin's closest aide had just called me and said that Peres was coming for Israel and that Rabin would not come. The president then got on the phone with Rabin. He tells Rabin, "I think you need to be here." I'm listening, on the line.

Rabin says, "Mr. President, it would be very awkward for you if I come, because then Arafat will come."

Clinton kind of looks at me and says, "It won't be awkward for me. I thought it was going to be awkward for you."

"No, no. I really don't want to come, because it would be awkward for you, Mr. President."

Clinton's getting exasperated now. "No, no. It won't be awkward for me. We'll take care of all the arrangements. Don't worry about that. You need to be here. It's really important that your people see that you're behind this agreement."

He gets off the phone and he looks at me and he's all red-faced and he says, "You might be the Middle East expert, but I'm telling you he wants to come."

So I got on the phone to Rabin's aide again and I said, "What the fuck is going on here? I just heard Rabin on the phone and he's blaming Clinton. He's saying that Clinton doesn't want him to come. Let me tell you, Clinton wants him to come."

"No, no, no. It's a bad idea. He's not going to be there with Arafat. Forget about it."

A couple days later we went in to brief Clinton again, before he was to announce in a Rose Garden press conference that we were taking the PLO off the terrorism list, because otherwise there was no way *anyone* from the PLO could come.

Dennis Ross: Before Clinton goes out to announce there's going to be a signing ceremony at the White House, he asks, "So what happens if they ask about Arafat?" Martin Indyk and I both chime in at the same time saying, "Say that they've agreed it can be done at the level below the leaders."

Martin Indyk: "Say that we've sent invitations to the PLO and to the government of Israel and we've been informed that Abu Mazen* will be coming for the PLO and Shimon Peres will be coming for the government of Israel."
He listens. He nods his head.
He goes out and makes the announcement. Second question is: "Is Arafat coming?" He says, "We've sent invitations to the PLO, the government of Israel." So far so good. Then: "And it's up to them who they want to send."

Dennis Ross: We get back into the Oval Office and the first thing the president says is, "I know what you told me, but I think this makes more sense." This was Clinton the leader / politician thinking it's better if it's done at the highest level.

Martin Indyk: Within one hour we had a call from Hanan Ashrawi† saying that Arafat was watching the press conference and he wants to inform the president that he'll be coming. We went in to tell Clinton and he said, "Get me Christopher." He talked to the secretary of state: "I want you to tell Rabin, 'Arafat is coming and the president wants you here.'"
Christopher called Rabin. "The president wants you here." Rabin's response was, "What can I do? The president made me do it."
The point of the story is that Clinton understood far better than I did that if this was going to work, Rabin and Arafat had to be clearly identified with it. The two leaders had to be there to signify that they, not their lieutenants, were the ones making the peace. Their absence would have been an indicator that this wasn't the real thing.
Clinton understood that from the get-go. He was not as hung up as we were on Arafat's terrorist past. He said, "This is going to be a hell of a risk. The only way it's going to work is if both of them get behind it and the United States gets behind it." That's what that picture from the signing is about. Rabin and Arafat, and Clinton with his arms around them.

The signing took place on September 13, 1993, on the South Lawn of the White House.

*Palestinian leader also known as Mahmoud Abbas, Arafat's successor as president of the Palestinian National Authority.
†Activist and politician, at the time spokesperson for the Palestinian delegation to the talks.

This was now a partnership between the three of them; Arafat had suddenly become a full partner in the process. It was Rabin who brought him into the tent, but it was Clinton who understood that we're in a new world now. He wasn't going to let his Middle East experts get in the way of this one.

"Clinton gave a beautiful speech."

Before the ceremony, Bill entertained the two leaders in his office.

Dennis Ross: He was basically trying to make conversation. He knew there wasn't going to be much interchange between them. The truth was, Arafat was more open to it, but it was hard for Rabin. Rabin held Arafat personally responsible for the deaths of a lot of Israelis and specifically the worst attack, at Ma'alot,* where the kids were killed. It was a legacy he was overcoming.

I saw Rabin walk in, and Rabin was stiff. Up until the bitter end before this he was insisting Arafat couldn't come with a uniform on. I actually saw Arafat's closet once. That's all he had—like fifteen of these things.

Clinton got them to shake hands by creating an embrace. Literally. Bringing them together. They were both small men—Arafat particularly, but Rabin, too. Clinton was so much bigger. If you look at the video, Rabin hesitates and you can almost see Clinton getting ready to push him in.

Clinton knew you couldn't have this event and not have the picture of them shaking hands.

Martin Indyk: Clinton gave a beautiful speech in which he held out to Israelis and Palestinians the promise of "the quiet miracle of a normal life."

> A peace of the brave is within our reach. Throughout the Middle East, there is a great yearning for the quiet miracle of a normal life. . . .
> The children of Abraham, the descendants of Isaac and Ishmael, have embarked together on a bold journey. Together today, with all our hearts and all our souls, we bid them shalom, salaam, peace.[2]

What we discovered subsequently was that neither the Israelis nor the Palestinians particularly wanted the quiet miracle of a normal life. That was American naivete at work.

---

*On May 15, 1974, Palestinian militants entered a school in Ma'alot, a town in northern Israel, and took hostage a group of visiting high school students. When Israeli forces stormed the building, the gunmen opened fire on their captives, killing more than twenty of them. "West Bank Massacre: Decades of Violence," *New York Times*, February 26, 1994; "Middle East: Bullets, Bombs and a Sign of Hope," *Time*, May 27, 1974.

The Palestinians wanted other things—revenge, justice—and the Israelis wanted other things—security, or to get the Palestinians to acknowledge that they had lost and Israel had won. It was much more tribal than Clinton wanted to believe.

It's the great thing not just about Clinton, but throughout American engagement in the Middle East. There is this naivete, this basic assumption that this problem can be solved. It just requires a certain ingenuity and the stars aligned in the right way and good, effective American diplomacy, and some money. Every problem has a solution. That's the way we think as Americans.

People who live in the Middle East, including Israelis, have a different view of the world. They come from a very different experience. It's not the bounteous, optimistic experience of the American Dream.

As they say in the Middle East, not every problem has a solution, not every question has an answer.

30

Something Is Rotten in the State of Arkansas: Whitewater, the Scandal Begins

"It created this whole aura."

David Terrell: What a crock!

Whitewater, the all-purpose scandal that started with a bum land deal along an obscure river in rural Arkansas and ended with the near removal from office of the most powerful person in the world, entered the national consciousness with an article that appeared in the *New York Times* on March 8, 1992, two days before Bill's primary victories on Super Tuesday. "Clintons Joined S. & L. Operator in an Ozark Real-Estate Venture," the headline announced.[1]

At the root of the story lay the 1978 investment of $200,000 by Bill and Hillary, and friends Susan and Jim McDougal, in the purchase of 230 acres of woodland in northern Arkansas. The partners planned to subdivide the grounds and sell lots to retirees. But even though the area boasted some of the best fishing in the Ozarks, the enterprise came up empty, eventually costing Bill and Hillary around $40,000.[2]

The initial hook in the Whitewater affair—what from the beginning gave the tale its taint of unspecified corruption—was Jim McDougal's operation of a small savings and loan. Madison Guaranty went bust in 1989, one of hundreds of S&Ls to fail in the late 1980s and early 1990s, precipitating a massive government bailout of the industry. The *Times* article, written by the reporter Jeff Gerth, laid out a tangled web of business ties and tax deductions but revealed no actual and substantial wrongdoing. It was the first of many pieces, in the *Times* and elsewhere, to see a wisp of smoke and deduce a raging fire.

From March 1992 to the end of Bill's presidency, no one would prove any illegality by either Bill or Hillary relating to the ill-starred scheme to turn a buck by luring senior citizens to come to Arkansas and fish.

David Terrell: If you go to the property that was Whitewater, you'll find that it's very beautiful. It sits on a bluff above the White River and it really could be prime development property, except for the fact that it's on the wrong side of the river. You can't get there from here. There's no good road to it, and there's no bridge over the river up there. Now, Bill Clinton was governor at the time, and Jim McDougal was liaison from the governor's office to the Highway Department. If they'd been crooked about it, there would have been some attempt at building a damn bridge up there. There's just nothing to this whatsoever.

Now, his judgment—and Hillary's, for that matter—in going into business with people like Jim McDougal is just astounding. Jim was a smart guy and a charming guy, but you wouldn't buy a used car from him. He was loony as a tune.

Max Brantley: Whitewater was old stuff, it was nothing, it was penny-ante at best.

I don't think you can find anybody today in the national press who covered this story who can explain in a few words, in any kind of coherent or cogent fashion, what Whitewater was about, because it was nothing.

But it opened the door to other things. It created this whole aura that there must be something rotten down here in Arkansas, and if there is something rotten down here, Bill Clinton must be in the middle of it.

Douglas Brinkley: Whitewater was a cooked-up, ridiculous, empty story.

It was used for political purposes to try to bring Bill Clinton down.

"Bill had disturbed Jim's mama."

While a supermarket tabloid set off the Gennifer Flowers story, the scandal that led to Bill's impeachment was pushed by the Gray Lady of American journalism. And what set off the coverage was a textbook case of a classic Clintonian phenomenon: Someone made the mistake of thinking Bill agreed with her.

Fred Barnes: The *New York Times* gave it the legs it got. If it had been the *Arkansas Gazette*, it probably wouldn't have happened.

Ernest Dumas: The whole episode goes back to what Jim McDougal perceived as a slight. But of course Jim was sick all along.

Jeff Gerth came down for the *New York Times* to look at some kind of background piece on Bill Clinton. This was in April of '92. He already had contact here with Sheffield Nelson.* Sheffield, as it turns out, had just had contact with Jim McDougal, and Jim had told him some things about the Whitewater Development Corporation and Madison Guaranty and how Clinton had not done him right. Sheffield puts Jeff Gerth in touch with Jim McDougal. McDougal tells him all about this Whitewater Development Corporation.

Bill had known Jim McDougal for a decade by the time he went into business with him. In the sixties, McDougal had run William Fulbright's Little Rock office. The man Clinton met at that time was not the mentally ill, ruined S&L operator the world met in the 1990s.

When Bill became governor in 1979, he hired McDougal as his liaison to a number of state entities. Three years later, McDougal bought the savings and loan that he soon ran into the ground.[3]

McDougal got in trouble when the S&L crisis hit. Madison Guaranty went under. Clinton's securities commissioner, Beverly Bassett Schaffer, helped to put it under. Jim thought Clinton should have done more to help him.

He was broke and living in a little trailer out back of one of his friends' in Arkadelphia. And so Jim McDougal's mother ran into Bill someplace, and Clinton asked her how Jim was doing, and she said, "Oh, he's doing terribly." I don't know whether she said, "Can't you get Jim a job in state government?" But according to McDougal, Clinton told his mama that, yes, he'd find a job for him in state government. He never did. Jim's mama kept coming to Jim, saying, "Has Bill got you a job yet?" Jim said it just broke his heart that his mama was so hurt that Bill had not gotten him a job.

That was the slight: Bill had disturbed Jim's mama. You look back at the whole thing—what a bizarre thing this was because there was never anything to it.

*A Little Rock lawyer and onetime supporter of Bill who turned bitter enemy over what seems to be yet another case of mistakenly perceived agreement: Nelson believed Bill had promised to pass up a bid for reelection in 1990 so that Nelson could run in the Democratic primary. Instead, Nelson ran as a Republican, losing to Bill in the general election. Conason and Lyons, *Hunting*, 8–13.

The key thing was Jim McDougal's mama being upset. It saddened him so much to see his mama suffering about having been lied to by Bill Clinton.

"It wasn't just the partisan Republicans who were out to get him."

Ernest Dumas: The Whitewater story hung around, and the Clinton people had to respond to it, and other people started digging so you had more and more detail about an insignificant event, and eventually it became a frenzy, what with the herd mentality of reporters.

Whitewater, and all its eventual permutations, would prove a bonanza to the Republicans who had never accepted Bill's legitimacy.

Helen Thomas: He never knew a second in the White House when he was not being investigated. The ultraright gave him no quarter, they went after him from the moment he stepped into the White House. Every second, every breathing moment.

He showed an incredible naivete. They had him on target and he didn't do anything to defend himself. The pressure was unbelievable, but he didn't retaliate. He's a gentleman, really.

Know your enemy, for God's sakes. He didn't understand how far they would go. He didn't understand Washington.

Sam Donaldson: The Republicans had decided that all tactics were fair. They seized on this Whitewater business.

I would simply say that it's the duty of news organizations, if these questions are raised or if they find questions, to bring them to light. But at that point, how you proceed in investigating them and how the press conducts itself makes a difference. I can cite examples in this town where very smart politicians who were well liked got through a similar-type issue. By similar-type issue, I mean, "Here's smoke, let's see if there's fire." But unlike with the Clintons, when there's no fire it's pretty quickly dispensed with, and it's back to business as usual. Washington—if I can use the whole term—didn't much like the Clintons, and didn't much think that they were the kind of people you should bow down to. It wasn't just the partisan Republicans who were out to get him.

What made Whitewater possible was the uproar over the firings at the Travel Office. Travelgate led to Whitewater via Bill's kindergarten classmate, Vince Foster, the deputy White House counsel. Foster had been assigned to deal with the Travel Office firings. He also handled the Clintons' personal legal affairs—including Whitewater.

The lawyer from Hope became a target for Bill's enemies.

Alan Simpson: They just hounded him. It was ghastly to watch. Ghastly. It seems to me the *Wall Street Journal* was after him more than anyone else. But everybody was after him.

To the *Journal* editorial page, Foster was a Clinton crony, covering up for his corrupt old friends. The *Journal's* relentless attack on Foster reached its zenith in the ominous question one headline posed: "Who Is Vince Foster?"

It was all too much for Foster. On July 20, 1993, six months to the day after Bill's inauguration, Foster went to Fort Marcy Park in nearby McLean, Virginia, stuck the barrel of a revolver in his mouth, and pulled the trigger. "The WSJ editors lie without consequence," he wrote in his suicide note. "I was not meant for the job or the spotlight of public life in Washington. Here ruining people is considered sport."[4]

Nina Totenberg is the legal-affairs correspondent for National Public Radio.

Nina Totenberg: Vince Foster was the custodian of the personal Clinton dealings, and so when he committed suicide, the *Wall Street Journal* editorial page went on something of a tear, and so did some reporters. They had the idea that he killed himself because he knew something that would be harmful to the Clintons and didn't want to jeopardize the presidency.

Whitewater was complicated. It was a land deal, it was a subject that was obscure, to say the least, not easy to explain. But the idea that somebody who's very close to the president, a boyhood friend, suddenly kills himself out of nowhere, and he's the central contact point on Whitewater, is something everybody can understand, and people wonder if something's being hidden. It became the reason a special prosecutor had to be appointed.

The key to what followed was the handling of the files in Foster's office after his death.

After Foster killed himself, the deputy attorney general sent over two career guys from the Justice Department, very well-regarded guys. Frankly, any idiot would've told you, "Look, you seal the room. You let them have access to anything. These are not people who have improperly trashed politicians in the past." Instead, Bernie Nussbaum, who was a New York, Wall Street, take-no-prisoners lawyer, never really understood Washington, and he didn't understand how this would look.

Bernard Nussbaum was Bill's first White House counsel.

So he didn't seal the office and he removed all the personal files, which then opened up the Clinton administration to the suspicion that files had been improperly removed, purged, never found, and that's not a bell you can unring. You're stuck with it.

The media did not report Nussbaum's removal of the files until December 1993. The news accounts further revealed that among the material removed—and now in the possession of Bill and Hillary's private attorney—were papers that dealt with Whitewater and Madison Guaranty.[5]

Suicide, hidden files—what more did one need to discern the nefarious doings at the heart of this White House? William Safire, the conservative pundit for the *Times*, was among the loudest and most suspicious of the columnists and editorial writers who now put two and two together and got five.

William Safire, January 6, 1994:

> What terrible secret drove Vincent Foster, the Clintons' personal lawyer, to put a bullet through his head? . . .
>
> Vince Foster improperly kept the potentially damaging records of that [Whitewater] deal in his White House office. Surely crossing his mind after the furor over the abuse of power in travel office patronage was the potential of far greater disgrace or prosecution in a money-and-influence scandal.[6]

Between the first *Times* article in March 1993 and the discovery of the files twenty-one months later, Whitewater had been a sleepy scandal no one much followed. Now, its period of dormancy was over.

"Any logical person would have to come to that conclusion."

Robert Fiske: Republican senators were calling for Janet Reno to appoint an independent counsel since the three-judge-court statutory procedure had expired.*

The New York attorney Robert Fiske was appointed first Whitewater independent counsel on January 20, 1994.

There was a code of federal regulations that allowed the attorney general to appoint someone with a title of independent counsel who would have exactly the same powers as somebody appointed under the statute.

She was pushing back. "No, no. If you want an independent prosecutor, reenact the independent-counsel statute. Then I'll apply to the three-judge court, and they can appoint somebody. Because if I appoint somebody, people will say, 'How can somebody who's supposed to investigate the president have the appearance of independence if they've been appointed by someone who reports to the president?' "

---

*A post-Watergate ethics reform authorizing a judicial panel to appoint an independent counsel to investigate high-ranking federal officials. The law had lapsed in 1992 when Republicans voted against its extension.

But then some of the Democratic senators, like Moynihan and Bradley,* began calling for her to do it.

Pat Moynihan: "Yep. Yep. Nothing to hide. Do it."[7]

And then President Clinton himself, when he was abroad, made a public statement asking her to do it. At that point, she did.

Bill made the decision while in the Czech Republic on the way to Moscow.[8] He later wrote:

> It was the worst presidential decision I ever made, wrong on the facts, wrong on the law, wrong on the politics, wrong for the presidency and the Constitution. Perhaps I did it because I was completely exhausted and grieving over Mother.[9]

Virginia had died days before.

During the 1970s Robert Fiske, a Republican, had served as U.S. attorney for the Southern District of New York.

Robert Fiske: I had been appointed by President Ford, and then, in a fairly unusual development, was continued on by President Carter. I think I had a reputation for being nonpolitical and independent. I think that's why they picked me.

The New York attorney Mark Stein worked on Fiske's staff at the Office of Independent Counsel.

Mark Stein: We worked constantly. I went to the office, I worked from 8 in the morning until 11 at night, I went home and slept. Everybody else was doing the same thing. Bob made it very clear we weren't going to be doing this forever.

The team was entirely apolitical. Nobody was asked about their politics when they joined.

Foster's death drew Fiske's attention.

The press started heating up, and word started traveling around, with people saying, "Why did he commit suicide?" or even, "Did he commit suicide?" "Was it related to his knowledge of Whitewater?" Bob Fiske decided that it was important to make this part of his investigation, because of everything swirling around.

*Bill Bradley (NJ).

After Rush Limbaugh suggested to his dittoheads that Foster "was murdered in an apartment owned by Hillary Clinton," the stock market took a tumble. European traders, an analyst at Lehman Brothers explained, "were afraid Hillary Clinton was involved in a murder. They hate that."[10]

Robert Fiske: The report on Foster said that we concluded it was a suicide committed in Fort Marcy Park.

I knew ahead of time that this was a supercharged thing politically. I guess the theory was that he knew so much bad stuff about the Clintons that they had him killed.

I knew that if we did indeed find that it was a suicide, some people weren't going to accept it. But we thought that the report was so well done and so well reasoned that any logical person would have to come to that conclusion.

We had retained four prominent medical examiners to assist in the investigation. One was the chief medical examiner for New York City. The second was the chief medical examiner from Seattle. The third was the chief medical examiner for the armed forces. And the fourth, from the FBI, had been the chief medical examiner of the District of Columbia.

I remember going to a meeting where they were giving their conclusions. One of the issues was whether Foster had been murdered and then moved to Fort Marcy Park. I remember Charles Hirsch, the New York medical examiner, saying, "Impossible."

I said, "Why?"

"He was wearing a white shirt. When they found him, he was in a sitting position on a sort of hill with his feet down. His shirt was spotless. Because he was on the hill, all the blood had rushed down to his legs. When they put him on the stretcher, blood rushed back up and by the time they got him to wherever they were taking him, his shirt was bloody. There's simply no way that anybody could've shot him somewhere else and moved him to Fort Marcy Park and have his white shirt be as spotless as it was."

I said, "I've dealt with a lot of expert witnesses over my career and it's always, 'On the one hand, on the other hand.' 'We can say this to a reasonable certainty.' Nobody ever says 'impossible.'"

He said, "That's the way I feel about it: absolutely impossible."

"David Hale was a liar, crook, and thief."

The key to the case against Bill was the testimony of David Hale, a municipal judge from Little Rock already in legal trouble.

Ernest Dumas: David Hale was a political hack. He got to be a municipal judge, but he was never a friend of Bill Clinton's.

By the eighties, David Hale had an investment company—he got money from the Small Business Administration and made loans. In the '80s, Hale and McDougal were working together on some projects. David Hale made a loan of $300,000 to Susan McDougal to set up a business, but actually Jim took that money and was using it for real-estate development. Of course, they didn't repay the loan.

When Clinton got elected president, the SBA then came down, did an investigation, and determined that David Hale's operation was all a fraud. So they referred the thing to the new U.S. attorney Clinton had appointed. She brought indictments against David Hale, and in '94, when there was a special prosecutor appointed, he cut a deal that said, "Bill Clinton tried to get me to make that loan to Susan McDougal."

Robert Fiske: That was probably the principal allegation that called for the appointment of a special counsel, because here was a probate judge in Little Rock making an allegation that on its face, if true, meant that the president, while governor, had committed a federal crime.

Max Brantley: David Hale was a liar, crook, and thief who was willing to say whatever needed to be said to knit together the McDougals and these financial organizations in a way damaging to Bill Clinton.

Kent Rubens: There's nothing Hale had that would indicate that he had any credible evidence to give, number one. Number two, anybody who knows Bill Clinton knows that Clinton just wouldn't do something like that. Now would Clinton tell somebody that Jim McDougal was a good guy? Yeah. Fine. But money is not the key to Clinton's being. Hell, I accuse him of never having reached in his pocket and paid for a meal in his life. He's been on the government bandwagon the whole time. But you'll never convince me that Bill Clinton ever did anything in order to make a nickel. It ain't in him.

Fiske struck a plea deal with the disreputable Hale. Why?

Robert Fiske: This is classic. Every time you bring a case based on the cooperation of one of the people who were involved in the crime, you have the same issue. We did not want to bring a case against anyone based solely on the testimony of David Hale. After he pled guilty, we went through the process of trying to find evidence to corroborate his allegations. It would only be if you had the corroborating evidence that you would then decide to bring the case.

We were very much in the process of corroborating his story on a different issue—which led to the indictment of the McDougals and Governor Jim Guy Tucker*—when I left in September of '94. But no one ever brought the case based on the allegation that involved the SBA. That was never corroborated. It certainly wasn't by the time I left, and we were working on it.

Ernest Dumas: There was never anything other than Hale's account. That's all Kenneth Starr ever had. They never came up with anything to support it.

Robert Fiske: There never was a charge against the president. We were very careful when we filed the indictment against David Hale. We never alleged that the president was a coconspirator.

"I always thought that was a bit of a crock."

In June, Congress renewed the independent counsel statute, and Bill signed it. "I drove another nail in my own coffin," he later wrote of the signing.[11] Now a three-judge panel appointed by Chief Justice William Rehnquist would name the independent counsel.

Robert Fiske: As soon as the statute was enacted, I was told that the attorney general was going to ask that I be reappointed; at that point, I thought I would be. Because it was so logical: We'd been in place, we'd been doing it for six months. But when it didn't happen in the first week, then I began to think, "Maybe there's an issue here." But I still thought I would be reappointed right up to the end.

On August 5, 1994, the panel made its choice: Kenneth W. Starr, formerly George H. W. Bush's solicitor general and earlier a judge on the D.C. Court of Appeals, to which he'd been appointed by Ronald Reagan.

The reason the three-judge court gave for replacing me was the same reason that Janet Reno had given for being reluctant to make the appointment in the first place: an appearance of a lack of independence. They thought it was important that the person they pick be someone different from the person she had picked. That was the reason that they gave. It had nothing to do with the quality of the work that I was doing.

*All found guilty of fraud in a joint trial in 1996. Tucker, as well as some knowledgeable observers, have called the charges trumped up and the verdict unjust.

Nina Totenberg: I always thought that was a bit of a crock. Bob Fiske was a person of great integrity. Nobody had ever suggested that he was in the bag to anybody, and he was a lifelong Republican. I think he would've been trusted by both sides to come to a reasonable conclusion.

Robert Fiske: As far as I was concerned, I thought there was absolutely no objective basis for doing this. It was simply a question of appearance.

We had a terrific staff of people, and we were going around the clock to get it done. But there must have been some perception out there. I don't know.

In terms of the aggressiveness, the fact of the matter is that I was appointed in January of '94 and I was replaced in August. And what was accomplished in those few months is pretty extraordinary. When I left, I told the FBI and the IRS we were expecting to bring a number of indictments against a number of people, including Governor Tucker and Webster Hubbell,* in the next few months. All of those cases were brought by Ken Starr, based in substantial part on the investigations we had done that were well on their way to being concluded.

Ken Starr was a stalwart of the Federalist Society, the association of conservative lawyers that had steadily increased its influence in Washington since its founding in 1982. He had conferred with the attorneys representing Paula Jones and had argued on television that her sexual-harassment case against Bill should go forward despite the claim by Bill's lawyers that, as president, he was immune to private civil suits while in office.[12]

Nina Totenberg: He had given advice to the Paula Jones team, and he didn't have any prosecutorial experience. He had served in the Justice Department, but as solicitor general, and that's why I thought he was a particularly unfortunate choice: He didn't bring to bear the kind of judgment he would have brought in areas with which he was more familiar.

Harold Ickes: He had a very good reputation. He was considered a skilled appellate judge; he sat on one of the federal circuits. He was considered an outstanding lawyer. But something happened to him, and whatever good judgment he had was cast aside, and he became a tool of the hard-line Republicans who hated Clinton and wanted to get him out at any cost.

---

*Under investigation for fraudulent billing practices while at the Rose Law Firm, Hubbell resigned as associate attorney general in March 1994. He pleaded guilty a year later and served eighteen months in prison.

Others didn't think Starr changed at all.

Barney Frank: Starr was one of these guys who agreed that Clinton was a terrible man and that all he stood for had to be destroyed.

The Democrat Barney Frank is a longtime congressman from Massachusetts.

There's no question in my mind that when the judges appointed Ken Starr, they knew they were getting a right-wing hatchet man.

One member of Fiske's team disagrees.

Rusty Hardin, a Texas attorney, was hired by Fiske and remained in place briefly under Starr.

Rusty Hardin: I know that Ken Starr was not motivated by personal animus toward Clinton. He's gotten a bad rap.

The White House viewed the new prosecutor with suspicion.

Dee Dee Myers: If you looked at who his friends were and what his politics were and how he got the job, I don't think there was a lot of optimism.

31

Golfing with Willie Mays:
Bill Among Friends

"It calms him."

Whenever possible, Bill would escape the pressures of his job by returning to Arkansas.

Carolyn Staley: He still says that his staff can tell when he hasn't been home, that he gets short-tempered, that he gets a little less fun to be with. When he comes to Arkansas and has a chance to see friends, have barbecues, see the seasons, he recenters. It's refreshing for him.

Paul Leopoulos: Every time he came home he would stay at Hillary's mom's house in Little Rock. Not at a big expensive hotel. We'd go up there and play hearts until like 5 and 6 in the morning, all night long, and we had more fun. He would tell us all these stories, oh my gosh, amazing stuff.

The northern California resident and Arkansas native Martha Whetstone tried to supply some friendly faces whenever Bill visited the Bay Area.

Martha Whetstone: A year or two ago, after he was president, I said to him, "You know what I love about you? I love the fact that you do not ever trade up or trade in your friends. Once you're a friend you're always a friend."

And Clinton said, "I really pride myself on that. You know, when I go to Little Rock, the first night I'm there I always try—even when I was president I tried—to play cards with my friends from high school." When he was president, almost every trip he came out here we tried to get together with friends and give him a refuge to have a good time and just be normal—gossip, play cards, go to lunch, have some laughs. He needed that.

Carolyn Staley: The way he describes it, it calms him, reminds him who he is. There's unconditional love. He can be sure of the people he's with, and that they really want to be with him. We'd eat barbecue and play cards, and if he wanted to talk about some issue, we'd talk about it.

If he wanted to talk about the Middle East, we'd go for two hours and talk about the Middle East. It would go nonstop. He'd be on a roll. But many times he'd go into this shutdown: Let's just play cards. Let's just watch a basketball game. You'd get a sense real quickly about whether or not he wanted to talk.

It's a safe place.

"Hey, get you a Coke?"

When he couldn't go to Arkansas, Bill brought Arkansas to him.

Carolyn Staley: I was over there a good bit.

During the 1990s, Carolyn Staley worked in Washington.

I would be in my office about 4 o'clock, and I'd get a call: "Bill's showing a movie tonight. Can you come over?"

"Yeah, love to."

There would be popcorn, salted and unsalted—you'd go in, pick up a bag of popcorn, sit in the movie theater, and watch a screening.

Martha Whetstone: I was having dinner with him one night when he was president and he said, "How are your girls?"

I said, "Fine."

"I'd like to see them."

"You would?"

"Yeah, I'd like to see them. Bring them to Washington. Come spend the night at the White House with me."

So we go to the White House and we get a picture of them sitting in their jammies on his lap. He knew what a thrill it would be for my kids. And the other thing when they were there that night, he had dinner with them and sat between them and served their plates.

Paul Leopoulos: The first time I went up there was a month or two into his presidency. Hillary and Chelsea were gone, on some trip. So he was there by himself in the living quarters. They put me in the Lincoln Bedroom, which is just down the hall from their suite. We talked and bullshitted and all that, and played games and stuff.

You know, at first I avoided calling him because I didn't want to bother him—he's got all these things he's got to do. But I heard Bush Sr. and his wife on Larry King. King asked, "What's the thing people don't know about the White House?" And they said, "It's a very lonely place. Nobody will call you. Everybody thinks you're too busy." And I went, Oh, my God. So, I started calling him and writing him letters, and he'd write back. He needed his friends.

Martha Whetstone: He was always writing notes: "Keep in touch." "Make sure you keep in touch with me." "Don't lose touch."

Joe Purvis: Picture this: We're sitting in the solarium at the White House eating bacon and eggs or something like that, biscuits, and here comes a guy in a pair of jogging shorts and a T-shirt. "Hey, get you a Coke?" And he reaches in and hands you a Coca-Cola and sits down. We talked for probably an hour and a half—my wife and I; David Leopoulos may have been there that weekend as well. There's just the four of us up there, although of course, they've got Secret Service people. He gets interrupted by the ushers with a couple of national security calls and stuff going on in Bosnia. And just as he sits down, while he's sweating and wiping himself off with a towel and drinking a Coke, he says, "We just dodged a bullet in Bosnia," and doesn't elaborate.

Paul Leopoulos: I went up there many times. You know how the Republicans said later that he sold the White House to the highest bidder and all that crap?* Bullshit. There were more middle-class people from Arkansas who

*See Chapter 46 regarding the allegations of improper fund-raising for the 1996 reelection campaign.

spent the night at the White House than there would have been in any of those other administrations. He shared the White House with a whole lot of people across Arkansas.

Not all his guests came from Arkansas.

Chevy Chase: My wife and I were down in Washington because Ted Kennedy had asked us to host a fund-raising breakfast for him.

Chevy Chase is an actor.

The night before, there was a dinner for Ted Kennedy, a large dinner; we were there, and the Clintons arrived. There was a big hullabaloo. He was president.

One of the Secret Service people—I gather it was Secret Service—came over to our table and asked if we would spend the night at the White House. I said I didn't think we could, because we had the early breakfast for Senator Kennedy the next morning. "But thank you." He said, "Oh, that's all right. We'll get you there."

That Cadillac or Lincoln or whatever it is—the door must be six hundred pounds. The glass in the window is three inches thick. Sitting in the back there with him waving, me waving—what the hell. And the little flags and, oh, my gosh. The fact that everything stops. You have the motorcycles and black SUVs and whatever. People in Washington are used to it. I ain't used to it. I'd never sat in that car with the president. That was fun.

We went in around the back of the White House. We get in a small elevator to go to the private quarters—it's about 10 o'clock, 9:30. And when we get out of this little elevator, Bill walks immediately around to his right, to a little kitchenette, and goes into the fridge. I hear a muffled, "I know you must be hungry, Chevy."

"No, I just had a huge dinner over at the Ted Kennedy event."

He appears from the kitchen, leading us out to the Truman Balcony, which is the most beautiful place to sit on a beautiful evening. And he's sitting with an ice cream cake, like a Baskin-Robbins kind of thing that has been suspiciously cut up from before. He's clearly been working on it like a chipmunk over the last week or so. And on top of that, just in case Jayni and I might be thirsty, Chelsea comes out with a six-pack of Diet Pepsis.

It was memorable sitting there, I was encouraging him to get into Bosnia —I mean, one doesn't encourage the president, particularly one like me who knows so little and pretends to know so much more. He was sticking his fork in there and talking, while he ate, about the national interest.

The next morning I stepped out in the hallway in my underpants and I see that the president's there in his shorts and sneakers and a T-shirt with two Secret Service guys. Both of them are holding his arms, leading him into the elevator. And he gives me this look, like Snoopy, as if to say, on the one hand, "Goodbye. Nice having you," and on the other hand, "I gotta go work out." My sense of it was that he was kind of being made to do something he didn't want to do. I don't know what they did. I guess they ran or something. He had great legs, really strong legs. Linebacker legs.

"How does he have time?"

In addition to his exhaustive knowledge of college basketball and his facility with crossword puzzles, in addition to his detailed understanding of trade deals with Japan and sewerage systems in Topeka (or so it seems), Bill also knows his baseball.

Martha Whetstone: I got him together with Willie Mays. He was like a child.

I do his golf games out here when he comes—I'd submit a list of potential people for him to play with. He's a frustrated athlete, so I would sometimes put athletes with him—Jerry Rice, Steve Young, and a couple of other Forty-Niners. At one point I submitted Willie Mays. And Clinton's like, "You think Willie Mays would play golf with me?" I said, "I think so." He almost forgets sometimes—it's like, "I think you're president of the United States."

Anyway, we were at a dinner in the Peninsula and Willie Mays is my table partner. I said, "Willie, I called the Giants to ask you to play golf with the president of the United States. Didn't they tell you?" He goes, "No, Martha, they must have thought it was a joke." He didn't know the president, so I took him over and said, "Mr. President, we called Willie to play golf with you, but he says the Giants didn't put the message through. They probably didn't believe me when I said that I was calling on behalf of you." So the president says, "Willie, if this woman calls you, it's the real thing. You better take the call."

Clinton and Willie have gotten together numerous times. Willie gave the president a lot of his original jerseys as a gift, which was a big deal thing. They just love each other.

The president is a big baseball freak, I don't know if people know that about him. He can tell you the box scores, he knows every detail about baseball. It's scary because you think, "How does he have time?"

Baseball seems to be a recent addition to Bill's store of knowledge—in 1995 Taylor Branch found him unacquainted with one of the game's most familiar statistics: Lou

Gehrig's streak of 2,130 consecutive games.[1] Apparently his friendship with Willie Mays has inspired him to bone up.

He can tell you statistics, what the standings are. In the office in Harlem, he is going point for point with Willie. "What do you think about this and blah, blah, blah, and who's the best hitter?" He'll have his thing about who's going to win and what individual players are doing, what their batting averages are.

I said, "Clinton, you're scary."

32

Rebuke:
The 1994 Midterm Election

"There was something going on."

As the midterm elections of November 1994 approached, Republicans smelled blood.

Scott Reed: Our focus in '94 was bashing Clinton, raising a ton of money, and recruiting the best candidates we could everywhere, because by April or May we started to feel the tide was rising. He'd made a few missteps—they'd had the health care debacle. So every piece of direct mail we did, and we did millions of pieces, was very tough anti-Clinton.

We were getting an incredible response. Incredible! We'd come in on Mondays, and we'd have boxes of mail to the ceiling. That gave us a sign there was something going on.

On November 8 the GOP trounced the Democrats.

Robert Rubin: There's one point clear in retrospect. You got to the end of '94, the economic program hadn't really had enough time. The thing was working, it was substantial. This was the beginning of a terrific period economically. But people hadn't experienced enough of it for it to have political resonance.

Scott Reed: The election result was a combination of rebuke of Clinton for overshooting the runway on a couple of things and the arrogance of power of the Democrats on the Hill—just their being in power for too long. It wasn't just Clinton.

Dick Armey, a Republican from Texas, served eighteen years in the House of Representatives. He was House majority leader for the last eight, 1995–2003.

Dick Armey: The most graphic thing we knew about President Clinton in 1994 was the health care overreach. But there was a general attitude across America that this guy's just too slick, he's a con guy. He had the nickname Slick Willie. I think a lot of people said, "We just don't trust him."

Dan Glickman: Gingrich was a provocateur. He was a revolutionary. His predecessor, Bob Michel, was a go-along legislator.

Bob Michel: Newt and I had our differences, obviously. During the Clinton years, their whole campaign was predicated on trashing Congress or trashing the government.

Bob Michel of Illinois spent thirty-eight years in the House, beginning in 1957. He served as Republican leader—always in the minority—from 1981 until his retirement from Congress in 1995.

When Newt became leader, he did nothing to encourage our members to be collegial. Just the opposite: "They're our enemies, treat them like it. You've taken forty years of crap, time to stick it back to them."

The Republicans had not controlled the House of Representatives since January 1955.

Sam Donaldson: Newt Gingrich and his merry band in the House said, "Enough of this cooperation! Enough of this being a minority party! We're gonna make it war, and all tactics are fair in love and war. We're gonna destroy the Democrats. They were successful in planting in the public's mind that these people were corrupt, and then secondly, that they had become tired. That the Democratic Party's ideas had become tired.

Clinton's perceived overall failure played into that.

"God, gays, guns, and Clinton."

To give candidates all over the country a platform to run on, Gingrich, Armey, and their cohort of House Republicans came up with the Contract with America, a document promising prompt action on ten major initiatives. Among the measures the Contract called for were tort reform, a cut in welfare spending, and term limits for members of Congress.[1]

But at the heart of the 1994 Republican congressional campaign lay Bill Clinton. Three Democrats who lost in November discuss the dynamics.

Kansan Dan Glickman lost his bid for reelection to a tenth term in the House. Dave McCurdy of Oklahoma gave up his House seat to run unsuccessfully for the Senate. Senator Harris Wofford of Pennsylvania lost his bid for reelection.

Dan Glickman: The biggest issue was guns. The president pushed the assault-weapons ban in the crime bill, which I voted for. It was a killer for me because I lost my blue-collar base.

Bill won passage of two gun-control measures during his first two years: the 1993 Brady Bill, mandating a waiting period before a person could buy a handgun, and the 1994 assault-weapons ban, which was contained in the crime bill and banned the sale of certain military-grade weapons.

NAFTA, which I supported, also turned off the blue-collar base. Plus, I was viewed as a tax raiser because of my vote on the budget. And the president himself became an issue with the health care plan. He wasn't very popular at all at that time.

Dave McCurdy: I talked about globalization, competitiveness, education, all those kinds of things. My opponent talked about "God, gays, guns, and Clinton." That was the mantra. Clinton, in his autobiography, mentions "God, gays, and guns." But he leaves out the "and Clinton."*

They did an ad showing me seconding Clinton's nomination at the convention in '92. By the end of the speech they morphed my face into Clinton's. It's a common tool now, but boy, in '94, this was high-tech. And it was effective. It was killer. Clinton's ratings in Oklahoma at the time were probably 25, 30 percent.

Harris Wofford: We could chart well over 200,000 votes that changed from the 1991 election because of abortion and, secondly, guns. The gay issue was there, but it was small.

And the health care failure. If we had succeeded with even a first step, I would have easily won.

Andrew Friendly: We saw the writing on the wall before the elections, when members of Congress didn't want the president to come to their districts to campaign for them. The president's popularity was in the tank.

•   •   •

*Clinton, *My Life*, 630. Bill does the same in his discussions with Taylor Branch (*Clinton Tapes*, 221).

Leon Panetta: It was clear we were going to take a hit; I don't think anybody thought we were going to take that big a hit. But President Clinton knew that we had pushed people to vote for taxes in the budget plan. We had pushed people to vote for gun control. We had pushed people on health care, on trade. A lot of Democrats had taken some very tough votes.

We knew that the Senate might be in trouble. I don't think we ever expected we'd lose the House, because we had a pretty good margin. Late afternoon on Election Day, George Stephanopoulos came in and said, "This is going to be a real landslide."

On November 8, 1994, the Republicans gained fifty-four seats in the House—knocking off even Tom Foley, the Democratic speaker from Washington—and eight in the Senate to take control of both chambers. Twelve governor's mansions changed hands, with the liberal lion Mario Cuomo losing in New York to a little-known state legislator from Peekskill, and the media star Ann Richards giving way in the Lone Star State to a baseball-team owner with the middle initial W.

From Bill's press conference, November 9:

> Q. Yesterday not a single Republican incumbent lost in any race for Governor, House, or Senate while the Democratic Party, your party, suffered its worst losses for decades. Do you view this as a repudiation of you, or is there another common denominator in this election that we're missing?

> The President. Well, I think that I have some responsibility for it. I'm the President. I am the leader of the efforts that we have made in the last 2 years. And to whatever extent that we didn't do what the people wanted us to do or they were not aware of what we had done, I must certainly bear my share of responsibility, and I accept that.[2]

Part IV

Recovery
1995–1996

33

Picking up the Pieces:
The Aftermath

"He finally exploded."

Harold Ickes: He had campaigned hard around the country making the case for what his administration had done, what the Democrats had done. The constant thematic with him was, "Harold, if I could just tell everybody what we've done, we could certainly stay the course."

It was a real slap in the face to Democrats, to the Democratic Congress, and to the Democratic president. It had a profound effect on him.

Rebuked, Bill & Co. faced an uncertain landscape as they pondered reelection in 1996.

Terry McAuliffe: On election night 1994 they had a party at the White House.

In 1994 the finance chairman of the Democratic National Committee, Terry McAuliffe would become finance chairman and cochairman of Bill's 1996 campaign. Bill later named him to chair the DNC.

Wasn't much of a party. At some point the president said, "Come on, Terry, let's go outside and have a beer." So we went up to the Truman Balcony, just the two of us, and I had a cigar and a beer. He doesn't drink. He chewed on a cigar. It's such a magnificent sight when you're sitting up there. Thomas Jefferson's looking you right in the eye. I said, "Tonight was a rough night for us. But I'm telling you, these guys are gonna overreach, they're gonna become intoxicated with power, and it's gonna help you get reelected."

He perked up a little bit, but it was hard. He'd lost the House and the Senate. And he was worrying about his own reelection in 1996.

Dan Glickman: I think he was stunned. He got the biggest spanking, probably, that he'd ever gotten.

A lot of us who had lost went down to the White House. He was in an apologetic mood. He said, "I hope that I didn't cause your problems. These are tough issues, and sometimes you have to make tough decisions. But I'm convinced we will ultimately prevail, because we're in the right."

Henry Cisneros, then secretary of housing and urban development, caught Bill in a different mood.

Henry Cisneros: We had a meeting of a small group within a week after the election.

The president was livid. Frustrated. Angry beyond words. People were criticizing things like his schedule and his allocation of time, basically putting it all back on him for what happened in the election. He finally exploded. "You're the guys who run my schedule and make me do everything, who don't ever give me time to think or focus." He completely blew up.

But in that same conversation came the beginnings of a concept, which was, if it's going to be ugly, you may as well make it a showdown between yourself and Gingrich, because we think that Clintonism at its best, articulated cleanly, has more support than Gingrich and his Contract with America. Make this the battle of the Titans. Let it be a test of ideas.

Harold Ickes: At Christmas I was at the White House, but everybody else was out of town. It was a very sour, very depressing time for him. But at bottom Bill Clinton is as tough a fighter as you've ever seen, notwithstanding his ease of personality. He decided that this was something he was going to take on, that he could revive himself and come back.

People don't understand how tenacious he is.

"There were a couple thousand people screaming."

Harold Ickes: I was very concerned that there would be a primary against him in 1996. Terry and I put together a fund-raising program and started raising money. I wanted to make sure we could head off any possible primary —Jesse Jackson was talking about it, there was chatter about Dick Gephardt.

Terry McAuliffe: I went to the White House on December 27 for breakfast. I said, "Listen, don't worry. I'm gonna take care of the money." He looked at me like I was from Mars. I said, "Mr. President, have I ever lied to you before?"

"No."

"Okay, then. Forget it. We're not gonna talk about this anymore." I smacked my hand down on the table for emphasis and hit my fork and the fork went whizzing by his ear. I thought, "Oh, my God, I almost killed him." I ate my scrambled eggs with a spoon. I was not going to crawl on the floor to go get my fork back.

There were a lot of naysayers. When I was writing the fund-raising plan, I was watching Sam Donaldson on television saying, "Bill Clinton has no chance to win again. He can't even win a Democratic primary. He ought to get on Air Force One and fly around the world and just have a fun time."

Doug Sosnik: When I was hired in the beginning of '95 to be the White House political director, the president said to me that he thought he'd get reelected, but he wasn't sure.

Doug Sosnik joined the White House a year into Bill's administration. He remained for six years, holding a number of senior positions, including political director.

What he wanted to be sure of was, win or lose, after the election he didn't want any regrets. One of the things he would insist upon was that in the second two years of his first term, he would be in control of his presidency. He would be doing what he wanted to do, and not, as he felt he had the first two years, have others driving his agenda.

But I think it took a good three or four months for him to get recentered off the shock of the '94 election.

Terry McAuliffe: We had these big meetings in the White House where I'd lay out my very aggressive fund-raising plan. I said to him, "We have to do it this way, because we have to scare off primary opponents."

Bill Bradley was thinking of running.

I said, "We're gonna do our first event in New Jersey. We're gonna raise a million bucks, and I've rented the biggest hall in the state." Well, everybody at this big meeting at the White House was horrified. Mickey Kantor said, "What if you fail? Then you've ruined the president."

God bless Hillary. She said, "Why is any one of you asking Terry McAuliffe a question about money?" The president said, "That's right. This meeting is over." That was the end of that. And sure enough, we went and did it.

When they walked into that hall in New Jersey, the president and Hillary, the vice president and Tipper, there were a couple thousand people screaming. That was the kickoff of the reelect.

One potential opponent was a person who had gotten the better of Bill at the beginning of the administration. Bill continued to fear him.

Terry McAuliffe: The only one the president and I did talk about a lot—and he was very worried—was Colin Powell. People had convinced the president he was going to run.

Throughout 1995 two questions swirled around Powell, whose partisan leanings were unknown when he retired from the army in September 1993. In November 1995 he gave his answers: Yes, he was joining the Republican Party, and no, he would not run for president.[1]

Doug Sosnik: Any Democrat running could have drained us of our resources. If you look at what we did in '96 to Dole, it was based on our ability to avoid a primary and thus get ready in '95, so that when there was a Republican nominee, we could flatten him.

34

Relevant:
Newt versus Clinton

When the 104th Congress went to work in January 1995, Bill had a rival for the national spotlight.

Joe Gaylord: There's no question that Newt was thrust into the role of leader of the opposition.

Joe Gaylord was a key political adviser to Newt Gingrich.

For having led us out of the wilderness after forty years he was hugely admired by grassroots Republicans across the country. And because this hadn't happened in so long, the news media paid so much attention to everything he did or said that by definition he became the alternative president. That lasted for a while.

To many people in the country, it was always Newt versus Clinton.

For the first few months of 1995 one combatant had the upper hand.

Clinton was stumbling around badly.

Bill, at a White House press conference, April 18, 1995, after being asked if he worried about his voice being heard above the Republican domination of "political debate":

> The Constitution gives me relevance. The power of our ideas gives me relevance. The record we have built up over the last 2 years and the things we're trying to do to implement it, give it relevance. The President is relevant here, especially an activist President. And the fact that I am willing to work with the Republicans. The question is, are they willing to work with me?[1]

After working for other Republican lawmakers, Arne Christenson joined Newt Gingrich's staff in January 1995.

Arne Christenson: There was a belief for a while that you could drive policy from the House, that, in peacetime, on domestic issues, the House could be the center of gravity for policy. To some degree, that did bear itself out. But, obviously, the veto gives the president incredible leverage and relevance. Maybe when he said it we took it too lightly, because it was a very important point. The president is always relevant.

35

Pastor to the Nation:
Oklahoma City

"He rose to the moment."

Don Baer: The turning point started with this speech he gave to the American Society of Newspaper Editors, in Dallas, on April 7, 1995.

Don Baer joined the White House in early 1994 as Bill's director of speechwriting. He would later be White House communications director.

It was basically, "I was not sent here to stack up a pile of vetoes. I was sent here by the American people to get things done and that's what the Congress and I should be doing."

A lot of what we were trying to do was to present the president as the person who could define the common ground for Americans, away from the fringes.

Then, out of the blue, came Oklahoma City.

Moments after 9 A.M. on April 19, 1995, Timothy McVeigh parked a rented truck filled with more than two tons of explosives next to the Alfred P. Murrah Federal Building in Oklahoma City, Oklahoma. The twenty-six-year-old army veteran and radical militia sympathizer aimed to kill a large number of U.S. government employees to mark the second anniversary of the federal raid on the Branch Davidian compound in Waco, Texas, an action he considered emblematic of the government's tyrannical oppression of the nation's citizens.* The truck exploded at 9:02, killing 168 people, most of them federal employees, as well as 19 children, most of whom were attending the day care center on the building's ground floor. By 11, police would pull over McVeigh for driving without a license plate; soon law-enforcement authorities would connect him to the explosion and would also arrest his accomplice, Terry Nichols.

Nichols would be sentenced to life in prison. McVeigh would be sentenced to death. On June 11, 2001, in a federal prison in Terre Haute, Indiana, he was executed by lethal injection.[1]

The bombing took place only hours after Bill had protested to reporters of his "relevance" at the previous evening's press conference.

Mike McCurry: Everything swung into, "How do we get on top of managing the information that we need in order to know exactly what's going on?" Because all sorts of crazy stories were out there immediately, most of them focused on: "Was this an act of Arab terrorism?" Clinton was determined to be very careful.

Leon Panetta: He said, "Don't jump to conclusions. We're going to investigate."

Don Baer: Oklahoma City was an incredible opportunity. It's horrible to talk about it as an opportunity—it was searing to experience it with him. It took your breath away, in terms of sheer emotive quality, to go into that huge cow palace in Oklahoma City on the Sunday afternoon when we flew down there for the president to do the memorial service.

---

*On April 19, 1993, federal agents raided the headquarters of the sect headed by David Koresh, ending their fifty-one-day siege. Four agents of the Bureau of Alcohol, Tobacco and Firearms and some eighty members of the cult died in the raid. Janet Reno, the new attorney general, had cleared her decision to conduct the operation with Bill, but she took public blame.

The service, held on April 23 at the Oklahoma State Fair Arena, was titled "A Time for Healing."

You saw an arena full of ten thousand or more people, all silent, many of them in tears. He rose to the moment in such an incredible way, expressing the national grief and the resolve that the country wanted: to know that this could not stand.

As he comforted the bereaved families at the service, Bill also made the larger point of defending the work of government employees.

Bill, April 23, 1995:

> This terrible sin took the lives of our American family, innocent children in that building only because their parents were trying to be good parents as well as good workers, citizens in the building going about their daily business and many there who served the rest of us, who worked to help the elderly and the disabled, who worked to support our farmers and our veterans, who worked to enforce our laws and to protect us. Let us say clearly, they served us well, and we are grateful. . . .
>
> To all the members of the families here present who have suffered loss, though we share your grief, your pain is unimaginable, and we know that. We cannot undo it. That is God's work. . . .
>
> To all my fellow Americans beyond this hall, I say, one thing we owe those who have sacrificed is the duty to purge ourselves of the dark forces which gave rise to this evil. They are forces that threaten our common peace, our freedom, our way of life.
>
> Let us teach our children that the God of comfort is also the God of righteousness. Those who trouble their own house will inherit the wind. Justice will prevail.
>
> Let us let our own children know that we will stand against the forces of fear. When there is talk of hatred, let us stand up and talk against it. When there is talk of violence, let us stand up and talk against it. In the face of death, let us honor life. As St. Paul admonished us, let us not be overcome by evil, but overcome evil with good.[2]

Henry Cisneros: As an observer up close I felt a change in the tenor, in the vibrations after Oklahoma City, because all of a sudden the American people saw. First of all, they saw the logical result of the venom and the hatred as it impacts a young man whose mind was so twisted by it that he ended up killing 168 fellow Americans. It was like, "Enough! Enough, enough, enough! Innocent people are dying. And where's our country going?" There was that subconscious sense about it to me.

And the second thing was that the president acquitted himself well through this, much as Reagan was the great comforter after the *Challenger* explosion.* Clinton was dignified in his response, dignified with the families, dignified as the mourner, dignified as the comforter, dignified as the spokesman for the country. The Republicans' fundamental view of him was, "This is a person who didn't deserve to be president, who is flawed morally." And here he was, taking on the moral mantle in a completely sincere and effective way.

I thought that that was a turning point. I felt the turn in the country and in him. All of a sudden, a lot of the things that were trivial about the presidency —the conversation about does he wear boxers or briefs, and things like that which demeaned the presidency†—disappeared. And in their place was a more sober person who knew he was dealing with big, ugly forces in the world. The gravitas descended upon him.

Leon Panetta: Oklahoma City showed the president's ability to bring the country together. One of his great strengths is the ability to heal.

Jonathan Alter: Oklahoma City was a real turning point because people realized that all this right-wing nuttiness actually had consequences.

It wasn't just people yelling on the radio; people could die from this right-wing nonsense. And then Clinton gave a pitch-perfect eulogy. One of the things that was very effective was that he didn't seem to be responding in a vitriolic way. You would never catch him saying, as George W. Bush did, that if you don't agree with me, you're on the side of the terrorists.

His rhetoric was much more subtle. So even when he was trying to pin down and stigmatize the other side, he did it skillfully and intuitively, and he could do it extemporaneously. He seemed like a person of generous spirit even when he was sticking it to the other guys. That's a world-class skill.

"Over and over again, we used the words radical and extreme."

Leon Panetta: It was at a time when there was a lot of anger. You had a lot of these little armies out there, people with guns. It was a moment when the

---

*The *Challenger* space shuttle exploded on January 28, 1986.

†In April 1994, at a forum aired by the cable channel MTV, a seventeen-year-old girl asked Bill, "Mr. President, the world's dying to know. Is it boxers or briefs?" Bill was taken aback. "I can't believe she did that," he said, but only after he answered her question, "Usually briefs." William J. Clinton, "Interview on MTV's 'Enough Is Enough' Forum," April 19, 1994, American Presidency Project, http://www.presidency.ucsb.edu/ws/?pid=49995.

country could have gone in the wrong direction, but he had a calming effect. There was a speech he gave in Michigan, about the groups out there trying to create disruption in our society. It gave him the platform to again present to the people what he was really about and who he was.

Don Baer: It was the commencement speech at Michigan State—Michigan, of course, being one of the key homes of the militia.

That speech was really written about the radical extremist forces—not the Republicans in Washington, but those forces that were spewing hatred about the American government and certain people in government, all that stuff that was directly involved in Oklahoma City.

Bill, Michigan State University, May 5, 1995:

> I say to you, all of you, the members of the Class of 1995, there is nothing patriotic about hating your country, or pretending that you can love your country but despise your government.[3]

Mike McCurry: It wasn't consciously trying to tie conservative extremism in the House to the militia groups. But it was very clearly a statement about extreme rhetoric that declares government is not the solution, it's the problem. Even that Reaganesque language* had a sinister side that fueled a lot of those guys who were way out there. Clinton felt that some voice had to stand for the value of us working together as a nation. This was the heart of what Clinton was about as president: rescuing the positive use of the tool of government for the American people. The threat to that was these hostile forces that were completely antigovernment. Our rhetoric was subliminally a way to push Gingrich and the Republicans more and more to the extreme side.

Over and over again, we used the words *radical* and *extreme* interchangeably to discuss the priorities of the new Republican leadership in Congress—to get the public to recognize that the Republicans' agenda was radical.

Bill, February 24, 1995, at a joint press conference in Ottawa with Canada's prime minister: "I do not think the American people expect nor support these radical right-wing measures that are coming out of these House committees."

June 23, 1995, speaking to five Democratic governors in a conference call: "I believe that their plan"—the Republican budget proposal—"is still too extreme."

August 1, 1995, at a White House press conference: A Republican bill featured

---

*From Ronald Reagan's first inaugural address, January 20, 1981: "In this present crisis, government is not the solution to our problem. Government *is* the problem."

"extreme anti-environment provisions"; the Republicans favored "extreme budget cuts."

October 19, 1995, speaking to reporters at the White House: Republicans should "turn back from passing extreme measures that will never become law."[4]

Leon Panetta: He's endured a lot of hate throughout his political career, and a lot of people who had almost a blind hatred. He used to talk about that, how there were these groups and people who were that way.

How he grew up in Arkansas plays an awful lot into what Bill Clinton is all about. He saw the good and the bad. He saw what was happening with blacks. He saw what was happening with poor people. He saw what was happening with people who drink. All of those created a compassion in him that is one of his great strengths. In the end, he really does care about people.

And so when it came to these right-wing groups and militias, he knew what they were about. He'd seen it in Arkansas, he knew the kind of hatred that was out there. I think he viewed this as a moment where he could stand up and say to these people, "No, this country is not about where you want this country to go."

During the 1990s, the Reverend J. Philip Wogaman was pastor at Washington's Foundry United Methodist Church, which Bill and Hillary attended regularly.

J. Philip Wogaman: In Oklahoma City, he was a pastor to the nation. He was in church two Sundays after that, and I greeted him at the door as he was coming in. I said, "Mr. President, if, after politics, you are looking for another position, I think you'd make a fine pastor." He smiled and said, "I'm not a good enough person."

36

End of an Era:
The Road Back

"I've never met anyone quite like him."

Harold Ickes: Leon Panetta came back from a meeting and said, "I need to take a shower."

I said, "What are you talking about?"

"This guy, Charlie. He's just awful."

"Who are you talking about?"

"Charlie."

"Charlie who?"

"This guy Dick Morris."

"Is that asshole over there?"

Although Dick Morris had been instrumental in Bill's Arkansas political rise, the brash pollster and strategist had for several years been advising mostly Republican politicians, like Mississippi Senator Trent Lott, when Bill asked him in 1995 to help with his own reelection.[1] Because of Morris's toxic reputation, Bill at first kept the consultant's involvement secret from most people in the White House.

Andrew Friendly: At the beginning there were only a few of us who knew that he was talking to Dick Morris at all. The code word was Charlie: "Charlie's calling." Once people found out, there was a great deal of resentment.

Harold Ickes: Morris is without a moral center. He could advise Hitler or he could advise Mother Teresa—on the same night.

Mike McCurry: Morris was a pure political animal. I've never met anyone quite like him. He could not see anything except political consequences—there was no right and wrong, no best interest of the country.

When he learned that Morris was whispering in Bill's ear, Leon Panetta had Morris and the other top political aides attend strategy sessions with Bill every Wednesday night.

Mike McCurry: You could see Clinton always figuring out, "Half of Dick Morris's ideas are truly brilliant and half of them could get us all thrown into jail." His figuring out which were good ideas, and using them, was the whole art of the Clinton-Morris relationship.

Harold Ickes: Clinton's view was that Morris was the best there was at seeing the dark side of politics.

Doug Sosnik: He could filter through the best of Dick and keep out the worst of Dick. The best of Dick was pretty good. The worst of Dick was pretty bad.

Harold Ickes: I could hardly stand to be in Dick Morris's presence, but the president wanted him. He's the president, it's his call; if I didn't like it, I could leave.

Morris thought he had the run of the government. He was calling up cabinet secretaries. Literally calling them up saying that he was speaking for the president of the United States and he wanted to visit them and go over their programs. Leon and I said, "Fuck him. He's not running the government," and went to the president about it and clamped down.

"He started taking on smaller issues."

Michael Waldman: I'll never forget sitting with the president in the Cabinet Room at a meeting in December of '94 with a bunch of policy aides. He said, "It's been a rarity in American history that the public wanted a strong, permanent central government, and right now they don't want that. But we have to be careful not to do anything that's going to make it impossible for the public to get that when it once again decides it wants that." And he said, "We need to get some things done that will start showing people what they like about government again." So, there was a long-term strategy behind some of the incremental shorter-term things in that period.

School uniforms. Curfews. That kind of thing. There were a whole host of "values initiatives," the purpose behind them being, in part, to emphasize the role of government as an empowering device for families. The V-chip was another initiative like that.

Mike McCurry: These small initiatives gave people a sense of what Clinton really cared about as president.

Harold Ickes: I think that President Clinton understood, and I think the Democrats in Congress understood, that there was a new day at hand. The era of big government was over, to quote a former president of the United States.

Bill, State of the Union Address, January 23, 1996:

> We know big government does not have all the answers. We know there's not a program for every problem. . . .
> The era of big government is over. But we cannot go back to the time when our citizens were left to fend for themselves. Instead, we must go forward as one America, one nation working together to meet the challenges we face together. Self-reliance and teamwork are not opposing virtues; we must have both.[2]

The three sentences that completed the latter paragraph were hardly noticed. What *was* noticed was the apparent pronouncement, by a Democratic president, of the death of FDR's New Deal and LBJ's Great Society.

Harold Ickes: I'm not sure he ever meant that, because there's no question that he is a real believer in what government can do. But I think he came to understand that he had to approach it in a much different way, and he started taking on smaller issues. He was ridiculed for some of the issues; I thought some of them were a little goofy myself.

But essentially, he set about prosecuting a set of issues that would help everyday Americans, that everyday Americans could understand, and that he could prosecute successfully against Republican opposition. And the Republicans found him a very tough guy to deal with.

It really came to the fore with the government shutdown.

37

This Town Ain't Big Enough: Shutdown Showdown

If Bill's preaching in Oklahoma City installed him as the nation's comforter in chief, it was his battle with Newt Gingrich, beginning in early 1995 and culminating in the two government shutdowns at year's end, that cemented his place as protector in chief—protector of average Americans against the depredations of a band of extremists out to make middle-class lives less secure and less safe. Cultural issues had sunk Bill in 1994, casting him as champion of homosexuals and persecutor of gun owners; in 1995, bread-and-butter issues would recast the national argument and complete Bill's rehabilitation in the eyes of the public.

And yet, for all the credit he accrued among the American people in 1995, he never achieved the standing he'd sought during his first two years in office: as a leader transforming the nation for the better. Rather, he assumed the role of fierce defender of the status quo, admired not for things he did but for things he prevented others from doing.

"This will burn itself out."

Don Baer: President Clinton recognized by the beginning of '95—and I remember his phrase—that the Republicans were going to "burn themselves out." He said, "The country doesn't want the radical approach that they are presenting and that they will be known for. This will burn itself out."

As a consultant to the Democratic National Committee, Paul Begala gave political advice to Bill. He left the nation's capital to return to his native Texas just before Labor Day.

Paul Begala: The last day I was in Washington, in August of '95, I went for a run with Clinton. It was humid and hot. Both of us had gained a lot of weight during the campaign, and both of us were losing it—we were proud of that, two fat boys trying to jog off the fat. It was at Fort Myer.* He was pointing out where the Lincoln conspirators had been hanged and all this historical stuff.

I was very grounded in the here and now. I'd worked on the Hill and I knew Gingrich a little bit. I told him, "Newt and those guys think they can roll you."

"They can't think that."

"Yeah, they think they're going to roll you, in particular on the Medicare cuts."

"I couldn't be that lucky. That's going to give me a Gary Cooper moment. They wouldn't be that stupid."

His favorite movie is *High Noon*.

"That's the easiest kind of leadership," he said. "I just say no and I win. The harder thing is if they want to make a deal and then I've got to compromise."

I said that they thought he was weak. He said, "They're misreading me." That was a frequent misjudgment of Clinton. He has a bar of steel in his spine. For all of the child of an alcoholic trying to bring people together, he's also the child of an alcoholic who threw his father against the wall and said, "Don't you ever touch my mother."

Sure enough, it all played out exactly as he said. December comes around, they come in with the budget and he points to that desk, the *Resolute*.† He tells Dick Armey, "If you want somebody to sign this budget you're going to have to put another president behind that desk, because I will never do it."

A lot of people mistake his desire to pull people together as weakness. He views it as strength. He's capable of Gary Cooper leadership, but he thinks it's overrated and cheap.

*Military facility adjacent to Arlington National Cemetery in Virginia.

†Elaborately carved wooden desk used by many presidents since Queen Victoria presented it to Rutherford B. Hayes in 1880. It was constructed from timbers of a British ship, HMS *Resolute*. "Items from the Oval Office: The *Resolute* Desk," Jimmy Carter Library, http://www.jimmycarterlibrary.org/tour/ovaloffice/popup/desk.html.

If Bill was Marshal Will Kane, the virtuous lawman played by Gary Cooper in the 1952 western, he faced a made-to-order Frank Miller, the outlaw determined to lead his gang in gunning down the marshal and busting up the law and order he'd brought to the frontier.

Fred Barnes: Clinton had an opponent who was unattractive and whose strategy was flawed and that was Newt Gingrich, who thought he could govern Washington from Capitol Hill. You can't do that. It doesn't work.

Bob Dole: Dumbest thing Newt ever did was shut down the government. If there was ever any doubt about Clinton's reelection—probably wasn't much —there wasn't after that.

Dumb, dumb, dumb.

"This was a critical moment."

Perhaps the most consequential decision Bill made in 1995 was his adoption, with modifications, of the Republicans' goal of a balanced budget.

Alice Rivlin: In early '95 Gingrich was going gangbusters for deficit reduction and Clinton was losing his nerve. His focus wavered because he was being told by the political people, "We told you so. This is bad politics. If you hadn't done the deficit reduction, you wouldn't have lost."

The Republicans were proposing getting the budget balanced in seven years. At the time that seemed like a terrible thing.

Michael Waldman: In the spring of '95, in a televised speech, he said he was for a balanced budget in ten years. That was controversial within the Democratic Party, but he felt it gave him firm ground on which to stand and say, "Well, what kind of balanced budget?" He would always talk about wanting "a balanced budget that honors our values by protecting Medicare and Medicaid, education and the environment." MMEE—those were his budget priorities.

Doug Sosnik: This was a critical moment for Clinton running his own White House. The conventional wisdom in the West Wing and among the Democratic leadership on the Hill was that the Republicans should be forced to figure out how to enact the platform they had run on and not be bailed out. Clinton felt differently.

Bill, June 13, 1995:

> It took decades to run up this deficit; it's going to take a decade to wipe it out. Now mind you, we could do it in 7 years, as congressional leaders

propose. But the pain we'd inflict on our elderly, our students, and our economy just isn't worth it. My plan will cut the deficit year after year. It will balance the budget without hurting our future.[1]

The issue that above all triggered the shutdown was Medicare.

Chris Jennings: The Republicans had their own health care agenda: a $270 billion cut in Medicare over five years, just gigantic.

The Republicans were also proposing tax cuts, largely benefiting the wealthy, totaling $240 billion over the same period.[2] The near 1:1 correspondence between the tax cuts and Medicare cuts handed Bill a ready-made argument that "the congressional majority appears to be choosing for the first time ever to use the benefits we provide under Medicare . . . as a piggybank to fund huge tax cuts for people who don't really need them."

"My fellow Americans," he said, "this is a big fight."[3]

Plus $180 billion in Medicaid cuts.

We hadn't vetoed a bill yet, we hadn't had a major fight with the Congress yet, so this was a test: What is Clinton going to do? The Democrats in Congress were strongly pushing us to just attack these cuts, send veto messages, oppose, oppose, oppose. Saying, "You don't have to engage with these people. The president is always trying to split the difference; he's going to undermine our negotiating capability."

The president heard that. We defined what these cuts would mean. We said how many people would be affected, what districts would be affected, how many children would be cut off, how many elderly women, how much premiums would be going up. But the president didn't have his bearings back until we went through the painful process of developing our own balanced budget, which required some savings in Medicare and Medicaid, but drops in the bucket relative to what they had been talking. We did this at his insistence. Some of us questioned the advisability of going down this path, but in the end he proved it was exactly the right thing to do.

The moment he had an alternative, he became a tiger.

"It was one of those moments you never forget."

The bickering between Bill and Gingrich grew more heated over the summer of 1995 and into the fall. With no accommodation reached by September 30, when the government's fiscal year ended, Congress enacted a "continuing resolution" that authorized funding to keep the government running through November 13 but didn't settle the points of contention between the two sides. As that date approached, the Republicans decided to make their stand, refusing to pass another continuing resolution that did not advance their agenda.

Mike McCurry: In meetings I sat in on when the Republican leadership came to the White House, there was a very clear dynamic, with some of these guys, like Don Nickels* and Dick Armey, just not wanting to deal with Clinton. You could see them dripping with contempt.

Meanwhile, you could see Gingrich and Clinton saying, "What about this?" "What about that?" There was a give-and-take.

Leon Panetta: I was concerned, others were concerned, that he might give in to Gingrich in order to avoid the possibility of a shutdown.

The president said, "Let's try one more offer on Medicare to see if we can get a deal." I was responsible for making the presentation in the Oval Office. I had a chart that I was working with, and an easel pad. In the room it was Bob Dole, Dick Armey, Newt Gingrich, Dick Gephardt, Tom Daschle,† the vice president, myself, and the president.

I made the presentation, nervous. Bob Dole said, "That makes some sense." Dole would have cut a deal five days before. But Gingrich said, "Oh, no, I can't do that." Bill Clinton then said—it was one of those moments you never forget—"I can't do what you want me to do. It may cost me the election, but I don't think it's right for the country." It was a courageous moment, because he might very well have been drawing a line that would lose him the election. He might have been giving them an issue that could kill him. For Bill Clinton to say that—I mean, Bill Clinton is a guy who wants the presidency more than any person on Earth—it was an important moment.

Soon after that, they sent another bill, he vetoed it, and it shut down the government.

On November 14, 800,000 federal workers—about 40 percent of the nondefense workforce—found themselves on furlough.[4]

Chris Jennings: I think if you ask him, that might have been one of the proudest moments of his administration. I know it was for the people who

*Conservative Republican senator from Oklahoma, then fourth-ranking member of the leadership.

†Democrats Gephardt of Missouri and Daschle of South Dakota were the minority leaders of the House and Senate, respectively.

worked for him. Sometimes you do things that people on the political side say you shouldn't. That's when people say, "He's bigger than the polls." A lot of people who care about poor people say that that was his shining moment.

That confrontation and the ultimate veto sent a signal that the president did have a line he would not cross. And from that moment on, it made him a far more effective negotiator, a far more effective executive-branch leader, a far more effective administrator of government. In the White House you could feel the presidency had become stronger as a consequence of that conflict and his willingness to stand up.

Mike McCurry: We weren't sure we had the winning card. When the last drive for a deal failed I remember a sense of gloom around the White House: Boy, this may be a really bad thing for us politically. Nobody felt that this was going to be a triumph.

As soon as the government closed, however, public opinion began to swing Bill's way.

Doug Sosnik: TV cameras showed people at the Washington Monument— they can't get a tour, because the government's closed. People can't get Social Security checks. All of a sudden, the shutdown showed people what happens when you don't have the government. It became real. And they started looking around, saying, "Why is the government shut down?" It quickly became clear that the Republicans were pursuing something other than the interests of the country.

Leon Panetta: The shutdown gave the president, for the first time in his administration, the ability to clearly present to the American people what he was about. The toughest thing during the first two years was to grab a message: What is Bill Clinton about? What the Republicans did when they shut the government down was give him a great opportunity to present a message. And the message was: "I'm not these guys, I care about you. I want to help people improve their lives. That's what I'm about."

"Dole had no use for the whole process."

Arne Christenson: Remember, Dole was running for president.

Doug Sosnik: Dole recognized that he was in a Faustian bargain: Despite Gingrich's unpopularity in the country, he was popular in the Republican Party. Dole couldn't have any daylight between himself and Newt Gingrich.

Dole recognized, while it was happening, the damage that the shutdown was going to do to him.

Bob Dole: We could do a shutdown for a weekend—other Congresses had done it, Democratic Congresses. Okay, let's do it for three, four days. But the president couldn't lose. You talk about handing somebody something on a platter. Finally a couple of senators—we told Newt, "This is crazy."

Scott Reed: Dole used to go to meetings with these guys and he was the only one who asked the question, "What's the end game? You guys are talking about shutting down the government, and closing down the monuments, but what's the end game?" The shutdown was devastating, devastating on how it branded Dole and the Republican Party as mean-spirited and out of touch.

Mike McCurry: Dole had no use for the whole process. I don't think Dole liked Gingrich very much.

Interviewed by the author in September 2007, while Gingrich was making his customary noises about running for president, Dole was asked, "You're not like Newt Gingrich, are you?"

Bob Dole: I don't want to be like Newt. Newt's a very smart guy in many ways, but when he comes around to saying all of the Republicans running for president are pygmies (except him, of course), that tells you about all you need to know about him.

He could never be elected, so I don't think he's going to run, I think he's just having a lot of fun. But apparently when he's on Fox, the numbers go up. I don't watch it when he's on.

Joe Gaylord: In many ways, Clinton and Gingrich were alike. They had a voracious appetite for policy, they knew a lot about a lot. They were both well read. I think, actually, they liked one another.

Mike McCurry: I think Clinton liked him a lot. They had way too many similarities.

Age, physical demeanor, interests, a wide-ranging intellectual curiosity, a strong ability to argue and hold a position. And probably a fundamental insecurity, too. Kind of like, "Do people really like me? Do people really get what I'm about?"

They early on established a relationship where they could talk turkey to each other.

Gingrich has said, and his staff has said, that Gingrich would come back from these meetings and be kind of mesmerized with how interesting Clinton was, and how charming. They'd go crazy: "You went down there and gave away the store again, didn't you?"

Arne Christenson: Where Bill Clinton is most mesmerizing is that he can communicate with whoever's in front of him in a way that really can capture them. I had a bit of a view into the way he worked with Newt, with Trent Lott, and with Denny Hastert.*

With Newt, he was always the policy wonk, the other smartest person in the world. They were going to solve these problems together. With Trent, he was much more the southern-boy dealmaker. With Denny, he was the principled midwesterner trying to hit an honest bargain with the farmer across the table.

It's hard to find many people in Washington who weren't subject to Clinton's charms in some way.

Jonathan Alter: Clinton read Gingrich, which isn't that hard to do. He figured out who Gingrich was and played on Gingrich's public recklessness. So whereas Clinton would usually say the right thing in public in this period, Gingrich would almost always say the wrong thing, and Clinton knew how to exploit that without overdoing it.

Gingrich certainly had said the wrong thing in October 1995 when he let slip his prediction that Medicare would "wither on the vine." He tried to walk the statement back; Bill didn't let him: "When they say those things, it's clear that the Republicans come not to praise Medicare but to bury it."[5]

That's where the skill comes in, in the day-to-day. And Gingrich was being advised by zealots who thought they had been put on Earth to turn America into a right-wing nation. Clinton read that we were still basically a moderate country. He was more in tune with where the country really was.

Usually, the person who understands the country better wins those things, and Clinton clearly did.

The shutdown ended after six days, when Bill consented to the seven-year target for a balanced budget and the Republicans agreed to send him a "clean" continuing resolution and promised "adequate funding" for Medicare, Medicaid, education, and the environment—whatever "adequate funding" meant.[6] But the truce was set to expire after a month, and the government shut down again in

*Speaker of the House (R-IL), 1999–2007.

December. The second shutdown was not as drastic as the first—Bill had in the interim signed appropriations bills covering much of the government—but it lasted longer, three weeks. Republican militants in the House did not want to give in, but in January, Gingrich and Dole, reading the opinion polls, realized that the shutdown had to end. Budget talks, including threats of shutdown, continued, but there would be no drastic Republican cuts to the programs Bill had deemed essential.[7]

High noon had come and gone. The Miller gang had been vanquished. The marshal stood tall.

38

Shalom, Chaver:
The Death of Yitzhak Rabin

"He was in tears."

On the evening of Saturday, November 4, 1995, Israeli Prime Minister Yitzhak Rabin addressed the more than 100,000 people gathered in Tel Aviv's Kings of Israel Square to show their support for the Oslo peace process—and to answer increasingly virulent demonstrations staged by its opponents. As the rally concluded, the seventy-three-year-old politician walked toward his car. Before he could enter the vehicle, Yigal Amir, a twenty-five-year-old Jewish law student, fired his pistol three times at him. Two bullets struck Rabin, who was pronounced dead less than two hours later at Tel Aviv's Ichilov Hospital.[1] The assassin, who was apprehended immediately, was among those ardently opposed to Oslo: Rabin, he said at his arraignment, had wanted "to give our country to the Arabs."[2]

Rabin was shot at 9:30 P.M. Tel Aviv time. In Washington, it was 2:30 in the afternoon.

Anthony Lake: I gave Clinton the news Rabin had been shot. He went out on the putting green to wait, because he couldn't stand to sit in his office. He wasn't putting—maybe a little bit—he was just standing there. Then I got the news that Rabin had died and I had to walk out there to tell him. It was as if somebody had punched him in the stomach.

Mickey Kantor: I called Clinton immediately. He was in tears.

Mike McCurry: He was openly weeping.

At about ten minutes to six, Bill stepped out to the Rose Garden to issue a statement. It was one of the few occasions he has ever appeared on television visibly shaken:

> I want the world to remember what Prime Minister Rabin said here at the White House barely one month ago, and I quote, "We should not let the land flowing with milk and honey become a land flowing with blood and tears. Don't let it happen." . . .
>
> Yitzhak Rabin was my partner and my friend. I admired him, and I loved him very much. Because words cannot express my true feelings, let me just say, *shalom, chaver*—goodbye, friend.[3]

Jonathan Alter: Rabin had been one of the only older mentors he's ever had in politics. What's amazing about him is that there was no father figure, for a fatherless child, who guided his political career.

Martin Indyk recalled Bill's first encounter with Rabin, during the 1992 campaign.

Martin Indyk: Clinton was very nervous about meeting him the first time around, and quite in awe of him. Rabin was older, about the same age his father would have been. And so Rabin became something of a father figure to him.

Dennis Ross: There's no question there was admiration; he clearly looked up to him. But was he a father figure? I myself said it at one time, but I'm not sure it's the most apt description.

He came to look at Rabin as someone who was the embodiment of what I would call real virtue. He saw Rabin as the embodiment of the Israeli experience—someone who fought as a kid, spent his whole life in the military, and then became a statesman. This kind of growth, this reflection of Israel's experience, this capacity to move from being a warrior to being a peacemaker—I think it had a profound effect on Clinton.

He admired the quality of Rabin's mind—you couldn't deal with Rabin and not be impressed. Rabin was the most analytical person, certainly the most analytical leader, I ever dealt with. Every meeting he would give you an analysis, and he'd spell it out and it would be incredibly systematic. I used to say if Rabin has made up his mind on something, forget it. You have no possibility of moving him because he's thought it through.

But he was also completely intellectually honest, and Clinton saw this. If reality proved his assumptions to be wrong, he would say so. Strength of character, intellectual honesty, personal virtues, extraordinary experiences—all of which came together to impress President Clinton.

And then the courage to run tremendous risks for his nation and for himself.

Clinton in March '93 says to him, "You take risks for peace and we'll act to minimize those risks." So when Rabin is assassinated, Clinton takes it personally: I told him to take risks for peace and now he's dead. He felt it profoundly.

Rabin always operated on the premise that being close to the president of the United States was an important objective for any Israeli prime minister. At first he looked at Clinton as someone who was new to all of this. He felt that part of his responsibility was almost to educate Clinton about the realities of the Middle East. As time went by he came to respect Clinton in terms of someone who had a capacity to learn quickly. He saw something else: He saw Clinton's capacity to connect with other leaders, and he saw how meaningful that was.

Rabin had a tough exterior, blunt, no-nonsense. Clinton is someone who can talk about anything. Small talk, big talk—doesn't matter, he can do it. Small talk for Rabin was like an oxymoron: What's the point?

In some ways he was a perfect fit with Clinton. But warmth, it's just not who Rabin was. It's exactly who Clinton was.

"You can almost see him lift Peres's spirit."

The sudden loss of a friend and mentor was not the only reason Rabin's death rattled Bill.

Dennis Ross: Clinton was shaken as well because he saw that everything was built around Rabin. He was the core of this process. How were we going to deal without him?

Martin Indyk: I was at the hospital where Rabin was lying dead. I was trying to reach the White House, but I couldn't get through. Suddenly the phone rang on the hospital reception desk. I picked it up, instinctively. It was the White House. They said, "The president is on the line," and he sounded completely devastated. I said, "The funeral will be within twenty-four hours. That's the Jewish tradition, to bury the dead straight away." He said straight out, "I'll be there."

Dennis Ross: It was a given for him.

It wasn't just because it was the right thing to do, it was also that he felt this personal connection to Rabin. And he owed it to him to act on what he was trying to do.

On the plane flying over for the funeral, I was telling him how Peres said it should have been him, not Rabin.

Shimon Peres, foreign minister under Rabin, had become acting prime minister upon Rabin's death. Eighteen days later, he would assume the post officially.[4]

I said to him, "One of the things you've got to do when you're there is buck up Peres. Peres is carrying this incredible weight. He and Rabin were rivals for fifty years. They were never close friends, but they were staples in each other's lives.

"Peres was the dreamer. Rabin was the guy who was grounded. Peres could afford to be the dreamer because Rabin was grounded. Rabin could be grounded because someone else was dreaming. Now Peres doesn't have that. You have to reassure him."

And so when Clinton first sees Peres, he walks up to him and Peres extends his hand and Clinton puts him in a big bear hug, and you can almost see him lift Peres's spirit. I was really struck by it. I saw Clinton hug people all the time; it was not a big deal. But at this moment the embrace almost made Peres feel, "Okay. I can do this."

It was not just a literal embrace, but a figurative embrace: "I'm here for you. I'm really here for you, and what I represent is here for you. What you need, you can count on."

People say a picture is worth a thousand words. Well, this embrace, this hug, was worth all the talking points. Whatever he had to say, the hug did more.

Bill delivered one of the eulogies for the fallen leader.
Bill, Jerusalem, November 6, 1995:

This week, Jews all around the world are studying the Torah portion in which God tests the faith of Abraham, patriarch of the Jews and the Arabs. He commands Abraham to sacrifice Yitzhak. "Take your son, the one you love, Yitzhak." As we all know, as Abraham in loyalty to God was about to kill his son, God spared Yitzhak. Now, God tests our faith even more terribly, for he has taken our Yitzhak.

But Israel's covenant with God, for freedom, for tolerance, for security, for peace, that covenant must hold. That covenant was Prime Minister Rabin's life's work. Now, we must make it his lasting legacy. His spirit must live on in us.

The Kaddish, the Jewish prayer for mourning, never speaks of death but often speaks of peace. In its closing words may our hearts find a measure of comfort and our souls the eternal touch of hope: "*Oseh shalom bimromov hu ya'aseh shalom aleinu ve'al kol Yisrael, ve'imru amen.*"*

And *shalom, chaver*.[5]

---

*"He Who makes peace in His heights, may He make peace upon us, and upon all Israel. Now respond: Amen." Rabin had spoken these words at the signing of the Oslo Accords on the White House lawn. Translation from Rabbi Saul J. Berman, *The Rabbinical Council of America Edition of The Art Scroll Siddur* (Brooklyn: Mesorah, 1987), 57.

Dennis Ross: The speech at the funeral is riveting. When he leaves Israel after the funeral the headlines in Israel are *"Shalom, Chaver."*

"He's a real person."

Dennis Ross: The mix of Clinton's empathy with his capacity to learn anything was a wonderful marriage because when you're asking people, especially in historic conflicts, to do the hardest things they're ever going to have to do, the one thing you have to be able to do is prove that you understand why it's so hard for them.

The way you do that is by showing how well you understand their predicament, and by mastering the detail to the point where you may know it better than they do, so you really can explain that you understand why it's so hard. He could do that brilliantly.

One time with King Hussein I told him that Hussein felt that we didn't sufficiently appreciate what we were asking him to do.

The meeting between Bill and the Jordanian monarch took place in June 1994, as negotiations were under way to reach a peace agreement between Jordan and Israel.

Hussein had sent him a letter with an annex of specific requests, and Clinton, without a note, went through each of the items in the annex. It just blew Hussein, and all of Hussein's team, away that he knew the minutiae of what was important to them, including certain kinds of debt forgiveness and giving them status as a major non-NATO Ally* so that they could get certain excess equipment. Just ticking this off.

And then he sort of leans over—and Clinton would get right in somebody's face—and says, "I know you want F-16s,† I know you want complete debt forgiveness. I'd like to give it to you. I really would like to give it to you. But I've got to tell you, we need the Congress to do that, and I can't do it unless you're prepared to meet with Rabin. If you're prepared to meet with Rabin, I can get you everything you want.

"So let's think about how you could do that. If there's anything I can do to make it easier for you, you tell me and I'll do it."

He's already won Hussein over by going through the details of what the request had been, and then he goes to the much bigger-ticket items, and he does it in a way that makes Hussein say, "Yeah, I want to find a way to do that."

---

*Privileged status granted by the United States to closely allied non-NATO countries. Jordan received the designation in 1996.

†The F-16 is a U.S. fighter jet.

Afterward I got a message from the Jordanians saying that was the best meeting the king's ever had with any American president.

A similar scene had taken place in Geneva five months earlier, when Bill met with Hafez al-Assad to urge the Syrian president to make peace with Israel.

What Clinton did was go through the issues in a way that presidents don't normally do. Assad had met with President Bush, whom he thought highly of, he'd met with Carter, he'd met with Nixon. He'd met with every American president.

I had said to Clinton, "One thing about Assad, he thinks that every westerner he ever meets with doesn't appreciate the constraints he's under. They think only *they* have public opinion."

So Clinton says to him, "I know there are things that are really hard for you to do. I know that you've got your own people who expect certain things from you."

Bill acknowledged that for Assad, a deal must include the return to Syria of the Golan Heights, held by Israel since the 1967 war.

He goes through this in a way that says, "I know what you want. You want the land back and I know there's no peace if you don't get the land back. I know that. And I know *how* you get it back is important to you because you've got these domestic pressures. And people may not appreciate that." But then he says, "Let me tell you what Rabin's problems are."

In return for the land, Bill told the Syrian, Rabin needed guarantees of peace and security.

Assad came over to me afterwards. He knew me with Bush and Baker, and here I am with Clinton.

Compared with other presidents, Assad told Ross, Bill "knows our problems better and he is committed to solving them."[6]

It was his way of saying, "You know how I felt about President Bush, but I've never met an American president like this. He's a real person."

That's what he said: "He's a real person."

39

I'll Show You Mine If . . .
The Big Mistake

Mike McCurry: The shutdown was odd in many ways. You were not allowed to set foot on the campus unless you were deemed essential. I had my staff calling me from home saying, "Whatever we can do from home we will do." And I'm thinking, "There's really nothing going on here. I'm going to have to do a briefing at some point, but we have the interns."

And that was exactly where Monica came from, because the interns were running the show. Because they weren't paid, they could show up and answer phones and staff the functions. I ran the White House Press Office with a bunch of college kids.

On the evening of November 15, 1995, day two of the first shutdown, Monica Lewinsky encountered Bill in Leon Panetta's West Wing office. There she flipped the back of her jacket to reveal to him the portion of her thong panties that showed above the waistline of her trousers.[1] Had Bill been appalled by such behavior—and told the people running his office that this presumptuous young woman needed a talking to, or a relocation, or a boot out the door—historians would have no reason to mention him in the same sentence with Andrew Johnson. But he wasn't and he didn't, and three years later Congress made him only the second U.S. chief executive to suffer the indignity of impeachment.

Shortly after his glimpse of Lewinsky's lingerie, Bill and the twenty-two-year-old intern from Beverly Hills were making out in the office of George Stephanopoulos. "What an incredible, sensual kisser," that woman, Miss Lewinsky,* thought to herself. They went back to work, but two hours later they were once more in

---

*In reports of Bill's famous denial that he had "sexual relations with that woman," Monica's honorific is often rendered as "Ms." In the White House transcript, however, it is "Miss." William J. Clinton, "Remarks on the After-School Child Care Initiative," January 26, 1998, American Presidency Project, http://www.presidency.ucsb.edu/ws/index.php?pid=56257&st=&st1=.

Stephanopoulos's office, where Monica performed fellatio on Bill. Ever the multi-tasker, Bill took a phone call from a member of Congress during the act. Before his new friend could bring him to "completion," as the Starr Report* would later helpfully point out, Bill had an attack of—conscience? regret? neatness?—and told Monica he didn't want to climax with her. Two evenings later, as Monica was helping distribute pizza to White House personnel working overtime—she brought the president two vegetarian slices—Bill and Monica made whoopie once more, this time in Bill's bathroom off the Oval Office. "It was the first I had seen him without a shirt," Monica would recall, "and he sucked in his stomach. I thought it was the cutest thing."[2]

The president and the intern would enjoy ten sexual encounters over sixteen months. Only the last two times would Bill allow himself to reach "completion"; in so doing he spilled his DNA on his partner's blue dress, which she'd bought at the Gap.[3] In 1998 that DNA would have a story to tell.

Jonathan Alter: November 1995 was the beginning of the resurrection, the beginning of the humiliation. You've got both Bill Clintons: You've got the responsible Clinton who is rolling up his sleeves and trying to reopen the government and break the stranglehold of radical Republicans, and you have the heedless Clinton with his pants unzipped. Solid and squalid, cautious and reckless.

Super-smart and super-dumb. On some level he had to know that when he grabbed Monica Lewinsky in George Stephanopoulos's office and started making out with her, that it was not going to end well.

He knew she was a talker, he knew that if Linda Tripp didn't come along, the thing would get out some other way. Part of classic tragedy is when the hero knows that he's got this flaw that's going to bring him down.

I think in his mind the shutdown was his last chance to save his presidency. He didn't know he was going to have a second term. All the chips are on this. We know now that he ended up winning, but he didn't know that at the time.

Clinton once said, Everybody's got their addictions. And everybody in his family had their addictions. His stepfather was an alcoholic. His brother was a cocaine addict. His mother liked to gamble. Sex happened to be his addiction. Addiction is extremely self-destructive—you're in the grip of a force more powerful than yourself.

I love this line from Dr. Jekyll in the Robert Louis Stevenson story: "The lower side of me, so long indulged, so recently chained down, began to growl for license." I think that's what was happening to Clinton at that time. He saved his presidency and he destroyed it simultaneously.

*Ken Starr's report to Congress, issued in September 1998.

40

A Commander in Chief (Finally) Commands: Bosnia, Solved

"He understood that an absolute catastrophe was looming."

The war in Bosnia continued during 1994, and the United States and its NATO allies continued to dither. In February a Serb mortar attack killed sixty-eight Muslim civilians in a Sarajevo marketplace. Starting in April, NATO would mount sporadic, limited air strikes on Serb positions. The attacks did little more than reroute or delay Serb movements—they did nothing to alter the course of the conflict—and thus earned their derisive nickname: "pinprick strikes."[1] U.N.-NATO troops remained on the ground in Bosnia but were too small in number to defend the beleaguered Muslims.

That autumn the situation continued to deteriorate.

Anthony Lake: It was a mess. The State Department had recommended a policy of "containment"—i.e., you can't fix Bosnia, so let's keep it from running across its borders, and I agreed with my staff, who were very hawkish, that we had to go along, and Clinton did, too. This was a bad decision, in retrospect.

In December, Bosnia's Serbs and Muslims agreed to a four-month cease-fire negotiated by Jimmy Carter. The truce went into effect on New Year's Day 1995.

Once the cease-fire expired at the end of April, the Serbs picked up where they had left off. On July 6 they commenced a savage attack on the town of Srebrenica, one of the six "safe areas" established by the United Nations in 1993, forcibly expelling some twenty-three thousand women and children and slaughtering nearly eight thousand men and boys. When Srebrenica fell on July 11, the Serbs directed their attention to the remaining enclaves.[2]

Richard Holbrooke: Several events in May, June, July of '95 convinced the president that he had to get more engaged. The overarching reason was that he understood that an absolute catastrophe was looming and that we were going to get pulled in one way or the other. The triggering event was Srebrenica.

We had committed ourselves to a NATO plan that involved significant use of American forces to pull the NATO forces out of the enclaves. I argued that we were now involved either way. If the British and the French and the Canadians and others withdrew, we would assist them in a withdrawal that would be followed by a Rwanda-style slaughter. And if we were going to use force anyway, why not use the force to bomb the murderers rather than withdraw the U.N.?

Jim Hoagland: What Holbrooke succeeds in doing is to persuade Clinton that the issue is not Bosnia, the issue is NATO.

Richard Holbrooke: He understood fully that what was now at stake was not only the future of the Balkans but America's role in Europe.

As Bill and his advisers planned sterner measures, in consultation with European allies likewise ready at last to put a stop to the genocide, he dispatched Holbrooke to pressure the Serbs.

Richard Holbrooke: On our first attempt to get into Sarajevo three of my four colleagues were killed. That happened on President Clinton's birthday, August 19. He was in Jackson Hole, Wyoming.

Because Milošević would not allow Holbrooke and his team to fly into Sarajevo, they were forced to navigate a treacherous mountain road. Robert Frasure and Joseph Kruzel of the State Department and Nelson Drew, an air force colonel on the staff of the National Security Council, died when the French armored personnel carrier in which they were riding went off the road and rolled down the steep slope. Holbrooke and General Wesley Clark, riding in a U.S. Army Humvee, were not hurt.[3]

We spent the night in Sarajevo in a state of shock, sleeping on cots in an office with firing audible all over.

We got through to President Clinton at Jackson Hole. He asked us to come back with the remains, and then we'd reconstitute the mission. His instruction to us was, "Make clear to everyone you're coming back, that we're not getting out." That was a very, very important thing. It was a simple message, but sometimes simple messages are the most dramatic.

We came back to Washington. We said farewell to our three colleagues at Arlington. President Clinton came for the memorial service. We met in the chapel at Fort Myers afterwards.

President Clinton was dynamic and vigorous that day in telling us to get back out right away and not stop. Throughout the rest of the negotiation, he left us alone most of the time, but at critical moments he intervened. Those interventions were immensely important.

The men who died were exceptionally good men. He knew them. We couldn't back away after losing three of five on our original negotiating team. And perhaps lurking in the back of his mind were the events of two years earlier in Mogadishu.

By August of 1995, President Clinton was a foreign policy president, seasoned in international negotiations and understanding the use of power and its symbols.

Anthony Lake: If you've got power, you then have responsibility. You can't run away from it.

On August 30 NATO aircraft began Operation Deliberate Force. The bombing campaign involved 3,515 sorties before it ended fifteen days later, when Bosnian Serb leaders agreed to NATO's demands. Among those terms were a commitment to refrain from attacks on the safe areas and a removal of heavy weapons from the area around Sarajevo. The siege of Sarajevo, which had begun more than three years earlier, had come to an end.[4]

"It's our failure or our success."

Richard Holbrooke: President Clinton never wavered in his decision to commit American troops to enforce a peace agreement. The American public was heavily against it in polls. On October 30, 1995, the House of Representatives voted three to one for a nonbinding resolution that the administration would not deploy troops to Bosnia without prior congressional approval. Gingrich, who was then speaker, called the vote "a referendum on this administration's incapability of convincing anyone to trust them." The president's response through his press spokesman, Mike McCurry, pleases me to this day: The president "will live up to his responsibilities as commander in chief and be true to his oath of office. If he needs to act to protect America's interest in the world, he will act."

We were two years past Somalia, a year and a half past Rwanda. The president was asserting the commander in chief prerogatives he must exercise from time to time.

A critical decision was where to hold the peace talks. I felt we couldn't control the talks unless we hosted them. President Clinton decisively backed the recommendation that Tony Lake and I made. That was critical: Our hands can't be washed here; it's our failure or our success.

Talks opened November 1 at Wright-Patterson Air Force Base, in Dayton, Ohio. The American delegation, headed by Holbrooke, hosted presidents Franjo Tuđman of Croatia, Alija Izetbegović of Bosnia-Herzegovina, and Slobodan Milošević of Yugoslavia, as well as a delegation of Bosnian Serbs.

On November 20, 1995, when the Dayton Accords tottered on the brink of failure, President Clinton made a phone call to President Tuđman to urge him to make an agreement. He really put the pressure on. That was a critically important call.

On November 21 we got an agreement.

Under the deal, Bosnia was kept intact, but with a weak central government and with its territory demarcated into three autonomous regions, one for each of the three major ethnic groups: Serbs, Muslims, and Croats.

In three years of war, 100,000 people had lost their lives.[5]

Dayton significantly enhanced his global stature. A month after Dayton we were all in Paris at the Elysée Palace signing the formal agreement. He was the dominant figure in that room.

In Paris only months before, Jacques Chirac had lamented that the post of world leader was vacant. The job had now been filled.

He was the president of the United States, and the United States had ended this war. The Europeans had been unable to do so.

It turned out the United States did have a dog in this fight. And that dog succeeded.

"That's an order from the commander in chief."

Richard Holbrooke: On November 22 we met at the White House in the Situation Room. The president and the vice president, very unusually, both came to the meeting.

We had clear reports that the military—not General Shali but others—were not going to support this agreement. If they didn't support it, we weren't going to get the money appropriated. Vice President Gore said that Dayton was well worth taking the gamble on. And then he paused and he looked directly at the military representatives in the room and said, "I want to make an important practical point regarding the Joint Chiefs and the Pentagon. I've had lots of conversations with Congress. They have told me our military representatives on the Hill usually leave audiences more uncomfortable than when they arrived. I'm not saying the military is trying to undercut our policy, but they're losing us votes up there." People were stunned at the harshness of it. The deputy secretary of defense was acting secretary that day. He responded, "We need answers that Shali and his colleagues can feel comfortable with."

President Clinton stepped back in. "The diplomatic breakthrough in Dayton has given us a chance to prevail in Congress and in the nation. We can't promise Congress zero casualties, but we have to convey a high level of confidence in our capacity to carry out the mission. Your people have body language. It's not a question of being dishonest, but we can't close this deal without Pentagon support." And then President Clinton looked directly at General Shalikashvili and said, "I know there's been ambivalence among some of your people—not you, Shali, but some of your people—about Bosnia. But that's in the past. I want everyone here to get behind the agreement." And then Clinton and Gore got up and left the room.

That was a decisive moment, when the president of the United States— especially with the vice president next to him—delivers a message that crystal clear to the chairman of the Joint Chiefs of Staff. That's an order from the commander in chief, and the military are good, loyal people. They will obey.

Shali, who is a very good man, got the message and stuck with it.

Bill, November 27, telling Americans of his decision to send twenty thousand U.S. troops to Bosnia as part of a sixty thousand–strong NATO force:

> The people of Bosnia, our NATO allies, and people all around the world are now looking to America for leadership. So let us lead.[6]

Richard Holbrooke: The president believed that the U.S. had a strategic national security interest in European stability and security. So he set out to do three things simultaneously. The first and most urgent was to settle the crisis in Bosnia. The second was to enlarge NATO. So we set out to bring Poland, the Czech Republic, and Hungary into the alliance.

The three nations entered NATO in 1999. The alliance would further expand in 2004, with the admission of seven additional states formerly in the Soviet orbit.

And the third thing was to improve relations with Russia. It took the skills of a political genius, Bill Clinton, to do this, because he had to convince the Russians that the enlargement of NATO was not an anti-Russian act. He did it by summoning all the skills that make him the best political thinker in the modern era.

The relationship with Yeltsin was critical. And the reason President Clinton was so brilliant with Yeltsin is that he understood Yeltsin as a political figure, not simply the abstract symbol of Russia. He saw Yeltsin's strengths and flaws, and Yeltsin had a lot of both. He worked Yeltsin in a beautiful way.

There had been questions raised after the Cold War about whether we were still committed to Europe. President Clinton resolved those decisively with the enlargement of NATO, the settling of Bosnia and later Kosovo, and the Russian relationship.

Each one of these interrelated acts in Europe has been well reported, but not as an integrated strategic whole. Nobody's ever given President Clinton the full credit he deserves.

41

Ballot-Box Missionary:
Irish Troubles, Irish Votes

"You couldn't have been better, Mr. Governor."

During the 1992 campaign, recently retired Congressman Bruce Morrison sought out his law school classmate to impart some advice:

Bruce Morrison: "Pay attention to the issue of Northern Ireland, which cuts broadly in Irish America, even among people who have been here generations."

Morrison has a special connection to Irish Americans for his sponsorship in Congress of a visa program for citizens both of the Republic of Ireland and of Northern Ireland, which remains part of the United Kingdom.[1]

I knew, first of all, that Bill Clinton is a child of the civil rights movement in the United States. He was in Oxford during '68–'69, and in Northern Ireland at that point there was a civil rights movement that was patterned on the U.S. civil rights movement. It was big news in Britain.

In 1969, after the peaceful Catholic civil rights efforts of the late sixties disintegrated into violence, British troops arrived to keep the peace.[2] The situation, however, only got worse, as Ulster's Catholic minority chafed under Protestant domination and paramilitaries from both communities employed violence in pursuit of their political goals.

Among Americans strongly identifying themselves as Irish, sympathy in the conflict known as "the troubles" has lain squarely with the (mostly Catholic) Republicans, who favor reuniting the six northern counties with the Republic to the south, and against the (mostly Protestant) Unionists, who favor continued union with Britain.

Now, it wasn't something he paid a lot of attention to for the next twenty years in Arkansas, where there's not much of an Irish-American community and where ethnic politics is usually about black and white, not Irish or Italian or whatever, like in a northeastern community. But when you tell him there are forty-four million Irish Americans and that this struggle has meaning to them, you've said all you need to say for him to check that box on the list of things to know about and to respond to.

As deputy political director of the campaign, Christopher Hyland worked to generate support among a broad variety of ethnic communities. One of them was Americans of Irish descent.

Christopher Hyland: I worked to build bridges to Irish Americans—we had hundreds of letters, meetings, discussions with them. Even though some important people associated with the campaign opposed the idea, I championed peace in Ireland as a cause for the campaign and beyond. What Bill Clinton achieved in Ireland turned out to be, arguably, the jewel in the crown of his foreign policy.

Bruce Morrison: There was one major event, on April 6 in New York, just before the primary.

This was a tradition. A coalition of Irish American organizations in presidential campaigns would hold a gathering called the Irish American Forum.

Raymond Flynn: We invited all the candidates for president to show up at Rosie O'Grady's function room.

In 1992 Raymond Flynn was mayor of Boston. He left that post the following year to become Bill's ambassador to the Holy See.

Bruce Morrison: The questions were prepared in advance and given to the candidates. They were expected to pander. They weren't expected to come if they were going to say, "I'm on the British side." I said to the campaign and to Clinton himself, "There is no British-American vote."

Raymond Flynn: Bill Clinton called me before the forum, and he asked if he could meet with Paul O'Dwyer* and myself beforehand. There had been a

---

*A veteran Irish-American Democratic politician from New York City.

conspicuous absence of political interest, presidentially, by both Democrats and Republicans prior to that.

Bill Clinton met with Paul O'Dwyer and me for two or three hours. It was amazing. He was so interested. Asked every pertinent question. When he left the meeting with us, we went over to the forum. Well, Bill Clinton really amazed the crowd.

Afterward he came up to me and Paul O'Dwyer and he said, "How do you think I did?" Paul O'Dwyer said to him, "You couldn't have been better, Mr. Governor, you did an outstanding job." I mean, it took us twenty years to build up that kind of understanding and awareness of the issue, and here's Bill Clinton talking—you would have thought that *he* was the person who was involved in the peace-and-justice movement in Northern Ireland for twenty years. That's how convincing he was. He stole the show.

Bruce Morrison: A peace envoy and a visa for Gerry Adams were among the questions at the April event, and he said he would do it.

Irish-American activists urged Bill to promise that he would appoint a special U.S. envoy to Northern Ireland and issue a visa to Gerry Adams, president of Sinn Fein, the political arm of the leading Catholic paramilitary group in Northern Ireland, the Irish Republican Army. Before that time, the U.S. government had refused to allow Adams to visit the United States on the grounds that he represented a terrorist organization.

George H. W. didn't have a clue about Northern Ireland. There was nothing. This issue was always run out of the State Department, and it was a very anglophile policy.

Nancy Soderberg: During the Cold War the U.S. never wanted to upset Britain on anything. Basically, Britain told us to butt out of Northern Ireland, and we did.

Raymond Flynn: Every person who was at the meeting—and it wasn't just individuals belonging to the Ancient Order of Hibernians or the Friendly Sons of Saint Patrick; some were Republicans, some Democrats, some liberal, some conservative—they all walked out determined that Bill Clinton was their candidate for president of the United States.

That was probably the only time that Irish Americans ever voted as a bloc, except for Kennedy in '60. They voted with pride for Governor Clinton.

•   •   •

Irish Prime Minister Albert Reynolds met with Bill on Saint Patrick's Day 1993.

Albert Reynolds: He sent everybody away, so we had a long chat about the situation in Ireland. He explained to me that it became an issue during the presidential election over there.

Albert Reynolds served as taoiseach, or prime minister, of the Republic of Ireland from 1992 to 1994.

He needed to be involved because, he says, as one politician to another, "You'll appreciate that the Irish vote is so important in the United States, and that I'm starting to look at the next election."

I said, "Yeah, I do.

Clinton became identified with the Irish issue, and so, he said, he couldn't get elected again if he wasn't seen to do something for the trouble in Ireland. He did his sums, and saw that if he didn't hold the Irish-American vote, he wouldn't get reelected.

It was politics. It had to be looked at, and looked after.

"I have expectations of him."

As the Clinton administration began, the issue of the Adams visa offered the first test of the commitments Bill had made to Irish Americans in 1992.

Bill faced opposition to the proposed visa from within the administration.

Bruce Morrison: The FBI went nuts. And they tried to stop it at the State Department.

This issue was taken over by the White House; Warren Christopher didn't play a role at all.

Nancy Soderberg headed up administration policy on Northern Ireland from her post on the National Security Council.

Bruce Morrison: There were lots of these kinds of people who were excluded from the United States. Nobody ever feared that they were going to do damage to the United States. It was who they were. They had a label: They're "terrorists." They're "communists." They're whatever.

In January 1994, Bill granted Adams a two-day visa to attend a conference on Northern Ireland in New York.[3] In exchange, Bill wanted the IRA to agree to a cease-fire in Northern Ireland.

What Adams's visa meant to Clinton was: This is my tool for sending a message to Gerry Adams that I'm not afraid of him, but I have expectations of him and I will not be shy about letting him know what I think is the right thing to do.

Nancy Soderberg: By August we still didn't have the cease-fire. I said, "Well, that's it. It's over." But then they did it on August 31.

Six weeks later, Protestant paramilitary organizations followed suit, and conditions in Northern Ireland improved dramatically.[4]

Bruce Morrison: From early on President Clinton came to have a politician's respect and affection for Gerry Adams, because he saw in Gerry Adams real political skills. He saw in Adams a kind of spark and a genius. A strategic sense that he clearly liked and respected. Gerry's a very charismatic and likable human being.

During the fall, Adams visited the United States again. He did not come face to face with Bill, as his supporters had hoped, but Bill did make it possible for him to meet with members of Congress and senior White House aides.

In March 1995 Bill allowed Adams into America once more, and the two politicians finally exchanged their first handshake. The setting was an annual congressional celebration of Saint Patrick's Day.[5] The Irish-American congressman Pete King was there.

Peter King: It really hit the fan the day Adams came to Capitol Hill for the speaker's lunch. I was walking over there at the same time President Clinton was arriving, so I said, "Mr. President, happy Saint Patrick's Day." It was pandemonium as far as the police and security. He said to me, "I'm catching more shit because of you Irish." And he laughed.

I said to him, "I don't know if it's any consolation to you, but I was talking to my mother today and she said, 'If you see the president, wish him a happy Saint Patrick's Day.' I said, 'How about me?' She said, 'I'm worried about Bill Clinton today.' " He got a big kick out of it.

So we go upstairs to the lunch and it was this crazy thing. They had Adams at one table and the president at another table, but they weren't meeting. There was this whole protocol: Adams couldn't go over to the president's table, because he's the president of the United States, and Clinton thought he couldn't walk over to Adams. They're sitting ten feet away from each other! President Clinton said to a woman on his staff, "When am I going to meet this guy?" They're laughing, and she comes over to me. I go to Tony Blankley, who was Gingrich's guy, and he goes, "The Irish government doesn't want him to meet Adams." So I go over to the Irish ambassador. He goes, "No. I haven't said anything like that." I go to the Irish prime minister's people. "He hasn't said that." Finally Gingrich comes over to me and says, "Here's what we've done. John Hume"—the moderate nationalist leader of the SDLP*—"will escort Gerry Adams up to meet the president." There were five or six of us who knew what was happening. Everyone else was listening to Irish music, and drinking beer, and eating their corned beef and cabbage.

So they met, and it went well. And then the president invited me to come up. And then Tom Manton† came over, and President Clinton said to him, "Can you imagine this poor bastard?" He's looking at me. "His own mother's going to vote for me, but she's not sure about him."

He remembers everything you tell him.

In January 1995 Bill took a major step toward fulfilling his promise to name a U.S. envoy to Northern Ireland. Because the British government objected to the appointment of a political envoy, Bill selected George Mitchell, just retired from the Senate, as an economic representative. Mitchell proved to be an inspired choice. His involvement with Northern Ireland expanded until he was named to chair the process that produced the Good Friday Agreement of 1998.

Bruce Morrison: Bill Clinton changed American policy 180 degrees. He went from an American policy of hands off to putting America's weight not against Britain, not against Ireland, not in favor of the IRA, none of that—in favor of a peace process. In favor of action.

The other thing was, there was a long-standing British approach to "the troubles." The British approach was do a deal in the middle. Get the moderates to agree, and marginalize the extremists. A total failure, because the "extreme," so-called, had deep support in the community, even among people who wouldn't be for violence of any kind, but who viewed it as done on their behalf.

Clinton's policy was an inclusive policy. Reach out to the extremes. Get them in the tent and preach politics—a viable political mechanism to supplant violence, which is what has happened.

Clinton gave Adams a visa to come to the United States. That was risky business, meaning, "If I, the most powerful man in the world, take a political risk to let you in the door, then I can ask you to reciprocate by taking your own risks to make peace." Asking the weak to do the right thing while the strong sit back is not very persuasive. When the powerful say, "I'll put my

---

*Social Democratic and Labour Party. The SDLP favored a united Ireland, but unlike Sinn Fein, it opposed the use of violence.

†Democratic congressman from New York.

political interests on the line," they're saying, "If I can do it, you can do it, because I have more to lose."

It's at the heart of why the peace process worked. It was saying: "We're not going to play out all of history and all of the bad things you ever did. Tomorrow's another day.

"I don't believe in violence, so I'm going to demonstrate to you that you can be a champion for your people with a ballot box. I'm willing to be a missionary for that, and I'm willing to take political risks for making that true."

That's peacemaking. Clinton did that.

"It was the ultimate Bill Clinton moment."

On November 28, 1995, Bill left on Air Force One to visit England, Northern Ireland, and the Irish Republic, before moving on to Germany and Spain.[6]

Bill's trip helped to "concentrate the mind," British Prime Minister John Major said the same day, as he joined his counterpart from the Republic of Ireland, John Bruton, in London to announce the start of "preparatory" talks aimed at opening full-scale, all-party peace negotiations the following February.[7]

Two days later, Bill stood in Belfast's Donegall Square, where he was given the honor of throwing the switch to light the city's Christmas tree. Tens of thousands, Catholics and Protestants, came to cheer the first sitting American president to visit Northern Ireland.[8]

Nancy Soderberg: The whole country turned out for us. Driving around Northern Ireland, the crowds kept getting bigger and bigger and bigger. Young people, in particular, came out to see this man who had stuck his neck out for them.

Clinton loved it. The whole trip, he was moved by the reaction from the people. It was the ultimate Bill Clinton moment: There's no better politician to convey hope and empathy for people's troubles than Clinton, and he did it in spades.

Pete King was there, too.

Peter King: We met him in a factory over in the Catholic section of West Belfast and then we went over to the other side of Belfast, the Protestant section, to meet with the Unionist leaders.

I try to keep my own biases out of it,* but in the Catholic section of Belfast

---

*King is Catholic.

it was unbelievable. These people had felt totally isolated from the rest of the world their whole lives, and suddenly you have the president of the United States in West Belfast. I'm willing to bet that 99 percent of the politicians in the south of Ireland have never been to West Belfast. It was like going to Beirut. You just didn't do it. And here you have the president of the United States going through in a slow motorcade. People were holding their kids up, the whole thing. In Derry, which is an overwhelmingly Catholic city, the crowds along the way were, again, just phenomenal.

From Northern Ireland, Bill headed south.

After he spoke in Dublin, he was really intent on finding his Irish roots. They've never really been able to track down his Cassidys,* but they found a Cassidy's Pub in Dublin. First of all, there was still heavy smoking in Ireland —believe me, in those places it was like going into a fire—but they had no smoking that day. Because of his allergies, I guess. He was at the bar—you would have thought he was one of the neighborhood guys. They gave him a beer but he didn't drink it—he doesn't drink; that's the one vice he doesn't have. But he was bullshitting, talking to these Irish guys, joking, slapping them on the back. He was so relaxed, they're coming up and slapping *him* on the back. The Secret Service guys were thinking, "What's going to happen here?"

There was a formal dinner that night, but he seemed much more comfortable in that pub.

On February 9, 1996, Bill's work on Northern Ireland suffered a setback as the IRA broke its seventeen-month truce, setting off a bomb in London's Docklands district that killed two people. Another seventeen months passed before the IRA reinstated its cease-fire.[9]

Bruce Morrison: The interesting thing about Clinton, in contrast to some lesser folks who have worked on this policy, is he never took the reverses personally. It was never, "Hey. I did all of this stuff for them and look at them." It was always future-oriented, keeping your eye on the ball and continuing to work on the project. And being on the phone, and meeting with all of these two-bit nothings from Northern Ireland he would meet with on or around Saint Patrick's Day. People who, if you took their political equivalent in the United States, would never get a meeting with the president

---

*"Papaw," Bill's maternal grandfather, was Eldridge Cassidy.

of the United States. We're talking about people who had one seat in a 109-member assembly representing a country of 1.5 million people. It's like a minority member of the Delaware legislature—whom would *he* get to meet with at the White House?

There was a level of personal investment that was unshakeable.

Peter King: My father, who was raised by Irish immigrants, died before Bill Clinton became president. But going back to when I was first involved in the issue, he said that he would never have the patience to put up with all of these Irish people. He said they could drive you crazy. Well, maybe that's what appealed to Bill Clinton. They can find so many things to argue about and so many minute arguments to make—they can debate every issue to death. He thrived on that. This was stuff that would make somebody else throw them out of the office and say, "I'm fed up with this." He would go back and forth with them.

A number of people in Ireland—political leaders—talked about Bill Clinton's feeling for the nuance and the detail, not just of the factual issues, but of the personalities and psychologies involved. I guess this is going to sound bad, but who better to understand the most dysfunctional political system and the most dysfunctional fight in western Europe than Bill Clinton? He seemed to thrive on that type of chaotic behavior.

42

A Deal. With the Devil?
Ending Welfare as We Know It

"He was ready to do it."

Tom Brokaw: One of his enduring legacies will be welfare. That was a bold step.

Acting on his campaign promise to "end welfare as we know it," Bill in June 1994 submitted a bill that would for the first time impose a time limit on the payment of welfare. To help recipients make the transition "from welfare to work," the proposal called for $9.3 billion to be spent on job training, child care, and job subsidies.[1] But by this time Bill's health care initiative, and with it his legislative might, had taken such a battering that Congress never took up his welfare proposal.

The following year, the Republicans who had taken over Congress began working on a far different version of welfare reform: It would end the federal entitlement to benefits under Aid to Families with Dependent Children and slash as much as $69 billion of federal funding over five years.[2] Twice the Republicans passed their legislation; twice Bill vetoed it.

But during the summer of 1996, Republicans softened their bill—a little. Responding to Bill's concerns, they increased funding for day care and softened provisions pertaining to eligibility for Medicaid and food stamps. The end of the entitlement, however, and budget cuts of $55 billion remained. Bill still had two bones to pick with the Republican bill—cuts in food-stamp funding and denial of benefits to legal immigrants—but he decided to sign the legislation, with the intent of correcting those flaws later.[3]

Bill, August 22, 1996:

> I signed this bill because this is an historic chance, where Republicans and Democrats got together and said, we're going to take this historic chance to try to recreate the Nation's social bargain with the poor. . . . We can change what is wrong.[4]

Tom Brokaw: I thought it showed real political courage on his part to do it, because it ran straight against the grain of the liberal Democrats who were his base.

Congressman John Lewis (D-GA):

> Where is the compassion? Where is the sense of decency? Where is the heart of this Congress? This bill is mean. It is base. It is downright low-down. What does it profit a great nation to conquer the world, only to lose its soul?[5]

Arne Christenson: The change in welfare reform from an entitlement to a time-limited program was a huge, huge compromise of everything the progressive Democrats had been for, for at least a generation.

Robert Rubin: I, myself, was not in favor of welfare reform. Welfare reform was very popular, but it was not popular with some of the president's own colleagues.

Joe Lockhart: He believed that the deal on the table was not only a good deal politically, it was also good policy and he was ready to do it.

Henry Cisneros: I thought that, as advantageous as it was politically, too many people were going to be hurt. I was wrong. Welfare reform was the right thing to do substantively and politically.

It's turned out for the most part good—that is to say, there's been an impetus for people to get training, get jobs, become self-sufficient. It established a Democratic approach for a new way of reaching the marginalized, though I am not naive about the fact that too many people today are left without resources. But welfare as it existed was not the way.

"It was a very punitive approach."

Max Brantley: Welfare reform was viewed as a slap in the face to many of his old friends, the Edelmans, particularly.

Peter Edelman, who served on the Senate staff of Robert F. Kennedy, held high positions in Bill's Department of Health and Human Services.

Edelman resigned from HHS in protest of his old friend's signature on the 1996 legislation.

Peter Edelman: Let's be clear what he was talking about when I went into the government.

What he had said in the campaign was that a person had to have a job by the end of two years on welfare; if they did not have a job, public funds would supply a job. And if public funds were unavailable to supply a job, then the person could stay on welfare. That was the substance of what he meant by "end welfare as we know it."

The system needed reform. We needed to change it to make it more work-oriented, but in a positive way.

But after 1994, Bill's plan was moot.

The Republicans have taken over Congress. This is the major event. They're saying, "End welfare as we know it? We know how to do that. We will end the entitlement to welfare," which had never been in the conversation until then. "We will put in hard time limits," which had never been in the conversation until then. The only thing that carries over is the phrase "end welfare as we know it," which had enormous political power.

The difference is fundamentally this: If you take away the idea of entitlement, and you say this is a block grant and the states can decide who may get welfare, then no one has an enforceable right to anything. The second thing is, since the '96 law there's a huge culture of "Make those people take a job, any job, doesn't matter what job, doesn't matter whether they've been trained for it." If they're in community college trying to better themselves, you can make them leave the community college to take some menial job. It was a very punitive approach.

Lawrence O'Donnell: It is fair to question what, if anything, the president really believed about welfare policy, given what his plan was compared to the plan he surrendered to.

Peter Edelman: He did not have to sign the bill. Political advisers—not Dick Morris, but Leon Panetta, Harold Ickes, George Stephanopoulos—all urged him to veto the legislation, or said to him that it would not be fatal to his re-election chances; indeed, it might even help, because of his standing up for a principle.

Clinton made a brilliant political deal for himself: The deal was, implicitly, the Republicans get to keep the House because they can point to this achievement, and Clinton gets reelected president. As far as the Republicans were concerned, he was going to be reelected anyway.

He took out election insurance.

Joe Lockhart: There were two or three problems with the bill. His point was, "I'm not going to rest until they're fixed," and he did get the fixes.

Clinton is a piece of Dick Morris and a piece of Peter Edelman; we all want to see him as one person, and it's just not true. I remember how pleased he was with himself after the things were fixed, when he could go back to his liberal friends and say, "I told you I was gonna get this done, and I got it done, and I was right and you were wrong."

Peter Edelman: It's become a kind of automatic reflex in the public debate to say that welfare reform was a success. It's a more complicated story than that.

Robert Reich: I think he could have held out for a better bill. You see, in order to get people genuinely off of welfare you've got to provide them with job training, education, income support while they're getting skills. Child care, health care. You've got to give them a support system. They may get a job, but the objective certainly is not just to move them from the ranks of the jobless poor to the working poor. You want them to have upward mobility.

I think it is wrong for both Republicans and Democrats now to look upon welfare reform and say it was a big success.

It's far too early to declare victory over poverty.

More than any other single act during his eight years as president, Bill's signing of the Personal Responsibility and Work Opportunity Reconciliation Act of 1996 embodies the notion of Clinton as Rorschach test: Was his signing of this Republican bill an act of courage for its defiance of his political base? Or was it a craven maneuver to secure reelection on the backs of the poor? Did he give in when he should have held out? Or were his compromises worth making in order to achieve significant positive change in the life of the nation?

Brave statesman or political opportunist? Benevolent pragmatist or betrayer of principle?

It depends on how you read the inkblot.

43

Slippery or Steadfast?
Shapeshifter

"You didn't know where he was going to be."

Bill's shift toward the center in 1995 and 1996, his outmaneuvering of Republicans on their signature issues of crime, welfare, values, and fiscal responsibility, won him comfortable reelection. But the tactic only intensified the mistrust of many critics to his right and to his left.

Fred Barnes: He brought out some primal instincts among conservatives.

Arne Christenson: I interpret the venom much more in terms of personal unreliability than in terms of ideology—there are a lot of strong liberals who don't attract venom. I didn't think Clinton was an intransigent liberal. There was just a sense that you didn't know where he was going to be from one day to the next.

Joe Lockhart: The hatred was that they were out of power and he was smarter than they were. Every time it came to a battle of wits, a power play, he won. The government shutdown killed them. They were so sure that they were right, but he so outplayed them that they wanted him gone.

Joe Gaylord: There was a feeling among conservatives that Clinton was duplicitous and untrustworthy. And that his use of language was so carefully contrived as to be misleading. That he was not a reasonable partner in the administration of state affairs. And that grew into a venomous dislike—and not just dislike; it was that he became despicable in their eyes. It created a huge cavern in the country.

Arne Christenson: I suppose you'd say most of the intense hatred was on the right, but there was a lot of discontent on the left toward Bill Clinton. Because they weren't sure where he'd end up.

Douglas Brinkley: He became successful because he co-opted the Republicans' issues. He became a centrist. He became a conservative Democrat.

Peter Edelman: My view of Bill Clinton is net favorable by a wide margin. However, I have strong disagreements with him on a few things, like welfare. Whether he did these things out of conviction or to broaden the reach of the Democratic Party, it doesn't matter. For example, I also disagree with major elements of the Crime Bill of 1994: It created "three strikes and you're out" and fifty-five new counts of capital punishment in federal law. The way welfare reform was done elevated politics over principle.

Lawrence O'Donnell: I don't think there was liberal governance during the Bill Clinton years. Gingrich forced big spending cuts on Clinton, but in '93 Clinton started with what, for Democrats, were extraordinary spending cuts.

It was actually, as of that time, the most conservative governance we had had.

Douglas Brinkley: Rhetorically, particularly in the black community, he stayed a liberal, but record-wise he was successful largely because he was almost undistinguishable from Republicans.

One liberal Democrat, however, is not so hard on Bill.

David Bonior: I never thought he was a conservative. I thought he could have gone further and done more, but any efforts to reach beyond a centrist position were squashed with the failure of health care. And then, of course, with the failure of retaining the Congress.

It remains to be seen how progressive Clinton could have become if he'd had a Democratic Congress to work with, but he was relegated to working with a reactionary Congress. And so he had to settle for smaller initiatives and not very big systemic changes.

I'm not extremely critical of him. I would have wished for something else, but we didn't have something else.

"I couldn't live with myself if I didn't do this."

One of Bill's bravest performances took place just after his world had come undone in the 1994 midterms.

Robert Rubin: In late 1994, Mexico started moving toward a currency crisis. Nobody in Washington saw it until it happened.

Lawrence Summers: Mexico moved from being a poster child of a successful emerging market to the brink of default inside of three weeks. They devalued on December 19, and there was a panic.

The question of whether they'd be able to pay their debt was very much in doubt by early January.

Robert Rubin: The fear that we had was that Mexico would go into a real economic crisis—in a country already with a very large number of poor people. It would increase illegal immigration to our country. It would add to drug trafficking and crime. Mexico was also a big market for us. It had all kinds of ramifications.

Beyond all that, we were worried that it might spread to other countries, and then you could have a global economic crisis.

Lawrence Summers: When the president decided to offer Mexico a very large loan, it was enormously controversial: It was the largest financial commitment the United States had made to another country since the Marshall Plan. It seemed to come out of nowhere. There was no absolute guarantee of being paid back. There was much resentment of Mexico in America. It became a free-for-all.

The president made a decision to seek legislative approval from Congress for loan guarantees.

Robert Rubin: The leadership in Congress said they would support us. But very quickly, they all backed off. To his credit, Gingrich was the one who most stuck with us.

Lawrence Summers: When it became clear that the legislation would not pass quickly and that Mexico was on the verge of default, the president then decided to authorize the use of the exchange stabilization fund.

The Treasury Department's exchange stabilization fund is by statute to be used, at the treasury secretary's discretion, for regulation of international currency exchange rates. However, Bill's use of the fund to rescue Mexico was not the first time a president had drawn upon it, without congressional consent, to make loans to a country in crisis.[1]

Robert Rubin: I think it was remarkable what he did. He loses terribly in November of '94, and here we come to him in January of '95, telling him we have an idea that can cause him to lose the support of the American people totally. We told him there had been a poll in the *L.A. Times* that said that 80 percent of the American people did not want to provide assistance to Mexico to deal with the crisis.

My guess is we weren't talking for more than ten or fifteen minutes when he said, "Look, I don't want to discuss this. I mean, I want to learn about it, but you don't have to persuade me it's the right thing to do. Let's do it."

Lawrence Summers: He said, "Look, there's a lot of chickenshit stuff that goes on, but the way the system is supposed to work, we make our best judgments and if we make them right, good things happen, and if we make them wrong, bad things happen. And that's how it ought to be. I couldn't live with myself if I didn't do this, because it's the right thing to do."

The package worked; Mexico did not default. In the end, the United States not only recouped the $20 billion it had advanced but even netted a profit of $500 million on the transaction.[2]
The author noted to Robert Rubin that Bill Clinton's detractors consider him a political coward, a man without a core.

Robert Rubin: I know they do. It's very common. I think it's an astonishing claim.

If you think about it, in that first year he was there, he put in place a fiscal program that was serious. It had real assumptions, it wasn't rose-colored glasses. And the evidence of how difficult it was, was how powerfully he was attacked. The budget passed by one vote in the House and no votes in the Senate.

He did gun control, which was very difficult. Health care didn't pass, but it certainly was an act of courage to try it. NAFTA was toxic with the AFL-CIO—they were natural allies of his, and he fought for it. Chinese accession to the WTO was deeply controversial within the AFL-CIO; he did it.

I would argue just the opposite of those claims.

Lawrence Summers: It had to do with courage at a few key moments. As president, when it was really important, he did the right thing by his lights rather than the political thing. That was deficit reduction, that was investing heavily in Russia. That was supporting aggressive bailout responses in Mexico, in Korea, and Brazil.* That was committing American prestige and force

---

*South Korea in December 1997, Brazil in October 1998.

to Bosnia and Kosovo. When the stakes were high, the right decisions were made against political pressure. Was there tremendous political pragmatism about lots of other things? Of course. And where one looks back and sees errors having been made, they were less considered errors, where a judgment was made to elevate politics over substance, than decisions that look enormously consequential in hindsight but didn't get the thought they deserved at the time, like Rwanda.

When the stakes were very high, the courage was very great.

Jonathan Alter: Clinton looked like a guy who just did what was popular and was always eager to please, but in reality he did make more of the tough choices, unpopular choices, than I expected him to make. Before Clinton became president, I thought he would shy away from making those out of his eagerness to please.

My take on him was that he was a man born out of his time. I think Clinton wanted to live in the sixties, when there was a lot of money for big, bold experiments. Instead he comes in and has to worry about the bond market. He has to become an Eisenhower-like president.

He could have been a great president if he'd been president at a different time. But the 1990s will be remembered as a relatively placid and prosperous era when we had the luxury to indulge in tabloid stories ad nauseam. After 9 / 11 a sex scandal would not have been that big a deal. He was never really tested by fire, despite Bosnia and Somalia, the way other presidents have been. The era doesn't have the weighty, tragic arc of other periods of history. The real action during the Clinton presidency was in the business world.

Interwar presidents are not usually regarded as great presidents. We don't know how Clinton would have responded to 9 / 11. But we do know that he was more attentive to America's place in the world than his successor and that he remained hugely popular throughout the world for the duration of his presidency. And that is very, very important for the national interest of the United States.

44

Piece of Cake:
Reelection

"There's no way you can beat Clinton."

Sam Donaldson: I thought it was breathtaking when Bill Clinton declared, "The era of big government is over." Signing the welfare-reform bill against the wishes and vocal condemnation of the leftist members of his party was another indication that he couldn't get tagged like other Democratic nominees. And so by the end of the second two years, he was back. He'd positioned himself as a president who could get things done, who had helped save the country at the time the Republicans wanted to shut it down.

And he was running against Bob Dole.

In the 1996 GOP primaries Dole faced opposition more vehement than viable—most notably from plutocrat wannabe Steve Forbes and pitchfork waver Pat Buchanan. In February, Buchanan took New Hampshire, while Forbes took Delaware and Arizona, but then Dole ran the table, wrapping up the nomination by the end of March.

Bob Dole has been a fine public servant. But in that contest in 1996, Dole, the last of the World War II veterans to run for the presidency, simply looked old, and his ideas looked old, compared to Bill Clinton.

Jack Kemp: Everybody in the country knew about Bill Clinton.

The late Jack Kemp, the former football star, congressman, and secretary of housing and urban development, was Dole's running mate in the fall.

There wasn't one thing that Bob Dole or I could have told the American people different. They knew him. They elected him. They liked him.

Peace and prosperity. Reagan couldn't have been beaten in 1984 and, in my opinion, Clinton and Gore could not very well have been beaten in '96.

Bob Dole: It was uphill all the way. The economy was good—fortunate for the people but unfortunate for me politically. It stayed good through '96. What do you want? That I go out and say I wish the economy were bad so you can vote for me?

I got a seven-page handwritten letter from Nixon going all through it. And he's pretty good. The last paragraph said that if the economy was good, forget it. There's no way you can beat Clinton.

"It was a total linkage."

Scott Reed served as Bob Dole's campaign manager from January 1995 through Election Day 1996.

Scott Reed: I thought that Clinton was vulnerable. Ninety-four had been a historic rebuke.

But '95 was a tough year for us because the Democrats started advertising in June. The "Dole-Gingrich Monster" ads.

Paul Begala: Dole-Gingrich. Every ad said that.

Arne Christenson: They really ramped up in November and December when they had footage from some of the budget negotiations. They always had Newt and Dole in grainy black and white, with this sinister music in the background, and then the president coming on in vivid color making his stand for all that is good.

"Dole-Gingrich vote no—no to America's families," said the narrator in a commercial that aired during the spring of 1996.[1]

Paul Begala: Gingrich was out of central casting in a way that Bob Dole could never be. Dole was essentially agreeable, pleasant, accommodating, a war hero. He was your Uncle Bob, whom you may disagree with on politics but you had this huge respect for. They could have never demonized him without Newt. Newt was everything Dole wasn't. He was like a Thomas Nast* cartoon of a right-wing thug: Overweight, bombastic, and given to hysterical rants. He blamed liberals for Susan Smith—the woman in South Carolina who murdered her children. Woody Allen left his wife for his wife's adopted daughter—and that was the Democrats' fault. He says these crazy things. He was a gift.

---

*Influential American political cartoonist, 1840–1902.

Harold Ickes: It was a total linkage of Dole with Gingrich. There were a couple of spots where they morphed into one another.

Medicare, Medicaid, Social Security, saving the Department of Education. We kicked the shit out of them. Gingrich and the Republicans, the Shi'ites in Congress, became the touchstone.

Dole tried like hell to gently divorce himself from Newt. He never could. We tied him up. It was brutal.

Craig Smith: We had done a lot to make Gingrich seem like the bad guy. We weren't *not* going to take advantage of that.

Doug Sosnik: If you look at polls from, say, mid-January '96 until Election Day, there's an amazing consistency. Despite all the running around, all the money spent, all the ads, the die was cast in December '95, early January '96, by the government shutdown.

"Age made a difference."

Dan Glickman: I think Dole and Clinton liked each other. I never heard either one of them say anything ad hominem or personally bad about the other. Ever.

I always thought President Clinton thought of Dole a little bit like the father he never had. And I thought that Dole admired Clinton a bit for his ambition and brashness and romanticism. They were different types of personalities, obviously, but the one thing that tied them together was that they were both legislative activists. They wanted to accomplish things.

Joe Lockhart: Now he loves Dole. At the time I think he had a lot of respect for him. They did not have a bad relationship going into '96. Clinton is the unique person who can like and respect someone even if he knows they don't like or respect him because he's just that way. He has an enormous reservoir of goodwill. It doesn't take a lot to get him pissed off for five minutes. It takes a lot to get him to write somebody off.

Bob Dole: Toward the end of the campaign we had all these "Dole in '96" signs and they changed it to Dole *is* 96. I thought that was pretty cute.

Joe Lockhart: He was a World War II veteran whom everyone honored but in the public's mind was not necessarily a guy who had a twenty-first-century mindset.

Bob Dole: Age made a difference. Some people wondered if I'd still be around, particularly since I'd had pretty serious injuries,* and Clinton was rugged. But it was a good time for Democrats. They had a good candidate. If you believed in his philosophy, why not keep him?

Joe Lockhart: The Dole campaign was not the best run in the world. There were verbal gaffes that Dole had trouble getting out of.

Campaigning in Kentucky in June, Dole discussed the state's most valuable crop, tobacco: "We know it's not good for kids. But a lot of other things aren't good. Some would say milk's not good."[2]

Bill pounced. In his weekly radio address a few days later, he cited his efforts to restrict the marketing of tobacco to youngsters—another of his 1995–1996 "values initiatives," and one Dole opposed.[3]

> When political leaders . . . oppose our efforts to keep tobacco away from our children, they continue to cater to powerful interests, but they're not standing up for parents and children.[4]

Joe Lockhart: The way politics works, it's not enough for someone to say something silly. Someone has to go in and exploit it and stir it up a little bit.

In 1992 Bill's campaign had harassed President Bush with Chicken George.

Craig Smith: In the '96 campaign we had Butt Man. We had somebody dressed like a big cigarette following him around. We got to the point where we actually had the instructions for making the Butt Man costume posted on the Internet, so you could be your own Butt Man and go to Dole events. We would go to some Dole events and there would be like ten Butt Men walking around.

On August 15, in his speech to the Republican Convention in San Diego, Dole made an even more damaging error:

> Age has its advantages. Let me be the bridge to an America that only the unknowing call myth. Let me be the bridge to a time of tranquility, faith, and confidence in action. And to those who say it was never so, that America has not been better, I say, you're wrong, and I know, because I was there. And I have seen it. And I remember.[5]

Scott Reed: Clinton turned it around on us pretty quick and made it into "a bridge to the twenty-first century."

---

*Wounded in action in Italy in 1945, Dole had lost the use of his right arm. In July 1996 he turned seventy-three.

Bill, August 29, 1996, to the Democratic convention in Chicago:

Now, here's the main idea: I love and revere the rich and proud history of America. And I am determined to take our best traditions into the future. But with all respect, we do not need to build a bridge to the past. We need to build a bridge to the future. And that is what I commit to you to do.

So tonight, tonight let us resolve to build that bridge to the 21st century, to meet our challenges and protect our values.[6]

Game, set, match.

Craig Smith: Here was Dole, not only looking like he was from a previous generation but we had these quotes from him basically saying, "I don't want to go forward. I want to go back." People said, "Look, I'm not sure I like everything that Bill Clinton does, but we can't go back." People know that elections are more about tomorrow than they are about yesterday. Instinctively. And we positioned Bob Dole as the candidate of yesterday.

When Bob Dole gave us that line about the bridge, it was just too easy.

"Why wouldn't I remember him?"

Joe Lockhart entered Bill's employ in March 1996 as the campaign's press secretary.

Joe Lockhart: I started working for him and heard the story that Clinton has the ability, when he's talking to you, to make you feel like you're the only person in the world. Heard that and heard that. I'm a skeptic. I'm like, He's just good.

One time we had been on a campaign trip for eighteen hours. We pulled into Paducah, Kentucky, at two in the morning. We said to him, "Everybody is tired, sir. There'll be a few people at the hotel. Wave at them." One of the things I used to tell him was, "You keep the press up until four in the morning, you're gonna get worse press. They have to stand there and watch you until you go to sleep."

We get there and there aren't twenty people, there are two hundred people, so he's like, "I've got to go. These people have been waiting here for two hours." We're like, "Okay, just go shake a few hands. Please, let's go to bed."

So he's shaking hands and he motions for this guy in the crowd to come up to the front. They start to talk. It's now 2:30 and they talk for twenty minutes. Clinton is animated; I mean, really animated. You don't know whether he's mad, whether it's his long-lost brother, but he's very engaged. Finally, he goes inside.

The press were all like, "Who is this guy he was talking to?" I said, "I'll find out." So I go and I grab him and I say, "Who was that guy?" And a very excited president says, "That's Charlie So-and so."

I'm like, "Okay. Help me out. Who is he?"

"In 1986 when I was at a national governors' meeting, I was assigned to write a white paper on education reform, and he was the staff member of So-and-so"—a Republican governor. "We stayed up all night in his room and we wrote it," and blah, blah, blah.

"That's a really interesting story. So you've stayed in touch?"

"No. I haven't seen him since that night."

I looked at him and said, "That was ten years ago and you saw him one time?"

He looked at me and goes, "We did this whole thing. Why wouldn't I remember him?"

I thought, "This is for real," because you can't fake that. You can't, after the thirty-seventh eighteen-hour day in a row, be genuine with every person unless you really are, and he was.

I told the press the story and they all nodded like, "Yep, that makes sense."

"Clinton worked with Gingrich to get stuff done."

Doug Sosnik: As long as possible, we stayed inside the bubble of the presidency, communicating on a daily basis to the American public what President Clinton was doing on their behalf. That really worked.

Scott Reed: The killer for the election was welfare reform. We had a three-legged stool. Taxes, defense security, and the third leg was always going to be welfare reform.

Clinton had vetoed the bill twice. We were like, "Now we have an issue." Twice! It wasn't once, it was twice.

We were going to roll out *our* welfare reform. But Republicans passed the welfare-reform bill again and sent it to Clinton for the third time. We begged Trent Lott* not to do it.

Bob Dole: I don't think Lott at that time was a big Bob Dole fan. He is now.

Scott Reed: It was going to be a pillar of our campaign. And what did they do? They passed it.

It was devastating. It was absolutely devastating.

---

*Lott had succeeded Dole as majority leader when the Kansan left the Senate in June.

Doug Sosnik: Starting with the '92 election and through the first term, a lot of Republicans felt like we were taking their issues, and welfare was the biggest one left on the table. If the president were to perform in that area, we would gnaw more and more into the middle part of the electorate.

Joe Lockhart: The Republican leadership in early July of 1996 sacrificed Bob Dole so that they could keep Congress, and very openly. I don't think there was anyone who stood up in front of a camera or microphone and said so, but it was pretty clear.

We could have taken the House back that year, but the Republicans, by getting enough done, kept their majority. There were some Democratic leaders on the Hill who were upset that Clinton signed these bills, because they wanted to have this fight. But it made sense for us.

Arne Christenson: Clinton worked with Gingrich to get stuff done, and then the Republican majority was able to run on accomplishments.

Joe Lockhart: From July to August, just before the Republican convention, was probably the most productive legislative month in his eight years. We got Kennedy-Kassebaum, the minimum wage, and welfare reform. He signed those three bills on three consecutive days, which basically sealed Bob Dole's fate. The president brought the Republicans to the table, got something done, and the only person who wasn't standing there shaking hands was the Republican candidate for president.

On August 20 Bill signed legislation increasing the hourly minimum wage by ninety cents. The following day he signed Kennedy-Kassebaum, named for its two chief sponsors, Ted Kennedy (D-MA) and Nancy Kassebaum (R-KS). The most touted of the bill's provisions enabled Americans to hang onto their medical coverage when they switched jobs or lost one.[7] On the twenty-second he delivered the coup de grace, welfare reform.

Dole tried to rain on each of Bill's three parades, but when the president signed welfare reform, which had passed with the vote of just over half the Democrats on Capitol Hill but every Republican save two, Dole's campaign could only echo Bill's critics on the left when it sputtered, "By selling out his own party, Bill Clinton has proven he is ideologically adrift."[8]

Working hand in glove with a Republican Congress more interested in saving itself than its nominee, Bill had used the power of his office to render his opponent, essentially, irrelevant.

Bob Dole: There were two or three things Congress did in the last couple of months that didn't help me any. Maybe they helped Congress.

• • •

Joe Lockhart: Clinton woke up the day after the midterm election in 1994 and said, "This isn't working. What are we going to do?" The process changed. It didn't change what he was for and what he wanted to get done, it changed *how* to get it done. He had to change focus a little bit. It's the way of the world.

He was much more effective from January 1, 1995, on, and got more effective every year.

After the votes were counted on the night of November 8, 1994, a second term for Bill seemed unthinkable. But on November 5, 1996, Americans returned him to office, and it wasn't close: Bill took 49.24 percent of the popular vote—agonizingly short of a majority, allowing his detractors to continue taunting him as a president by plurality—to 41 percent for Dole and 8 percent for Ross Perot, who had run once more as an independent. And Bill trounced Dole in the electoral college, 379–159.[9] Congressional Republicans got what Bill had made possible for them: They held on to both chambers, adding two seats to their majority in the Senate while losing only eight in the House.

That evening, Bill returned to the steps of the Old State House in Little Rock to celebrate his triumph in "the last election in which I will appear on the ballot" as a victory for the politics of moderation: "Tonight we proclaim that the vital American center is alive and well."[10]

Arkansas Senator David Pryor, who had hosted a party for Bill in the afternoon, spoke for many in hoping that the reelected president would enjoy a second term free from the tormentor who had burdened the first:

> I think the biggest round of applause you could get in Arkansas is say, "let's get this election over with and let Ken Starr go home." We feel we've pretty well had it for a long time . . . and we just feel like still there's nothing there.[11]

Oh, there was something there.

Part V

Humiliation
1997–2000

45

Reckless, Stupid, Human:
Wasting a Precious Gift

Bill, Second Inaugural Address, January 20, 1997:

> The American people returned to office a President of one party and a Congress of another. Surely they did not do this to advance the politics of petty bickering and extreme partisanship they plainly deplore. No, they call on us instead to be repairers of the breach and to move on with America's mission. America demands and deserves big things from us, and nothing big ever came from being small. Let us remember the timeless wisdom of Cardinal Bernardin,* when facing the end of his own life. He said, "It is wrong to waste the precious gift of time on acrimony and division."
>
> Fellow citizens, we must not waste the precious gift of this time.[1]

"Why do something so stupid?"

Almost a year into Bill's second term, Sam Donaldson received a change in assignment.

Sam Donaldson: Roone Arledge, who was then still president of ABC News, said to me, "I want you to return to the White House as our White House correspondent." I'd served twelve years covering Presidents Carter and Reagan; I didn't want to go back. But when the president of your news division says, "I want you to do it," you do it. I thought, "The second term, not much going on. I can handle this."

One week later, the Monica story broke.

Elaine Kamarck: The second term was blown up because of Monica Lewinsky. There *was* no second term.

*Joseph Bernardin, the recently deceased archbishop of Chicago.

All policy—all *serious* policy—stopped, because to do anything big you have to use some political capital. Clinton needed all his political capital to keep himself from being thrown out, so basically nothing happened in the second term.

Ron Fournier: He squandered the last three years of his presidency. Three years is a long time in the presidency of a talented man, and they were thrown away.

Andrew Friendly: Why do something so stupid? You're feeding into exactly what they think about you.

John Breaux: I don't think there's any argument that it was reckless behavior. It was also human behavior.

"It would have been a signature contribution from the president."

Bill opened his second term with an ambitious goal.

Janet Yellen served as chair of Bill's Council of Economic Advisers from 1997 to 1999.

Janet Yellen: The president very much hoped to be able to make progress on Social Security. That was a high priority.

Social Security had long been considered politically untouchable—the "third rail of American politics," certain to electrocute anyone who dared lay a hand on it. Bill was serious about grabbing it.

Right at the beginning of Clinton's second term—maybe not the first week, but early on—we started having small group meetings, almost weekly, to discuss Social Security reform.

Elaine Kamarck: It was an unbelievably fabulous policy perspective. To have a president who was reelected—in a sound victory—facing budget surpluses? Unheard of.

Bill Clinton was the one doing this. Entitlement reform was clearly part of what the second term was supposed to be about.

Janet Yellen: We hoped to make some progress on Medicare, but we decided that Social Security was the easier problem to deal with. We thought we had good ideas for how to reform Social Security, and that became a huge objective. It would have been a signature contribution from the president. It's something he wanted as part of his legacy.

It required political courage and the willingness to ask for sacrifice from some people. And he was willing to take it on.

If the impeachment hadn't happened, would we have been able to achieve a bipartisan compromise? I don't know. When I talked to some well-connected Republican economists about the prospects for a bipartisan Social Security solution during Clinton's second term, they told me to forget it.

Democrat Charles Stenholm of Texas served in the House from 1979 to 2005.

Charles Stenholm: There's not a doubt in my mind that had Monica Lewinsky not happened, we would have had a Social Security reform bill. Monica Lewinsky blew that out of the water.

Jonathan Alter: With no Monica would Clinton have been able to get serious Social Security reform in 1998? Yes, but I think it would have been along the lines of what Reagan did in 1986, which nobody remembers. He changed things around the margins, solidified it for a couple more decades. So it's not like Clinton would have made profound changes in American life if it hadn't been for Monica Lewinsky.

Bob Kerrey: There's no question, the scandal cost him a lot. There's also no question that he accomplished a lot in the last few years of his presidency.

In November 2005 Bill addressed an academic conference on the Clinton administration at Hofstra University, Hempstead, New York. At one point in the speech, which took the form of an apologia for his presidency, he read a list of his administration's achievements during its last year, 2000. He was reading the list, he said, in part because he was "sick and tired" of people saying how much could have been accomplished had there been no impeachment. Among the items on the list were the setting aside of wilderness lands, a trade bill regarding Africa, China's entry into the World Trade Organization, expansion of child care and after-school programs, efforts to battle drug trafficking in Latin America, sequencing the human genome, and expansion of the national-service agency AmeriCorps.[2]
Elaine Kamarck heard the speech.

Elaine Kamarck: Look, the government is always accomplishing things because it's a government of laws not men. It runs on its own, and there were certainly lots of things that he could get accomplished even while the impeachment was going on.

But what he couldn't get accomplished was anything that required the expenditure of significant political capital. There's nothing on that list that was a fight.

You can't be under impeachment and go into the House of Representatives and pick a fight on something else. Not going to happen.

"The American people never left him."

Mickey Kantor assessed Bill's affair with Monica Lewinsky, and the public's response.

Mickey Kantor: It was not a Phi Beta Kappa move on his part. Some would call it stupid. It was not high crimes and misdemeanors.

Now, he created the situation. No one held a gun to his head. It was his fault and he would say the same thing. What's fascinating is from day one to day end of that situation, the American people never left him. Never. No matter what was revealed. Never, never, never left him.

Fred Barnes: I kept thinking, month after month, from January 1998, when the Monica Lewinsky scandal broke, "Once the public really understands what's here, they are going to turn on Clinton."

They never did. His presidential approval numbers were up in the 60s and stayed there. Amazing. You know why? One, most Americans didn't think his crimes were that serious. Two, they liked him a lot. And three, those were good times economically. You get all those together—he sailed right through.

Douglas Brinkley: The dilemma for his presidential legacy is, if I walk into my class and ask students, "John Kennedy, what do you think of?" their answer will be, "Ask not what your country can do for you, ask what you can do for your country." If I say, "Ronald Reagan," they'll say, "Mr. Gorbachev, tear down this wall." Bill Clinton's sound bite that will live eternally is, "I did not have sex with that woman, Miss Lewinsky." The finger wag is an eternal film clip.

Look how moving he was at Oklahoma City. He gave this extraordinary speech after the bombing, filled with love and regret and pain and anguish. I don't think it could have been a better written or delivered speech; it should live on in the annals of oratory. But it gets forgotten. What they remember is "I did not have sex . . ." And "It depends on what the meaning of the word *is* is." When his name comes up even today on any show—you turn on Leno or Letterman—it's usually in a sex joke.

The pop culture has painted him as a sexual pervert. I don't think he is, but the fact of the matter is, his reputation includes a great deal of that. That lives on for people.

46

Big Bucks Bedroom:
Scandal of the Year, 1997

But first . . .

The name Monica Lewinsky would not surface until 1997 ended, and the to-do over the Whitewater land deal had, for the most part, run its course by the time 1997 began. However, the first year of Bill's second term did not lack for a scandal to keep the press and the opposition nipping at his heels. The subject was the fund-raising for Bill's reelection.

Information had begun to trickle out during the last few weeks of the 1996 campaign concerning illegal fund-raising by the Democratic National Committee. Most ominous in the reports were suggestions that the government of China, through laundered campaign contributions, was purchasing influence with the president of the United States.

In 1997 the trickle became a flood. The revelations may not have exposed unlawful behavior on Bill's part, but they were embarrassing all the same. For example, the media reported that attendees at White House "coffees" with the president, held to reward political donors and entice potential donors, had included an arms merchant from China and a mobbed-up securities swindler from New Jersey. Attention also focused on the Lincoln Bedroom, and on the people who slept there and in other guest rooms at the White House. More than nine hundred individuals had enjoyed Bill's overnight hospitality during the first term, including not only ordinary people from Arkansas and beautiful people from Hollywood but also people who owed their close personal friendships with Bill solely to the size of their checkbooks and a willingness to open them to the Democratic Party.[1]

Hearings in the House and Senate found little to pin directly on Bill, but the proceedings, along with the press, helped paint a sordid picture.

New York Times, editorial, February 27, 1997:

> Having turned the White House residential quarters into a Democratic con-
> tributors' playground and sleepover camp, President Clinton now tells us
> that the Lincoln Bedroom was not for sale and no one was actually prom-
> ised anything in return for money. That may be so, but the image of guests

racing in and out of White House bedrooms like something out of a Feydeau farce makes it clearer than ever that Mr. Clinton was presiding over an operation that was out of control and demeaning to the government.[2]

As the second term began, Bill asked Paul Begala to return to the White House.

Paul Begala: I told him I didn't want to defend the '96 reelection. I thought the fund-raising they had done was excessive. I didn't think it was illegal, but I was not impressed. He said, "That'll be six weeks of hell, and then we'll have four years to run a country."

The president believed that the health care plan went down in part because the opponents had money to advertise it and we didn't. That hung over him leading to '96, and he was persuaded that he needed lots of money for early advertising. That set in motion a whole series of things. They were the same things other presidents had done, but they were a little much for me.

Terry McAuliffe: He had I don't know how many, eight hundred, guests in the White House during the first term. Six hundred were people he'd known forever. Understand, the president didn't have Kennebunkport. He didn't have Crawford.* He didn't have a home to entertain in. And when he invited these personal guests, he paid for it out of his pocket. If I'm up there and I have a Diet Coke, he pays for that, the president personally. This was a way for him to bring in old friends.

Paul Begala: Nobody passed a hat at the White House, but you had your donors in. His predecessor did it, his successor did it. Doesn't make it right. What he would say is, "My opponents tried to use it to investigate me up the wazoo, but nothing came of it because I didn't break any laws. What they didn't like was, I beat them at their own game."

*The homes used for vacations by the first and second President Bush, respectively. Bill and Hillary had owned homes in Fayetteville and Little Rock but sold the last of them shortly after Bill reoccupied the governor's mansion in 1983. They did not become homeowners again until 1999, when they bought their Dutch colonial in Chappaqua, New York.

47

Nailed!
Linda and Lucianne

Meanwhile . . .

"We talk every night."

Lucianne Goldberg: Tony Snow,* who had been a longtime friend of mine in Washington, called me and said—this must have been in, oh gosh, '96— "There's this great gal who worked for me when I was a speechwriter at the White House."

Lucianne Goldberg is a New York literary agent specializing in conservative themes.

She spent the Bush years there and now she's at the Clinton White House, and she is very upset about what she's seeing—the differences between the Bush White House and the Clinton White House. She wants to write a book about it.

I said, "Have her get in touch with me." So she did.

Goldberg paired the woman, Linda Tripp, with a conservative columnist to work on a book proposal. The outline the two came up with didn't interest Goldberg, but some months later Tripp reached out to Goldberg again.

I said, "Okay, I'm listening. What have you got that's different from what you sent me?"

"He's having an affair with a twenty-three-year-old girl on the White House staff."

"How do you know something like this?"

"She's befriended me. We talk every night."

---

*A conservative columnist and former speechwriter for the elder President Bush who would later serve as White House press secretary for the younger.

I was shocked. We'd all heard rumors that he fooled around, but I didn't think it would be this close to the home fires.

I said, "If you want to write this, I have to have proof. I can't go on your word that this is happening. Have you got any physical evidence?"

"No. I just have these long phone calls with her."

"Go to Radio Shack, get yourself a cheap tape recorder. Plug it in your phone and when she calls you, tape it."

So that's what she did. She went and bought a tape recorder and she started taping the calls.

I told my husband as soon as I hung up, "If we ever wanted to get Clinton, this is the way to do it. We're not going to do it with deals or schemes or foreign policy or the economy or Whitewater or some old, stupid crime when he was governor. This is the one thing everyone can relate to. From the truck driver and the maintenance worker in the park to the Supreme Court—they all get it. All you have to do is prove it."

It was politically fail-safe. A lot of people had come to me with anti-Clinton stuff—crazy murder stuff and that he killed Vince Foster. None of that stuff, to me, was ever going to harm him in any way. But with a story like this, bingo, you have everybody's attention.

"He was a four-flusher, a con man."

A premier practitioner of Clinton hatred, Goldberg addressed the phenomenon.

Lucianne Goldberg: Couldn't stand the man. Can't to this day.

It wasn't his politics. I save a special place in hell for true liberals, but I don't think he was one. He was DLC, very much not a liberal. It was that I thought he cheapened the office.

I thought the Clintons were thoroughly unpleasant people. I come from the South and I know that guy. He was every sleazeball I ever went to high school with. He was the guy who would lean out of the car and bang on the side of the door when you walk by on the street. He was the not-so-cool seducer all women had known. I just didn't like him. It was a visceral thing. You talk to any Clinton hater and they're vague about it.

He didn't play by the rules. He was a four-flusher, a con man. He didn't deserve to be there. He lied his way there, and he lied when he got in there.

I'm such a Reaganite, and Reagan to me was so elegant that it was just a visceral offense that this man was in that office.

He was sleazy, and this proved it. This encapsulated it. That's what excited me so much about it, that it spoke to that sleaziness in a way that nothing else he did could.

When this came to me I thought, "Good. Here's a way to let people know for sure what kind of person he is."

48

Pants on Fire:
The Jones Deposition

"This is extremely serious for the president."

On May 8, 1991, Paula Corbin—she would later marry Steve Jones—and a coworker were staffing the registration table at a conference put on at Little Rock's Excelsior Hotel by their employer, the Arkansas Industrial Development Corporation. According to Paula Jones, a state trooper approached her to say that the governor wanted to meet her in his room. The officer accompanied the twenty-four-year-old woman upstairs, leaving her alone in the room with Bill. There, Jones would claim, Bill clumsily tried to seduce her—"I love the way your hair goes down your body"—then exposed himself, asking her to "kiss it." Horrified, she responded, "I'm not that type of girl," and left the room.[1] Bill would deny that any such thing took place.

On December 20, 1993, an issue of *American Spectator* magazine hit the newsstands with a cover story that relayed a truckload of Saturnalian tales about life in the Arkansas governor's mansion while the nation's new president was the state's chief executive.[2] Later, responsible journalists would note fatal flaws in the article: gross factual errors, the financial motivations of the Arkansas state troopers telling the stories. But for the time being, the mainstream media dutifully passed on the scurrilous charges in the scandal it dubbed "Troopergate."

Among the lurid accounts was tucked one easy to miss: A woman identified only as "Paula" spent an hour with the governor in a hotel room during a reception in Little Rock. In February 1994, Paula Jones appeared at a Washington press conference organized by the Conservative Political Action Committee and told her tale of sexual harassment by Bill.[3] Four years later, her case would provide the occasion for lawyers to question Bill under oath about Monica Lewinsky.

Jones filed her sexual-harassment suit against Bill in May 1994. Beginning the following month, Bill's attorneys repeatedly sought to have the case put off until he left office, but no court would agree with their contention that entanglement in private civil litigation would "distract a President from his public duties, to the detriment of not only the President and his office but also the nation that the Presidency was designed to serve."[4]

The case went all the way to the Supreme Court, which heard arguments in January 1997. Joining Bill's private attorneys in seeking a delay was the government's advocate before the High Court.

Nina Totenberg: Clinton went to great lengths to make it appear that he was unconcerned with this case, while at the same time, the night before the argument, he was calling the solicitor general of the United States making suggestions for arguments. He was preoccupied with this.

On May 27, 1997, the High Court issued its ruling.

"It was a stunning decision—a slam-dunk for Paula Jones," Totenberg said at the time.[5]

Justice John Paul Stevens, writing for the unanimous court, made what may have been the most boneheaded prediction in the history of jurisprudence: If the Jones lawsuit were "properly managed by the District Court, it appears to us highly unlikely to occupy any substantial amount of petitioner's time."[6]

The ruling meant that the suit would go forward. It also meant that attorneys for Paula Jones, in accord with sexual-harassment law, would be permitted to ask all manner of questions about Bill's sex life in order to establish a "pattern of conduct."[7]

Nina Totenberg: The Jones case was very damaging to the president. I don't care what he says, he lied about his relationship with Monica Lewinsky. It may not, strictly speaking, have been perjury, because perjury involves intent to deceive and making a literally untrue statement. He was trying very carefully to avoid saying anything literally untrue.

He clearly knew what he was doing.

In mid-November 1997, Linda Tripp and Lucianne Goldberg decided they had enough information on tape to make their move against the president they despised. And so they got word of the Clinton-Lewinsky affair to the lawyers representing Jones.[8] On December 5, the Jones attorneys faxed to Robert Bennett, the lawyer defending Bill in the suit, their witness list, which included a long roster of women alleged to have had some sort of sexual interaction—consensual sex, harassment, rape—with the president. The next day, as Jeffrey Toobin has reported, Bennett and his team met with their client in the Oval Office to go over the list. When they came to Monica, Bennett told Bill that the Jones lawyers were asserting that she and Bill had had a sexual liaison. Bill responded, "Bob, do you think I'm fucking crazy? . . . The right has been dying for this kind of thing from day one. No, it didn't happen."[9]

At 2:30 A.M. on December 17, Bill called the woman he indeed *was* fucking crazy enough to have had a sexual liaison with. He notified her of her name's appearance on the list. Ken Starr's office would later charge that in this conversation Bill obstructed justice by advising Monica to file a false affidavit in the case. But Monica would repeatedly deny that Bill ever told her to lie, and her account of the phone call suggests that Bill was thinking of ways she might tell the truth but not the whole truth—the approach he would later take in his own testimony.[10]

When Monica did file her affidavit a few weeks later, however, she did lie, stating that she "never had a sexual relationship with the President."[11]

Meanwhile, through a network of anti-Clinton lawyers providing advice to the Jones legal team, Ken Starr's office got wind of Linda Tripp and Monica Lewinsky.[12] On January 12 lawyers from Starr's office interviewed Tripp. Three days later they met with the deputy attorney general, Eric Holder, to request jurisdiction over the Lewinsky matter.

Ken Starr's investigation had taken him from a land deal to the firings at the Travel Office to a variety of alleged financial irregularities on the part of the Clintons and their associates. But Bill's sex life?

The connection made by Starr's lawyers began with Webster Hubbell, already in trouble with the Office of Independent Counsel.

Solomon Wisenberg, an experienced prosecutor from Texas, served in the OIC under Ken Starr.

Solomon Wisenberg: Around the time Hubbell was working out his plea deal, he got over $700,000 in consulting fees. One of the people who arranged a consulting contract with him was Vernon Jordan; he'd arranged it with one of Ron Perelman's companies.

Linda Tripp told us that Vernon Jordan was helping Monica Lewinsky to get a job in order to shut her up, and that Vernon Jordan has told her it's okay to lie in the civil deposition.

Bill had asked Jordan to help Monica find a job in New York. Jordan's efforts did land her a position—with Revlon, a company owned by Perelman. There is no evidence that Jordan advised her to lie in the Jones case.[13]

The thinking was, That's a good enough hook.

At the request of the Justice Department, the three-judge Special Division that had appointed Starr gave its assent to the expansion of jurisdiction. The decision was made without Starr's office disclosing, to the Justice Department or to the three-judge panel, the indirect contacts it had had with the Jones lawyers—a connection that Justice officials later said would have resulted in the assignment of the matter to another prosecutor.[14]

Ken Starr was now officially investigating Bill's attempt—allegedly criminal—to keep his private affairs private.

Meanwhile, negotiations had nearly produced a settlement to the Jones case, with Bill offering his accuser $700,000. The deal broke down, however, when Jones's husband and her "adviser," the California media maven Susan Carpenter-McMillan, both avid Clinton haters, upped their side's demands: They insisted that in addition to the cash, Bill deliver a forthright apology for the wrong he had done Jones. Bill and his lawyers would not even entertain the idea. "If you want ten dollars and an apology," Bob Bennett told the Jones attorneys, "you're not going to get it."[15]

Bill would have to testify, under oath, about his sex life.

Their advice to settle rejected, the Jones legal team withdrew from the case.

James Fisher was among the new group of lawyers who took up Jones's case beginning in September 1997.

James Fisher: The important theme of the Paula Jones litigation was that Bill Clinton misused his power as the chief executive of the government of the State of Arkansas.

The witnesses to the primary incident with Paula Jones were already well identified and had been interviewed by several people. To the extent we were able to prove similar misconduct in other incidences, that would tend to support the proposition that Paula was telling the truth, that she hadn't just made up facts.

The Jones lawyers found current and former state troopers who claimed Bill had used them in the service of his sex life—to approach women, to make arrangements, to deceive Hillary. None of the information the Jones lawyers had found in Arkansas, however, would prove as consequential as the story given to them by a former White House employee.

We didn't speak to Linda Tripp before we put Monica Lewinsky's name on the witness list. Linda Tripp had told someone who told someone who told someone—through however many links it went in the communication chain, the rumor got to us that this was something worth investigating.

Linda talked to us the night before Bill Clinton's deposition. All of this is happening in about a one-week period. We realized then: This is extremely serious for the president.

"He became visibly shaken."

On Friday, January 16, 1998, prosecutors from Ken Starr's office confronted Monica Lewinsky at the Pentagon City Ritz Carlton Hotel, where they famously spent hours in a vain attempt to gain her cooperation in the investigation. During a break in the discussions, Monica went to a pay phone to try to warn Bill that their secret had been discovered—she called Betty Currie, Bill's secretary, who had helped conceal the affair, but got no answer.[16]

The following day, when Bill sat in the offices of a Washington law firm to be deposed for the Jones case, he did not know that the jig was up.

James Fisher questioned the witness.

James Fisher: You could have cut the air with a knife. He entered the room with a great flourish as we were all sitting there waiting. He's a very charismatic man with a lot of personal magnetism. It was unlike any deposition I've ever taken or any that I'll ever take again.

There were six lawyers sitting on the other side glaring at me, radiating hate waves. There were Secret Service people. I tried to focus on the questioning, but it was hard not to be distracted.

While sexual-harassment law allowed Fisher to go through Bill's sexual history with a fine-toothed comb, Fisher sought a way around asking questions that forthrightly described body parts and sexual activities.

I was trying, as we were trying throughout this process, to refute the notion that we were the ones pushing things off into the area of the salacious.

Fisher came up with a three-part definition of "sexual relations" for the purposes of the proceedings; Judge Susan Webber Wright kept only one part:

> . . . the person knowingly engages in or causes—
> Contact with the genitalia, anus, groin, breast, inner thigh, or buttocks
> of any person with an intent to arouse or gratify the sexual desire of any
> person.[17]

While the definition would trip Bill up, it would also give him his out. Later, he and his defenders would justify his denial of engaging in sexual relations with Monica by contending that the definition was one-sided—that it applied, as it were, to only the pitcher, not the catcher.

James Fisher: I don't think the language permits that construction, but that's the position the president took. The way he was interpreting that definition was not how that statute had ever been interpreted.

And besides, as Monica would tell Ken Starr's office, Bill did touch her genitalia and breasts.

Remember, his onus as a witness is to tell the truth, the whole truth, and nothing but the truth. She performed oral sex on him.

> Q. Did you have an extramarital sexual affair with Monica Lewinsky?
> A. No.
> Q. If she told someone that she had a sexual affair with you beginning in November of 1995, would that be a lie?
> A. It's certainly not the truth. It would not be the truth.
> Q. . . . And so the record is completely clear, have you ever had sexual relations with Monica Lewinsky, as that term is defined in Deposition Exhibit 1, as modified by the Court. . . .
> A. I have never had sexual relations with Monica Lewinsky. I've never had an affair with her.

If you look at the definition and the wording of my questions, there's absolutely no doubt he was telling a lie.

Nina Totenberg: Since when is oral sex not sex? You have to be eighteen to think that. Maybe that's Bill Clinton's problem. Maybe, when it comes to sex, he has the mentality of an eighteen-year-old.

James Fisher: He also flat out lied about whether he was ever alone with her,

> Q. At any time have you and Monica Lewinsky ever been alone together in any room in the White House?
> A. . . . I have no specific recollection, but it seems to me that she was on duty on a couple of occasions working for the legislative affairs office and brought me some things to sign, something on the weekend. That's—I have a general memory of that.

and about whether he had gotten gifts from her that he remembered.

> Q. Has Monica Lewinsky ever given you any gifts?
> A. Once or twice. I think she's given me a book or two.
> Q. Did she give you a silver cigar box?
> A. No.

Fisher also questioned Bill about gifts he'd given to Monica.

> Q. Well, have you ever given any gifts to Monica Lewinsky?
> A. I don't recall. Do you know what they were?
> Q. A hat pin?
> A. I don't, I don't remember. But I certainly, I could have. . . .
> Q. Do you remember giving her a gold brooch?
> A. No.[18]

David Terrell: Bill Clinton never forgets anything. The way to know he's lying is when he says, "I don't remember."

James Fisher: It was when I asked Bill Clinton about those gifts that the blood drained out of his face and he realized he was doomed. He became visibly shaken at that point.

Monica would eventually tell Ken Starr that she gave Bill some thirty gifts, while Bill gave her about eighteen.[19]

Nina Totenberg: He clearly lied in the deposition in the Paula Jones case.

And he could've gotten out of it. All he had to do when asked about Lewinsky was say, "I need to talk to my lawyer," and then tell his lawyer that the other side had something. His lawyer would have gotten him out of there, and he would have settled the case.

He wasn't prepared to face his wife, so instead, he lied in the civil proceeding, and he didn't tell the truth to his lawyer.

The case could have been settled right there.

49

The Bombshell Wears a Beret:
Enter Monica

"This is a real story."

In the early morning hours (Washington time) of Sunday, January 18, less than a day after Bill had given his deposition, Matt Drudge published what he had been told by a lawyer connected to the Jones case.[1]

Mike McCurry: The Drudge Report hinted over the weekend that *Newsweek* had killed some story on some sexual liaison that Clinton had had.

Newsweek's Michael Isikoff, who had been in contact with Lucianne Goldberg and Linda Tripp, as well as with the OIC, wanted his magazine to publish his findings on Monica in the issue about to go to press, but his editors decided against it. Drudge's initial post focused on the *Newsweek* angle: "NEWSWEEK KILLS STORY ON WHITE HOUSE INTERN." Drudge did not, in this item, mention the name of the "young intern" who was "sexually involved with the love of her life, the President of the United States." But he did in subsequent posts over the three-day Martin Luther King holiday weekend.[2]

Everyone's initial reaction was, "This is bizarre beyond words. This is such an overreach by the scandalmongers that we'll finally get some relief. Maybe we can use it to humiliate the scandal crowd and put them in their place."

There had been this long exhausting year of 1997, with all the campaign-finance stories. And then discovering that we had all these confidential personnel records from the FBI.* Every time you turned around, the collective umbrella of Whitewater had expanded off in a different direction. Now, here's one that's so ridiculous people will say, "Come on. Let's stop this nonsense."

Because this one is so utterly absurd.

In its Wednesday, January 21, issue, the *Washington Post* became the first mainstream newspaper to report the story.

Obviously, then it became a whole different thing. That's when I finally had my sinking feeling. The night the story was breaking, Tuesday, someone told me that the *Post* is going with a story about Clinton having a relationship that is going to get him in trouble in the Paula Jones case. I got Peter Baker of the *Post* on the line, and he said, "It's our understanding that there's been an expansion of the role of the independent counsel to investigate a matter involving Clinton and an intern named Monica Lewinsky."

I said, "That Monica? That can't be right."

We knew who she was because she used to flirt excessively with Stephanopoulos. She would hang around George's office all the time, asking if she could go to Starbucks for him.

Whenever the general subject of his sex life had come up, the conclusion was, "There's no way he could be fooling around, because he's got Secret Service guys here all the time. Even if he wanted to, there's no way he could pull anything off." Even if Clinton has got a history, he likes to fool around, he gets palsy-walsy with people, no one imagined, "This guy might be doing something that could be very damaging."

The sinking feeling was, this is a real story, not a stupid story. Baker said,

---

*In 1996 a congressional investigation of Travelgate discovered that several hundred FBI personnel files, of past and present executive-branch employees, had been in the improper possession of the White House Office of Personnel Security. While Bill's opponents made much of "Filegate," the material had come to OPS because of nothing more nefarious than a bureaucratic snafu—and one that neither Bill nor Hillary had anything to do with.

"Mike, this sounds like a serious deal. This is not some gossipy thing we're putting in the Style Section."

Craig Smith: I saw the report and I was going, "What?"

Paul Begala: Vertigo. It was dizzying and awful.

Mike McCurry: Clinton had three scheduled interviews, because we were preparing for the State of the Union address. We always would do a series of interviews to tee up the State of the Union. Obviously, in every case, he got asked about this story. And the language of his denial, in the interview with Jim Lehrer, was in the present tense. He said, "There *is* no sexual relationship." I didn't pick up on it at the time, but when the thing got transcribed, all the press came and said, "Why is he using the present tense?"

Bill, interviewed by Jim Lehrer of PBS's *News Hour,* January 21, 1998:

> Mr. Lehrer. Mr. President, welcome.
> The President. Thank you, Jim.
> Mr. Lehrer. The news of this day is that Kenneth Starr, the independent counsel, is investigating allegations that you suborned perjury by encouraging a 24-year-old woman, former White House intern, to lie under oath in a civil deposition about her having had an affair with you. Mr. President, is that true?
> The President. That is not true. That is not true. I did not ask anyone to tell anything other than the truth. There is no improper relationship. And I intend to cooperate with this inquiry. But that is not true.
> Mr. Lehrer. "No improper relationship"—define what you mean by that.
> The President. Well, I think you know what it means. It means that there is not a sexual relationship, an improper sexual relationship, or any other kind of improper relationship.
> Mr. Lehrer. You had no sexual relationship with this young woman?
> The President. There is not a sexual relationship—that is accurate.[3]

Sam Donaldson: On the first day that it broke I realized he was lying. Not because I'm so smart, or because anyone told me, but Jim Lehrer properly asked him a question about the charge of a sexual liaison with a White House intern. The answer we were listening for was one word: "No." I didn't hear it.

Did you rob a bank this morning? What's your answer?

When I hear a bunch of words to a direct question that can be answered, "Yes," "No," "No comment," "Up yours," but with a direct answer—I've dealt with politicians in this town for forty-five years—I know there's a big problem. So I suspected immediately, as did most of the other reporters in the press room, that it probably was true. It was a terrible time after that, because the White House went to ground, the wagons were circled.

"We just kept painting."

Harris Wofford headed the Corporation for National and Community Service, which encompasses AmeriCorps and other volunteer programs, 1995–2001.

Harris Wofford: I was with Clinton just as the Monica matter broke publicly. It was the Martin Luther King federal holiday. Every year, Clinton did some service.

We were at a high school in Washington. Clinton and I, with two Ameri-Corps members and the teacher and about six students, were painting the walls. Work was going on in classrooms all over the school.

We were told that at some point the press is going to come in and they've been strictly instructed, "No questions, just a photo op." We should continue painting and not be diverted by them.

So the moment comes, and thirty people crowd into one end of the classroom. The photos were going click, click, click, click, click, as we're painting. And Sam Donaldson shouts, "Mr. President, did you have sex with Monica Lewinsky?" We just kept painting. "I guess you didn't hear me. Mr. President, did you have sex with Monica Lewinsky?" Clinton said, "This isn't the time to talk about that. We're doing something else today, Sam."

He went back to painting, and the press finally left. As they were going out, this high school senior said, "Do they really talk to the president of the United States like that?"

Mike McCurry: Our collective wisdom was: There needs to be a stronger denial.

His movie friend, Harry Thomason, was staying at the White House. He's the one who coached and rehearsed Clinton on "I did not have sexual relations with that woman, Miss Lewinsky." It was the best possible evidence of how in-the-dark we were that we wanted him to go out there and make a forceful denial of this whole thing so that we could all put the matter to rest.

Sam Donaldson: He came to the Roosevelt Room for an occasion of some other purpose, at the end of which he made his famous finger-wagging declaration that he'd not had any sexual association with that woman, Miss

Lewinsky. He said later that he'd forgotten her first name. Oh, come on, really? I don't think so.

Bill was there on the twenty-sixth, the day before he was scheduled to deliver his State of the Union address, to talk about a new after-school child care initiative. At the end of his remarks on the policy, he tacked on a few sentences:

> Now, I have to go back to work on my State of the Union speech. And I worked on it until pretty late last night. But I want to say one thing to the American people. I want you to listen to me. I'm going to say this again. I did not have sexual relations with that woman, Miss Lewinsky. I never told anybody to lie, not a single time—never. These allegations are false. And I need to go back to work for the American people.
> Thank you.[4]

Paul Begala: The denial was so vigorous. I thought, "Well, okay." I believed the denial.

Ron Fournier: I walked out of that event shaking, because I knew he wasn't telling the truth. I was as convinced as I possibly could be.

Nina Totenberg: I guess I sort of believed him initially, because I thought he wouldn't be that categorical. I thought it was a dangerous thing to go out on a limb like that if it wasn't true. I confess, I thought the whole hunt for the dress was insane. I thought it was a crazy idea to think that somebody would keep a dress with the president's semen on it. I was wrong.

It was surreal, but his detractors were right about Monica, down to the nth degree. I certainly don't think he harassed her or anything like that. I think that she was fixated on him, and Bill Clinton loves to be loved. It may be excessive to say that she stalked him, but she was certainly in hot pursuit, and he didn't throw her out.

He was incapable.

"People completely misread Clinton."

If Bill had to "go back to work for the American people," so did his White House staff. Bill took steps to insulate his aides from the legal issues, but that separation from the subject dominating the news and their thoughts made work difficult.

Mike McCurry: The lawyers were the ones dealing with Clinton on it because we weren't supposed to. We had no sense of cohesion and coherence as a staff because we didn't know what to make of it. I remember a lot of conversations with my colleagues, asking, "Do you think this is true?" We all kind of said, "Who knows?" Very few of us believed that there was anything as gruesome as what was later reported in the Starr Report.

It was awkward around Clinton in the early days of this thing, knowing that this is the elephant in the room, but you're sitting there trying to have a conversation about, "You're meeting with the prime minister of Hungary and here's what the issues are." You're trying to conduct business as usual.

It was a really peculiar thing. I'd sit in the senior staff meeting and everyone would report on what they were going to do that day: The governors are coming in for this, the task force on that is meeting. When it came around to me I'd say, "Same old, same old. You know what I'm doing." I was out there getting pummeled on Monica every day.

The feeding frenzy. You saw this excitement over a huge breaking story, because in the first couple of days there was a sense that Clinton was going down.

Paul Begala: People completely misread Clinton on that. They all thought he was going to resign. Everybody in Washington—the Democrats, the Republicans, the media, everybody.

Craig Smith: I knew it would never lead to a quick resignation. That's not Bill Clinton's way.

Paul Begala: By the next Sunday, Sam Donaldson was speculating as to who would be in the Gore cabinet, who would be Gore's vice president. That was crazy.

Sam Donaldson: I said, "If the evidence demonstrates that he's not telling the truth, he'll resign, and it could be within a week," or words to that effect.
Of course, I was wrong.

The people at the other end of Pennsylvania Avenue were also reacting to the news.

Bob Kerrey: Oh, my God, an intern. He's toast.

Doug Sosnik: I had conversations with the president in which I told him that at the end of the day he was most vulnerable not from the Republicans but from the Democrats. The Republicans couldn't remove him from office; the Democrats could.

Paul Begala: The first seventy-two hours, the Democrats in Congress were ready for him to go.
What changed it for them was the polling.

Although internal White House polling showed a quick drop of 15 percentage points in Bill's popularity, a public poll taken days after the story broke found, to the contrary, that America's appraisal of his job performance had not significantly altered: A healthy 56 percent approved, statistically unchanged from a month before. The nation's view of Bill's character, however, did take a hit, with only 40 percent saying he shared their values, down from 55 just before he won reelection.[5] The public had known about Bill's reputation in 1992 but elected him anyway. In 1998, and through the remainder of his term, Americans would see a rogue and a scoundrel—who was good at his job. "This isn't about me, it's about you," Bill had said in 1992. The public had agreed with him then, it agreed with him now.

Paul Begala: The public saved Clinton. I think from the beginning they thought the allegation was true. But they also saw it was ginned up by his political adversaries to drive him out of office. I'm not one who believes that Clinton needed months of lying to prepare the public for the shocking news that he had cheated on his wife.

Joe Lockhart: It was wild and it was crazy, but it was very clear what we had to do, which was set aside whether any of the attacks were right or wrong, take out all the judgments. We were trying to survive.

I don't know the answer to this, but it's not an unreasonable theory that if he had stood up there that day and said, "Here's what happened. Let me try to put it into some perspective. Let me tell you how sorry I am," he would not have lasted as president.

Sam Donaldson: Bill Clinton is a man-child in one body. The man side of him is so impressive: the best natural politician I've ever seen; the president who knew more detail about more issues that come to the presidency than anyone I've ever seen. You go down the whole list; so impressive. Then you go to the child side of him, and you want to gently shake him by the neck and say, "Get out of the sandbox. You can't play with interns any more. You can't not keep to a schedule. You can't make 2 A.M. phone calls to anyone in the world just because you have insomnia."

It's all the same person.

"But then he gave the State of the Union."

On the evening of January 27, Bill went before a joint session of Congress to deliver his annual State of the Union address.

Joe Lockhart: He went up there against all odds and said, "You know what? This doesn't matter. I'm the president. This is what we're gonna do and if you think coming after me is more important than saving Social Security and providing health care and education, I'll have that fight with you every day."

Michael Sheehan: He welcomed working on the speech, because it was a chance not to think about all the other stuff. It was almost, in a weird way, a refuge.

With the federal budget finally coming into balance—years earlier than anyone had anticipated—the most celebrated line in the speech dealt with the disposition of the coming trillion-dollar surplus:* "Save Social Security first."[6]

Peter King: During those first few days, I don't think you could even find one Democrat who said a good word about him, but then he gave the State of the Union.

I called the White House switchboard to let Clinton know that I was going to stick with him. (I mean, it was in the first ten days. I didn't know it was going to go on all year.) He got back to me from Camp David. He told me it was untrue: "This is a bad rap. They're out to get me." He seemed in a fighting mood.

From then on, I thought he was going to make it through. The public never supported impeachment.

The whole thing was a high-wire act, looking back on it. Once he survived the initial onslaught and was able to get up and deliver the State of the Union—I mean, with all of that going on. I don't know how the guy does it.

50

Scandal? What Scandal?
Compartmentalization

Once the initial revelations had sunk in, and once the State of the Union was done, once it became clear that neither the scandal nor Bill was going away, the White House and the president needed a modus operandi to carry on doing the people's business.

*That number would nearly quintuple by the time Bill left office.

Paul Begala: Podesta,* took charge right away. He said, "We're going to have this team of lawyers and a couple political people. They will handle this. Everybody else, swim in your lane. Don't ask, don't get involved."

We settled on a formulation, which was for him to say to the public, "I have a job to do. I'm going to focus on that job"—and then, in fact, do that job.

A few of us—me, Rahm Emanuel,† Doug Sosnik, Podesta—were in both worlds.

I would be there with him and the lawyers, and we would hash out the latest leak or allegation. It was so painful, personal, awful. Your mind would be reeling and your heart would be sick. And then—I mean, one minute later—Bob Rubin and the economics team would come in. And it would be as if the other never happened. I'm still in the last meeting. I'm still trying to grapple with what's going on in that world. But Clinton had this remarkable capacity to shift. When he said, "I'm focusing on my job," that's when he really told the truth. He was distracted when we were dealing with the scandal—terribly—but then he was able to shut it off, move on to the next thing. It was amazing.

The job, I think, was therapeutic for him, because he was able to forget his other worries. These policy sessions consumed most of his time.

Chris Jennings: What I thought was phenomenal was how he could compartmentalize and focus: "Okay, we have this priority. If we lose focus, so will the public, the Congress, and the press. Don't get distracted." We did event after event after event, and I was around him all the time. I never ceased to be amazed by his laser-beam attention to the issue at hand. I could not comprehend how he could do it, but he did it.

I'm sure there were times that his anger and frustration, particularly with himself, got him down. I mean, he's human. But he's not human relative to the rest of us on this.

And it wasn't just my issues. It was everyone's issues. Everyone always said, "How does the guy do this?"

Charlene Barshefsky: His directive to all of us was: "The American people hired us all to do a job. Do your job."

But you could see the toll it was taking on him, and the result was, you bothered him less. He comported himself, as did the first lady, in the most graceful way one possibly could under those circumstances.

But he seemed older to me. More ragged. Somewhat preoccupied.

*John Podesta, then White House chief of staff.
†Then a senior adviser to Bill.

Lawrence Summers: Ninety-five percent of the time you would not have known that anything else was going on.

It seemed extremely impressive to me, but people do what they have to do. There really wasn't a whole lot of alternative for him but to keep moving. And that's what he did.

51

The Puritan and the Pol:
Starr versus Clinton

"Clinton outfought him, no question about that."

If the pursuit of policy resided in one White House compartment, in another dwelled the pursuit of political survival.

Sam Donaldson: The White House employed four tactics, which proved successful: They lied, they stonewalled, they delayed, and they attacked. They attacked the independent counsel, they attacked the press, they attacked the vast right-wing conspiracy.

It was a grim time at the White House.

Fred Barnes: They politicized it and made it a partisan issue. It was a shrewd strategy and it worked. When you see the votes on impeachment in the House and conviction in the Senate, they were overwhelmingly party-line votes.

Sam Donaldson: Ken Starr didn't pay much attention to the very important maneuvering for public opinion. The president not only paid attention, but he and his people knew exactly how to do it.

Ken Starr, April 2, 1998:

We don't deal in politics. We work in the realm of facts and law, and not public relations.[1]

Fred Barnes: Clinton outfought him, no question about that.

Starr's moralistic tone, his doughy, unexpressive face, his flat, nasal voice, his self-righteous comments doled out mornings at his Virginia curbside as he took out the garbage—put together, it meant that the opposition to Bill was personified in a man whom the public simply didn't like, much as it had not liked Newt Gingrich during the government shutdown of 1995–1996. As relentlessly as the two men tormented Bill, he was in a way fortunate to have them as his prime antagonists.

On April 1, two and a half months after Bill's deposition in *Jones v. Clinton*, Judge Susan Webber Wright dismissed the lawsuit. Writing that while Bill's "alleged conduct, if true, may certainly be characterized as boorish and offensive," she found in the evidence no "basis for a claim of criminal sexual assault." As to Monica:

> Whether other women may have been subjected to workplace harass-
> ment, and whether such evidence has allegedly been suppressed, does
> not change the fact that plaintiff has failed to demonstrate that she has a
> case worthy of submitting to a jury.[2]

In other words, Bill's tryst with the intern was legally without relevance to a case that was legally without merit. But Starr, speaking to reporters outside his home, said that Wright's finding would not affect his investigation:

> Our facts are very different. Our scope is very different. . . . It doesn't
> matter who wins and who loses in the civil case. What matters from the
> criminal law's perspective is, were crimes committed?[3]

Joe Lockhart: There's nothing the president did that came anywhere near providing grounds to remove him from office, not even close. Having said that, a smarter, more savvy prosecutor bent on removing the president probably could have done it.

But Starr overplayed his hand. It became clear that his only focus was bringing down the president, and he just wasn't very good at it. He did not go about it methodically and politically. He went about it morally and he tripped himself up because the country wasn't in the same moral place as he was. The country didn't believe that the president should be removed from office because he violated his marriage vows.

In September 1998 the attorney Gregory Craig, a friend of Bill and Hillary's from law school, would leave a post in the State Department to coordinate White House legal strategy on impeachment.

Gregory Craig: He kept saying, "I have a duty to investigate, I have a duty to pursue. I have a duty. I have a duty."

In that same session in front of his home Starr recalled an old TV show:

> You are all too young to remember a wonderful program called Dragnet.
> Just the facts, ma'am, Jack Webb would say. And that's something that I
> always remember, "just the facts."[4]

Gregory Craig: It's like he had no discretion as to where the investigation should go and how it should be conducted. To him it was all black and white: He had a duty and he did it. It showed inexperience and zealotry, a bad combination.

Although Bill mostly held his tongue in public, letting others carry the fight to Starr, in private he was furious.

Terry McAuliffe: He was madder than hell at these guys and what they were doing to him. Listen, they were going after his reputation, they were trying to put him in jail.

And then they sent hundreds of these agents down to Arkansas and harassed people. Totally innocent people had to get lawyers and were bankrupted. It really ate at the president and Hillary to see their friends subjected to that. He would tell me stories of how the FBI had gone to their house or shown up at their office and embarrassed them and threatened them. It just killed him.

"Bill Clinton does weird things to people."

Michael Emmick: Ken Starr is one of the nicest guys you would ever want to meet.

The veteran prosecutor Michael Emmick worked on Starr's team.

He is interested in fairness as a matter of procedure. I never saw a hint of his religiousness having any role in any of our decision making.

There was a civil case, the Paula Jones case. There were serious allegations of obstruction and perjury. There was plausible evidence supporting those allegations, and we were charged with the obligation to investigate those allegations.

Nina Totenberg: I understand the idea that lying about sex under oath is still lying, but this is one of the things that seasoned prosecutors learn: Sex is something people cannot *not* lie about. We don't normally prosecute people for lying about sex. What we do is, we penalize them in civil suits. The Jones case was a civil suit. It's not unheard of for a judge to say, "You lied. That's it. You lose." Usually it doesn't get referred to a prosecutor at all.

There was a Cotton Mather* feeling about Ken Starr at that time, which I

---

*Puritan minister connected to the Salem witch trials of 1692, during which he stated that "an Army of Devils is horribly broke in upon the place which is our center." No Clinton hater ever put it better.

had never detected before about him and I have not detected since, and I have no explanation for it.

Bill Clinton does weird things to people. This is a guy who drives people wild —in part because he's so successful, and his opponents think he's a phony. But that's very hard to prove to the American public, because people like him.

That's galling to people who think he's a duplicitous son of a bitch.

52

Respite:
A Tour of Africa

As previous presidents have done when embattled at home, Bill turned his attention overseas—in fact, all over the globe: toward Africa, Northern Ireland, the Balkans, the Middle East. Paralyzed in domestic policy, in foreign policy Bill chalked up important achievements—and one grand failure.

He began with a continent usually neglected by American presidents.

"He put on kente cloth."

On March 22, seventeen days after Vernon Jordan completed a second day of testimony in front of Ken Starr's grand jury, nine days after the transcript of Bill's Jones deposition was made public, seven days after Kathleen Willey told *60 Minutes* that Bill had tried to force himself on her in the Oval Office in 1993, Bill left Washington to begin a six-country, twelve-day tour of Africa.[1] The first stop was Accra, the capital of Ghana.

Joe Lockhart: We fly all night; then there's about a twenty-mile trip into Independence Square—on both sides of the road it's ten people deep.

Sharon Farmer: There were huge crowds everywhere.

Joe Lockhart: It's like 110 degrees. We get there and it's the most people I've ever seen anyplace. We hear stories: People have walked for two days to get there because they live a hundred miles away.

Ghanaian officials estimated that the crowd at Independence Square numbered more than half a million.[2]

Sharon Farmer: Dust, dirt, hot as hell, but the enthusiasm—the cheers, the roar. It was a tremendous sound. And he put on kente cloth. That's the first time I ever saw a white guy do that.

Bill, March 23, 1998, Accra, Ghana:

> *Mitsea mu. America fuo kyia mo* [My greetings to you. Greetings from America]. Now you have shown me what *akwaaba* [welcome] really means. Thank you, thank you so much.[3]

Joe Lockhart: It was a great event, but it set off a series of great events.

It was one amazing appearance after another, where you realized the power of the U.S. president. Six or seven million people came out those twelve days to see him. From that point in his life, he will always be someone who cares about Africa. He's there three times a year now.

No American president had ever thought Africa was important enough to go there and spend ten days. But this was a president who was saying, as leader of the lone remaining superpower, "Africa is so important that I'm going to take twelve days of my presidency and devote it solely to this issue." Part of it also was just the magnetism of Clinton, this great leader who's respected around the world.

Princeton Lyman: He apologized in Rwanda.

Bill, Kigali, Rwanda, March 25, 1998:

> The international community, together with nations in Africa, must bear its share of responsibility for this tragedy. . . . We did not act quickly enough after the killing began.[4]

Princeton Lyman: Americans don't apologize very often. It didn't overcome all the animosity over Rwanda, but it did make an impact.

In Senegal, he had the sea behind him and he basically apologized for slavery, which no American's ever done.

Bill, Goree Island, Senegal, April 2, 1998:

> In 1776, when our Nation was founded on the promise of freedom as God's right to all human beings, a new building was dedicated here on Goree Island to the selling of human beings in bondage to America. Goree Island is, therefore, as much a part of our history as a part of Africa's history.[5]

There's a respect that comes from Clinton. A lot of our dealing with other countries and cultures is patronizing. We say, "Oh, yes, Your Excellency," and all the rest, but it's not real. With Clinton it's very real, and that comes across to the Africans.

Joe Lockhart: We spent as much time in little villages as we did at big public rallies. There is a natural connection he has with people, particularly children. Most politicians do these events because they're good photo ops. They *are* good photo ops, Clinton knows that, and they build support. But these places inform Clinton. They make AIDS real to him. They make malaria and dysentery real to him. They motivate him to do something. He is as engaged talking to a sick three-year-old as he is talking to Nelson Mandela.

I've been around a lot of politicians who'll get back in the car and say, "Okay. Can we go to the bar and get a drink now?" Clinton will get in the car and talk incessantly about the event he was just in. Sometimes you want to say to him, "I was there, sir. You don't have to recount the whole thing." But he's doing it because he's internalizing it.

We went to this community that had gotten a grant from USAID* to buy computers, but the computers were still in boxes. He said, "Why aren't they set up?"

They said, "The grant only covered this much, and we need more money."

That's all he talked about for three days, and guess what? That problem got solved, and it didn't just get solved in that community. Everybody at USAID heard the story of Clinton saying, "What are we doing? It's taunting them to give them half the solution." That's just not common among politicians.

"I feel your pain." A lot of politicians feel your pain. He takes it a step further. He tries to do something about it.

"Mandela went out of his way to praise him."

In the middle of the trip, Bill visited South Africa. The emotional high point of the stay was the tour of Robben Island he received from Nelson Mandela, who had been held there for eighteen of the twenty-seven years he'd been a political prisoner before his release in 1990 to negotiate an end to the apartheid regime. Mandela showed him the tiny cell where he'd slept and the quarry where he'd broken rocks.[6]

Princeton Lyman: He thought Nelson Mandela was one of the great heroes —as most people do. He had tremendous admiration for Mandela's ability to come out of prison and adjust to the modern world, and then to carry through this successful negotiation.

Nelson Mandela has this extraordinary dignity about him, combined with a kind of a humbleness. I think Bill Clinton understood that right away.

*United States Agency for International Development, the federal organization that administers nonmilitary foreign aid.

Joe Lockhart: Clinton was heavily influenced by Mandela, in that during all the trial and tribulation that culminated in Monica, Clinton was struggling for a reason to hold on, to say, "This is all worth it. I'm not going to succumb to my worst instincts and lash out at my enemies." And the thing that always went off in his head, and he would say this, is how generous Mandela's spirit was in forgiving all of his oppressors. I think he came to realize that the way to survive and even grow in these times was to take on that Mandela spirit.

Princeton Lyman: When Clinton was under so much criticism over the Monica Lewinsky thing in 1998, Mandela went out of his way to praise him on that trip to South Africa, to take his hand in public and walk up the stairs with him, and deflect all the questions from the reporters. It was a demonstration of how much mutual admiration had grown between them.

Lyman was asked whether Bill's relationship with Mandela seemed similar to that with Yitzhak Rabin.

These are strong figures, courageous people, taking great risks and doing so for the right reasons and the right causes. I think that's the kind of person Clinton saw himself as: Someone who came back against odds.

He always used to call himself "The Comeback Kid." Clinton is aware of his own magic.

53

Today's Word Is *Is*:
The Grand Jury

"Did I hear what I just thought I heard?"

Abbe Lowell: The president was cornered, put in a position where an average person would never be put. He had no option not to testify in the grand jury once Ken Starr wanted to make it a public event. And yet, testifying in front of the grand jury was a setup.

The attorney Abbe Lowell served as counsel to the Democratic minority on the House Judiciary Committee during the impeachment hearings.

Average people can take the Fifth Amendment. Public officials, let alone the president of the United States, cannot.

After months of delay, Ken Starr's office finally reached an immunity agreement to secure Monica's testimony—and get their hands on the blue dress and the semen that stained it—at the end of July.[1] In the Map Room on August 3, Bill rolled up his sleeve so that the White House physician, in the presence of an attorney from Starr's office, an agent of the FBI, and Bill's lead personal attorney, David Kendall, could extract a sample of presidential blood. DNA analysis quickly confirmed that the two fluids indeed came from the same body.[2]

With Starr's grand jury set to convene in the White House to hear his testimony on Monday, August 17, Bill could no longer deceive his wife. On the morning of Saturday, the fifteenth, according to accounts written by both Bill and Hillary, the cheating husband woke his unsuspecting wife to confess his sins. For the next couple of months, Bill would sleep on the couch.[3]

Solomon Wisenberg was one of three lawyers from Starr's office who questioned Bill on the seventeenth, in the same Map Room.

Solomon Wisenberg: I had nothing to do with negotiating the ground rules—right off the bat we were at a disadvantage. Number one, it's not in the grand jury room, it's at the White House. Number two, there's a four-hour time limit, which is perfect for somebody like him who can give a speech every time you ask a question.

I thought it was very important to be tough, to treat it like a cross-examination. I figured he was a hostile witness who was not going to tell the truth.

I do believe that he ended up perjuring himself at the grand jury. In fact, there's no question of it in my mind.

Nina Totenberg: He's trying not to commit perjury before the grand jury. That's where that stupid sentence comes from: "It depends what the meaning of the word *is* is." The sentence is hairsplitting to the point of ridiculousness.

Solomon Wisenberg: When he said that I thought, "Did I hear what I just thought I heard? Boy, he really fucked up." Because I thought basically he was doing very well.

It was in answer to a very important question.

At the Paula Jones deposition they were using this false affidavit of Monica Lewinsky to try and limit the questioning of President Clinton about Monica Lewinsky. His lawyer, Bob Bennett, gets up and says, "Your honor, they're asking these questions in bad faith, because I've got an affidavit here that says there is no sex." I was outraged by that: You're causing your lawyer—and Bennett doesn't know that the president's lying—to use an affidavit that you know is fraudulent to try to keep a question from being asked.

> Q: The statement of your attorney, Mr. Bennett, at Paula Jones's deposition ... "Counsel is fully aware that Ms. Lewinsky has filed, has an affidavit which they are in possession of saying that there is absolutely no sex of any kind in any manner, shape or form, with President Clinton." ...
>
> Whether or not Mr. Bennett knew of your relationship with Ms. Lewinsky, the statement that there was "no sex of any kind in any manner, shape or form, with President Clinton," was an utterly false statement. Is that correct?
>
> President Clinton: It depends on what the meaning of the word "is" is. If the—if he—if "is" means is and never has been that is not—that is one thing. If it means there is none, that was a completely true statement. . . .
>
> Q: I just want to make sure I understand, Mr. President. Do you mean today that because you were not engaging in sexual activity with Ms. Lewinsky during the deposition that the statement of Mr. Bennett might be literally true?
>
> President Clinton: No, sir. I mean that at the time of the deposition, it had been—that was well beyond any point of improper contact between me and Ms. Lewinsky. So that anyone generally speaking in the present tense, saying there is not an improper relationship, would be telling the truth if that person said there was not, in the present tense; the present tense encompassing many months. That's what I meant by that.

In addition to parsing verb tenses, the examiner and the witness dissected the definition of sexual relations used during the Jones testimony. Bill admitted that his encounters with Monica "did involve inappropriate intimate contact" but continued to maintain that they "did not constitute sexual relations as I understood that term to be defined at my January 17, 1998, deposition."

The dialogue turned surreal.

> Q: If a person touched another person, if you touched another person on the breast, would that be, in your view, and was it within your view, when you took the deposition, within the definition of sexual relations?
>
> President Clinton: If the person being deposed—
>
> Q: Yes.
>
> President Clinton:—in this case, me, directly touched the breast of another person, with the purpose to arouse or gratify, under that definition that would be included.
>
> Q: Only directly, sir, or would it be directly or through clothing?

President Clinton: Well, I would—I think the common sense definition would be directly. That's how I would infer what it means.

Q: If the person being deposed kissed the breast of another person, would that be in the definition of sexual relations as you understood it when you were under oath in the Jones case?

President Clinton: Yes, that would constitute contact. . . .

Q: And you testified that you didn't have sexual relations with Monica Lewinsky in the Jones deposition, under that definition, correct?

President Clinton: That's correct, sir.

And so forth and so on—and on and on and on.[4]

Solomon Wisenberg: It would have been much easier to say, "Look, did you touch her breasts or not?" But he had already said, "I'm gonna answer hypothetical questions only."

What he's saying is, "I said I didn't have sexual contact. I agree that if I touched her breasts, that would be sexual contact. And I didn't have sexual contact." He didn't want to say, "I touched"—"or didn't touch"—"her breasts." If he had said, "I didn't touch her breasts," he would have clearly been perjuring himself. Because he did touch her breasts. Monica has no reason to lie about that. Also, it makes no sense. Under his interpretation, he's sitting there getting a blow job and never touching her in any sexual area. He's patting her on the head or something.

Monica, August 26, 1998, describing in a deposition to the OIC her first sexual encounter with Bill:

. . . he touched my, my breasts with my bra on, and then either—I don't remember if I unhooked my bra or he lifted my bra up, but he—this is embarrassing.

Q: Then he touched your breasts with his hands?

A: Yes, he did.

Q: Did he touch your breasts with his mouth?

A: Yes, he did.

Q: Did he touch your genital area at all that day?

A. Yes . . . he put his hand down my pants and stimulated me manually in the genital area.

Q: And did he bring you to orgasm?

A. Yes, he did.[5]

Solomon Wisenberg: The key was, we had a right to ask this question because we were looking at whether or not he had committed perjury and obstruction of justice in a sexual-harassment lawsuit.

"The grand jury's tougher."

Solomon Wisenberg: I try to remind people that he's the only president in U.S. history to be found in contempt by a court.

In April 1999, two months after the impeachment ordeal ended with Bill's acquittal by the Senate, Judge Susan Webber Wright would issue a thirty-two-page ruling in which she held Bill in contempt of court for his testimony in the Jones deposition.[6]

The record demonstrates by clear and convincing evidence that the President responded to plaintiff's questions by giving false, misleading and evasive answers that were designed to obstruct the judicial process.

This false testimony, said the judge who was taught at Arkansas Law School by Professor Bill Clinton, "undermined the integrity of the judicial system."[7]

When Susan Webber Wright ultimately found him in contempt of court, she said he answered untruthfully in the deposition with an intent to obstruct the proceedings. It was based on two things: One, his statement that he didn't have sexual contact with her was laughable. Two, which people tend to forget, he repeatedly testifies at the Jones deposition that he was never alone with Monica Lewinsky. Clearly, when you have fellatio with somebody six to ten times, you're alone.

In Jones, it's clear. It's a perjury and obstruction. The grand jury's tougher because he knows what we know and he knows about the DNA test. So I would say that his perjury there was his repeating of his statement that he didn't have sexual contact with her, saying he had told the truth in the deposition.

Solomon Wisenberg: He was alternately brilliant, combative, dishonest, petulant, good at gobbling up time with set speech answers. There were many parts when the president appeared to be quite angry, flushed in the face. It wasn't like he was shouting or screaming—he kept his control—but he was obviously not happy with the questioning.

The president left the room abruptly when it was over. We were packing up our things, and then he comes back in with a big grin, like it's a church supper in Arkansas and he's running for county sheriff, and goes around shaking everybody's hand on the team, saying, "Y'all did a great job."

I was amazed by that.

54

Speech Defect:
An Unapologetic Apology

"He vented."

Nina Totenberg: He gave that speech in August where he finally had to admit everything, but he couldn't bring himself to apologize to the American public for lying to them. It was a very defensive speech, and it's not that he didn't have other drafts in front of him. He did.

Bill, August 17, 1998:

Good evening. This afternoon in this room, from this chair, I testified before the Office of Independent Counsel and the grand jury. I answered their questions truthfully, including questions about my private life, questions no American citizen would ever want to answer.

Still I must take complete responsibility for all my actions, both public and private. And that is why I am speaking to you tonight.

As you know, in a deposition in January I was asked questions about my relationship with Monica Lewinsky. While my answers were legally accurate, I did not volunteer information. Indeed, I did have a relationship with Ms. Lewinsky that was not appropriate. In fact, it was wrong. It constituted a critical lapse in judgment and a personal failure on my part for which I am solely and completely responsible.

But I told the grand jury today, and I say to you now, that at no time did I ask anyone to lie, to hide or destroy evidence, or to take any other unlawful action.

I know that my public comments and my silence about this matter gave a false impression. I misled people, including even my wife. I deeply regret that. I can only tell you I was motivated by many factors: first, by a desire to protect myself from the embarrassment of my own conduct. I was also very concerned about protecting my family. The fact that these questions were being asked in a politically inspired lawsuit which has since been dismissed was a consideration, too.

In addition, I had real and serious concerns about an Independent Counsel investigation that began with private business dealings 20 years ago, dealings, I might add, about which an independent Federal agency found no evidence of any wrongdoing by me or my wife over 2 years ago.* The Independent Counsel investigation moved on to my staff and friends, then into my private life. And now the investigation itself is under investigation.† This has gone on too long, cost too much, and hurt too many innocent people.

Now this matter is between me, the two people I love most, my wife and our daughter, and our God. I must put it right, and I am prepared to do whatever it takes to do so. Nothing is more important to me personally. But it is private. And I intend to reclaim my family life for my family. It's nobody's business but ours. Even Presidents have private lives.[1]

Sam Donaldson: Early that evening we knew he was going to address the nation—a draft of a speech was circulated, written by a couple of his strong supporters. It was a wonderful example of how to fall on the mercy of the court, beg forgiveness, go forward, and perhaps escape. If he had delivered that speech that night, he might have escaped impeachment on the floor of the House.

Michael Sheehan: He vented. And the message was designed for the people who agreed with him instead of everybody else. I think he got some bad advice.

Joe Lockhart: The speech was a disaster. He gave that speech in anger, and I'm telling you, that was when we all thought this could turn on us.

The public did not like that speech. We knew that, we had our own numbers. At this point, there's really only one game. You don't want to get impeached by the House—we're going to fight that, but you know what? We don't have control of it. What we do need to do is make sure the Democratic

---

*The San Francisco law firm Pillsbury, Madison and Sutro had undertaken an exhaustive investigation into Whitewater on behalf of the Resolution Trust Corporation, the federal agency set up to deal with the savings-and-loan crisis. The report, issued in December 1995, found "no basis to charge the Clintons" with misconduct in connection with Whitewater. The national press had paid the report cursory attention at best. Conason and Lyons, *Hunting*, 176–177, 199; "The RTC Investigation," CNN, http://www.cnn.com/ALLPOLITICS/1997/gen/resources/infocus/whitewater/rtc.html.

†Bill may have been referring to the supposedly confidential review of complaints against the OIC begun in the summer of 1998 by the Justice Department's Office of Professional Responsibility. Gormley, *Death of American Virtue*, 590–592.

caucus stays together in the Senate.* The Democratic caucus in the Senate hated that speech. They had gone from being ready to throw the president out earlier in the year to calming down and feeling better about it. They didn't feel so good for the next two weeks. We got reports of people saying, "This is untenable. We can't defend it." That eventually calmed down, but it was a moment of real peril.

"I apologize to all of you."

Joe Lockhart: He apologized about five times.

Bill, September 11, 1998, to religious leaders gathered at the White House National Prayer Breakfast:

> I have been on quite a journey these last few weeks to get to the end of this, to the rock bottom truth of where I am and where we all are. I agree with those who have said that in my first statement after I testified I was not contrite enough. I don't think there is a fancy way to say that I have sinned.

Bill went on to say that he had asked forgiveness of those he had hurt—his family, his friends, his staff, his cabinet, Monica and her family, and the American people. But to be forgiven, he needed to show both "genuine repentance" and

> a willingness to give the very forgiveness I seek; a renunciation of the pride and the anger which cloud judgment, lead people to excuse and compare and to blame and complain.[2]

Nina Totenberg: Yeah, well, a lot of people didn't believe that contrition. I think it was a little convenient, myself.

He apologized in private as well as in public.

Doug Sosnik: After people came back from Labor Day, after they had digested the Starr Report and everything else, the president went to different groups of people to apologize to them. He had a cabinet meeting. He had a

---

*Under the Constitution, a president is impeached by a simple majority in the House, which Republicans at the end of the 105th Congress controlled with 227 of 435 seats. The issue then goes to trial in the Senate, where removal from office requires a two-thirds vote. In the 105th Congress, in session at this time—and in the 106th, in session when the trial took place—Republicans held 55 of the Senate's 100 seats; to convict, therefore, they would need the votes of all their senators plus at least a dozen Democrats.

Democratic Senate leadership meeting, with Daschle bringing in about a dozen senators. The president spent a couple of hours in that meeting, explaining himself and the mistakes he made, apologizing and getting reactions. The same with the House.

The meeting with Democratic senators took place on September 10.

John Breaux: It was in the private quarters, upstairs. It was very, very personal. He talked about the fact that he'd let everybody down, including us. He was basically saying, "Look, I messed up on something that was very personal, and I apologize to all of you for that." It was a very powerful moment.

He held another meeting in the residence later that day.

Dan Glickman: I call it the highest-priced group-therapy session in the history of the United States of America. The president had all the cabinet and all the senior staff there.

We went around the room, and everybody told the president what they thought. The meeting lasted for hours. Some of the cabinet members, like Donna Shalala, were furious and told the president that. Others, particularly the Arkansas crowd, were "You're a good man, Mr. President. We all sin. You'll get through this." And then there were the rest of us, who didn't know what the hell to say. We just fumbled through it. I think I said that life is filled with bumps and the easiest thing to do is to admit your mistakes and move on, and most people will be forgiving. I think that's what I said, but frankly, I don't really remember. I just wanted to get out of there.

It was one time when I saw a lot of people not being obsequious to a president. The tendency when you're with the president is to hunker down and not say much. The women were very, very direct with him.

That meeting was instrumental as a safety valve so that nobody left the cabinet, even those who felt they had been deceived by him.

That was really amazing when you think about it. Nobody left.

55

Sine Qua Non: Ulster's Peacemaker

"God, is he always that way?"

Only a week after Bill returned from Africa, Catholics and Protestants in Northern Ireland, in talks chaired by George Mitchell, reached a historic accord. Promising "a fresh start" after the "tragedies of the past," the Good Friday Agreement, signed in Belfast on April 10, 1998, set out a schedule for disarming the militias and held both sides to a "total and absolute commitment to exclusively democratic and peaceful means of resolving differences on political issues."[1]

Peter King: How could he find the ability to focus and concentrate? The Saint Patrick's Speaker's Lunch in March of '98—that was a day or two after Kathleen Willey was on *60 Minutes,* and the Good Friday Agreement came just a few weeks after that. He went to Ireland in September of 1998—Belfast, Dublin, and Limerick City. That was just a few weeks after his testimony before the grand jury. While we were in Ireland, Joe Lieberman went on the Senate floor attacking him.*

My mother's family was there, and he met with all of them. You'd never know anything was up. Coming back on the plane I had fallen asleep; he came back and woke me up to update me on the private meetings he'd had with Trimble† and Adams, talking as if everything was fine. The following

---

*On September 3, Connecticut Democrat Joe Lieberman took the floor of the Senate to say that "something very sad and sordid has happened in American life when I cannot watch the news on television with my 10-year-old daughter anymore." "Excerpts from Senator Lieberman's Talk on President's Personal Conduct," *New York Times,* September 4, 1998. Philip Roth, in the prelude to his novel *The Human Stain,* refers to these words as he describes the revival during 1998 of "America's oldest communal passion, historically perhaps its most treacherous and subversive pleasure: the ecstasy of sanctimony." Philip Roth, *The Human Stain* (New York: Houghton Mifflin Harcourt, 2000), 2.

†David Trimble led the (Protestant) Ulster Unionist Party.

week we were at the White House. It had been planned, an Irish celebration. That was the day the Starr Report came out. He seemed a little shellshocked, but again, he went ahead with it and gave a great speech.

Somewhere in early December of 1998 there was a big dinner in downtown Washington. All of the leaders were in—Gerry Adams, John Hume, David Trimble. I was sitting in the audience, the president was there on the dais, and a White House staff person came down and said, "The president would like to see you after dinner." So, near the end I go out into a hallway behind the stage. It was like a 1930s movie, some crummy-looking hallway, and he was in a room. He'd been meeting with Gerry Adams—Hillary was there, too. Then they leave, and it's just me and the president.

He wanted to meet with me on impeachment, because the vote was coming up. We're talking about who I thought was with him and who he could talk to. He was perfectly focused and even humorous. He was imitating Robert Byrd, how this was the moment Byrd was looking forward to— being like a Roman senator with a toga.

Impeachment was about a week or ten days off.

King recalled a scene from Bill's 1998 trip to Ireland.

Peter King: We were in Dublin, and I was sitting at a table with the bishop of the Church of Ireland, which is Anglican; in my Catholic mindset he would have been the enemy, but he was a great guy.

This was the day Lieberman spoke against him. Clinton comes over to the table and asks the bishop if he's met me or not, and he says yes. And Clinton goes, "Now, this man is a sinner." He's going on and on about all of these sins I have to atone for. I'm thinking, "Joking is fine, but you'd think he'd be reluctant in that climate to be talking to a clergyman about somebody's personal sins."

When he walked away, the bishop said to me, "God, is he always that way?"

I said, "Yeah. That's the way he is."

"He was the glue and he was the inspiration."

Peter King: When Adams and Paisley sat down, that was the culmination of eight hundred years.

In March 2007 an iconic photograph came out of a historic encounter: Gerry Adams and Ian Paisley, the Protestant firebrand who led the Democratic Unionist Party, held their first face-to-face discussions. Although the two former enemies didn't shake hands, they did hold a joint press conference. They announced their agreement to set up a coalition administration of the North as a follow-up to elections in which Sinn Fein and the DUP had solidified their status as the province's two leading parties.[2]

Going back to when Bill Clinton gave Gerry Adams the visa in January of '94—the day before he gave that visa, if you said to someone that there was going to be peace in Ireland and the U.S. is going to be a factor in it, people would have said, "What are you, crazy? This has been going on forever."

There's a direct line. He gave Adams a visa in January of 1994. The IRA called a cease-fire in August of '94. Clinton had Adams to the White House in 1995. Then the British started meeting with Adams, and Clinton appointed Mitchell as the envoy. Clinton stayed involved after the IRA broke the cease-fire. Dealt with all the parties. Saint Patrick's Day, which had been just a ceremonial event here every year, became a key negotiating point. Everyone started coming here for that. David Trimble and Gerry Adams did not talk to each other in Ireland. They would come here, and they would sit down with Bill Clinton separately, and he would be an envoy back and forth between the two of them. It was amazing.

George Mitchell gets a lot of credit for the peacemaking, and he deserves it. But it was Bill Clinton who did it.

Bruce Morrison: Bill Clinton didn't do it alone. He didn't invent the idea, and people had to do this after he was gone, but the central organizing event would not have occurred without him. In fact, it was defined by him.

More than that, the shape of the process, the conceptual framework that was imposed from the outside on people who had a much narrower view of how to do this, came from him and from people working with him. Not to denigrate anybody else's contribution, but he was the glue and he was the inspiration.

And it teaches a lesson, if people will learn it, because it is about getting past the labels to the substance of how you actually get people who hate each other to live with each other, which is the world's pressing problem.

The lesson to draw is that the way you use power is by example and by persuasion. Not to say you don't have to defend yourself with military power under certain circumstances, but real change comes from persuading people that it's in their own interest to change. And the way you do that is to show them that you actually care about the change from their perspective, as well as your own.

That's a powerful tool. To make people feel like he's thinking about them, not just thinking about himself.

That's Bill Clinton's gift.

56

Softcore:
The Starr Report

On September 9, 1998, Ken Starr delivered his report on the Lewinsky matter, all 445 pages of it, to Congress. On the eleventh, at Newt Gingrich's command, the report was published on the Internet; on the twelfth it appeared, in whole or in part, in newspapers around the country.

The highlight (or lowlight) of the report—the material everyone turned to upon first seeing the document—was a comprehensive, dated account of the "sexual encounters" between the president of the United States and his young friend, details definitely included. Among the items the report contained were:

> During their encounter on New Year's Eve, 1995, Bill "stopped [Monica] before he ejaculated" because, Monica told investigators, "he didn't know me well enough or he didn't trust me yet."

> During their encounter on January 7, 1996, Bill, Monica said, "was talking about performing oral sex on me," but she declined the offer because she was menstruating at the time.

> On January 21, 1996, Monica asked Bill whether their relationship was "just about sex," or did he "have some interest in trying to get to know me as a person?" To which, according to Monica, Bill replied, laughing, that "he cherishes the time that he had with me."

And the topper:

> On March 31, 1996, while Hillary was in Ireland, Bill telephoned Monica at her desk and "suggested that she come to the Oval Office on the pretext of delivering papers to him." She did, carrying a folder containing a gift for him: a Hugo Boss necktie. A Secret Service agent admitted her to the Oval Office. The lovers walked toward Bill's private study just off the Oval. Then:

>> In the hallway by the study, the President and Ms. Lewinsky kissed. On this occasion, according to Ms. Lewinsky, "he focused on me pretty exclusively," kissing her bare breasts and fondling her genitals. At one

point, the President inserted a cigar into Ms. Lewinsky's vagina, then put the cigar in his mouth and said: "It tastes good." After they were finished, Ms. Lewinsky left the Oval Office and walked through the Rose Garden.

The report also detailed Monica's gifts to Bill (among them a frog figurine, reflecting Bill's "interest" in frogs),* and Bill's gifts to Monica (a hat pin, "a pair of joke sunglasses").[1]

Larry Flynt is the publisher of Hustler *magazine.*

Larry Flynt: I wrote Starr a letter saying he's done something that I'd been trying to do for twenty-five years and had never been able to do: This man has expanded pornography to where no one thought it would go.

It's in our schools, our libraries, and online. It was a stupid thing to release that.

Nina Totenberg: It didn't make Starr look good. I understand the desire to put detail in, in order to flesh out the evidence, but when you're dealing with the president of the United States and a sex scandal and nobody is victimized —we're not talking about underage people or anything like that—I thought it did not make Starr look good.

Solomon Wisenberg: We felt like we needed a tremendous level of detail so that there would be no doubt that he had had sexual contact and that he had lied about it.

Michael Emmick: I guess when you ask a question about a level of detail, there are a couple of questions that come to mind. One is, "Compared to what?" How much detail could there have been?

You wouldn't really be able to portray what they had in a believable way unless you could provide some level of detail to show that this actually happened. We tried to be as circumspect as we could.

Barney Frank: Nobody believed that. They did it to discredit Bill Clinton. The sexy stuff, the business about the cigar—nothing turned on that. They thought that would further discredit him in people's eyes. No human being in the world thinks that whether he did or didn't put the cigar in his mouth after putting it in her vagina had any legal basis. Nobody.

*Actually, it was Hillary who was interested in frogs, placing her extensive collection of frog knickknacks on display in the family parlor of the White House residence. Branch, *Clinton Tapes*, 178, 396.

Solomon Wisenberg: I can't sit here and say to you that nobody on the team was in any way happy that this might embarrass the president. As a straight technical matter, did we need that matter of detail? I think yes. Could it have been packaged in a better way? Yes.

Gregory Craig: It was an effort to drag the president through the mud, to destroy his character in the public domain. It was an abuse of power of the worst kind. I think the American people saw it for that.

It was calculated, it was premeditated, it was grotesque.

57

For Mature Audiences Only: A Committee, a TV Show

"The parties were far apart."

The Starr Report closed with eleven possible grounds for Bill's impeachment, each backed, it said, by "substantial and credible information." The alleged acts behind grounds one through ten were: false testimony at the Jones deposition and before the Starr grand jury; obstruction of justice in the Jones case by, among other actions, helping Monica get a job in New York in exchange for her false affidavit; and obstruction of justice in the Starr investigation by lying about his relationship with Monica to people who would appear before the grand jury. The last ground cited the private and public lies and evasions (including "I did not have sexual relations . . . ") Bill had committed since the Monica story went public: Such behavior was "inconsistent with the President's constitutional duty to faithfully execute the laws."

Now that it had made the Starr Report public, Congress had to figure out what to do with it.

The late Henry Hyde (R-IL) chaired the House Judiciary Committee.

Henry Hyde: Obviously, perjury is very serious. Especially from the president.

As time went on it became more and more evident that if we walked away from it, it would be almost a dereliction of duty. There was a responsibility to take seriously the lying before the grand jury in federal court and the efforts made to put the fix in on Paula Jones. If the Republican Party had any reason for existence, all this conduct, from a president who was denying it, required some response.

The first question the Judiciary Committee needed to decide was whether to begin a formal inquiry on impeachment.

Howard Berman: I had a meeting with Henry Hyde in late summer.

Howard Berman (D-CA) served on the Judiciary Committee.

It was before the Starr Report came out, but we knew it was coming. He said to me, "We're going to do this really straight. Howard, if *you* aren't going to be voting for impeachment, *I'm* not going to be voting for impeachment." In other words: This is not an effort to get the president. We're going to exercise our responsibilities dispassionately.

Now, events down the road changed his mindset.

On October 5 the panel voted to recommend to the House that the inquiry begin. Three days later, the full House accepted the advice, and the Judiciary Committee got to work on its investigation.

The committee's tally on October 5 was 21–16, along strict party lines.[1] What had happened to Hyde's vow to make the process bipartisan?

Barney Frank: Henry never meant it, apparently.

Frank was another Democrat on the committee.

Or, a more charitable interpretation is that he would have been willing to do that if he were in charge, but he was overruled.

Henry was not calling the shots. Strategically, Tom DeLay* was, and I think Henry got swept up in it.

Tom DeLay was driving this whole operation, and in his mind it was a very positive one. He saw it as a way not just to get rid of Bill Clinton but to discredit Democrats. That's why it was never bipartisan.

Gingrich was the overall enabler, but it was DeLay's passion more than Gingrich's. That was my sense.

Hyde recalled the situation differently.

Henry Hyde: Gingrich and DeLay had nothing to do with it. They did not interfere. They never talked to me. They were the leaders of the party, but the impeachment process had a life of its own.

*R-TX, then the House majority whip.

Asa Hutchinson (R-AR) also served on the committee.

Asa Hutchinson: My view is that even if we somehow came up with some type of compromise as to how to move forward, it would ultimately have broken down in a partisan divide. The parties were far apart in their view of it. Democrats said this is something that doesn't merit a serious look at impeachment. The Republicans said that allegations of lying under oath and obstruction of justice do merit such consideration.

"They thought Bill and Hillary Clinton were wizards."

The argument between the two sides boiled down to a simple question: Was the case about sex or about subverting the legal system?

Henry Hyde: The White House was very resourceful in arguing that this was persecution for sexual misconduct.

The press still buys it. We insisted that the problems were perjury and obstruction, which were serious, not trivial.

Barney Frank: People kept saying, "It wasn't the sex act. It was the lie."

But for DeLay and the right-wing constituency, it *was* the sex act. This fifty-year-old married man had oral sex with this young woman. They were appalled by that.

I think the real moment of demoralization for the Republicans came when they realized that the public on the whole was not nearly as outraged by the nature of the act as they thought it would be. In fact, I think that's part of the reason why they decided they'd get rid of Clinton.

That was the whole problem with the Republicans. They thought Bill and Hillary Clinton were wizards who had somehow enchanted America out of its moral moorings. A lot of these people felt they'd gone to sleep in a Norman Rockwell painting and woke up in a Bosch triptych; that, all of a sudden, perversity and abortion and homosexuality and pornography were popular. And so they were appalled that the president was not being repudiated by the American people for having had oral sex with a woman of a young age.

If you were calculating purely politically, you would have abandoned it at some point. But DeLay and the people around him really believed that the Clintons and their Hollywood friends had somehow stolen the country.

And so they, and the Republican base, didn't want to impeach Bill Clinton. They wanted to drive a stake through his heart. He was this creature who was destroying their country and they had to destroy him.

"Sit down and shut up."

In addition to overseeing the White House legal effort, Greg Craig was also charged with keeping House Democrats in the president's camp.

Gregory Craig: By the time I got there in the middle of September, the Democratic members of the Judiciary Committee and of the House were so angry at Bill Clinton that they didn't want to see anybody from the White House.

They were still angry about what had happened to them in 1994—they totally blamed that election on Clinton. That, and the fact that the president had misled them about Lewinsky in January of '98. I'll give you an example. George Miller, a liberal Democrat from California, environmentalist, education guy—you would have thought he'd be a Clinton supporter. When I walked in the room he said, "Sit down and shut up for twenty minutes. I've got to ventilate." He spent twenty minutes telling me how he would never trust Bill Clinton, how he and many other Democrats were very, very angry at Bill Clinton. He went down the bill of particulars: President Clinton had destroyed the Democratic Party, he was responsible for giving the House of Representatives to Newt Gingrich. There was a level of anger that was astonishing. And then he said, "We're going to work hard to save his tail, but this is not a labor of love for us."

Barney Frank recalled the mood among his fellow Democrats.

Barney Frank: It started out with, "Oh, the stupid bastard. He's so irresponsible." There was frustration, irritation, and anger at him. But it soon transformed into anger at the Republicans for overdoing it.

Their extremism drove Democrats back into an emotional commitment to him.

Gregory Craig: There were two other people the Democrats were even angrier at than Bill Clinton, and those were Tom DeLay and Newt Gingrich. The Democrats saw this as a coup by extreme right-wing Republicans seeking to destroy a moderate, reforming, Democratic president.

"It elicited a big ho-hum."

A week after they published the Starr Report on the Internet, the Republicans on the House Judiciary Committee sought to press their advantage by releasing the videotape of Bill's four-hour appearance before Ken Starr's grand jury.

On September 21 the three major broadcast networks, the three major cable news networks, and a variety of international outlets broadcast the testimony, in full or almost in full—the broadcast nets did cut away for a few minutes here and there to spare viewers the most sordid parts, as did NTV, the German network airing the tape. Nielsen estimated that 22.5 million Americans tuned in.[2]

Barney Frank: In August and September, many people thought Clinton was gone. I really had the sense, "This is gonna be a losing cause."

I was resigned to taking the unpopular role of defending Clinton. The day the grand jury testimony was released, I was steeling myself. I thought people might react negatively. But people said, "Oh, is that what this is about? The stupid bastard went and had oral sex with a kid? Shame on him. Now what's for dinner?"

That's when the tide began to turn. People thought that the grand jury testimony being televised, which Starr insisted on, was going to destroy him. Instead, it elicited a big ho-hum.

Peter King: The testimony was supposed to be devastating, it was going to destroy him. Watching the phone calls come into my office the first few minutes of the telecast, it was, "Look at this guy. He's a bum. He should be impeached. He's terrible." But then the sympathy built up. People were saying, "Who the hell is this Ken Starr to be asking the president of the United States these personal questions?"

It wasn't the left-wing Democrats who were coming to his defense. It was more the Irish and Italian people in their fifties and sixties, American Legion types, people who I'm sure never voted for him. They just felt, "Hey, this has gone too far. Knock it off."

That's when I felt he was going to beat it.

Jonathan Alter: The single most embarrassing day in the history of the American presidency was the day the grand jury testimony aired on national television. All day. Here was the president discussing the most intimate sexual details on national television. The president of the United States, talking about whether he touched a woman's vagina. It was unthinkable.

While the video was playing, Bill addressed the United Nations General Assembly in New York; some broadcasters displayed the two performances via split screen. He then traveled downtown to the campus of New York University.

In the afternoon I went to a conference on the Third Way* at NYU, cosponsored by Tony Blair and President Clinton. Afterwards there was a reception.

*Bill's New Democrat centrism, internationalized.

Both the president and first lady were there, on opposite sides of the room. I thought, "There's no way he's going to want to talk to me. I'm from *Newsweek,* for God's sake, land of Michael Isikoff." But he pulls me over, puts his arm around me—he's in a very upbeat, almost disturbingly upbeat, mood—and he says, "You know what those Latin American presidents were telling me today over at the U.N.?"

"No. What, Mr. President?"

"They said, 'In our countries when they have a coup d'état they use real bullets. You're lucky.'" And then he laughed.

58

DeLayed Reaction:
The Midterms and the Majority Whip

"It was unprecedented."

Howard Berman: I'll never forget Newt Gingrich telling me in mid-October, because we had lockers near each other in the House gym, that he thought they were going to pick up twenty seats. They lost five. And he resigned as speaker.

As the 1998 midterm elections approached, Republicans thought they had a winning issue.

Arne Christenson: There was a lot of talk about, "This is the elephant in the room. Is there any way that we can use this?"

Joe Gaylord: There were four or five different firms that we had producing spots for the congressional committee. All of them were focus-grouped and tested.

The ads had nothing to do with impeachment. They had everything to do with sex. There was one ad that featured two women speaking to one another, saying, "I don't know what to tell my kids."

Arne Christenson: Most people went in expecting, just because of everything going on, that the Republicans would pick up seats.

Nina Totenberg: It was a giant miscalculation on their part. They thought that having the impeachment before the midterm election would be great for them. Instead, people came to see impeachment as a disproportionate punishment for the crime.

Craig Smith: In the 1998 election, Bill Clinton—under threat of impeachment, with the party almost bankrupted, in the sixth year of a presidential term— picked up seats in Congress. That hadn't happened since 1832. And the only reason it happened then was because the U.S. added several new states so there were more members of Congress to elect. It was unprecedented.

In fact, the balloting marked only the second time since the Civil War that a president's party increased its share of Congress in any midterm.[1]* On November 3, 1998, the GOP not only lost five seats in the House but also failed to net any gains in the Senate. Clintonites celebrated in particular the fate of Republican Senator Al D'Amato, the pugnacious New Yorker who fell to Representative Chuck Schumer. In 1995 D'Amato, as chairman of the Senate Banking Committee, had held a series of hearings into Whitewater and assorted other alleged mischief committed by Bill while governor of Arkansas. The sessions were noisy but accomplished little other than embarrassing D'Amato for the lack of substance to back his wild accusations.

Arne Christenson: What we didn't anticipate was the difference in intensity between the two bases due to what had happened in the six weeks before the election. If the election had been held September 1, it would've been a lot different, probably. But as more and more of the sordid details of the case came out, people began to be repulsed, not only by the case, but by the people who seemed to keep bringing up the sordid details.

"No Tom DeLay, no impeachment."

The midterms did not provide the only expression of popular opposition to impeachment.

Henry Hyde: I had some great experiences. One, I was leaving the Hyatt Regency on New Jersey Avenue after breakfast one morning. I'm going up the escalator, and I heard this huge hissing sound. I turned around. The entire lobby was hissing me: It was a meeting of the United Auto Workers. I waved happily to them. Another time I'm driving home down Route 7, and a woman pulls up in her car and rolls her window down. So I rolled mine down. She said, "I hope God strikes you dead." I said, "Have a nice day."

I did have three bodyguards who were very capable people.

---

*FDR's Democrats had done it in 1934. George W. Bush's Republicans would do it in 2002.

• • •

With the election results in, the lame-duck House had to make a decision.

Peter King: On Election Day 1998, impeachment was dead as far as everyone knew. All the House Republicans met in mid-November—that's when we elected Bob Livingston to be the speaker and Gingrich left. It was a two-day conference, and I don't think one person mentioned Bill Clinton or impeachment.

Two things happened over the next few weeks, really over Thanksgiving:

One is that there were the interrogatories that were sent to Bill Clinton. In the answers he basically gave the impression of stiffing the committee, so that got it motivated again.

Two days after the election, Hyde & Co. sent Bill a set of eighty-one questions— each one beginning with "Do you admit or deny . . ."—dealing with various aspects of the case: Monica's initial affidavit, the gifts, Monica's job search, Bill's conversations with Betty Currie, and the like. Bill and his lawyers delivered their responses the day after Thanksgiving. They answered each question carefully, revealing nothing newsworthy.[2]

If the Republicans expected Bill to suddenly admit to perjury and obstruction of justice, and throw himself on the mercy of the committee, they were disappointed.

Henry Hyde: The answers to some questions, I thought, could best be characterized by the term *smart ass*. They weren't as serious as we were.

Peter King: Two, Tom DeLay—and I give him political credit for being able to organize this—realized that in both parties, unless it's an unusual year, incumbents are going to get reelected. You don't face opposition from the opposing party, your threat comes from within your own party, from your base, in a primary. And the base of the Republican Party wanted Bill Clinton impeached.

That was the fear put into Republican members of Congress. The Christian radio stations, the hard-core conservative talk shows—all of that was mobilized over that two- or three-week period. I knew Republicans who had told me they were dead set against impeachment. Suddenly, they came back in December and, almost without our realizing it, the ground had shifted under everyone.

This was DeLay.

Jonathan Alter: No Tom DeLay, no impeachment. He was driving the train.

On paper, Tom DeLay, as majority whip, was only the third-ranking Republican in the House, behind Speaker Gingrich and Majority Leader Armey. But the House did not run on paper.

Peter King: Gingrich was basically a nonfactor.

The speaker had private reasons for avoiding the issue.

Barney Frank: Newt Gingrich, by then, was on his second wife and working on the third. Newt was never a true believer on this right-wing social stuff. Certainly not in his own life.

Peter King: Armey was not really that strong at that time. DeLay was the most powerful inside guy. Whether it was K Street* or the conservative media, he controlled it, and he really put the heat on.

I don't know if Tom ever even spoke to anyone himself. He didn't have to. The word was just out there.

Jonathan Alter: The Republicans knew that the country was basically with Clinton on the issues—it's a centrist country. The scandal gave them what they saw as a way of breaking his presidency. They were so zealous, they never accepted that the public wasn't with them.

Clinton was onto this, he understood it. And that's part of what gave him his equanimity, his calm amidst the storm.

In December, as the full House was preparing to vote on articles of impeachment, one poll recorded that 62 percent of Americans opposed impeachment. Bill's job approval rating? A lofty 65 percent. Public opinion had, basically, held fast for Bill the entire year.[3]

Some other numbers help explain why:

By the beginning of December 1998 the unemployment rate had dropped to 4.4 percent, nearly the lowest in some thirty years. Over the previous twelve months the Consumer Price Index had risen a paltry 1.5 percent.

On New Year's Eve the Dow Jones Industrial Average would close 16 percent higher than it had a year before, with the Standard and Poor's 500 up 27 percent, and the NASDAQ up 40 percent.[4]

James Carville was right: It was the economy, stupid. But the Republicans in Congress didn't care.

---

*Street where many large D.C. lobbying firms have their offices. After the Republican victory in 1994, DeLay and the conservative über-activist Grover Norquist launched the K Street Project, a bare-knuckle—and successful—effort to force lobbying firms to hire Republicans and fire Democrats.

59

Impeach the Rapist!
Fifty Boxes, Four Articles

"We had fifty cartons full of documentary evidence."

If the House at large needed prodding, post-midterms, to resume the drive toward impeachment, Henry Hyde and his fellow Republicans on the House Judiciary Committee never pulled back.

Abbe Lowell: After the election, there began to be talk of some sort of censure. But the people who were pushing impeachment never relented— Chairman Hyde, the leadership—they were just regrouping.

The means that the Republicans used to reach their end was, they were having Republican members of Congress go into the evidence room to look at raw material that had been acquired but was not part of the impeachment recommendation or the proceedings in the House. The so-called allegations of sexual assault against Juanita Broaddrick, and all those things.

Although Juanita Broaddrick, a resident of Van Buren, Arkansas, had filed an affidavit in the Jones case denying rumors about Bill and her, she told a different story to staff working for David Schippers, the counsel to the Republicans on the Judiciary Committee. Broaddrick alleged, to the committee and later on *Dateline NBC*, that in 1978, Bill Clinton, attorney general of the State of Arkansas, had raped her.

There were numerous "Jane Doe" stories—Broaddrick was Jane Doe number 5—included in the boxes of supplementary evidence members were viewing.[1]

Bill McCollum, a Florida Republican, served on the House Judiciary Committee.

Bill McCollum: The material was in an office building behind the Rayburn Building. It was under guard, it was secure.

Henry Hyde: We had fifty cartons full of documentary evidence. There wasn't one Democrat who would walk over there to look at the evidence.

Gregory Craig: The Juanita Broaddrick stuff.

First of all, it was twenty years old, some of it. The Juanita Broaddrick allegation took place at a time when he was attorney general of the State of Arkansas. It was never included in Kenneth Starr's allegations, was not part of the Starr Report, was never discussed in the House Judiciary Committee, at least not in public. The president's lawyers never had a chance to look at it, refute it, examine it, cross-examine it. It just sat there like a heap of stinking garbage in the corner.

Schippers claims that he changed the votes of at least fifty people using this evidence.

Abbe Lowell: We live in a country that has rules and regulations. What happened to President Clinton in impeachment wouldn't happen to a person accused of murder in most trials in the United States in terms of secret evidence, non-cross-examination, manipulation of evidence. One of the extraordinary things about the impeachment process was that at a time when we should have been acting at our best, the process was acting at its worst. At a time when partisanship should have been thrown out, as it was in the best part of Watergate, partisanship was at its worst. At a time in which we should have been holding on to the protections guaranteed in the Constitution and treating impeachment as the Founders intended, as the equivalent of killing a king, we treated it as if it were no different from a thirty-second TV ad to gain seats in Congress.

Arne Christenson recalled the atmosphere on the Hill during this time.

Arne Christenson: I had a young woman working for me who used to work for a Republican member of the Judiciary Committee. She had set up this event in the Capitol Dome and done a great job. The president spoke at the event. We told him she was the one who'd organized it, so afterwards he called her over and thanked her. And he said, "Sometime you should come down and use the presidential box at the Kennedy Center." Something like that—some throwaway line.

Well, her old boss—who served on the Judiciary Committee and was looking at all the boxes—called her over and told her, "I never want you talking to that man again."

"I was saying the obvious."

On the morning of November 19, Ken Starr took his seat in front of the House Judiciary Committee. He would occupy it well into the evening. He started with a two-hour opening statement, then faced questioning from members and counsel.

Abbe Lowell questioned Starr for an hour.

Abbe Lowell: My goals were to show, first, that there was no "there" behind the allegations. Starr said Clinton told Monica Lewinsky to lie, but she said in her deposition that she was never told to lie by anyone, including the president. The headline of the impeachment referral was not supported by the actual evidence.

And then to show that this was a process that had been skewed, that had been biased. Starr had had meetings with Linda Tripp, he had been supported by Republican conservative groups. There had been a long process of, if it's not Whitewater, it's Travelgate; if it's not Travelgate, we gotta find something.

At one point Lowell sought to encapsulate the story: "The president wanted to conceal his private improper relationship from anyone he could. As my daughter would say: 'Duh!' "[2]

The president had an illicit affair, and when it was discovered, he lied about it. I was saying the obvious, which is, who in America, in that situation, doesn't do what the president did, and how does that rise to the level of being an impeachable offense? And as I was ticking off that litany, this dawned on me.

Who would have thunk it, I spent four years in college and three years in law school, and the best way of describing a very important constitutional moment was in a teenage phrase.

We were impeaching a president of the United States for being caught in an improper relationship as a married man, and the allegation was—whether proven or not—that he lied about it.

I mean, really. Duh.

"They ruled it out of order."

With the votes on impeachment approaching, in the Judiciary Committee and then in the full House, some Republicans and some Democrats still tried to avert the crash.

Peter King: I proposed censure. I had spoken with several other Republicans —I was the one who was going to float it, and they were supposed to back it up. They never did.

Barney Frank: We offered censure on the floor and they ruled it out of order. They could have had a four hundred–plus vote for censure, but they held on and said, "No, we gotta throw this man out of office."

On December 11 and 12, the Judiciary Committee approved four articles of impeachment:

Article I: Perjury before the grand jury.
Article II: Perjury in the Jones case.
Article III: Obstruction of justice.
Article IV: Perjury and abuse of office in his response to the eighty-one interrogatories.

Every Democrat on the committee voted against all four articles; every Republican save one voted in favor of all four. The exception was Lindsey Graham, of South Carolina, who voted against Article II on the grounds that perjury in a civil deposition did not warrant impeachment.[3]

The issue would now move to the House at large. In the meantime, Bill had a trip to take.

60

Amazing:
A Speech in Gaza

Dennis Ross: Arafat comes over to me—it was just before we went to Wye—and he said, "It's amazing that with everything that's happening to him, he's ready to do this. We'll never forget it."

In October 1998 Bill summoned Israeli Prime Minister Benjamin Netanyahu and Palestinian leader Yasir Arafat to the Wye River conference center on Maryland's Eastern Shore. Nine days of negotiations, with Bill intimately involved, yielded the Wye River Memorandum, signed by Netanyahu and Arafat. Aimed at the implementation of Oslo and of the Interim Agreement of September 1995, the document outlined steps to be taken to transfer land in the Occupied Territories from Israeli control to either full or partial Palestinian control, as well as measures each side would take to enhance the other's security.

Another provision of the agreement called for Bill to be invited to a meeting of the Palestinian National Council, during which the body would renounce the articles in the Palestinian National Charter (or Covenant) that called for the abolition of the State of Israel.[1] On December 14 Bill arrived in Gaza to attend and address the gathering.

Martin Indyk: We were just about to go into the hall where he was to give the speech when he was pulled aside by an aide and told something that knocked the wind out of him. He was really, I would say, panicked. He said to Hillary, "I'm in trouble now. I'm in real trouble."

The aide may have told Bill that Christopher Shays of Connecticut, a moderate Republican representative who had opposed impeachment, had just announced that he was wavering.[2]

She took him by the arm and led him into a holding room. We all waited outside. I don't know what happened in there, but about twenty minutes later he came out of that room and he got up and gave the most amazing speech.

Dennis Ross: This was Clinton at his phenomenal best, finding a way to connect with people, wherever they were.

Martin Indyk: We'd put in a lot of time trying to get the speech right, but most of it he ad-libbed.

Dennis Ross: The part he ad-libbed, which was half the speech, was an effort to reach out to Palestinians, to connect with them, but also to say how they would have to change. He was as much preacher as teacher in that speech.

Before Bill spoke, about three-quarters of the more than five hundred delegates assembled raised their hands, then rose to their feet to support Arafat's decision to revoke the articles.[3]

Bill, in Gaza, December 14, 1998:

> It is an interesting thing to contemplate that in this small place, the home of Islam, Judaism, and Christianity, the embodiment of my faith was born a Jew and is still recognized by Muslims as a prophet. He said a lot of very interesting things. But in the end, He was known as the Prince of Peace. And we celebrate at Christmastime the birth of the Prince of Peace. One reason He is known as the Prince of Peace is He knew something about what it takes to make peace. And one of the wisest things He ever said was, "We will be judged by the same standard by which we judge, but mercy triumphs over judgment."
>
> In this Christmas season, in this Hanukkah season, on the edge of Ramadan, this is a time for mercy and vision and looking at all of our

children together. You have reaffirmed the fact that you now intend to share this piece of land without war, with your neighbors, forever. They have heard you. They have heard you.

Now, you and they must now determine what kind of peace you will have. Will it be grudging and mean-spirited and confining, or will it be generous and open? Will you begin to judge each other in the way you would like to be judged? Will you begin to see each other's children in the way you see your own? Will they feel your pain, and will you understand theirs?[4]

Dennis Ross: I was crying. Literally, I was speechless. Nabil Sha'ath* said afterwards, "We should use the tape in our schools."

Martin Indyk: At the end the Palestinians stood up and cheered. They had tears in their eyes. I went up to Hillary and embraced her. I said to her, "He's an amazing man." She said, "He certainly is."

Dennis Ross: It was the same thing in Israel. He and Netanyahu gave a speech to Israeli youth. Netanyahu didn't connect with them, Clinton did.

In Gaza before his speech, Bill had met children whose fathers were being held in Israeli prisons. Two evenings before, in Israel, Bill had met with Israeli children whose fathers had been killed by Palestinians.

Ross recalled the scene when a Palestinian girl told Bill about her father's absence.[5]

When this little kid began to cry, our interpreter, who was translating, began to cry, too. So Clinton put his arm around our interpreter and sort of held him as he was trying to interpret.

He has this capacity to understand people at the level that moves them. Now, that means he has to immerse himself enough in their reality to understand it. That's what sets him absolutely apart from anybody else.

Martin Indyk: He could feel their pain. Simple as that, you know.

*A close aide to Arafat.

61

Bad Guys:
Going After Bin Laden and Saddam

With the Judiciary Committee's work in hand, the full House was ready to move forward with the matter of impeachment. Before it could vote, however, two events —one foreign, one domestic—intervened.

"We used a missile attack."

The foreign event in December was a companion piece to one that had taken place in August.

Samuel Berger: Al-Qaeda was not distinctly on our radar screen until the mid-nineties, and then particularly after the bombing of our embassies in Africa. At that point, al-Qaeda became something that we paid a great deal of attention to.

On August 7, 1998, at about 10:30 A.M. local time, terrorists exploded massive bombs at two U.S. embassies in Africa: in Nairobi, Kenya, and Dar es Salaam, Tanzania. More than 220 people died in the well-coordinated attacks—the bombs went off only a few minutes apart—including twelve Americans. More than 4,000 people were injured.[1]
A week later, Bill's national security principals informed him that both the FBI and the CIA had traced the bombings to al-Qaeda.[2]

William Cohen: During that time, we really intensified the hunt for bin Laden.

William Cohen, a Maine Republican, left the Senate to become secretary of defense for Bill's second term.

We had intelligence at one point that bin Laden was going to be at a certain training camp in Afghanistan with a group of his associates.

Samuel Berger: The president decided that we should make an attempt to kill him.

William Cohen: We had to be hundreds of miles away, off in the water. How do you kill an individual long-distance? We used a missile attack.

We missed bin Laden—he'd left a few hours earlier—but we did do substantial damage to some of his cohorts. Killed quite a few.

On August 20, U.S. warships in the Arabian and Red Seas launched some seventy-five cruise missiles in retaliation for the embassy bombings. More than sixty of the missiles were directed toward an al-Qaeda training compound near Khost, Afghanistan. Another thirteen struck a pharmaceutical factory in Khartoum, Sudan, that Bill and his administration believed was involved in the manufacture of VX nerve gas and was tied to both bin Laden and the government of Iraq.[3]* Bill was determined, after the pair of carefully timed attacks four hundred miles apart by the terrorists, to show that the United States could simultaneously hit two targets some twenty-five hundred miles apart in what was labeled Operation Infinite Reach.[4]

That was the only time in my tenure we felt we had a shot at bin Laden.

Some Republicans criticized the strike—some of them used the phrase "firing expensive missiles to kick dirt in the ass of a bunch of camels." But we thought it was the best chance we had of getting bin Laden.

Those criticizing the strike cited more than its failure to kill its primary target. Some pointed to the movie *Wag the Dog,* released just weeks before the Monica story broke, in which a fictional U.S. president wages a concocted war against Albania to divert attention from a sex scandal. The attack on bin Laden, some Republicans noted, came just three days after Bill's grand jury testimony and poorly received speech. "I just hope and pray," said GOP Senator Dan Coats of Indiana, "the decision that was made was made on the basis of sound judgment and made for the right reasons, and not made because it was necessary to save the President's job."[5]

Samuel Berger: The president was very clear that we would conduct national security policy as if there were no political challenges here at home.

---

*Later, that description of the Sudan facility would come into serious doubt. Indeed, before the strike some analysts in the government raised questions, but their warnings did not, apparently, reach Bill. James Risen, "Question of Evidence: A Special Report; To Bomb Sudan Plant, or Not: A Year Later, Debates Rankle," *New York Times,* October 27, 1999.

"Saddam is in breach."

Republican bad-mouthing of Bill's use of the military would grow even louder when Bill took action to counter another threat.

On October 31 the secretary of defense was on his way to Asia.

William Cohen: I was over Wake Island, flying to Hong Kong, when I had a call from the White House saying, "You've got to come back." So we landed on Wake Island, refueled, and flew back. Had a meeting in the Situation Room, and the president said, "We're going after Saddam."

Since the end of the 1991 Gulf War, Saddam Hussein and the West had played cat and mouse over weapons inspections conducted by the United Nations and the International Atomic Energy Agency, while the Iraqi president chafed under economic sanctions and "no-fly zones" over 40 percent of his country.[6]

Saddam blocked inspections in October 1997, but the following month, under both diplomatic pressure and the threat of force by Bill, he agreed to give inspectors a free hand. By that time, inspectors had informed U.S. authorities that Saddam no longer had the capacity to produce components needed for a nuclear bomb, but they still suspected that he was producing biological and chemical weapons.[7]

Hugh Shelton: The big surprise came later from the fact that he didn't have weapons of mass destruction. I said many times when I was the chairman, "We think the man has WMD." That was what the intelligence community kept telling us.

Despite his pledge, Saddam was soon restricting inspectors' access to key locations. Diplomacy from the United Nations and the State Department, as well as open talk from Bill about air strikes, persuaded the Iraqi leader to relent, but not for long. On October 31, 1998, he put a stop to all inspections and monitoring.[8]

Bill and his national security team looked at the data they'd recently collected.

William Cohen: There were lots of activities we had been picking up: Barring inspectors from various suspect sites, backing trucks up to the sites, and then five hours later letting inspectors back in. So we decided, in conjunction with the British, that we were going to take out his missile production facility.

The day we were launching—we actually had planes taking off—we got a signal from Saddam that he was prepared to let the inspectors come back and do their job.

The date was November 14.

So the president called off the operation. He said, "I just said today that if Saddam cooperates, we won't take any action. Now he's sending a signal he's going to cooperate. I don't have any choice. I'm going to keep my word."

The deal was that Ambassador Butler would go in for the first two weeks of December to determine whether Saddam was serious about allowing inspections to go forward.

We said, "If this time Saddam doesn't comply, we're going to go."

The president said, "That's the deal."

On December 15 Richard Butler, the Australian leading the U.N. inspection team, reported to the Security Council that Iraq had refused to provide documents vital to the search for chemical and biological weapons and was not allowing surprise visits by inspectors to Ba'ath Party headquarters in Baghdad.[9]

The president came back from Israel and Gaza. Once he landed, we had a meeting in the Situation Room. He looked around and said, "What do you recommend?" All of us said, "Mr. President, as we discussed last time, if this didn't work out, we were going to go." He said, "Yeah, you're absolutely right. I'm satisfied we've done everything we can to satisfy the requirements here. Saddam is in breach. Let's do it."

There was no hesitancy once he felt he had exhausted all the diplomatic initiatives. When it came to issues like that, the president never hesitated.

Beginning on the sixteenth, U.S. and British forces fired hundreds of missiles on Iraq, looking to crush Saddam's capacity to produce and deploy unconventional weapons. Targets over the seventy hours of Operation Desert Fox included missile factories, airfields, and command posts, as well as installations of the Republican Guard, the elite military force that provided the backbone of the dictator's power.[10]

Bill, December 19, 1998:

> We began [planning for the operation] with this basic proposition: Saddam Hussein must not be allowed to develop nuclear arms, poison gas, biological weapons, or the means to deliver them. . . .
>
> Saddam must not be permitted to defy the will of the international community.[11]

"This place is about to boil over."

House Republicans were scheduled to debate and vote on impeachment on December 17, the day after Desert Fox began.

Hugh Shelton: About, I don't know, a week before the impeachment, they announced when the vote's going to be, and the first thing that happens is Secretary Cohen and I look at one another and shake our heads, because the Republicans will accuse the president of "wagging the dog," which was not the case at all. And so we went over to the White House to make sure they understood the situation, but that we stuck with our recommendation of the date to do it. The decision was made to keep the plan in place. A lot of things went into determining when would be the best time to hit them. We had been through all that.

Representative Gerald Solomon (R-NY), December 16, 1998:

> It's obvious they're trying to do everything they can to postpone the vote in order to get as much leverage as they can. For him to do this at this unbelievable time is just outrageous.[12]

William Cohen: The day the attack was launched I got calls from Newt Gingrich and Bob Livingston. They said, "This place is about to boil over."

"What are you talking about?" I said.

"The Republicans. They're in an uproar. You have used and misused the military to divert attention from the president's problems."

"Under no circumstances was that ever a consideration."

"We need you to come up to Capitol Hill."

"Fine. When?"

"Tonight."

So there was a session. This was December 16. Seven o'clock at night I went up to a closed session of Congress.

George Tenet,* the chairman, myself, and Ken Bacon.† That was it. The chairman had some charts, Tenet spoke a bit, but for the most part it was me speaking, for three hours, in the well of the House of Representatives.

I can't say that all 435 members were there, but the place was filled. When I walked into that chamber, it was poisonous. The Judiciary Committee was ready to report out the impeachment resolution the next morning, and they thought that I had allowed the Pentagon to be used to divert attention from it.

I ended by saying, "I would put all of my public career on the line to assure you that at no time did President Clinton ever give any consideration to his personal problems. This was strictly a military operation. It was recommended by me and by the chairman of the joint chiefs." By the time we finished, they were on their feet applauding.

It was one of the critical moments of his presidency.

---

*Director of central intelligence, 1997–2004.

†Chief spokesman, Department of Defense.

"You had to deal with some realities."

On September 26, 2006, Chris Wallace interviewed Bill on *Fox News Sunday*. "Why," Wallace asked Bill, "didn't you do more to put bin Laden and al-Qaeda out of business when you were president?"

The line of questioning ignited Bill's temper. Jabbing Wallace in the knee, pointing his finger in Wallace's face, Bill laid into the reporter.

> Clinton: I think it's very interesting that all the conservative Republicans, who now say I didn't do enough, claimed that I was too obsessed with bin Laden. All of President Bush's neo-cons thought I was too obsessed with bin Laden. They had no meetings on bin Laden for nine months after I left office. . . .
> Wallace: Do you think you did enough, sir?
> Clinton: No, because I didn't get him.
> Wallace: Right.
> Clinton: But at least I tried. . . . They ridiculed me for trying. They had eight months to try. They did not try. I tried. . . .
>
> And you've got that little smirk on your face and you think you're so clever. But I had responsibility for trying to protect this country. I tried and I failed to get bin Laden. I regret it. But I did try.[13]

Richard Holbrooke: As far as September 11, 2001, goes, he wasn't president. And he had set into motion efforts against Osama bin Laden and al-Qaeda which were dismantled, downgraded, and neglected by his successor. I've never understood how anyone can hold him accountable for these things when he was more aggressive in dealing with them than his successor.

Hugh Shelton: There was always a desire to put some people on the ground in Afghanistan to try to find bin Laden to kill him, capture him. But you had to deal with some realities. To get into Afghanistan, you have to overfly Pakistan or Iran, either one of which is going to tell bin Laden that you're coming. And what about the Taliban? When do we say, "Okay, that's it. You either turn bin Laden over to us by tomorrow or you'll pay the price"? We had all of Omar's* stuff—all of the government buildings, everything—targeted. There was a military option to level them, but instead we kept delivering messages saying, "You've got to quit this. We want you to turn him over."

Of course, they never did.

In order to convince the American people and the Congress, if you're going to invade another country, you've almost got to have a smoking gun.

---

*Mullah Omar, leader of the Taliban.

You had the Taliban and bin Laden linked to the embassy bombings. But could you gain public support for invading another country knowing that you probably will not get the main man you're going after, and then you're going to own that country? It was an easy sale right after 9/11 to go in and try to get bin Laden and pay back the people who were supporting him. But that wasn't true back then.

"We focused on the threat intensely."

The United States had no advance notice of the embassy bombings, but the following year, thanks to good intelligence and better luck, authorities did uncover plans to terrorize people around the world during an upcoming celebration.

Samuel Berger: In November of 1999 we got information that there were going to be multiple attacks—in Jordan and in the United States—at the time of the millennium transition from 1999 to 2000.

We focused on the threat intensely. I convened the principals—the secretary of state, the secretary of defense, the director of central intelligence, the chairman of the joint chiefs of staff—in the White House, every day for an hour, for a month as we paid attention to breaking the threat.

We took it very seriously.

Authorities broke up two separate conspiracies. A plot to kill U.S. and Israeli tourists by a series of explosions in Jordan was halted after Jordanian authorities intercepted a telephone call between plotters. A plan to bomb Los Angeles International Airport, was foiled after a customs agent found bomb-making materials in the car of an Algerian man trying to enter the United States in Port Angeles, Washington.[14]

Bob Graham: The president had set the direction that we were going to take terrorism seriously.

On August 6, 2001, at his home in Crawford, Texas, President George W. Bush received his daily national security briefing, this day titled "Bin Laden determined to strike in US." Bush, unlike Bill when faced with an imminent threat, did not order emergency meetings of his national security principals. Nor did he cut short his summer vacation. Instead, when the briefing had ended, he told the CIA officer conducting the session, "All right. You've covered your ass now."[15]

Thirty-six days later, bin Laden did "strike in US."

62

The Hypocrisy Police:
Bob Livingston, Porn Star

The second interruption in the drive toward impeachment came from the ruler not of a nation but of an adult-entertainment empire.

"They started yelling, 'No, you resign.'"

After the midterms, Republicans in the House wanted a change in leadership.

Arne Christenson: Within a couple days, Livingston announced that he was going to run for speaker. It was all based on the election results. If we had picked up ten seats, there would have been no concerns about Newt staying on.

Just three days after Election Day, Gingrich announced that he would step down as speaker and would resign from Congress after his current term ended in January.[1]

Bob Livingston, a Republican from Louisiana, would be the next speaker of the House.

Or would he?

Larry Flynt: Every single night when I would go home, I was watching the Clinton bashing. There was nothing else on the news. Maybe I'm naive, but being in the business I'm in and having the experience I have in my life, what happened to Bill Clinton was not that unique.

The only thing is, he got caught and he lied about it. Now, people tell lies for all sorts of reasons: to keep from hurting other people's feelings, to hide things. Some of them are innocent in nature. Many of them have to do with ego. Without having him on a couch, I would have a tough time saying where he fit in. But it was my feeling that this was a witch hunt. He wasn't charged with treason. He didn't rob the treasury. I thought maybe there's something I could do. I designed a full-page ad for the *Washington Post*. I offered up a million dollars for anyone who could prove that they had had an illicit affair with a senator or congressman.

The ad ran on Sunday, October 4, 1998.

Our phone lines got jammed. It was unbelievable, the response that I got.

We brought down four people, but the biggest was Livingston. I tried to make it clear in all of the interviews I did that what I did was not about exposing people's sex lives. I've spent years fighting that they be private. What I was exposing was hypocrisy.

On the night of December 17, Livingston convened a meeting of the Republican members of the House.

Asa Hutchinson: He admitted to the conference that he was being "outed," but he did not indicate that he was going to stop pursuing the speakership.

"My fate is in your hands," he told his colleagues.[2]

Larry Flynt: I remember the first statement Livingston made. He said, "I may have strayed from my marriage, but it was never with anybody who worked for me or a lobbyist or anyone else in the government." Well, we knew when he was making that statement that we had him, because one source was a federal judge in Louisiana, another was an intern in his office, and a third was a lobbyist on Capitol Hill.

On December 19, as the House of Representatives was debating impeachment, Livingston stepped to the well of the chamber.

Asa Hutchinson: It was probably the most dramatic moment I can recall during my time in Congress. When Bob Livingston said the president ought to resign, they started yelling, "No, you resign." And that's what he did.

Livingston:

> I cannot . . . be the kind of leader that I would like to be under the current circumstances. So I must set the example that I hope President Clinton will follow. I will not stand for Speaker of the House on Jan. 6.

Livingston also vowed to leave the House within six months.[3]

Asa Hutchinson: No one had any advance notice that this was what Bob Livingston was going to do.

Peter King: There was absolute silence on the floor. It was like the air had been sucked out of the building. Then, suddenly, people started running everywhere.

Abbe Lowell: The whole experience of being on the House floor during the impeachment debate and voting was one of the most emotional events I've ever eyewitnessed. And then, when Mr. Livingston walked to the well and said what he said, it was almost surreal.

That was a day. That was a day.

Larry Flynt: Livingston painted himself into a corner. When he resigned, the *New York Times* did an interview with him, and they asked him what he thought about me. He said, "Larry Flynt's a bottom feeder." The *Times* called me. I said, "Yeah, but look what I found down there."

Flynt's appeal in the *Post* yielded more information on Republicans than on Democrats. Speaking in early 2007, several months after publication of Republican Mark Foley's come-hither emails to congressional pages but before revelations about Republican party animals Larry Craig, David Vitter, John Ensign, Mark Sanford, and Chip Pickering (and, to be fair, Democratic lady-killers Eliot Spitzer and John Edwards), Flynt explained the discrepancy.

Democrats or liberals, for the most part, are not as uptight about sex as the people who sit across the aisle from them. Chances are, your Republicans are born in a conservative household, they're raised conservative, usually staunch churchgoers; when they leave home they join a conservative movement. It's hard to change that mentality.

It's like a pressure cooker. You always see these guys getting busted. Jimmy Swaggart pushed against me for fifteen years. When he got busted in a motel room in Louisiana, they found a copy of *Hustler* there.*

We're not the morality police, we're the hypocrisy police. I don't think you can be called any worse name in the dictionary than a hypocrite, and I can't think of anybody who succumbs more to the hypocrite label than a politician. You don't call a used-car salesman a hypocrite.

It doesn't matter whether they're Democrat or Republican. They live one life and advocate another.

Barney Frank: I think this was entirely justified by what the Republicans were doing. I've said this with regard to closeted gay people: "The right to privacy is not a right to hypocrisy. If you begin to attack other people for what you are yourself doing, then you have forfeited."

Flynt also dug up dirt on Bob Barr, a pro-impeachment congressman from Georgia. Allegations included adultery, payment for his wife's abortion—Barr was staunchly pro-life in public—and perjury during his divorce proceedings. Barr did

---

*In 1988 the flamboyant televangelist was exposed as a patron of prostitutes.

not deny the extramarital affair but did deny that he'd ever committed perjury or "encouraged anyone to have an abortion."[4]

Bob Barr represented Georgia in the House from 1995 to 2003.

Bob Barr: Regardless of what one believes, that a member of the House should never be divorced or remarried or not, it's utterly irrelevant to whether or not the House was conducting an appropriate inquiry.

The White House and Flynt both asserted that they were not working together. Barr doesn't buy it.

Certainly, common sense tells one that they were working in concert; I'm not sure anybody could argue with a straight face that they weren't. To me it's beyond obvious.

It was consistent with the way the White House went after anybody who went against them.

Larry Flynt: I stayed clear of people within the administration. Never made an effort to contact Clinton. I feel that the last thing a president needs is to be supported by a pornographer.

"I ran into him."

Larry Flynt: I know a couple of people associated with Clinton. I was told two or three different times that when the timing's right, Mr. Clinton would love to have dinner with you. Well, he's got to be careful where he goes and who he's seen with, so if it happens, fine. If it doesn't, that's okay.

But I ran into him. It was at a fund-raiser in Vegas for Jack Carter, Jimmy Carter's son, who was running for a Senate seat in Nevada in 2006. Clinton came in the room and he recognized me—I was about thirty feet away. He walked directly to me, stuck out his hand, shook my hand, and said, "I just want you to know you're my hero."

63

It's Official:
Impeached

With Saddam Hussein and Bob Livingston both taken care of, the full House could finally vote on impeachment.

Bill was working the phones up to the last minute.

Charles Stenholm: I was one of five Democrats who voted to impeach the president.

I spent thirty minutes on the phone with him the day before, with him trying to talk me out of casting the vote. I finally told him, "Mr. President, I can't. I've made too many speeches back home to kids. You break the law, you've got to pay the price. And Mr. President, you broke the law."

Pete King was one of four Republicans who wound up voting against all counts.

Peter King: Even if I didn't like him personally, I still would have voted against impeachment. I have a very strong idea of the presidency of the United States, and to me this was trivializing it.

Before the vote, Bill kept in touch with King.

Actually, quite a bit. He called me from his hotel room in Jerusalem. It must have been about 2:30 in the morning, when he was on that trip. It was on a Sunday night.

He was coming up with different members of Congress—moderate Republicans, liberal Republicans—asking me how I thought they would go. He would ask me to call them. I think it wasn't until the last few days that he realized it was hopeless.

On December 19, 1998, the House of Representatives approved Article I, perjury in the grand jury, 228–206, and Article III, obstruction of justice, 221–212.

Lindsay Graham's objection swayed enough Republicans to kill Article III, perjury at the Jones deposition, 229–205. That vote would leave pro-impeachment forces with only one perjury case to make in the Senate trial, perjury before the grand jury—where the alleged lying was about lying in the Jones deposition, and thus a layer removed from Bill's straight-out denials, at the deposition, of a sexual relationship with that woman.

And the absurdity of the charge killed Article IV, dealing with the eighty-one interrogatories, 285–148.[1]

After the voting ended, Democrats sat quietly as Republicans clapped each other on the back and asked Henry Hyde and other leaders of the effort to autograph their copies of the impeachment resolution.[2]

Congressional Democrats showed more spirit later that day, when two busloads of them appeared on the White House South Lawn for a pep rally with their embattled leader.[3]

Barney Frank: The night we voted impeachment, I did not go to the White House. I deliberately stayed away, because I didn't think he deserved to be treated as a hero. I just thought he deserved to be someone who wasn't impeached.

Peter King: That high-wire act that was his life—where I really felt it myself was after I voted against impeachment in December, and I guess the vote in the Senate didn't come until what, February?

During that period I had the dread that this guy is going to get caught with somebody else.

I spoke on the House floor. I did all the television shows. I was intellectually satisfied and politically satisfied I was doing the right thing, but I was at the edge as far as how much more I could withstand. If he did something crazy between December 19 and February, I'm dead.

I wanted that final vote to come to the Senate before something else came out.

In the meantime, those who had engineered impeachment had doubts as to the fate of their handiwork once it was taken up on the other side of the Capitol.

Nina Totenberg: I had a conversation with DeLay's press guy. I said to him, "What are you going to do if you actually succeed in impeaching him?"

It was before Christmas. He said, "We're going to wrap it up all in a nice, little package with a card that says 'Fuck you' to the United States Senate."

64

It's About Sex:
The Trial

"I happened to be in his path."

Jonathan Alter: At the end of 1998 I went to Renaissance Weekend and he, in his state of denial, gave a long speech—full of statistics—about how much better things were in the United States. And it was all true. It was the middle of the biggest boom in the history of the country, and a lot of people were coming out of poverty. He reviewed everything that happened that year, except that he didn't mention one word about the fact that just a couple weeks earlier he'd been impeached.

Usually right around midnight on New Year's Eve at these weekends, and for a period of sometimes a couple hours afterward, he and Hillary would stand around and talk to pretty much anybody who was there—a thousand people. On this particular occasion, however, they made a hasty exit. I happened to be in his path as he was leaving. I said, "I hope you have a better year next year, Mr. President."

He very abruptly said, "I hope the Constitution has a better year, Jon."

And he was on his way.

"We don't want to sully the floor of the Senate."

Once the New Year's noisemakers had been put away, the impeachment circus moved to the Senate. Henry Hyde named himself and twelve other Republican members of the House as "impeachment managers" to present the case—exhaustively, they thought—at the Senate trial. But some senators, including some from the GOP, wanted to get to the inevitable result quickly: The fifty-five Republicans had no prospect whatsoever of persuading a dozen Democrats to join them in casting the sixty-seven votes needed to separate Bill from his office.

From the beginning, tension arose between the eager House managers and the reluctant senators.

Henry Hyde: Senators are very sensitive to polls, and the polling on impeachment was never in our favor. The senators made a decision—I'm speculating on this—that this wasn't helping anybody get reelected. We were never made to feel welcome in the Senate, although we believed what we were doing was right and honorable and necessary.

Nina Totenberg: The Senate, if it ever was really interested in convicting Clinton, did read the tea leaves of the election.

On the morning of January 7, 1999, Chief Justice William H. Rehnquist swore the one hundred senators to "do impartial justice."[1] The second impeachment trial in the history of the American presidency had begun.

At a meeting with Republican and Democratic senators, the House managers proposed calling thirteen witnesses.

Asa Hutchinson: The senators stood there shaking their heads, saying, "You might be able to make the case for two or three witnesses, but you're not getting thirteen."

Bill McCollum: What we kept hearing from a couple of key senators was, "We don't want to sully the floor of the Senate with discussion about sex and about Monica Lewinsky."

Gregory Craig: The House managers didn't persuade the Republican senators that questioning Monica Lewinsky in front of the full Senate was necessary. I can remember Strom Thurmond* bellowing "No!" when that was put to him.

"I pointed around the chamber."

After a week of procedural wrangling and submission of pretrial briefs by the two sides, the presentations to the Senate began, first by the impeachment managers, who argued that Bill had committed grievous violations of the law, then by Bill's defense attorneys, who argued he had done no such thing.

The impeachment managers got their three witnesses—to question only in private and on videotape. They chose Monica Lewinsky, Vernon Jordan, and the White House adviser Sidney Blumenthal, whom they suspected of conspiring with Bill to plant false stories in the press. None of the witnesses gave the managers anything to bolster their case. One gave them something to cripple their case.

Nina Totenberg: What the prosecutors wanted was for Monica to say that the president had urged her to lie, and they never got that.

---

*The ancient Republican senator from South Carolina.

Monica, February 1, 1999, on her affidavit in the Jones case:

He didn't discuss the content of my affidavit with me at all, ever.[2]

The highlight of the trial came on January 21, when Dale Bumpers, the Arkansan who had just retired after twenty-four years in the Senate, delivered a speech in Bill's defense.

Dale Bumpers: The president had to talk me into that. I told him, "I'm not the right one to do this for you. Good lord. We grew up together in Arkansas and we're close friends. I wouldn't be credible."

He said, "You will. You can say things that nobody else can say, because you know me better than anybody over there. You can talk about our personal experiences."

After thinking it over for twenty-four hours, I agreed to do it.

Gregory Craig: Bumpers gave one of the greatest speeches in—well, in courtroom history.

Bill's attorneys had addressed the specific charges contained in the articles of impeachment, arguing that the evidence for both perjury and obstruction was flimsy. Bumpers provided a larger context.

Dale Bumpers, January 21, 1999:

> Well, colleagues, I have heard so many adjectives to describe this gallery and these proceedings—historic, memorable, unprecedented, awesome. All of those words, all of those descriptions are apt. And to those, I would add the word "dangerous," dangerous not only for the reasons I just stated, but because it is dangerous to the political process. And it is dangerous to the unique mix of pure democracy and republican government Madison and his colleagues so brilliantly crafted and which has sustained us for 210 years.

Dale Bumpers: I meant that if you can drum up charges and get a president impeached on as flimsy an excuse as this, that's dangerous, because there was not one single allegation that even came close to what the Framers of the Constitution intended in the impeachment language.

> This is the only caustic thing I will say in these remarks this afternoon, but the question is, How do we come to be here? We are here because of a 5-year, relentless, unending investigation of the President, $50 million, hundreds of FBI agents fanning across the Nation, examining in detail the microscopic lives of people—maybe the most intense investigation not only of a President, but of anybody ever.

"Here's a man who was unfaithful to his wife. That is not a high crime against the United States because if it was, you'd be guilty, you'd be guilty, you'd be guilty, and you'd be guilty"—I pointed around the chamber—"and wouldn't that be a ridiculous outcome?"

Gregory Craig: Everybody in the chamber was also grateful because he allowed us to laugh. Up until that moment—we had been going for a week—it was agonizing, it was solemn.

It was the H. L. Mencken joke.

> H. L. Mencken one time said, "When you hear somebody say, 'This is not about money,' it's about money."
>
> And when you hear somebody say, "This is not about sex," it's about sex.
>
> You pick your own adjective to describe the President's conduct. Here are some that I would use: indefensible, outrageous, unforgivable, shameless. I promise you the President would not contest any of those or any others.
>
> But there is a human element in this case that has not even been mentioned. That is, the President and Hillary and Chelsea are human beings.

There had been a concerted effort to turn Clinton into this monster. Bumpers did a great job bringing it back to basic human qualities and virtues.

Dale Bumpers: A famous politician in this country who shall remain nameless said, The thing in your speech that I liked best was when you said,

> Sure, you say, he should have thought of all that beforehand. And indeed he should, just as Adam and Eve should have . . .[3]

That pretty much did say it all.

That every one of the thirteen Republican impeachment managers was white, Christian, and male was not lost on the blacks, Jews, and women who made up the Democratic Party's base. Congressman John Lewis recalled sentiment in the African American community.

John Lewis: It's part of religious tradition and heritage that we take the position that we all are sinners. But people also felt this undercurrent, "Why are they jumping on Bill Clinton? Are they jumping on this man simply because he identified with us?"

John (Robert) Lewis, a hero of the African American civil rights movement, is a Democratic congressman from Georgia.

There was a feeling on the part of a lot of people that there was some history here. Bill Clinton may be the first person since Robert Kennedy to have this type of hold on the African American community. People thought they were trying to impeach, to get rid of, to silence someone who was standing up and speaking out for the needs of the black community. So people didn't like it. My own mother, who is the sweetest person you ever want to meet in your life, didn't become a registered voter until the voting-rights bill that was passed in 1965. When she saw what was happening to Bill Clinton, she said to me—she called me Robert—"Robert, tell them to let him alone." At the time she was in her eighties, and I think she was speaking for a lot of people. A lot of people said, "Let him alone. Let my president alone."

It was ownership. You'd hear people saying, "Don't let them impeach my man, don't let them impeach my president. He is my president, he is my man."

"The results are in the history books."

On February 12, 1999, the Senate finally made official what had been apparent for months: Bill would remain in office. All forty-five Democrats voted to acquit on both articles. Ten Republicans voted to acquit Bill of perjury before the grand jury, making the vote 55–45 against; five voted no on the obstruction charge, making the vote 50–50. Since neither article received sixty-seven votes, said Rehnquist, "it is therefore ordered and adjudged that the said William Jefferson Clinton be, and he hereby is, acquitted of the charges in the said articles."[4]

The Year of Monica was over.

Gregory Craig: It would be nice to be able to take credit for this fantastic trial that this dream team of lawyers conducted in the Senate. But if you go back and look at his record as president between September 15 and the vote in February in the Senate, you'll find it was one of the five-month periods where he achieved extraordinary things, internationally as well as domestically. I believe that he, himself, won the impeachment by that five- or six-month period of performing. He worked his butt off.

He won, against impossible odds, programs out of the Republican Congress. He got additional appropriations for smaller classrooms, more cops on the beat. His budget went through again. The economy was performing spectacularly. He visited Gaza, where the streets were lined with Palestinians waving the American flag, and addressed the Palestinian National Council.

His performance as president was breathtaking.

. . .

Years later, the two sides' assessments of the impeachment and trial of William Jefferson Clinton remain irreconcilable.

Asa Hutchinson: As a lawyer I never argued with the outcome of a jury verdict. And here the jury acquitted the president of the United States. Does that mean we should never have gone forward with it? No, what it means is that the process worked. The Constitution was upheld.

Gregory Craig: There were a number of areas where branches of government just got it wrong, and they piled up and piled up and piled up. The Supreme Court got it wrong in the Jones opinion, 9–0, that a president must respond to civil process under all circumstances, even a politically driven lawsuit like the Paula Jones case. The Justice Department failed in supporting Kenneth Starr's request to include the Monica Lewinsky investigation in his mandate.

Many people in the House of Representatives voted to impeach the president on the basis of evidence that was essentially garbage in the corner. If you look at the impeachment debate on the floor of the House of Representatives, it was all broad attacks—he lied here, he lied there, he obstructed justice—with not one word of discussion about the evidence. And so the House of Representatives failed miserably. The only place that came close to getting it right was the Senate.

He should never have been impeached. He should never have been forced to go to trial. I don't think the system worked.

Henry Hyde: I don't know that you could draw any hard and fast principle that was reinforced or enforced.

We had a reckless president. The results are in the history books: There will always be an asterisk by Mr. Clinton's name.

65

Seventy-Eight Days:
Kosovo

"Go ahead and bomb us if you want."

If the 1995 Dayton Accords did not usher in the peaceable kingdom in Bosnia, a modicum of normal life did return to that troubled land. But while Bosnia stabilized, Serbia destabilized, as the years of warmaking, coupled with economic sanctions imposed by the West, produced a crippled economy that led citizens to demonstrate en masse against the corrupt and repressive rule of Slobodan Milošević.

Milošević responded with more corruption and more repression. He also returned to the tactic that had worked before to strengthen his following in Serbia: coarse nationalist demagoguery. The target this time was a familiar one: the Muslim ethnic Albanian population that made up 90 percent of the residents of the Serbian province of Kosovo.

Milošević had been persecuting the Kosovar Albanians since the late eighties, shutting down schools, depriving people of their livelihoods; the nationalist sentiment he whipped up had helped to propel him to the Yugoslav presidency. But his treatment of the Albanians turned brutal after the Kosovo Liberation Army, an ethnic Albanian paramilitary formed to combat Serbian oppression, murdered a number of Serb police officers in March 1998. As KLA attacks intensified in the months that followed, so did Serb reprisals, resulting in 3,000 Albanians killed and 300,000 evicted from their homes.

Television cameras broadcast the tragic scenes, putting pressure on Bill to act.[1]

Hugh Shelton: It's the CNN effect. So there is a tremendous push to do something. "Let's do something." Well, what can America do in a hurry? You can't do anything in a hurry politically, diplomatically, or economically, but you can do something in a hurry militarily. The question was, "Can we stop ethnic cleansing with anything other than ground forces going in and taking over Kosovo?"

• • •

Richard Holbrooke: Milošević was willing to give Bosnia away because it wasn't the heartland of Serbia. But Kosovo was the Jerusalem of the Serb nation.

In Kosovo on June 28, 1989, on the six hundredth anniversary of the battle on the Field of Blackbirds that had ushered in half a millennium of Ottoman—and Muslim—rule over the Orthodox Christian Serbs, Milošević had addressed a crowd of Kosovar Serbs, saying, "No one will ever beat you again." The same year, he changed the Yugoslav constitution to revoke the autonomy Tito, the former ruler, had granted Kosovo.[2]

So for Milošević, Kosovo was the ballgame. He had risen to power over Kosovo, and he would fall from power over Kosovo.

A well-publicized atrocity in Kosovo proved the last straw for the West: In January 1999 the bodies of forty-five executed ethnic Albanian civilians, some of them grotesquely mutilated, were discovered in the town of Racak. In February, U.S. and European diplomats convened at Rambouillet, a chateau near Paris, where they agreed to present Milošević with an ultimatum: Remove most Serb troops from Kosovo, return autonomy to the province, and admit twenty-five thousand armed NATO peacekeepers—or face NATO bombing.[3]

Bill sent Holbrooke to Belgrade to communicate to the Serb leader the seriousness of the threat.

I told Milošević that if he didn't accept our final position, we would start bombing as soon as I left the country. He said, "You're a great country. Go ahead and bomb us if you want." I believe to this day that he thought the bombing would not be as intense as it was.

At exactly noon I looked at my watch and said, "It's 6 A.M. in Washington. They're getting up soon. I need to report to them." We stood up. He said, "Will I ever see you again?" I said, "That depends on what you do in the next few hours."

I never saw him again. The bombing went on for seventy-eight days.

On March 24 some four hundred NATO aircraft, along with missile launchers on several warships in or near the Adriatic Sea, commenced the bombing of Serb assets with attacks on army barracks, air-defense installations, and airports, among other targets.[4] Addressing the American public that day, Bill emphasized not only the need to save lives in Kosovo but also the imperative to ensure a "peaceful, stable, free Europe." Inaction "would discredit NATO, the cornerstone on which our security has rested for 50 years now."

But Bill's words that day revealed something more personal: Kosovo presented a chance for Bill to atone for his failure to stop two earlier genocides—in Rwanda and in Bosnia.

As he issued an apology of sorts for his poor performance on Bosnia—

The world did not act early enough to stop that war . . .

—his language was nearly identical to that which he used on his trip to Rwanda: "We did not act quickly enough after the killing began." As he had not in Rwanda, neither could he now bring himself to use the first-person singular pronoun: "the world" had not intervened in Bosnia, "we"—"the international community"—had ignored Rwanda.

After offering a rundown of the consequences of inaction in Bosnia—

. . . innocent people herded into concentration camps, children gunned down by snipers on their way to school, soccer fields and parks turned into cemeteries . . .

—he described the mindset he had himself adopted in 1993–1994 after reading *Balkan Ghosts*:

At the time, many people believed nothing could be done to end the bloodshed in Bosnia. They said, "Well, that's just the way those people in the Balkans are." But when we and our allies joined with courageous Bosnians to stand up to the aggressors, we helped to end the war. . . . We must apply that lesson in Kosovo.[5]

Despite his evasive language, Bill clearly recognized the mistakes he'd made during his first years in office. He was determined to do better.

"The object is to win."

Bill's most controversial decision regarding Kosovo came weeks before the bombing began, when he ruled out the use of American ground troops in combat there.[6]

Hugh Shelton: Now, you don't have to be a professor of military science to figure out that you're not going to stop ethnic cleansing with air power if that's something you want to do immediately.

In fact, not only did the air campaign not stop ethnic cleansing, it provided the Serbs an excuse to expand it exponentially, with the goal of evicting all Albanians from their homes. To achieve that end, Serb forces terrorized the Albanian population: They attacked Albanian towns with artillery, conducted summary executions of men of fighting age, and pillaged property. Altogether, they dislocated and dispossessed some 1.3 million Albanians. With no troops on the ground, NATO could do nothing to halt the catastrophe.[7]

William Cohen: There was great suspicion and skepticism and outright hostility by Republicans toward anything the president wanted to do militarily.

And, of course, impeachment had left Bill with minimal political standing in the halls of Congress.

I felt that I had a way of negating that hostility, but I couldn't do it if there was a land campaign involved. There was no support for it; if we had focused on that, we wouldn't have had the air campaign.

Hugh Shelton: The concern I had as chairman was whether or not we could orchestrate a plan that would use air power to make the price on the Serbs high enough that they would give up and go home. We started with military targets, but then went on up to energy capabilities and transportation. And we had it ratcheted up so that if you don't give up now, the price gets higher and higher.

In May, after two months of bombing and no sign that Milošević was ready to give in, Tony Blair urged Bill to develop a blueprint for a ground invasion. Reluctantly, Bill agreed, and planning began for an invasion by 175,000 NATO troops.[8]

Some would say that it was, in fact, the threat of ground forces that caused the Serbs to capitulate. That probably did figure into it. But I think the bottom line was, when the people put to the street against Milošević, it was all over. They were through with him.

Milošević announced his surrender on June 3. The bombing stopped six days later, when he agreed in writing to remove Serb police and troops from Albania, to allow entrance to 50,000 NATO peacekeepers, and to return autonomy to the province.

Some have called Bill's conduct of the Kosovo campaign immoral.

Lawrence Korb: When you're bombing from the air, you're going to have a lot of collateral damage. The whole purpose was to stop people from being killed.

You say, "I want to stop a hundred people from being killed. I can bomb, and I may kill two hundred to save one hundred. Or I can put ground forces in. I may lose five or six of our people, but I'd save not only the original hundred but also the other two hundred."

I think Clinton was so concerned about risking American lives that he ended up destroying a lot more.

Hugh Shelton: I was criticized in the *Washington Post* for fighting unfairly in Kosovo, because we were staying up above the clouds where the Serbs couldn't hit us and it was too clean. Well, our goal is to win. We're going to go after the guy in a way that he can't get to us, but we can get to him. If we've got to commit people to go take a ground target, then we'll do it, but you have to do it prudently. It's not that you are afraid to take casualties, but you want to minimize the numbers.

Lawrence Korb: I think Clinton would argue, "If I didn't do this I couldn't have done anything." Okay—*if* that was the case. But given the whole way he approached foreign policy decisions, I think in this case he just did not want to take a chance that if it didn't go well he would be blamed.

Hugh Shelton: The object is to win. It's to accomplish the mission with the least number of casualties.

And the Serbs had every opportunity to say, "We quit. We surrender. We'll get out of Kosovo. You can have it. We don't want it."

In September 2000 the people of Serbia decided they had had enough of Slobodan Milošević and his wars, and voted him out of office. The government of his successor arrested him the following March, and in June he was transferred to the custody of the International War Crimes Tribunal at The Hague. His trial, on charges of crimes against humanity, war crimes, and genocide, began in 2002. It was still in progress in March 2006 when he was found, in his prison cell, dead of a heart attack.[9]

Bill, at Ganimet Terbeshi Elementary School in Ferizaj, Kosovo, November 23, 1999:

> The time for fighting has passed. Kosovo is for you to shape now. . . . Will you be focused on hatred and past wrongs and getting even? Or will you be thinking about good schools for your children, new homes for them, new businesses, the effort to create genuine self-government to eradicate corruption and violence and give your children the joys of a normal life?

As once more the fatherless child, the alcoholic's stepson, imbued with magic the leading of "a normal life," the crowd interrupted him repeatedly to chant, "Clin-ton! Clin-ton!"[10]

66

Down to the Wire:
Camp David and the Clinton Ideas

"Clinton knew this stuff cold."[1]

In May 1999 the Israeli electorate ousted the Likud government led by hard-liner Benjamin Netanyahu and replaced it with a Labor government headed by Ehud Barak, a former general who vowed to follow in the peacemaking footsteps of Yitzhak Rabin.[1] From then on, through the final days of his presidency, Bill would invest enormous time and energy in seeking to bring about the peace his hero had died for.

First, Bill sought to broker a peace agreement between Israel and Syria. He called Barak and a Syrian delegation to a meeting at Shepherdstown, West Virginia, just after the New Year, 2000. There eight days of talks, with Bill's persistent involvement, failed to produce a deal, primarily because Barak hesitated. When Bill met Hafez al-Assad in Geneva in March, it was the Syrian president who rejected an agreement.[2]

With the Syria deal off the table, Bill turned his focus toward the Israeli-Palestinian conflict. After visits by Barak and Yasir Arafat to Washington in the spring, Bill called them to the presidential retreat Camp David for a summit meeting at which he hoped to hammer out a final-status agreement to end the conflict.[3] Taking place only months before Bill would leave office, the conference represented his chance to end his presidency with a magnificent achievement—one that had eluded other presidents for decades.

Dennis Ross: We were up at Camp David when Clinton was making the final phone calls to set the time. He had some unease, which was not surprising. You're going for a high-stakes summit, and the prospects of success were not that high. So why go for it? His view was, "If you don't try, nothing is possible."

Joe Lockhart: Clinton knows he's a smart guy and a persuasive guy, and that if he works hard enough, he can solve anything. Camp David was all of that coming together. He was like, "Let's put them all in a place where they can't escape me because I'll get them to an agreement."

I don't think it crossed his mind that he wasn't going to get this done.

Four main issues stood in the way of an end to hostilities and the establishment of a Palestinian state in the West Bank and Gaza, which Israel had occupied since the 1967 war: Refugees, and the Palestinian demand for the "right of return" to pre-1948 places of residence, including those in Israel proper (a deal breaker for the Israelis); borders between Israel and the new Palestinian state, especially as affected by any Israeli annexation of land taken up by settlements in the occupied territories; Israel's security and Palestinian sovereignty; and the status of Jerusalem.[4]

The summit began on July 11. Except for three days Bill took to attend a G-8 economic summit in Okinawa, he was intimately involved in the two weeks of discussions with the two leaders and their delegations.[5]

Joe Lockhart: Clinton knew this stuff cold, inside and out, to the point where Barak couldn't bullshit him, Arafat couldn't bullshit him. He knew the issues better than they did. He also knew their politics as well as they did.

He would say things like, "I know you're gonna tell me you can't sell this point at home, but let me tell you how you can. I know your coalition. If you go to this person and tell them this, they have to be with you on it." Barak was not a great politician. You'd see Barak's eyes saying, "How the fuck does he know all this stuff?"

With Barak it was like two bureaucrats going after each other on the details, a classic negotiation. Arafat seemed to be on a different plane; with him it was like a spiritual conversation. Clinton and Arafat would talk about the history, they would talk about his people.

Dennis Ross: Clinton read Arafat as someone who needs and craves acceptance, and sees himself as the head of a culture that emphasizes victimhood.

Arafat almost revered Clinton. Maybe *revere* is too strong a term—*revere* is how Clinton treated Rabin—but for Arafat, Clinton was huge. He was a symbol of America's power and he was a symbol of Arafat's acceptance on the world stage. He was a symbol of how he was being treated as an equal to the Israelis. Clinton was a master at making him feel comfortable.

There was one time at Camp David. Clinton blows up at Arafat, and Arafat almost begins to cry. Clinton says, "I've been here for two weeks and the only thing you've said is no. You haven't offered one damn thing."

For Arafat it was like, "How can you be this way toward me?" He couldn't handle it, and I don't think it was an act. A lot of things about Arafat were an act; he was nothing if not theatrical. But there was something about the relationship with Clinton that was huge for him.

Joe Lockhart: The reason that Clinton got so much out of Arafat was, he was the first one who treated Arafat as a leader. No one had ever shaken Yasir Arafat the former terrorist's hand and brought him in, in that way.

The underlying message that Clinton delivered was, "You didn't get here by yourself. You got here because we did this together and now you've got to take the next step."

Arafat just couldn't see it.

Clinton was demanding that he be a courageous leader of his people, but Arafat wasn't capable of doing it. He was incapable of being the Arab who gave up part of Jerusalem. Clinton expected that after this whole process everybody would raise the level of their game. Clinton did, Barak did. Arafat wouldn't move. It was an unbelievable scene at 2 in the morning (or whatever it was) when Clinton made his last play on Arafat at Camp David.

He started by being nice, then became not so nice, then got in Arafat's face. I don't remember the words, but he was questioning Arafat's manhood and questioning his courage to take this step for all of his people. Clinton didn't walk out at the end of that speech and say, "Let's give it an hour." Clinton came out and said, "He's not the man he used to be. He's not gonna do this. Let's go." He got in the car and left. It was over.

Martin Indyk has a different view of the summit and its outcome.

Martin Indyk: When we went to Camp David, we had no real idea of what we were doing. Don't forget, there had never been a final-status negotiation before. We unpacked the Jerusalem issue at Camp David. But instead of moving the process toward a solution, what we did was allow Arafat to use that issue to doom those talks. Jerusalem was his escape route at Camp David.

Bill and his team, along with negotiators for both sides, devised a variety of creative solutions to the vexing problems presented by Jerusalem, particularly sovereignty over the Temple Mount/Haram al-Sharif, the site of both the Western Wall, sacred to Jews, and the Dome of the Rock and al-Aqsa Mosque, sacred to Muslims.[6] But while Barak made substantial concessions on the issue, Arafat did not. Resisting Bill's intense lobbying, the Palestinian leader went so far as to deny Judaism's claim to the site, saying to Bill, strangely, that Solomon's Temple—the Hebrew temple built on the site around the tenth century BCE; the Western Wall is a remnant of the Second Temple complex, destroyed by the Romans in 70 CE—had been located in Nablus, not Jerusalem.[7]

Arafat could use Jerusalem as a way of avoiding what he saw as a solution imposed by Barak and Clinton. By the end of the administration, we had spent another six months negotiating these final-status issues—we had a much better idea of what might and might not work. But even then, when Clinton put his parameters down, we did not have workable solutions on the Palestinian demand for a "right of return" or for the Temple Mount / Haram al-Sharif in Jerusalem. And Arafat said no.

"Clinton wasn't prepared to give up."

The conference ended, with no agreement, on July 25.

Dennis Ross: At the end of it, the president's very down on Arafat, and the demonstration of that is how he handles the press conference. We've written a statement for him, and when he reads it beforehand he says, "This says Barak did things and Arafat just showed up."

I said, "That's right, because Barak made moves and Arafat didn't. Arafat doesn't get to come here and do nothing for two weeks and then get treated the same way as the Israelis." And he sort of nods and then he does it better, he does it sharper.

Another thing I say is, "Barak is the one who is exposed when he goes back because of the concessions he made here. Arafat won't be exposed; he can go back and claim to have defied us." So Clinton gets it in his head that he's got to do this to save Barak.

Bill, July 25, 2000:

> Prime Minister Barak showed particular courage, vision, and an understanding of the historical importance of this moment. Chairman Arafat made it clear that he, too, remains committed to the path of peace.[8]

Dennis Ross: Clinton wasn't prepared to give up. We were at the end of July, so he still had five months. He wasn't going to write it off.

I was much more pessimistic at that point. We'd demystified the issues, but I had doubts about Arafat. Clinton had doubts about Arafat but was still convinced he could persuade him. One thing about Clinton: Clinton sees these other guys as political animals and he feels he knows them.

In the fall of '94 we were coming back from having met Assad, and he says to me, "I knew people like Assad in Arkansas."

I say, "Well, maybe not exactly."

He says, "No, but I understand people who are afraid to make a move. I know what it takes to deal with someone like that."

On September 28 Ariel Sharon, under the protection of a thousand Israeli police officers, made a deliberately provocative visit to the Temple Mount. Sharon, who had succeeded Netanyahu as leader of the Likud Party, intended his one-hour stroll to make clear his opposition to any form of Palestinian sovereignty over the site. Violence broke out during the visit, as Arabs hurled stones and police responded with rubber bullets. Forty-eight hours later, fighting had spread throughout the West Bank and Gaza.[9] While Arafat may not have planned the outbreak, he did nothing to stop it.[10] The Second Intifada was under way.

Dennis Ross: At the end of October 2000 I said to the president, "Look, this is serving Arafat well. He's being thrust back in the center of the Arab world. Being identified with violence, being a victim, serves him better than trying to make peace."

"No, that can't be. It doesn't lead him anywhere."

He doesn't give up on Arafat. He still feels he can persuade him.

Martin Indyk: Clinton was affected at that point by a burning desire to get the deal. It was obviously an issue of legacy—his friend Rabin's legacy, not just his own. After the whole Monica Lewinsky affair, he did not want his presidency to be marked by scandal. Had he achieved the deal, he would have gone down in history as a great peacemaker. I think that his desire to get the deal affected his judgment about Arafat's sincerity.

Arafat took advantage of him. In October, Clinton summoned Barak and Arafat to Sharm al-Sheikh to try to head off the Intifada, which was only in its third week.

Bill and Egyptian President Hosni Mubarak acted as cochairmen of the two-day summit in the Egyptian resort city.

His aides advised him to take Arafat to the woodshed, to tell him that if he wanted him to make the deal, then he needs to stop the violence or there would be no effort by the United States. He had to put it very clearly to Arafat: "Cut this out or you can forget about me."

That's what his aides advised him to do.

But he didn't do that. Instead, when he started talking to Arafat about what was happening on the ground, Arafat promised that he would do the deal before Clinton left office. When Clinton came out of that meeting he told all of us, "I just had the most amazing conversation with Arafat." Right up until the last day, Clinton held out hope that Arafat would live up to his promise. It was only on his last day that he came to understand that Arafat had lied to him. And that's what he told George Bush. The day that they met in the Oval Office he said, "Don't trust Arafat. He lied to me and he'll lie to you."

"Clinton felt that Arafat was scared to death."

Through the fall, Bill and his team continued to work on a final-status agreement. Arafat visited the White House on November 9, Barak on November 12.[11] On December 23 in the White House Cabinet Room, Bill read to negotiators from both sides what, at Ross's suggestion, were called "the Clinton Ideas"—unlike a formal written "proposal," the orally presented Ideas would expire with Bill's exit from office, twenty-eight days later.

Dennis Ross: We didn't want Arafat to be able to pocket it and then say, "This is a starting point for negotiations, not the end point." The two sides had asked us to present our best judgment of what it would take to do a deal. It wasn't designed to be the opening.

The main points of the ideas were: Territory: a limited land swap. Security/sovereignty: withdrawal of most Israeli troops from the new State of Palestine; an international force to replace them. Right of return: Israel might accept a small number of refugees. Jerusalem: Arab neighborhoods of East Jerusalem would be in Palestine, Jewish ones in Israel; at the Temple Mount/Haram al-Sharif, each nation would exercise sovereignty over its own holy places.

In closing, Bill said that the agreement would mark the end of the conflict and the end of the violence.

While Bill did allow the two sides to quibble over the details—as long as they remained within the "parameters" he'd presented—the offer was, essentially, take it or leave it. The two sides each had five days to respond.

On the twenty-seventh, the Israeli cabinet assented to the deal, with reservations that Bill deemed to fall within the parameters. Arafat's side asked for more time.[12]

Dennis Ross: The people closest to Arafat were convinced he would do the deal. If you want to say that Clinton didn't read him right and I didn't read him right, neither did the people closest to him.

In the end, Clinton felt that Arafat was scared to death that if he made peace, he'd end up being a little fish in a little pond, with no one paying attention to him; as long as he didn't make peace, he still mattered. That fit the political lens through which Clinton saw leaders. My view was not a contradiction of that, but different. My view was that struggle defined Arafat. The cause defined him. When you have an end of conflict, there is no more cause and no more struggle. He couldn't live without struggle.

Martin Indyk offered a different explanation for the failure.

Martin Indyk: Had we gotten a peace deal between Israel and Syria in early 2000, Arafat would have grabbed what Barak and Clinton offered him. A deal with Syria would have led automatically to a deal with Lebanon. The other Arab states would have normalized relations with Israel. Arafat would have found himself running to catch up. Instead, when we lost the deal with the Syrians, Arafat was in the catbird seat and Clinton and Barak were running after him, because Clinton wanted the deal before he left office and Barak was in desperate political straits and thought a peace deal would save him.

For Arafat it was always a tactical game. After the beginning of the Intifada, a lot of Palestinians had been shot by the Israeli army. The Clinton deal would have required him to stand in front of his people at a time when they were really angry with the Israelis and say, "We got you a good deal. We got sovereignty over the Haram al-Sharif. But you are going to have to give up the right of return." He didn't have the courage to do that. If he'd had no choice, it would have been a completely different story.

Arafat fooled a lot of people, not just Clinton. Some would say he fooled Rabin, but I always thought Rabin had his measure.

It's not that Clinton's people skills failed him; it's too neat to say that was the problem. In addition to our having lost the Syrian deal, the situation on the ground was not in our control—Israelis and Palestinians were killing each other at the same time that we were trying to put this deal together. And it was the end of Clinton's administration. He didn't have any power anymore. He was a lame duck, he was out the door. So his ability to influence Arafat at that point was very limited.

I don't think his people skills could overcome those kinds of problems.

"Clinton was ready for one more go-round."

Arafat delayed his answer on the Ideas until January 2, when he met with Bill in the Oval Office. The Palestinian first told Bill he accepted the Ideas, but then raised a host of reservations so far outside the parameters that they made the deal impossible. Bill was incredulous: "His body language said no," he would write, "but the deal was so good I couldn't believe anyone would be foolish enough to let it go."[13]

Dennis Ross: Clinton knew at this point it was hopeless. He knew it was over, we all knew it was over. But because Barak was still desperate, Clinton was ready for one more go-round. Barak wanted him to come out to the region, and he was willing. Even in the last ten days of his presidency, he was ready to leap into the abyss. He'd said to Rabin, "You take risks for peace and I'll act to minimize them." Rabin paid for it with his life, in Clinton's eyes. That's what motivated him as much as anything.

I came up with one last idea, which was, "Why don't you call up Arafat and say that if he gets together with Peres and Shahak* for twenty-four hours, and they come to an understanding on the four core issues, you'll go out there. Maybe it won't be a final deal, but you'll go to concretize their understanding."

He calls Arafat and Arafat says, "I have to go to Morocco that day. Let's have Saeb† meet with Shimon Peres." My note to Clinton was something to the effect that he can't do it because he has a dentist's appointment.

In his last phone call with Arafat, Arafat says, "You've done more for the Palestinians than anybody else." Arafat was trying to be nice. Clinton tells him, "You made me a failure."

67

In Denial:
Bill Clinton and the Election of 2000

While Bill was concentrating on the Middle East, the American public was choosing his successor.

Michael Dukakis: Had Clinton not gotten involved with Monica Lewinsky, Gore would have won by fifteen points.

It's the only thing Bush had going for him. What else did he have? It was a very successful administration. Gore had been a part of it, an important part of it.

On the stump in 2000, Bush would end his speech by raising his right hand and placing his left on an imaginary Bible to act out a personalized version of the inaugural oath:

> When I become president, I will swear to not only uphold the laws of this land, I will swear to uphold the honor and the integrity of the office to which I was elected, so help me God.[1]

---

*Amnon Shahak, former chief of staff of the Israeli Defense Forces, and a participant in the negotiations.

†Saeb Erekat, a negotiator for the Palestinians.

Joe Lockhart: You might argue that the impeachment so weakened Gore that the Republicans got the White House back. It didn't. Gore messed up his campaign. Gore should have won.

Elaine Kamarck: In the first term Gore and Clinton had a great relationship. During the second term Gore was very angry at Clinton for the Lewinsky thing. So what had been a very strong partnership fell apart.

Joe Lockhart: Gore found Clinton's behavior abhorrent, but it was more than that. I think Gore for eight years chafed under the idea, "Who is this guy? I'm the guy who should be president." It was fine for the first couple years, then it got a little uncomfortable, then it got very uncomfortable when Clinton sometimes got in the way. Clinton tends to fill the stage. I don't sit around worrying about that because it was Gore's own doing, his own mental calculus, that caused him to come up short.

Gore's inability to come up with some positive way of using the Clinton relationship kept him from being president. Doing the I'm-going-to-ignore-him-as-a-way-of-showing-that-I'm-not-him was stupid.

Gore kept Bill at arm's length the entire campaign. He chose as his running mate the Democratic Party's anti-Clinton, Joe Lieberman. When Gore made plans to address a rally in Little Rock two weeks before Election Day, he didn't invite the town's favorite son to appear beside him.[2] Gore kept the Clinton administration's economic record—unprecedented job creation, a swollen stock market, minimal inflation—at arm's length as well, focusing instead on a populist appeal to differentiate his ticket from that of the Republicans: "They're for the powerful, and we're for the people."[3]

Elaine Kamarck: Al Gore was to be Bill Clinton's legacy. Al Gore faced the conundrum all through the 2000 campaign of trying to claim credit for Bill Clinton's record but not be too closely attached to Bill Clinton, because that turned off a big segment of voters. If Gore had had the political skills of Clinton, he could have walked that line, but that took a high level of political skill, and I don't think Gore had it.

On Election Day, Gore won the popular vote by half a million, but the result in the electoral college, and thus the identity of the new president, was not decided until a month's wrangling in Florida was halted by a 5–4 vote of the Supreme Court.

On January 20, 2001, Bill moved out of the White House. A few hours later, George W. Bush moved in.

There's no doubt that it was Clinton's fault. When you look at the exit polls for 2000, Gore's percentage of the vote in the various subgroups was either the same as Clinton's from 1996 or better, because he got more Democratic votes than Clinton did in 1996. With the exception of one category of voters. Guess which one?

Married women. What a surprise. Married women desert the Democrats —not totally, but they vote 6 points less for Gore than they did for Clinton in '96. That was not about environmental policy.

Several days after the Supreme Court handed George W. Bush the 2000 election, Gore met Bill in the Oval Office, where the men held "their first significant conversation in eighteen months," as the author John F. Harris described it. Not mincing words, Gore spent more than an hour telling Clinton that the Lewinsky affair had been the main reason he would not be the next president. Angrily, Clinton shot back that the loss was Gore's fault for his reluctance to stake his candidacy on the achievements of the administration he'd been part of for eight years.[4]

Douglas Brinkley: Clinton's in total denial about it. It's a misunderstanding of the damage he did. This does not mean that the people who went after him weren't zealots overstepping their bounds and putting partisan politics ahead of the national good. The impeachment spectacle grew so large it became ridiculous. So it's not that his critics don't deserve to be treated harshly in history, too, but he did nothing noble except have the chutzpah to defend himself, and to not completely crumble under ungodly pressure.

Elaine Kamarck: The Republicans were looking for a scandal, but he didn't have to give it to them. That's the bottom line, and until Bill Clinton himself can face that—I mean, come on. Come on. It wasn't the Republicans who had him fooling around with that little girl.

He was always reckless. It's his fatal flaw. He's blind when it comes to this, always has been. This was so much the way he behaved that the White House wasn't going to change him, although everybody hoped it would.

For George W. Bush to win the White House in 2000, an entire set of unlikely events had to occur—without any one of them, Al Gore would have become president: the candidacy of Ralph Nader; the butterfly ballot in Florida's Palm Beach County; the multipage ballot in Duval County; a Florida political establishment dominated by Republicans; a national press corps hostile to Gore; Gore's discomfort at campaigning, most evident in the three different personas he displayed in the three debates; and, of course, five justices on the Supreme Court willing to stop the counting of ballots in Florida and award the White House to the candidate they preferred.

But at the top of the list must go the Lewinsky scandal—generated by Republicans in Congress willing to seize on an episode of private behavior to bring down a man they loathed, but made possible by that behavior in the first place.

And so while Tom DeLay and Henry Hyde and Ken Starr didn't succeed in evicting Bill Clinton from the White House, they did evict Clintonism.

Bill's dalliance with Monica, therefore, cost the nation not only what might have been done between January 1998 and January 2001 but what might have been done, and what was done instead, over the eight years that followed:

Instead of responsible fiscal stewardship, endless red ink. Instead of a budget surplus bolstering Social Security or funding education and infrastructure, trillions squandered on upper-income tax cuts and an unnecessary war. In place of a Federal Emergency Management Agency run by competent professionals, a dumping ground for political hacks—thus, instead of a timely, compassionate response to a natural disaster, the drowning of New Orleans. Instead of a president turning his government upside down to stop an imminent threat of terror, a president whose reaction was a childish putdown and a return to clearing brush. Instead of judicious use of America's armed forces, an ill-begotten, counterproductive war, entered into deceitfully and conducted unforgivably. Instead of an America respected around the world, an America reviled around the world. Instead of a commitment to slowing climate change, eight years of denial that it exists. Torture, stem-cell research, wilderness conservation, mine safety—the list of Clinton policies repudiated by George W. Bush is practically endless.

And none of it would have happened had the president of the United States been able to control himself when a randy young woman showed him her underwear.

Dave McCurdy: He accomplished a lot. Unfortunately, the legacy is incomplete because of the personal failings.

Al Gore would have won had it not been for Lewinsky. That's a bad legacy.

Part VI

Citizen Clinton,
2001–

68

Parting Shots:
Leaving the White House

"Any VFW hall in America wouldn't like this guy."

With his tenure as the nation's chief executive about to end, Bill spent his spare time sorting through his eight thousand books and two thousand CDs—including his prized collection of the music of jazz saxophonists—choosing which to give away and which to take with him to the eleven-room home he and the newly elected junior senator from New York had purchased in tony Westchester County, just north of New York City.[1]

There was still time to make an impact in one area: the environment. In his closing days as president he issued a flurry of decisions, including one that prohibited commercial logging and the construction of roads in almost a third—fifty-eight million acres—of America's forests.[2]

Douglas Brinkley: One achievement of Bill Clinton that I'm appreciating more and more is his role with the environment at the end of his presidency. Bruce Babbitt one day came up and handed him a list of all the national parks that Theodore Roosevelt created, and said, "If you want to be a TR on the environment, this is what you've got to match."* After Theodore Roosevelt, FDR, and Jimmy Carter, he's probably our greatest environmental president. We wouldn't have the Grand Staircase–Escalante National Monument in Utah without him.

This is one side of him that's overlooked.

Before his exit, Bill had a saga to conclude. On January 19, his last full day in office, he agreed to a settlement with Robert Ray, who had succeeded Ken Starr as

---

*Babbitt, secretary of the interior throughout the Clinton administration, approached Bill with this challenge shortly before his first term ended. Douglas Jehl, "Transition in Washington: the Environment; How an Interior Secretary Helped to Encourage a Presidential 'Legacy,'" *New York Times,* January 19, 2001.

Whitewater counsel in October 1999. In exchange for Ray's giving up the possibility of indicting Bill on any charge connected to the Lewinsky matter, Bill finally copped to lying under oath in the Jones deposition—"certain of my responses to questions about Ms. Lewinsky were false"—relinquished his license to practice law for five years, paid a $25,000 fine to the Arkansas Bar Association, and pledged that he would not seek reimbursement of his legal fees necessitated by the Lewinsky investigation, even though, because he had not been indicted, he was permitted to do so under the independent counsel statute.[3]

After eight years in the maelstrom, Bill was free to become, quietly and without controversy, what he hadn't been in eighteen years: a private citizen.

Except that a new controversy would follow him out the door.

Just hours before noon on January 20, when the new president would be sworn in, Bill signed 176 presidential pardons and commutations.[4] One of them was for Marc Rich.

Marc Rich made his billions trading commodities, and it was one of them that got him into trouble with the law. In 1983 the U.S. attorney for the Southern District of New York, one Rudolph Giuliani, brought a fifty-one-count indictment against Rich related to his dealings in oil. Charges included tax evasion, fraud, conspiracy, racketeering, and trading with the enemy, the last stemming from his commerce in Iranian oil after the United States had outlawed trade with Iran following the taking of American hostages in Tehran in November 1979. Rather than face jail, he fled to Switzerland.[5]

As the end of the Clinton administration neared, Rich's attorneys, one of whom had served as Bill's White House counsel, petitioned Bill for a pardon of Rich. Arguing that the original charges should have been civil, not criminal, the lawyers did not tell the outgoing president that Rich had renounced his U.S. citizenship.[6] Also pleading on Rich's behalf was his ex-wife, Denise, who had donated more than a million dollars to Democratic endeavors, including the campaigns of both Clintons, and had pledged $450,000 to Bill's presidential library, to be built in Little Rock. One talk Denise had with Bill on the subject had occurred in December at a White House ceremonial dinner, where she interrupted his conversation with Barbra Streisand to draw him aside.[7] An array of Israelis and American supporters of Israel, where Rich had directed much of his substantial philanthropy, contacted Bill on the fugitive's behalf. One of them was Ehud Barak, whose approaching political demise—in early February, Barak would be soundly defeated at the polls by Ariel Sharon—generated feelings of guilt in Bill. Barak discussed Rich with Bill in three telephone conversations.[8] Opposing the pardon were some of Bill's closest aides, including his longtime protector Bruce Lindsey, then serving as a deputy White House counsel.[9]

The decision to pardon Rich spoiled what should have been a dignified departure from office. And it gave the Republicans one last opportunity to hold congressional hearings on the conduct of the forty-second president, which they did, in both the House and the Senate, in February and March.[10]

The Justice Department opened a preliminary inquiry, but Bill was saved from its clutches by his successor. "I think it's time to move on," said George W. Bush.[11]

Terry McAuliffe: Was the Rich pardon wrong? Absolutely. I didn't know about it till after. I said to the president as soon as I heard, "The guy renounced his citizenship. Come on. Any VFW hall in America wouldn't like this guy."

Joe Lockhart: The Rich pardon wasn't well thought-through on his part. But worse, there was no thought given to the infrastructure of how to go out and defend it.

As he left office, his transition staff was like two people, and none were press people who would be adept at noticing this. The Rich pardon was one of those things, I think, that he did to show that he could do it—it bugged him that there were people out there who had been treated badly like he'd been treated badly. He just picked some of them and said, "Whatever."

Jonathan Alter: I think he was tired and frustrated at the very end of his presidency, and not acting in a particularly rational way. For a while, it hurt him pretty badly.

Bill, defending the pardon in a *New York Times* op-ed, February 18, 2001:

> The suggestion that I granted the pardons because Mr. Rich's former wife, Denise, made political contributions and contributed to the Clinton library foundation is utterly false. There was absolutely no quid pro quo.[12]

Jonathan Alter: While I didn't think it was a straight quid pro quo for help for the library, I thought it was in the department of a fuck-you to his critics— that he would do what he wanted at the end of his presidency, and didn't evaluate or care what the reaction might be. He was pretty angry with both the legal system and the media by that point.

"They said he trashed Air Force One."

Paul Begala: There was also a nasty and deeply dishonest campaign by the new Bush White House to discredit him and his staff. That whole thing about how there was vandalism. It was all bullshit.

Jonathan Alter: There was bogus publicity generated by the Bush people that suggested that he and Hillary had stripped the White House of valuables and even taken the "W" keys out of the keyboards of White House computers.

Exactly how much damage was done is unclear, but a few pranksters—and only a few—may have committed some minor mischief, not only removing a W here and there but also leaving signs for the "Office of Strategerie" and loading the paper tray of at least one photocopier or printer with copies of a faux *Time* magazine cover, relayed around the Internet following Election Day, featuring a photo of Bush and the words "we are FUCKED."

Terry McAuliffe commented on the keyboards.

Terry McAuliffe: I'm sure they did that. Big deal. That's sort of a tradition for the White House staff.

Indeed, the outgoing Clintonites may have been taking revenge on the Bushies for pranks committed eight years earlier—posting signs reading "Draft Dodger," gluing headsets to telephones—when the elder George Bush vacated the premises so that Bill & Co. could move in.[13]

But with staffers of the nascent Bush 43 administration whispering their shocking tales of plunder and pillage in reporters' ears,[14] what was, at worst, a handful of childish pranks turned into

> trash dumped on floors, desk drawers emptied onto floors, pornographic pictures left in computer printers, scatological messages left on voice mail, and cabinets and drawers glued shut. (Brit Hume, Fox News Channel)[15]

And it wasn't only on Fox:

> Phone lines cut, drawers filled with glue, door locks jimmied so that arriving Bush staff got locked inside their new offices. (Andrea Mitchell, *NBC News*)[16]

Terry McAuliffe: They said he trashed Air Force One on the flight home to Chappaqua. You remember those stories?

The aircraft

> looked as if it had been stripped by a skilled band of thieves—or perhaps wrecked by a trailer park twister. (Columnist Tony Snow)[17]

There were about ten glasses broken. I was on the plane. You know what happened? The White House steward brought out a big cake and they had champagne on a tray. Sharon Farmer, who was the White House photographer, moved with her big lens, the tray fell. Glasses broke, glass got in the cake, we couldn't eat the cake. That was trashing the plane?

Acting on a request from the anti-Clinton congressman Bob Barr, the General Services Administration looked into the various allegations. Reporting in May, the

GSA would not say that no pranks had been committed but concluded that "there wasn't indication of real, significant, widespread damage."[18]

It was all false. It was about power. To the Republicans, Bill Clinton was taking away their power.

They had to make him look like trailer trash. They had to tear Bill Clinton down.

69

Convening Power:
The Clinton Foundation

Bill has led a double life since leaving the White House: As a public person he does good works; as a private person he pads his bank account. In 2008 he added a temporary third identity: he returned to being a political person—with disastrous results.

"It's the kids who are still dying."

Terry McAuliffe: It was hard for him. He was fifty-four years old when he left, and he had to go sit on the bench.

In 2002 *Newsweek*'s Jonathan Alter conducted Bill's first postpresidential interview. Bill spoke of his plans for his foundation.

Jonathan Alter: He was committed to using what he called his "convening power"—his ability to bring people together. And he succeeded far beyond my expectations.

Paul Begala: The president has always wanted to live a consequential life. He told friends that he had absolutely no interest in joining corporate boards. First, because he's an executive, not a board member—he likes running things—and, second, because I suspect it didn't fulfill his need to be part of something larger than himself, and to serve.

To construct the public side of his postpresidency, Bill started with the model fashioned by Jimmy Carter, before Bill certainly the most consequential ex-president since William Howard Taft served as chief justice of the United States from 1921 to 1930. Defeated in his bid for a second term, Carter returned to tiny Plains, Georgia, and opened the Carter Center in Atlanta.

Bill modified Carter's example to fit his own personality and ambitions. To begin with, although Bill, like Carter, hails from a small southern town, he wasn't about to return there to teach Sunday school. Homespun simplicity isn't Bill's style; he's more in his element with jet-setting glitz. His home base is a suite of offices on 125th Street in Harlem, New York City.

Second, since Carter had locked up the franchise on human rights and election monitoring, Bill had to look elsewhere. He took as his initial theme Third World health and development. The first and, as of spring 2010, still most important, initiative at the William J. Clinton Foundation—he's no longer plain old "Bill" (not always, anyway)—was the Clinton HIV/AIDS Initiative (CHAI), which extends treatment to people with the virus in developing nations. Another arm of the foundation, the Clinton Global Initiative, has raised billions to improve the lives of people around the world.

In recent years he's added work on, among other areas, climate change and childhood obesity. The latter was prompted by Bill's own health scare in 2004, when he underwent quadruple bypass surgery to correct for blocked arteries to his heart, and also, according to the foundation, by Bill's "own battle with childhood obesity" and "fondness for fattening food."[1]

Paul Leopoulos: An angel on this earth. He truly is an angel on this earth.

He could be sitting there smoking cigars, playing golf every day, like some of the other people who have been president before, but no, he's out there killing himself trying to save lives. That's an angel.

He's working far harder than anyone I've ever met in my life, and he will not stop. I don't think he's on a death mission or anything like that, I just say that he is working himself to death. He will die with a kid with AIDS in his hand.

One time, we were up at his apartment on the top floor of his library,* talking, a couple of old friends. Carolyn Staley said to him, "Bill I'm really proud of the article that was in *Esquire* magazine"†—it talked about his foundation and what it's doing. Good press. And he just sat there with a tear in his eye and he said, "They don't understand."

---

*On the third floor of the Clinton Library in Little Rock is a two-bedroom apartment for Bill's personal use.

†Joe Conason, "The Third Term: The Dawning of a Different Sort of Postpresidency," cover story, *Esquire*, December 2005. The cover headline reads: "Bill Clinton: The Most Influential Man in the World Starts Getting His Hands Dirty."

Carolyn said, "What do you mean, don't understand?"

He said, "It's not the kids we've saved, it's the kids who are still dying." And he said, "Until you can hold one of those kids in your hand, you will never understand."

People say, "Oh my God. I'm worried about him." Don't worry about him. He's doing what he wants to do. He's helping people. He's the happiest man on Earth.

The public health expert Dr. Jim Yong Kim is a cofounder, along with Dr. Paul Farmer and others, of Partners in Health, an organization that provides health services to underserved populations around the world.

Kim has worked closely with Bill on CHAI. He discussed Bill's efforts to fight worldwide HIV/AIDS during his presidency.

Jim Yong Kim: I don't think there was a single political leader in the world who did enough to face up to the problem during the 1990s. It was a group failure. If you ask President Clinton today, he would outline all the things he did. The Ryan White Act, for example, was really important. It provided access to HIV / AIDS treatment for a broad range of people in the United States.

But we didn't do enough to try to confront the epidemic in developing countries. What President Clinton says, and I believe him, is that he did look into doing much more in Africa but had a really difficult time because he was dealing with a Republican Congress starting from 1994.

If I were to give him a relative grade compared to the other leaders of the world, it would be A-, B+, because he did as much as or more than anyone else in the world. But in terms of what he should have done, I wouldn't give him such a good grade, because we now understand the devastating implications of doing too little too late in response to the African epidemic.

The changes that President Clinton did bring while in office were really important—to say a lot of the right things, not to castigate and marginalize people from the so-called "risk groups." He opened the White House to people with HIV / AIDS. He brought a whole new attitude.

In my heart of hearts, I wish President Clinton had done more in office, because his extraordinary brand of leadership could have turned the tide earlier. But, my gosh, looking at what he's done in the last several years, it is not at all an overstatement to say that he is one of the most important individuals working today in the response to HIV / AIDS.

"President Clinton was there."

When Bill was first plotting out the work of his foundation on the problem of worldwide HIV/AIDS, he met with Kim and other public health experts.

Jim Yong Kim: We told him the area that needed their attention most was HIV treatment—that was the huge dark area where we still had such a long way to go. And within treatment, I specifically said you should take on the issue of drugs.

Kim also met with Ira Magaziner, who ran Hillary's health care task force in 1993–1994. Magaziner has worked closely with Bill on CHAI and other foundation projects.

I said to Ira, "It's legal for poor countries to get generic medicines from India and other places, and there have been some announcements of price cuts, but we're not well enough organized to make sure that everyone takes advantage of them. And prices could go down more."

It's amazing what they've done.

The specifics of it were the following: Médecins Sans Frontières, Doctors Without Borders, had negotiated with a particular company to reduce the price of the triple-therapy drugs that they'd put it into one pill. The price had already gotten down to two or three thousand dollars per person per year. Still, that was too much for most countries, so MSF negotiated a price of $300. Ira called me one day when I was at the World Health Organization and said, "We're going to bring the price down to 140."

At first I was alarmed. I said, "Ira, if you bring the price down too low, it knocks other manufacturers out of the business."

Ira said, "It's not too low, don't worry. And others will get into the business because we are guaranteeing sales."

Magaziner drew mostly bad reviews for his work on the health care task force. Not so for his work with Bill's foundation.

Bringing Ira Magaziner into the AIDS struggle has made a huge, huge difference.

Paul Leopoulos: What Bill told me was, "You say to the drug companies, 'Would you rather sell a few drugs for a lot of money, or a lot of drugs for a little bit of money?'" It doesn't make any difference, business is business. The drug companies said, "We'll do it the way you want it, but you have to assure us prompt payment," and Bill said, "Done."

Jim Yong Kim: The price reductions have changed developing countries' notions of what's possible. A lot of other factors were involved, but President Clinton's getting it priced down to 140 was incredibly important.

The three-in-one pills are for first-line treatment, but people get resistant to those after time. Now there are second-, third-, and fourth-line drugs available in the United States for people who become resistant, but the prices of those drugs are very high, as much as ten times higher than the price of the first-line drugs. Whom are you going to call to bring those prices down? Most people in this business are relying on the Clinton Foundation.

Jim Yong Kim: The prices were just the beginning of the Clinton Foundation's impact.

They're doing projects on the ground, scaling up treatment in rural areas, taking over in places where no one else wants to be. They've gone around in a very deliberate process of finding what they call "care partners," who can actually do the job. That's what Partners in Health is—our specialty has been working in rural areas.

Their efforts were not wildly successful all the way across the board, but they had a great team in Lesotho, for instance, where the Clinton Foundation folks took care of the procurement and supply-chain management of drugs, and provided critical, high-level political support.

CHAI has been especially active in Africa.

In Africa he is an absolute hero. People in Africa think that President Clinton was the first American president who cared at all about Africa.

Let me tell you about the work in Lesotho. You can get to the highlands of Lesotho only by single-engine plane. You land on a grass runway on a plateau on top of a mountain—that's where we built our first clinic. President Clinton convinced the Irish government to give nine million dollars to get this project started. None of us could have gone to the Irish government and asked them for nine million dollars, but he got it done, and the Irish government gave the money to the government of Lesotho to treat poor people living with HIV.

You should see this place. It is in the middle of nowhere, on the side of a mountain, and President Clinton was there. The fact that he visits these places, the fact that what's coming out of his mouth is a positive, optimistic commitment to fixing these problems—that's the most important thing. That's why I say he's been absolutely one of the most important people in the global response to HIV/AIDS.

Princeton Lyman: He may take a little more credit than is due, because a lot of other people are working on these things, too, but he deserves a lot of credit. He's made it a big issue and he's done it.

And then he has the Clinton Global Initiative in New York every year. His personality is very important—so much, it seems, is wrapped up in the prestige of his own person. But that's the advantage of being who he is. Every ex-president decides how he's going to use his prestige. Clinton uses his for good causes.

Jim Yong Kim: One of the most important things that we need is convening power. Boy, President Clinton has as much convening power as any human on the face of the earth. His success in his postpresidential work has a lot to do with the fact that he can get a meeting with anybody, and he can talk just about anybody into just about anything. Working with him on a project makes us feel, "President Clinton's got your back."

"Bill Clinton says, 'Okay, let's go.'"

For decades, Western policy makers have been unable to see past obstacles that appear to make health and other services impossible to provide: a dearth of roads, clean water, electricity, trained providers. Kim has worked to change that attitude.

Jim Yong Kim: Let me put it this way: Coca-Cola can get a cold bottle of Coca-Cola almost anywhere in the world. If they can do that, come on, we can do clean water and food and basic primary health care services.

The problems in doing effective work in developing countries—Paul Farmer and I have said this a lot—should all be used as conversation starters, not conversation stoppers. To have President Clinton say, "Yeah, there are major problems, but let's go out and solve them"—that's the change in attitude we've needed for a long time. We've needed someone very prominent and very important and very persuasive to lead that charge.

He is not throwing up his arms in the face of these seemingly intractable situations. Bill Clinton says, "Okay, let's go. If infrastructure is a problem, we're going to build infrastructure. If clean water is a problem, let's work on clean water, too." He's using his huge range of contacts to help us do these things.

I've come to understand that political will, optimism, visionary leadership are critical in global health. We couldn't have possibly dreamed up a better scenario than to have him. He's been the cheerleader in chief, the optimist in chief in our effort to tackle AIDS in Africa.

Paul Leopoulos: He doesn't see a barrier, and he's been that way his whole life. I never heard Virginia say, "Watch out Bill, you can't do that," or "Be careful, be careful."

He doesn't see what *can't* happen.

Bill being Bill, of course, some people are still not moved by his good works.

Lawrence O'Donnell: It's all self-glorifying.

If we wanted to sit down and say, "Let's construct a path for glorification of Bill Clinton in a postpresidential environment," we could say, "It would be great if he did a lot of good works in Africa."

Look. My resistance to being impressed by Bill Clinton's charitable work comes from his obvious, desperate desire for me to be impressed by it. And his extremely calculated desire for me to be impressed by it. This is a person as calculating about public image as exists in the world.

He's as extreme a narcissist as politics produces—but he is, fundamentally, what politics produces. They're virtually all like him, to some lesser degree. But they are all somewhere on that narcissistic trip he's on.

It's inevitably part of what these people do.

"It was a huge media event all over China."

Bill's convening power hits its zenith every September when he hosts the conference known as the Clinton Global Initiative. Attending the New York gathering, which is timed to coincide with the annual opening of the U.N. General Assembly, are a panoply of high-octane national and international names in government, media, entertainment, philanthropy, and, of course, business—they're the ones with the deep pockets Bill cajoles them to dig into for projects across the developing world. Starting with the first CGI in 2005 through the 2009 edition, Bill has won commitments of some $57 billion to fund specific projects, from hospital construction in Kenya to free bicycles for survivors of the 2004 tsunami in Sri Lanka, from small loans for female entrepreneurs in Peru to the building of a kindergarten in Armenia, and even some tasks to be undertaken in the United States, like reduction of emissions from vehicles owned by the city and county of San Francisco.[2]

Attendees at the 2009 meeting included thirty-four heads of state and government, from Barack Obama to the prime minister of Papua New Guinea, and CEOs of Walmart, GE, Habitat for Humanity, and a host of other organizations, not to mention Demi Moore, Ashton Kutcher, and Martin Scorsese.[3]

Jonathan Alter: The Clinton Global Initiative has been a tremendous boon for the world.

He really does want to continue to make a difference.

Bill:

> The older I get, especially following my own brush with mortality, the more determined I am to try to prevent anyone younger than me from dying.[4]

Jonathan Alter: He's gotten a lot accomplished. He's kept at it, and he's serious about it. He's had the most productive ex-presidency in the modern era, and that includes Jimmy Carter, who often gets more credit than Clinton does.

Carter's done good work supervising elections and funding good causes, but Clinton has been more successful in leveraging his stature into more partnerships, more money, more good works, more innovation. Particularly on AIDS, but in a variety of other areas, as well.

Jim Yong Kim: Billions of dollars pledged through CGI, and he really pushes the donors to up the ante. Why would the titans of industry give all this money in the name of Bill Clinton? I've heard that many people are grateful to him. Many business people have told me that his steady hand on both the U.S. and the global economy was key to the great prosperity the world experienced during his presidency.

In terms of being able to turn on megawatt charm, nobody compares to Bill Clinton, and that matters. It's that personal charm, charisma, ability to read a situation, read people. It makes a huge difference. The fact that he can do it with rich people as well as with African health workers on the ground— that's one of his truly unique skills.

This is a guy who can get his head around a problem really quickly and has fantastic instincts about the right places to go to have an impact. People see him as a hero in the rest of the world.

I went to China soon after President Clinton went there. In China, he had meals with people living with HIV / AIDS. He hugged and kissed people with HIV / AIDS. It was a major media event all over China.

People thought you could get the disease from eating with people with HIV / AIDS. To see President Clinton doing what he did changed a lot of people's attitudes. He's such a respected figure. Chinese health authorities told me that President Clinton had an enormous impact.

Whatever deficiencies people accuse him of during his administration, boy, with what he's done recently—from drug prices to going to China and in a day changing the way people think about HIV / AIDS—he's more than made up for them in my view.

70

Chasing a Buck:
Making Multimillions Multinationally

The underside to Bill's globe-trotting, high-powered philanthropy has been his globe-trotting, high-powered personal money making.

During his nearly twelve years as governor, Bill was paid an annual salary of $35,000—Hillary had been the breadwinner before the family moved into the White House.[1] During his eight years as president he'd been paid more handsomely, but his annual income of $200,000 hardly allowed him to save enough to cover the expenses he faced upon leaving: his new home in Westchester, another in Washington to accommodate a senator's schedule, the sky-high legal bills he'd been presented by the lawyers who had battled Ken Starr on his behalf.

So, out of the White House, Bill and Hillary made up for lost time. Bill got started right away, raking in $9.2 million on the international speaking circuit—fifty-nine appearances in more than a dozen countries—in 2001 alone.[2]

That sum was only the beginning. According to records released in 2008 during Hillary's campaign for the Democratic presidential nomination, from 2000 through 2007 the pair had pulled down $109 million, including more than $10 million for two books by her, more than $29 million for two books by him, plus more than $50 million from his paid speaking gigs, which fetch as much as $425,000 a pop.

Bill also pulled down $12–15 million from his work as an adviser/rainmaker/walking advertisement—exactly what he did and how much effort he expended are hard to ascertain—for the Yucaipa Companies, a private-equity concern operated by one of his best postpresidential buddies, the California supermarket tycoon Ron Burkle. Another $3 million came from a consulting deal with another pal, Vinod Gupta, who ran the database provider InfoUSA.[3]

Lawrence O'Donnell: I had absolutely no surprises that after the presidency Bill Clinton would do virtually anything legal for vast amounts of money.

The emblem of Bill's troubling financial associations is a visit he made in September 2005 (and which the *New York Times* detailed in January 2008) to Kazakhstan with the Canadian mining financier and former film producer Frank Giustra on Giustra's private jetliner.[4] Ostensibly undertaken to announce a deal that would enable the nation's government to purchase discounted AIDS drugs, the excursion featured a lavish late-night dinner for the two men with the country's autocrat, Nursultan A. Nazarbayev, a holdover from Soviet days. At a news conference, Bill waxed effusive about Kazakhstan's bid to lead the Organization for Security and Cooperation in Europe, an international body concerned with promoting democracy. "I think it's time for that to happen, it's an important step, and I'm glad you're willing to undertake it," Bill said. Nazarbayev had long sought the office; many around the world, looking at his record of squelching democracy, had opposed it. Among them was the junior senator from New York, Hillary Rodham Clinton.*

Not more than forty-eight hours after Bill and Giustra left Kazakhstan en route to stops in India and China, Giustra's company signed preliminary accords with Kazakhstan's state-owned uranium authority to invest in three uranium projects there. The deal shocked the worldwide mining industry, since Giustra's company, just beginning in the uranium business, won contracts worth tens of millions of dollars, while more established firms were frozen out.

Did Bill know about Giustra's intent in visiting Kazakhstan? Bill's spokesman said that while Bill knew that his friend had business interests in Kazakhstan, the ex-president was unaware of "any particular efforts" and provided no assistance in this regard. Giustra said that he discussed the deal with neither Bill nor Nazarbayev, but the head of the Kazakhstan uranium agency said that Giustra did discuss it with Nazarbayev, and that the Canadian's friendship with Bill "of course made an impression." The Kazakhstan official hastened to add that the deal was concluded for sound business reasons. However, the official would later claim that an employee of the Clinton Foundation had come to Kazakhstan to argue adamantly that the Giustra deal be approved.[5]

Some months after he and Bill visited Kazakhstan, Giustra would make a secret $31.3 million dollar gift to the Clinton Foundation. He later promised $100 million more.

Lawrence O'Donnell: Everything that he's done for money is unseemly for a former president. He can go to any foreign country, and take any money for any purpose and speech, and enter into any investment scheme.

It's really just a personal notion of what kind of dignity do you want to maintain, and what kind of dignity do you think people expect of you? Clinton was right in assessing that there is no dignity expectation for him.

---

*When Nazarbayev garnered 91 percent of his nation's vote in a sham election three months after Bill's trip, Bill sent a letter of congratulations. "Recognizing that your work has received an excellent grade is one of the most important rewards in life," wrote the former Leader of the Free World whose middle name is Jefferson.

Let's stress something: No former president has to do a single thing for money. The government pays them a lot of money when they leave the White House. Just on Clinton's government pension and office infrastructure alone, the Clintons were going to live better than they'd ever lived in their lives. But that wasn't good enough.

Paul Begala: I don't ever participate in his commercial activities, but I don't think I've ever known anybody less interested in money than Bill Clinton.

He's just not terribly impressed with it. You might say, "Mr. President, this guy's coming in, and he's a multimillionaire," and it's like, "So what?"

But when he left office, because of who he is, he needed a big house that the Secret Service could defend. And then his wife decided to run for the Senate, so they needed a place in Washington.

And he had these crushing legal bills, and was determined to pay them.

Lawrence O'Donnell: I was not surprised that they would use the fake excuse of legal bills.

For one thing, he could have said, "I'm going to do speeches only until I get the money to pay off these lawyers." Besides, either one of their books would have taken care of the legal bills.

Just how much did Bill and Hillary owe to lawyers? And how much did the Clintons themselves end up paying? In March 2001 officials of a fund set up to pay the fees reported that it and a similar fund had paid $7.4 million of a total bill of $11.3 million, leaving $3.9 million.[6] In 2002 Senator Clinton's disclosure form revealed that despite earnings the previous year of $12 million for his speeches and her upcoming book, the couple had paid out only $1.3 million in legal fees for themselves and unspecified "former staff members." Listing amounts only by range, the congressional disclosure form stated that Bill and Hillary still owed lawyers between $1.75 million and $6.5 million.[7]

A report in 2009 pegged the bills at more than $14 million. A report three years earlier used the $11 million figure and noted that part of it was paid by Ron Burkle.[8] How large was this billionaire's gift to an ex-president and a sitting United States senator? How much did the lawyers finally receive? Who knows? What does seem certain is that Bill and Hillary paid relatively little out of their own pockets.

Good Bill, Bad Bill. Magnificent humanitarian in Lesotho, a smooth operator's front man (witting or unwitting) in Kazakhstan.

Incredibly, they really are two sides of the same person.

71

Bill in a China Shop:
Hillary for President, 2008

"This was his wife, whom he absolutely admires."

By 2008 memories of Marc Rich and Monica Lewinsky had receded; in their place was the image of a resourceful philanthropist who undertakes impossible tasks and gets them done. Bill could legitimately claim to be not only what *Esquire* called him in 2005, "The Most Influential Man in the World," but also among the most popular. Even in his home country, where people know his flaws, admiration for him was widespread and growing.

Then came Hillary's campaign for president.

Elaine Kamarck: In 2008 he wanted, desperately, to help his wife, and he was extremely rusty.

Jonathan Alter: His political skills had atrophied. And he handled himself in a way not befitting a former president. Whether it was born of his feeling like he owed Hillary, or his guilt or whatever, it was very disturbing. Not just to outsiders, but to his own friends and supporters.

Paul Begala: I think it was less lack of practice and more that this was his wife, whom he absolutely admires. I don't believe I've ever heard him say, about any criticism of Hillary, "Oh, yeah, that's fair." Which he'll say about himself all the time. The only time in 1992 that I remember him getting upset about an attack was in a debate in Illinois, when Jerry Brown attacked his wife. He was authentically furious—I thought he was going to punch him. He said, "You are not fit to stand on the same stage as my wife."

Days after he and Hillary and the brain trust managing her supposedly unstoppable march to the White House were stunned by Barack Obama's victory in the January 3 Iowa caucuses, Bill let loose his frustrations—toward the press, toward Ken Starr, and toward this newcomer who dared not only to oppose Hillary's candidacy but also to challenge Bill himself for first place in the hearts of Democratic voters. Appearing at Dartmouth College in Hanover, New Hampshire, he was asked about criticism of Mark Penn, Hillary's chief strategist, but quickly pivoted and unleashed an astounding rant:

> Let's go over this again. That is the central argument for his [Obama's] campaign: "It doesn't matter that I started running for president less than a year after I got to the Senate from the Illinois State Senate. I am a great speaker and a charismatic figure and I'm the only one who had the judgment to oppose this war from the beginning. Always, always, always."

Bill went on to challenge Obama's version of history. First, he claimed that the 2002 resolution authorizing President Bush to use force in Iraq—a resolution Hillary voted for and Obama, not yet in the Senate, spoke against—did not grant Bush a blank check, but was conditioned on the refusal of Saddam Hussein's regime to cooperate with U.N. weapons inspectors. He went on to cite alleged past equivocations in Obama's antiwar stance. Why, he wanted to know, had no debate moderator ever asked Obama,

> "You said in 2004 there was no difference between you and George Bush on the war, and you took that speech you're now running on off your Web site in 2004 and there's no difference in your voting record and Hillary's ever since?' "

In other words, Why is the press going so easy on Obama when it was so hard on me?

> Give...me...a break. This whole thing is the biggest fairy tale I've ever seen.

The "fairy tale" line is what got the headlines, but Bill wasn't finished venting his rage:

> What about the Obama handout that was covered up, the press never reported on it, implying that I was a crook? Scouring me, scathing criticism over my financial reports. Ken Starr spent $70 million and indicted innocent people to find out that I wouldn't take a nickel to see the cow jump over the moon....
>
> The idea that one of these campaigns is positive and the other's negative, when I know the reverse is true, and I have seen it, and I have been blistered by it for months, is a little tough to take. Just because of the sanitizing coverage that's in the media doesn't mean the facts aren't out there.[1]

Some commentators, including the veteran Democratic strategist Donna Brazile, a colleague of Begala's on CNN, saw a racial message in Bill's remarks at Dartmouth and elsewhere:

For him to go after Obama, using fairy tale, calling him a "kid," as he did last week, it's an insult. And I tell you, as an African-American, I find his words and his tone to be very depressing.[2]

Paul Begala: I remain, to this day, puzzled how any fair-minded person could say that had the slightest thing in the world to do with race.

He was, I think, historically accurate. It's not politically what I would have advised him to say, because while less constant than he was holding himself out to be, Obama was much more against the war than Hillary ever was. And so, for Democrats who were against the war, Obama was always going to be better. She did vote for it, and he did speak out against it.

But whether it was good strategy or not, it had nothing to do with race.

At Dartmouth Bill did not mention another factor that may have set off his outburst.

Jonathan Alter: He called Ted Kennedy the day after Iowa seeking his endorsement. And not only was Kennedy not going to break his neutrality to endorse Hillary, he was moving toward Obama. The conversation went really badly. Clinton belittled Obama, which made Kennedy furious.

He started to try to tell Kennedy that Hillary had really been against the war, and that the vote in the Senate had been just giving the president the authority to go to war—it wasn't really a pro- versus antiwar vote. Kennedy, the leading antiwar figure in the Senate at the time, was the wrong person to try that snow job on.

Kennedy endorsed Obama on January 28.

"He became like a caged animal."

Bill was out of control in New Hampshire, but where he really put his foot in his mouth was South Carolina. On January 26, the day of that state's primary, which polls showed Obama would win going away, a reporter asked Bill, "What does it say about Barack Obama that it takes two of you to beat him?"

Bill responded, through a tightly wrapped smile:

Jesse Jackson won South Carolina twice, in '84 and '88. And he ran a good campaign. And Senator Obama's run a good campaign here. He's run a good campaign everywhere. He's a good candidate with a good organization.[3]

Most pundits had much the same reaction as ABC's Jake Tapper:

Boy, I can't understand why anyone would think the Clintons are running a race-baiting campaign to paint Obama as "the black candidate."[4]

Paul Begala: That was the one thing that I thought was a fair criticism of him. He could have, should have, also mentioned that, for example, John Edwards won South Carolina and didn't win the nomination.

Bloggers—bloggers! Bill hadn't had to deal with *them* in 1992 and 1996— weighed in:

> It pains me greatly to write this post because—despite his many faults—I have long been an admirer of Bill Clinton. . . . Clinton is sullying his reputa-tion, harming the Democratic coalition, and setting back race relations in this country.[5]

The accusations of racism hit Bill hard.

Paul Begala: I talked to him during some of those times, and it was the unkindest cut of all. It didn't bother him when people accused him of murder —it was like, "Whatever. Crazy people say things." But this was said by some people he knew and admired and loved. You could say a lot about Bill Clinton, but this was the worst thing you could ever say about him. It was very painful, like a punch in the stomach.

Bill: "I don't have to defend myself on civil rights."[6]

Jonathan Alter: I don't think that Clinton ever intended to make a racial comment, and I understand why he's hurt by that charge, because that's not the kind of person he is. But I also think that it was a sign of his desperation, that he was trying to find any way he could to minimize Obama's victory in South Carolina.

But the comment was a sign of his carelessness, and his lack of understand-ing of the way things would be interpreted, or misinterpreted. The pundit types would have cut him more slack if he hadn't just finished lying about Obama being a Reaganite, because Obama made that comment about Rea-gan changing the trajectory.

Barack Obama, speaking to the editorial board of the *Reno* (Nevada) *Gazette-Journal,* January 14, 2008:

> I think Ronald Reagan changed the trajectory of America in a way that Richard Nixon did not and in a way that Bill Clinton did not. He put us on a fundamentally different path because the country was ready for it.[7]

Jonathan Alter: That was partly intentional on Obama's part. He knew how to push Clinton's buttons.

And he kept pushing.
Barack Obama, to ABC's *Good Morning, America,* January 20, 2008:

You know, the former president, who I think all of us have a lot of regard for, has taken his advocacy on behalf of his wife to a level that I think is pretty troubling. He continues to make statements that are not supported by the facts. . . . This has become a habit, and one of the things that we're going to have to do is to directly confront Bill Clinton when he's making statements that are not factually accurate.[8]

Jonathan Alter: Bill was lying about Obama having really been pro-war. And was privately claiming that Obama was using race. And was privately saying that Obama wasn't good for the Jews—which Obama was furious about.[*]

The behavior of Bill and Hillary—she added controversial statements of her own in 2008, most notably that Obama was not a Muslim "as far as I know"—cost them the good opinion of people who had previously held them in high esteem.

Lawrence O'Donnell: The Clintons have a single mode when it comes to people who are running against them. It doesn't matter how long they've been in politics or what color they are or what party they are. None of that matters. It doesn't matter if they agree with them 99 percent, which was the agreement rate on policy between the Obama and Clinton campaigns.

It's a willingness to do absolutely anything, and say absolutely anything, that they think will help them win. Anything, about anyone, at any time. When they were doing that to people like Kenneth Starr it was one thing. What it took to display those characteristics in an extremely negative light for former Clinton supporters was to see the Clintons do it against the first credible black candidate for president in American history. And see their unhesitating willingness to do it.

Bill may have had a strategy in mind as he went after Obama, but as the campaign went on he seemed more and more to be out of sorts, both baffled and buffeted by events. In April, as Hillary and Obama were contesting Pennsylvania's primary, he seemed to come unhinged.

In a telephone interview on a radio show in Philadelphia, Bill was asked about the Jackson comment in South Carolina. "Do you think that was a mistake?" said the host. "And would you do that again?"

Bill responded:

No, I think that they played the race card on me. And we now know, from memos from the campaign and everything, that they planned to do it all along.

*For more of Alter's reporting on the Clinton-Obama dynamic, see his book *The Promise: President Obama, Year One* (New York: Simon and Schuster, 2010).

Bill fulminated for another three minutes until the interview ended. Once he said "Bye-bye," he thought he was no longer on the air. He was, however, and listeners heard him say to whoever was next to him, "I don't think I should take any shit from anybody on that, do you?"[9]

Bad enough. But the next day his behavior turned truly bizarre.

Mike Memoli, a reporter working jointly for NBC and *National Journal,* asked, "Sir, what did you mean yesterday when you said that the Obama campaign was playing the race card on you?"

> Clinton: When did I say that, and to whom did I say that?
>
> NBC/NJ: On WHYY radio yesterday.
>
> Clinton: No, no, no. That's not what I said. You always follow me around and play these little games, and I'm not going to play your games today. This is a day about election day. Go back and see what the question was, and what my answer was. You have mischaracterized it to get another cheap story to divert the American people from the real urgent issues before us, and I choose not to play your game today. Have a nice day.
>
> NBC/NJ: Respectfully sir, though, you did say . . .
>
> Clinton: Have a nice day. [Continues shaking hands with supporters.] I said what I said, you can go and look at the interview. And if you'll be real honest, you'll also report what the question was and what the answer was.[10]

Elaine Kamarck: In his own campaigns, he was a very shrewd operator, really the best political strategist in the room. That sense seems to have left him in 2008.

Jonathan Alter: The best explanation that I heard from people who were close to Clinton was that he had been misled by Terry McAuliffe* into believing that it was over, and that Hillary had it in the bag. And so it was a very rude shock when Hillary lost Iowa, and then started losing all those caucuses. And so he got desperate and he became like a caged animal.

Elaine Kamarck: The Jackson comment was exactly the signal the black community needed. After Obama won Iowa, the black community began to move, big-time, to Obama, because they said, "Wow, this guy is real. He has just won in a lily-white state. That means he can really win." And so blacks who'd been for Hillary because, among other reasons, they didn't think a black would be able to win, suddenly changed their mind.

Now, a lot of that would have happened without Bill Clinton, but he

---

*Chairman of Hillary's campaign.

upped the ante. That's why it was such a bad move, and why it boomeranged so badly.

Jonathan Alter: Before long, the Clinton campaign wanted him muzzled.

He's not the kind of guy who would sit there and plan exactly how he was going to diss Barack Obama. But it came naturally to him. And it was another sign of his losing his chops, in that he was saying things that were not in Hillary's political interest for him to say.

He was getting the worst of both worlds. He wasn't doing anything to hurt Obama—in fact, the backlash against him was helping Obama. And he was tarnishing his own reputation.

72

Unintended Consequences: Clinton-Era Deregulation and the Financial Crisis of 2008–2009

If one highlight of Bill's legacy, his contribution to race relations, suffered in early 2008, another, his stewardship of the U.S. economy, came into question a few months later. Insofar as the federal government was responsible for the financial crisis and recession of 2008–2009, most commentators have cast blame on the policies of the Bush 43 administration. However, some experts have pointed as well to Clinton-era deregulation of the financial-services industry.

Bill did not invent deregulation of the American economy in general (begun in earnest during the Carter administration) or of the financial sector in particular (advanced during the Reagan administration, with disastrous results in the savings-and-loan industry). But he did continue the trend.

Critics have focused on two pieces of legislation. The Nobel laureate Joseph Stiglitz discussed them.

Joseph Stiglitz: I think most economists agree that both the repeal of Glass-Steagall and the refusal to do anything about derivatives contributed to the current crisis in many different ways. There's absolutely no doubt about that.

The Glass-Steagall Act of 1933 was a key component in FDR's attempt to prevent a repeat of the financial collapse that set off the Great Depression.

Glass-Steagall had required the separation of investment banks and commercial banks.

Elements of Glass-Steagall had been chipped away at for years, but the Financial Services Modernization Act of 1999—pushed in Congress by Senator Phil Gramm (R-TX), supported by Robert Rubin, Larry Summers, and Alan Greenspan, and signed into law by Bill—repealed it. Financial companies were free to grow into all-in-one behemoths offering just about every financial service imaginable—from investment banking to brokerage services, from commercial banking to life insurance.[1]

Stiglitz outlined two of the consequences.

One was, it worsened the "too big to fail" problem. The worst example of that was, of course, the development of Citigroup.

Citigroup was just one of the financial monsters made possible by the 1999 legislation and saved from ruin in 2009 by hundreds of billions of taxpayer dollars.

A second problem was, there were two very different cultures between the investment banks and the commercial banks. Commercial banks are entrusted with ordinary people's money; investment banks take rich people's money and "gamble." One is supposed to be boring, one's supposed to be exciting. By merging, you took the gambling mentality and applied that to commercial banks.

Stiglitz outlined the reasons for the repeal of Glass-Steagall—under a Democratic president.

Why did it happen? There were many factors that contributed to support for its repeal. If I had to name one: money. The financial industry became a very large campaign contributor to the Democratic Party.

A year after repealing Glass-Steagall, Congress enacted the Commodity Futures Modernization Act of 2000, again pushed by Gramm and signed by Bill, which shielded the complex financial instruments known as "derivatives" from government regulation. The folly of the system became apparent in 2008, as the overstuffed derivatives market brought the global financial system to its knees.

Derivatives had begun to grow in the late '80s. By '95, '96 it was recognized that they were extraordinarily dangerous. The chair of the Commodity Futures Trading Commission had tried to regulate the derivatives, but Summers, Rubin, and Greenspan pushed back hard. They won; you can say the country lost.

The obvious consequence is the check that we wrote for $180 billion to AIG. You might say it's the tip of the iceberg, as the country has paid a high price for the high level of financial risk taken, but even that amount is a pretty big check.

In the spring of 2009 Bill took a measure of responsibility for the meltdown of derivatives.

> I very much wish now that I had demanded that we put derivatives under the jurisdiction of the Securities and Exchange Commission and that transparency rules had been observed and that we had done that. That I think is a legitimate criticism of what we didn't do.[2]

But when asked in the fall of 2008 whether he regretted signing the repeal of Glass-Steagall, he answered, in part,

> No, because it wasn't a complete deregulation at all. We still have heavy regulations and insurance on bank deposits, requirements on banks for capital and for disclosure. . . . I have really thought about this a lot. I don't see that signing that bill had anything to do with the current crisis.[3]

Stiglitz commented on Bill's defense of the 1999 bill.

Let me put the best face on it.

Yes, in principle: If we had regulators who believed in regulation, they probably did have instruments they could have used to curtail the bad behavior. But the direction that we had taken on deregulation was reflected not only in the regulation but in how regulation was implemented. To give you an example, in '94 we gave the Fed more power to regulate mortgages. But we reappointed Greenspan, and Greenspan decided not to use those regulatory powers.

Republican presidents appointed Greenspan to the first, second, and last of his five terms as chairman of the Federal Reserve from 1987 to 2006. But Bill reappointed him to his third and fourth, in 1996 and 2000.

There were two reasons Greenspan was reappointed by President Clinton. One was that the president didn't want market turmoil. Markets like continuity. But also, Greenspan was very close to Rubin, and they both believed in the deregulatory philosophy. Greenspan's free-market attitudes were well known by the time he got reappointed by Clinton.

So I don't think President Clinton can walk away from responsibility for the deregulation, when he knew that the person responsible for enforcing regulation didn't really believe in it.

73

Envoy:
A Visit to North Korea

The beating Bill's reputation took on the 2008 campaign trail began to heal with his generous speech endorsing Barack Obama at the Democratic National Convention that August. Another opportunity to repair his image came a year later, because two American journalists strayed across a river in Asia.

On March 17, 2009, Laura Ling and Euna Lee, working on a documentary for Al Gore's Current TV about the trafficking of North Korean women into China, were captured by North Korean border guards on the frozen Tumen River separating the two countries. Three months later a North Korean court sentenced the two women to twelve years' hard labor for illegally entering North Korea and for "hostile" acts.[1]

The Obama administration called for the release of the two reporters, but normal diplomatic channels offered little chance of influencing North Korea's actions, especially after the rise in tensions following Pyongyang's testing, on successive days in May 2009, of short-range missiles and a nuclear weapon.[2]

Robert Gallucci, serving in the State Department, was lead negotiator for the Clinton administration in talks with North Korea that resulted in the 1994 Agreed Framework, which limited that country's nuclear program.

Robert Gallucci: The Obama administration responded to the North Korean nuclear test and missile tests with more and more enthusiasm for tougher and tougher sanctions at the U.N. It felt, presumably, that this was a right and necessary thing to do. But it did not put them in a good position to reengage the North Koreans.

The administration sought a way around the impasse. Hillary proposed sending a special envoy and suggested some names.

The two names floating around were Richardson* and Gore.

*Bill Richardson, Democratic governor of New Mexico, served as U.N. ambassador, 1997–1998, and in 1996 visited North Korea to arrange the release of an American captive.

The North Koreans, however, told the captured journalists they wanted Bill. The women conveyed the message to their families, who passed it on to Gore, who passed it on to the Obama administration, which asked Bill to make the trip.[3]

When I heard it was Bill Clinton I said: That's better, for two reasons. One, he doesn't go if there isn't a clear expectation he's going to return with these women. And second, since there's a larger policy issue here, of the stalled engagement with North Korea, someone of Clinton's extraordinary presence actually has a chance of moving us out of the trough we seem to be in.

In August 2009 Bill and a few aides flew to Pyongyang on a jet provided by another of Bill's rich postpresidential friends, the real-estate heir Steve Bing. After the former president and the North Korean leader Kim Jong-Il conferred, the North Koreans announced that they had pardoned the women.[4]

Al Gore was among those meeting the plane carrying Bill and the two reporters when it landed at Bob Hope Airport in Burbank, California. Shortly after the arrival Ling described the end of her captivity: "We were taken to a location and when we walked through the doors, we saw standing before us President Bill Clinton. We were shocked, but we knew instantly in our hearts that the nightmare of our lives was finally coming to an end. And now we stand here home and free."[5]

74

And Now?
The Future of Bill Clinton

Paul Begala: He probably had a harder time with Hillary's loss than she did. As soon as the primaries were over, she was ready to help elect this guy. I think it took him a little longer.

The feeling was mutual.

Jonathan Alter: It took quite a long time before Bill Clinton worked his way back into the good graces of the Obama team. There's still tension.

Shortly after Barack Obama won election on November 4, 2008, he began discussions with Hillary about her becoming secretary of state. Bill approved of her taking the job, but his enthusiasm came with the knowledge that his own activities would be scrutinized by people working for her prospective boss.

By the end of November the Obama team came up with a set of conditions under which Bill could become first spouse of Foggy Bottom. The one that stirred the most interest was the disclosure of the previously secret list of donors to the Clinton Foundation. It turned out that foreign governments had been generous supporters of Bill's work: Saudi Arabia, Australia, and the Dominican Republic had each contributed between $10 million and $25 million; Norway, Oman, and Taiwan were among those kicking in at least $1 million. Wealthy and well-connected individuals had opened their wallets to Bill as well, people like the son-in-law of Ukraine's president and an Indian politician who in 2008 had spoken with Hillary to urge cooperation between his country and the United States on civilian nuclear power. Most surprising, perhaps, was the presence on the list of onetime bitter enemies: Rupert Murdoch, the owner of Fox News, and Richard Mellon Scaife, who had financed the anti-Clinton research effort known as the Arkansas Project, which dug up Troopergate, which led to Paula Jones.[1]

Among the other conditions the Obama team laid out:

- No annual meetings of the Clinton Global Initiative outside of the United States;
- No new contributions to CGI from foreign governments;
- Approval by State Department ethics officials or the office of the White House counsel for each business activity and paid speech.[2]

Paul Begala: He was very impressed with how straight-up the Obama team was with him: We need this and this, but not that. And everything was just what they said. They asked him not to host any more CGI events overseas. He said, "I think they're good for the country, but if that's what you want, fine." And that was it.

He tells his friends that he's very happy.

When this book is published, Bill Clinton will be sixty-four years old. What will he do with the years—if his heart holds out, perhaps decades—left to him?

Maybe as former president he will finally produce his one magnificent achievement, a contribution on the order of universal health insurance in the United States or peace in the Middle East, the unattained goals of his two most noble and ambitious failures as president.

Greatness may be closer to Bill's grasp now than ever before. He is shorter on resources than he was as president—he is no longer supported by the vast apparatus, civilian and military, he once commanded. But the impediments he once faced have receded, too. No Republican Congress blocks him at every turn. No press casts doubt on his every move.

Not only have his external tormentors fallen away, his inner obstacles are less formidable as well. Does he still seek sexual gratification outside his marriage? Probably—rumors abound, and he is, after all, still Bill Clinton—but his private life no longer threatens to derail his public endeavors. Tom DeLay and Linda Tripp and Paula Jones and Ken Starr have moved on. His wife is not president; the national press cares little about ungentlemanly behavior from the man who is first gentleman of only the State Department, not the nation. If any of the CEOs, prime ministers, and movie stars who can help him advance his humanitarian work care about his private moral failings, he can always find others who don't.

Although he gives no sign of losing his driving curiosity, he has conquered the inability to set priorities that bedeviled the early years of his administration—he has restricted his foundation's portfolio to a handful of narrowly focused areas. His temper and his sense of aggrievement, so vividly on display during Hillary's campaign, seem irrelevant now, as well: Unless Hillary rethinks her 2009 announcement that she will not again run for president, or unless Chelsea seeks elective office, there will never again be a political campaign in which he is so personally invested that he is apt to make a public fool of himself. He is still mostly free to pursue his newfound interest in making money; indeed, the Obama administration may be doing Bill a favor by frowning upon some of his more questionable associations. But even if he makes the occasional trip to a Central Asian dictatorship and his traveling partner comes away with his pockets full, the *New York Times* may write about it, but few people will be bothered.

It is odd, certainly, to speak of a man as an underachiever when he spent a dozen years as a governor and eight as president. Yet, Monica aside, balancing the budget, promoting free trade, solving regional conflicts, and fending off Republican attacks, while impressive achievements, cannot leave history, or, one thinks, Bill himself, satisfied in the face of this man's remarkable talents.

Not long before putting this manuscript to bed I met with a speaker in this book— someone who served in the Clinton administration. The first thing this person asked me as we were sitting down was, "So, now that you're almost done with the project, what do you think of Bill Clinton?"

"You know," I replied, "I'm not sure."

"Yeah," this person said, "me neither."

Bill's work on HIV/AIDS has lifted the circumstances of millions. As the United Nations special envoy to Haiti, he is intimately involved in that land's effort to rebuild after the 2010 earthquake. But negotiating with drug manufacturers and seeing that medicines make their way up remote African hilltops, and even overseeing the reconstruction of a poor Caribbean nation, are child's play compared with another goal he has set for himself: fighting climate change, which affects not just those who carry a virus but everyone who breathes, and every economy of every nation on Earth. Bill has lamented that he faced no great challenge as president—that he was not in office during a time of war or depression. Here, then, is the greatest challenge of all. Can 2005's "most influential man in the world" bring enough influence to bear not only to affect climate change but to confront it with force and courage? Can he go beyond a pilot program that will make the Empire

State Building green and move toward meaningful, global solutions? Or will he leave the climate to Al Gore and come up with some other Gordian knot—nuclear weapons, maybe, or Israel and the Palestinians after all—that he and only he can untie?

Can he overcome his outsized flaws so that his outsized talents can work to maximum effect? Can Bill Clinton save the world?

Maybe now Bill Clinton will finally live up to his potential.

Epilogue:
Closing Argument

Sam Donaldson: I think Bill Clinton will go down as a successful president, but I don't think there will be a huge mark by his name. I don't see a legacy that so far has surfaced that future generations will go back to and say, "This started it, right here, and this man gets the credit, or he gets the blame, for what's happened since."

Charles Stenholm: I guess the first word to pop up—he wasn't a failure. Were it not for the moral indiscretions, it would have had a much better feeling about it. But I can say he wasn't a failure.

Walter Mondale: I'm sorry about the one mistake, everybody knows about it, no point in discussing it, but I think he's a very good person who tried very hard to help produce an America that is sensitive, that is fair, that tries to create hope instead of this bitterness. He tried to do the same thing internationally. I think he's got to go down as a very successful president.

Dave McCurdy: On balance, I believe Bill Clinton was an effective president. The Clinton administration should be credited with a number of major accomplishments. On the domestic front, his administration balanced the national budget and created a federal surplus, passed welfare reform, and expanded the earned income tax credit. In international affairs Bill Clinton spearheaded the successful Irish peace process, the Bosnia / Dayton Accords, and passage of NAFTA. He helped America navigate the early post–Cold War era and fostered one of the longest periods of economic expansion in our nation's history.

Bob Graham: What he did, particularly in the areas of economics and racial harmony, will be more fully appreciated twenty-five years from now than it is today.

The great economic achievement was that he put a tourniquet around a hemorrhaging federal fiscal policy. And actually did more than put a tourniquet. He closed the artery, and we were on a path to doing some extremely important fiscal improvements for the federal government. That was totally abandoned by the Bush administration.

Dick Armey: What's his legacy? To me it's that he got away with it. He's the accidental president who's the luckiest guy I've ever seen in politics; who is charming and seductive and charismatic; who had one or two good policy moments in terms of my interpretation of what's good for the country; and whose conduct was so boorish that the average family would probably have cut their college sophomore kid out of the will for it. He is, in my estimation, the most successful adolescent I've ever known.

Terry McAuliffe: Listen, how many people could go through what Bill Clinton was subjected to for eight years and come out as the most popular second-term president ever? Not many. It was because he could relate to the ordinary American and they could relate to him. He was one of us.

He got into politics the right way. I always say this guy gets out of bed every single day to give the average Joe a shot at the American dream.

Elaine Kamarck: He's burnished his image somewhat with the good works he's done, but also we went through an era of serious screw-ups by a president, so it makes the other stuff look trivial.

We elected this frat boy president in 2000 and nobody thought it would be much of a problem. Now look what he did. As it became clear that the war in Iraq was a self-inflicted wound, that it was the result of intentional choices that indicated very bad judgment, there was a forgiveness of Bill Clinton's human foibles compared to George Bush's foibles, which actually killed people.

Paul Begala: There's no doubt that Bush made Clinton look better.

Hillary used to say to Bill Clinton while he was president, "Your problem is, you make it look so easy." In that sense, Clinton might have caused Bush. I think Bush sat there in Texas, very modestly talented, and watched Clinton and thought, "I can do that."

It's the same way I can watch LeBron James and think, "I can do that." But then I go out in the driveway and I make a fool of myself.

Michael Dukakis: When you think about Clinton, you think of a guy who was very able, very competent, was able to do a lot of things, but, with an unfriendly Congress for six of the eight years, couldn't do a lot of things he would have liked to have done. Now, why did he have that Congress? Well, apparently because he had the guts to push for universal health care, so how can you fault him for that?

Bill Clinton's probably the ablest guy I've ever worked with in public life. You couldn't help liking the guy, but he was liked not only because he was a personable guy but also because he produced. This guy worked. He got things done.

Michael Kinsley: Number one, he made liberalism viable again. I had come to believe what the Republicans were saying, which was that the tides of history had turned and we would never have another Democratic president. He proved that wrong. And then the second thing he did—this was a benefit in political terms but also very good in terms of our country—he made Democrats the party of fiscal responsibility. And furthermore, he was fiscally responsible. He deserves enormous credit for that—because that's hard.

Bob Kerrey: He gave the nation the confidence that it needed in troubled times. I'm thinking particularly of the '95 attack on the Murrah Building in Oklahoma City. But other moments—to get Rabin and Arafat together, it's the poster child for Clinton's contribution because of his great gesture stretching his arms out, bringing those two together. It was those kinds of gestures that I think he'll be remembered for, as much as anything. He made people feel good about their country. He'll get high marks for that. He'll get high marks for intellect and energy and the willingness to really get down on a street level of policy.

Harold Ickes: His greatest accomplishment was his economic program. He thinks the toughest program he pushed through was his economic program in his first year. By one vote, and not one Republican voted for it. Something that he will tell you to his dying day.

I'm somewhat ambivalent about the change of welfare, but on balance as you look at the welfare system—and it's going to take another decade until enough studies are done—it was a pretty bold move. By doing that he helped get welfare off the Democrats' back. He helped get the tax-and-spend characterization off the Democrats' back. Clinton was a profound force in reshaping how people looked at Democrats.

I think there's an extraordinary record of accomplishment.

Lawrence O'Donnell: I don't think that his presidency amounted to very much. There was a two-year Clinton presidency, where if Clinton wanted to do something it would not necessarily get done but would get a fair hearing and a lot of legislative energy pushing it. And then there was a six-year Gingrich government, in which Clinton was allowed a small editing function on what the Gingrich government would do.

In those six years not a single thing that the White House wanted to do got done. The Gingrich government wrote the welfare-reform bill, where they took Clinton's slogan and made a law that said, basically, "We're gonna kick people off welfare." They imposed on him a welfare bill that prior to their taking over he had absolutely no relationship to.

The shutdown? Just theatrics. Did Clinton then not sign a Republican budget? It was mismanaged on the Gingrich side, and Gingrich, obviously, is a flawed human being. The Republicans were stuck in too doctrinaire a belief that the whole country hates government.

Throw in a grotesquely stupid scandal, involving his own personal behavior, that overtakes every day of his presidency for a year, and it becomes one of history's least important presidencies, in terms of actually setting some kind of direction or establishing some kind of principle that goes forward beyond that presidency.

What's the legacy? I don't get it. There's no lesson on how to be president —at all.

Leon Panetta: The real legacy of Bill Clinton is that he cared about people and wanted to improve their lives. In many ways it was taking his own story and making it America's story. He was a kid who could have gone in the wrong direction. He could have wound up in jail, but he worked his way up and he succeeded, and he wanted America to be able to share in that dream. That's why people feel good about him, because they know who he is—they know his weaknesses, but they also know what he cares about.

Jonathan Alter: Clinton has a wonderment at the world and a curiosity about change, and that is very appealing in an uncertain and fast-changing world, like, "Hey, there's this one guy who is actually paying attention to all this stuff and can help us to manage the transition." And that's why that "bridge to the twenty-first century," which became such a hackneyed slogan, actually did represent something. He didn't change the country, but he did help to manage people's understanding of a period of great change.

It was that conversation more than legislation that was the hallmark of his presidency. He had a thoughtful and educational conversation with the American people.

Robert Reich: He accomplished many, many good and important things, established a bulwark against Republicans, and repositioned the Democrats. But I'm sad we didn't accomplish more.

Now there are some more conservative Democrats who believe that if you maintain a fiscally responsible economy, get the budget deficit down, have free trade, and make a little improvement in public education, then everybody can partake of the American dream. I think that's wrong. I don't see any evidence of it.

We're faced with real, concrete problems. We've got massive numbers of people who don't have health care, and the middle class is being shafted. Our educational system is in shambles relative to what it should be. Inequality is out of control. Unless Democrats acknowledge the problems and engage them on the scale that's needed, what's the purpose of having a Democratic Party?

We've got to get back on that track. Call it liberalism, call it liverwurst, call it the New Deal, call it the *New* New Deal, call it populism. I don't care what you call it.

David Bonior: He ran an extraordinarily good economy. What part of that was what he did or was just being at the right place at the right time, I'm not prepared to judge. I suspect he walked into a very good technological renaissance and it drove the economy.

Because of the Congress he had, his policies were incrementalist. That's how you'd have to describe it. He did a lot of things, but none of them were transformational—with, perhaps, the exceptions of welfare reform and the 1993 budget. In terms of his foreign policy, if you set the trade stuff aside, he did a very good job.

He could have been so much better, I guess is my refrain. And in quiet times, when he's by himself, I'm sure he thinks about that as well.

Elaine Kamarck: I'm still mad at Bill Clinton from time to time. He had the intellect, he had the charisma, and he had the political opportunity to be another FDR when it came to what Americans cared about.

And he couldn't.

Harold Ickes: I consider Clinton a progressive of the first order.

Lawrence O'Donnell: He was far more conservative than Ronald Reagan.

Dick Armey: I know I'm being harsh, but I never could bring myself to believe that in the case of Bill Clinton I was dealing with a serious adult.

Terry McAuliffe: I always say he's like a giant Saint Bernard dog. He loves everybody and wants everybody to love him. What a guy!

Dan Glickman: What did Shakespeare say? "He was a man, take him for all in all." Above everything else, with all his foibles, Clinton is a real human being—the good, the bad, and the ugly.

Peter Edelman: Bill Clinton is a very, very complicated man.

Speakers in *A Complicated Man*

All interviews were conducted by the author, except those obtained from the Butler Center for Arkansas Studies of the Central Arkansas Library System and the Pryor Center for Arkansas Oral and Visual History at the University of Arkansas. Except for major governmental offices, positions listed are only those that pertain to Bill's schooling, his campaigns, his tenure as state attorney general, governor, and president, and his postpresidency.

Abbreviations

PrCtr   Pryor Center
BtCtr   Butler Center

Jonathan Alter	Journalist, *Newsweek* magazine.
Roger Altman	Deputy secretary of the treasury, 1993–1994.
Dick Armey	Member of the U.S. House of Representatives (R-TX), 1985–2003; House majority leader, 1995–2003.
Donald Baer	Director of White House speechwriting, 1994–1995; White House communications director, 1995–1997.
James Baker	Served under Presidents Reagan and Bush 41 as White House chief of staff (1981–1985, 1992–1993), secretary of the treasury (1985–1988), and secretary of state (1989–1992). As White House chief of staff managed 1992 campaign for George H. W. Bush.
Marie Baker	Distant cousin on Bill's mother's side. PrCtr.
Julie Baldridge	Director of consumer affairs, Arkansas attorney general's office, 1979–1981; press secretary, Arkansas governor's office, 1979–1980. BtCtr.
Fred Barnes	Journalist, Fox News and the *Weekly Standard*. For parts of the 1990s he wrote for the *New Republic* and appeared on *The McLaughlin Group*.

Bob Barr	Member of the U.S. House of Representatives (R-GA), 1995–2003. On House Judiciary Committee during impeachment proceedings.
David Barram	Silicon Valley executive; deputy secretary of commerce, 1993–1996; administrator, General Services Administration, 1996–2001.
Charlene Barshefsky	Deputy, then acting U.S. trade representative, 1993–1997; trade representative, 1997–2001.
Paul Begala	Political consultant; top strategist, with partner James Carville, in 1992 Clinton campaign. Consultant to the Democratic National Committee and political adviser to Bill, 1993–1995. Counselor to the president, 1997–1999. Political commentator, CNN.
Samuel "Sandy" Berger	Deputy national security adviser, 1993–1997; national security adviser, 1997–2001.
Howard Berman	Member of the U.S. House of Representatives (D-CA) 1983–. On House Judiciary Committee during impeachment proceedings.
Owen Bieber	President, United Auto Workers, 1983–1995.
David Bonior	Member of the U.S. House of Representatives (D-MI), 1977–2003; majority whip, 1991–1995; minority whip, 1995–2002.
Peter Bourne	Presidential adviser in the Carter White House. Biographer of Jimmy Carter.
Ellen Brantley	Judge, Little Rock. On University of Arkansas Law School faculty with Bill and Hillary. Assistant attorney general, Arkansas attorney general's office, 1977–1978. Wife of Max.
Max Brantley	Journalist, formerly with the *Arkansas Gazette,* now editor of the *Arkansas Times.* Husband of Ellen.
John Breaux	U.S. senator (D-LA), 1987–2005. Member of the U.S. House of Representatives, 1972–1987.
Douglas Brinkley	Historian, Rice University.
Tom Brokaw	Journalist, *NBC News.*
Marie (Clinton) Bruno	Cousin on Bill's stepfather's side.
Dale Bumpers	Governor (D) of Arkansas, 1971–1975; U.S. senator, 1975–1999.
Tommy Caplan	Classmate of Bill's (Georgetown).
James Carville	Political consultant; top strategist, with partner Paul Begala, in 1992 Clinton campaign. Political commentator, CNN.
Dale Charles	President, Arkansas chapter of the NAACP.

Chevy Chase	Actor.
Arne Christenson	Senior aide to Speaker Newt Gingrich, 1995–1999; chief of staff, 1996–1999.
Warren Christopher	Head of vice presidential search committee, then director of transition team, 1992. Secretary of state, 1993–1997.
Henry Cisneros	Secretary of housing and urban development, 1993–1997. Mayor of San Antonio, Texas, 1981–1989.
Dan Clinton	Cousin on Bill's stepfather's side. PrCtr.
Roy Clinton Jr.	Cousin on Bill's stepfather's side. PrCtr.
Liz Clinton-Little	Cousin on Bill's stepfather's side. PrCtr.
William Cohen	Secretary of defense, 1997–2001. U.S. senator (R-ME) 1979–1997; member of the U.S. House of Representatives, 1973–1979.
John Conyers	Member of the U.S. House of Representatives (D-MI), 1965–.
Gregory Craig	Washington attorney. Law school classmate of Bill's. Coordinated White House legal defense during impeachment period.
Rose Crane	Classmate of Bill's (Hot Springs, Arkansas); director of the Arkansas Department of Natural and Cultural Heritage, 1979–1981. PrCtr and BtCtr.
Patty Howe Criner	Classmate of Bill's (Hot Springs, Arkansas); scheduler, then press secretary in Arkansas governor's office, 1979–1981. PrCtr and BtCtr.
Bob Dole	Republican presidential nominee, 1996. U.S. senator (R-KS), 1969–1996; majority leader, 1985–1987, 1995–1996; minority leader, 1987–1995. Member of the U.S. House of Representatives, 1961–1969.
Sam Donaldson	Journalist, *ABC News.*
Joan Duffy	Journalist, formerly with the Memphis *Commercial Appeal,* the *Arkansas Democrat,* and United Press International.
Michael Dukakis	Governor of Massachusetts (D) 1975–1979, 1983–1991. Democratic presidential nominee, 1988.
Ernest Dumas	Journalist, formerly with the *Arkansas Gazette;* now a columnist for the *Arkansas Times.*
Peter Edelman	Counselor to secretary of health and human services, 1993–1995; assistant secretary of HHS for planning and evaluation, 1995–1996. Resigned in 1996 to protest welfare-reform legislation. Married to Marian Wright Edelman, a mentor of Hillary.
Michael Emmick	Attorney in Whitewater Office of Independent Counsel (appointed by Kenneth Starr), 1997–2000.

Sharon Farmer	White House photographer, 1993–2001; director of White House photography, 1999–2001.
Clay Farrar	Attended Hot Springs High School four years behind Bill. PrCtr.
Judy Feder	Principal deputy assistant secretary for planning and evaluation, Department of Health and Human Services; 1993–1995. Key figure in health care initiative.
James Fisher	Lawyer for Paula Jones beginning in September 1997.
Jimmie Lou Fisher	Arkansas state auditor (D), 1979–1981; state treasurer, 1981–2003.
Robert Fiske	First Whitewater independent counsel, 1994.
Ray Flynn	Mayor of Boston (D), 1984–1993; ambassador to the Holy See, 1993–1997.
Larry Flynt	Publisher, *Hustler* magazine.
Ron Fournier	Journalist, Associated Press; covered Bill in Arkansas and Washington.
Barney Frank	Member of the U.S. House of Representatives (D-MA), 1981–. On House Judiciary Committee during impeachment proceedings.
Andrew Friendly	Personal assistant (body man) to Bill, 1993–1994.
Al From	Founder of the Democratic Leadership Council, in 1985; led DLC, 1985–2009.
Judy Gaddy	Scheduler, special assistant for constituent affairs, Arkansas governor's office, 1984–1992. BtCtr.
Robert Gallucci	Longtime State Department and U.N. official. Chief negotiator with North Korea during 1994 nuclear crisis.
Joe Gaylord	Political consultant; adviser to Newt Gingrich.
Dan Glickman	Member of the U.S. House of Representatives (D-KS), 1977–1995. Secretary of agriculture, 1995–2001.
Lucianne Goldberg	New York literary agent specializing in conservative themes; aided Linda Tripp in exposing Lewinsky affair.
Bob Graham	U.S. senator (D-FL), 1987–2005; governor of Florida, 1979–1986.
Ernest Green	One of the "Little Rock Nine," the nine students who were the first African Americans to attend Central High School in 1957.
Paul Greenberg	Journalist, formerly with the *Pine Bluff* (Arkansas) *Commercial,* now editorial page director and a columnist for the *Arkansas Democrat-Gazette.* Long a harsh critic of Bill.
Stan Greenberg	Pollster for 1992 Clinton campaign. White House pollster, 1993–1995.

Conrad Grisham	Cousin on Bill's mother's side.
Robert Haness	Classmate of Bill's (Hot Springs, Arkansas). PrCtr.
Rusty Hardin	Attorney in Whitewater Office of Independent Counsel (appointed by Robert Fiske), 1994.
Jim Hoagland	Foreign policy columnist, *Washington Post*.
Richard Holbrooke	Diplomat: ambassador to Germany, 1993–1994; assistant secretary for European and Canadian affairs, 1994–1996; envoy and negotiator for Bosnia and Kosovo; ambassador to the United Nations, 1999–2001.
Asa Hutchinson	Member of the U.S. House of Representatives (R-AR), 1997–2001. On House Judiciary Committee during impeachment proceedings.
Henry Hyde	Member of the U.S. House of Representatives (R-IL), 1975–2007. Chaired House Judiciary Committee during impeachment proceedings.
Christopher Hyland	Attended Georgetown School of Foreign Service in class two years behind Bill; deputy national political director, 1992 campaign, with responsibility for ethnic outreach.
Harold Ickes	New York political consultant and lawyer; deputy chief of staff, White House, 1994–1997.
Martin Indyk	Veteran National Security Council and State Department official. Posts held during Clinton administration: ambassador to Israel (1995–1997, 2000–2001); assistant secretary of state for Near East affairs, (1997–2000); special assistant to the president and senior director for Near East and South Asian affairs, National Security Council (1993–1995).
Chris Jennings	White House senior health care adviser, 1993–2001.
Elaine Kamarck	Cofounder, Progressive Policy Institute (affiliated with the Democratic Leadership Council); ran "Reinventing Government" initiative, 1993–1997. Senior policy adviser, Gore campaign, 2000.
Mickey Kantor	Chairman, 1992 campaign; U.S. trade representative, 1993–1996; secretary of commerce, 1996–1997.
Laura Karber	Friend of Bill's (Hot Springs, Arkansas); wife of Mike.
Mike Karber	Classmate of Bill's (Hot Springs, Arkansas); husband of Laura.
Jack Kemp	Republican vice presidential candidate, 1996. Secretary of housing and urban development, 1989–1993; member of the U.S. House of Representatives (R-NY), 1971–1989.
Bob Kerrey	U.S. senator (D-NE), 1989–2001; governor of Nebraska, 1983–1987.

Jim Yong Kim	Physician and public health expert. Cofounder of Partners in Health, an organization that provides health services to underserved populations around the world.
Peter King	Member of the U.S. House of Representatives (R-NY), 1993–.
Michael Kinsley	Journalist. "From-the-left" host of CNN's *Crossfire,* 1989–1995; editor of *Slate,* 1996–2002.
C. Everett Koop	U.S. surgeon general, 1981–1989. Advised on health care initiative, 1993–1994.
Lawrence Korb	Military analyst. Assistant secretary of defense, 1981–1985.
Steve Kroft	Journalist, *60 Minutes* (CBS News).
David Kusnet	Chief speechwriter, 1992 Clinton campaign and White House, 1993–1994.
Anthony Lake	National security adviser, 1993–1997.
Paul David Leopoulos	Classmate of Bill's (Hot Springs, Arkansas).
John Lewis	Member of the U.S. House of Representatives (D-GA), 1987–. Hero of civil rights movement.
Joe Lockhart	Press secretary, 1996 Clinton campaign. Deputy White House press secretary, 1997–1998; press secretary, 1998–2000.
Abbe Lowell	Attorney; counsel to Democratic minority on House Judiciary Committee during impeachment proceedings.
Lonnie Luebben	Taught Bill at Hot Springs High School. PrCtr.
Princeton Lyman	Veteran State Department official, expert on Africa. Posts held during Clinton administration: ambassador to South Africa, 1992–1995, assistant secretary of state for international organization affairs, 1996–1998.
Gene Lyons	Journalist, Arkansas. Columnist, *Arkansas Democrat-Gazette,* coauthor with Joe Conason of *The Hunting of the President:* The Ten-Year Campaign to Destroy Bill and Hillary Clinton (St. Martin's, 2000).
Richard Mays	Attorney, Little Rock; Clinton supporter and fund-raiser. Appointed by Bill in 1979 to serve unfinished term on Arkansas Supreme Court. Member (D), Arkansas state legislature, 1973–1977.
Terry McAuliffe	National fund-raiser, 1992 campaign. Finance chairman, Democratic National Committee, 1994–1996. Finance chairman and cochairman, 1996 campaign. Chairman, DNC, 2001–2005. Chairman, 2008 Hillary Clinton campaign.

Bill McCollum	Member of the U.S. House of Representatives (R-FL), 1981–2001. On House Judiciary Committee during impeachment proceedings.
Dave McCurdy	Member of the U.S. House of Representatives (D-OK), 1981–1995.
Mike McCurry	White House press secretary, 1995–1998.
Thomas F. "Mack" McLarty III	Classmate of Bill's (Hope, Arkansas); White House chief of staff, 1993–1994; counselor to the president, 1994–1997, special envoy for the Americas, 1997–1998.
Merrill A. "Tony" McPeak	Retired four-star general, U.S. Air Force; air force chief of staff, 1990–1994.
Robert Michel	Member of the U.S. House of Representatives (R-IL), 1957–1995; minority leader, 1981–1995.
Walter "Fritz" Mondale	Democratic presidential nominee, 1984. Vice president, 1977–1981. U.S. senator (D-MN), 1964–1976.
Rudy Moore, Jr.	Campaign manager, Bill's first run for governor, 1978; chief of staff, Arkansas governor's office, 1979–1981. BtCtr.
Bruce Morrison	Classmate of Bill's (law school). Member of the U.S. House of Representatives (D-CT), 1983–1991. Involved in Northern Ireland issue.
Jack Moseley	Journalist, Fort Smith, Arkansas, *Southwest Times-Record*. BtCtr.
Brian Mulroney	Prime minister of Canada, 1984–1993.
Dee Dee Myers	Press secretary, 1992 campaign; White House press secretary, 1993–1994.
Bob Nash	Senior aide for economic development, Arkansas governor's office, 1983–1989; head of Arkansas Development Finance Authority, 1989–1992; undersecretary for small community and rural development, U.S. Department of Agriculture, 1993–1995; director of White House personnel, 1995–2001. BtCtr.
Roy Neel	Longtime aide to Al Gore; deputy White House chief of staff, 1993–1994.
Nathan "Mac" Norton	Attorney, Little Rock. Student of Bill's at University of Arkansas Law School; deputy attorney general for consumer protection, Arkansas attorney general's office, 1977–1979; chairman, Arkansas Public Service Commission, 1979–1983.
Robert Oakley	Longtime State Department official; special envoy to Somalia, 1992–1993 and 1993–1994.

Lawrence O'Donnell	Chief of staff, Senate Finance Committee under Chairman Daniel Patrick Moynihan during Clinton health care initiative; political commentator, MSNBC.
Leon Panetta	Director, Office of Management and Budget, 1993–1994; White House chief of staff, 1994–1997. Member of the U.S. House of Representatives (D-CA), 1977–1993.
Margaret Polk	Distant cousin on Bill's mother's side. PrCtr.
David Pryor	U.S. senator (D-AR), 1979–1997; governor of Arkansas, 1975–1979; member of the House of Representatives, 1966–1973.
Joe Purvis	Classmate of Bill's (Hope, Arkansas); son of Tom.
Tom Purvis	Resident of Hope, Arkansas; father of Joe. PrCtr.
Scott Reed	Republican political consultant; manager of Dole campaign, 1996.
Hugh Reese	Resident of Hope, Arkansas; husband of Myra.
Myra Reese	Cousin on Bill's mother's side; wife of Hugh.
Robert Reich	Classmate of Bill's (Oxford); secretary of labor, 1993–1997.
Albert Reynolds	Taoiseach (prime minister) of the Republic of Ireland, 1992–1994.
Alice Rivlin	Deputy director, Office of Management and Budget, 1993–1994; director, 1994–1996; vice chairwoman, Federal Reserve Board, 1996–1999.
Charles Robb	U.S. senator (D-VA), 1989–2001; governor of Virginia, 1982–1986.
Paul Root	Taught Bill at Hot Springs High School; special assistant for education, Arkansas governor's office, 1983–1987.
Dennis Ross	Chief Middle East envoy, 1993–2001. Filled the same role during the Bush 41 administration.
Kent Rubens	Attorney, West Memphis, Arkansas. Special chief justice, Arkansas Supreme Court, 1989; member (D), Arkansas House of Representatives, 1975–1981.
Robert Rubin	National economic adviser, 1993–1995; secretary of the treasury, 1995–1999.
Lottie Shackelford	Mayor (D), Little Rock, 1987–1991. Vice chairwoman, Democratic National Committee, 1989–.
Michael Sheehan	Debate / speech consultant.
Hugh Shelton	Retired four-star general, U.S. Army. Chairman of the Joint Chiefs of Staff, 1997–2001.
Alan Simpson	U.S. senator (R-WY), 1979–1997.
Rodney Slater	Aide in Arkansas governor's office, 1983–1987; member of Arkansas State Highway Commission, 1987–1993;

	director, Federal Highway Administration, 1993–1997; secretary of transportation, 1997–2001.
Craig Smith	Political consultant; worked for Bill in Arkansas and Washington, holding a variety of policy and political jobs, including deputy campaign manager and political director, 1996 campaign, and White House political director, 1997–1999.
Steve Smith	Managed Bill's campaign for Arkansas attorney general, 1976; chief of staff, Arkansas attorney general's office, 1977–1979; senior aide, Arkansas governor's office, 1979–1980. BtCtr.
Nancy Soderberg	Foreign policy coordinator, 1992 Clinton campaign; special assistant to the president for national security affairs and staff director, National Security Council, 1993–1995; deputy assistant to the president for national security affairs, 1995–1997; alternate representative, United Nations, 1997–2001.
Doug Sosnik	Democratic political consultant. At White House: deputy director of legislative affairs, 1994–1995; political director, 1996; counselor to the president, 1997; senior adviser to the president, 1998–1999.
Carolyn Staley	Classmate and next-door neighbor of Bill's (Hot Springs, Arkansas).
Mark Stein	Attorney in Whitewater Office of Independent Counsel (appointed by Robert Fiske), 1994.
Charles Stenholm	Member of the U.S. House of Representatives (D-TX), 1979–2005.
Joseph Stiglitz	Nobel laureate in economics, 2001. Member, Council of Economic Advisers, 1993–1995; chairman, 1995–1997.
Lawrence Summers	Undersecretary for international affairs, Treasury Department, 1993–1995; deputy secretary, 1995–1999; secretary, 1999–2001.
John Sununu	White House chief of staff, Bush 41 administration, 1989–1991; governor (R) of New Hampshire, 1983–1989. "From-the-right" host of CNN's *Crossfire,* 1992–1998.
John Sweeney	President, Service Employees International Union, 1980–1995; president, AFL-CIO, 1995–2009.
Strobe Talbott	Classmate of Bill's (Oxford); ambassador at large and special adviser to the secretary of state on the new independent states, 1993–1994; deputy secretary of state, 1994–2001.

Billy Tauzin	Member of the U.S. House of Representatives (LA), 1980–2005. Formerly a Democrat; switched parties in 1995.
David Terrell	Journalist, formerly with the *Arkansas Democrat, Arkansas Gazette,* and Memphis *Commercial Appeal.*
Helen Thomas	Washington journalist. Longtime White House correspondent, United Press International.
Nina Totenberg	Legal affairs correspondent, National Public Radio.
Mary Nell Turner	Resident of Hope, Arkansas. PrCtr.
Kathy Van Laningham	Senior assistant for education, Arkansas governor's office, 1988–1992. BtCtr.
Melanne Verveer	Attended Georgetown Institute of Linguistics and Languages during Bill's attendance at the School of Foreign Service. Deputy chief of staff, office of the first lady, 1993–1997; chief of staff, 1993–1997. Wife of Phil.
Phil Verveer	Attended Georgetown School of Foreign Service two years ahead of Bill. Husband of Melanne.
Michael Waldman	Special assistant to the president for policy coordination, 1993–1995; director of speechwriting, 1995–1999.
Martha Whetstone	Friend of Bill's from Arkansas.
Tom Williamson	Classmate of Bill's (Oxford); solicitor of labor, 1993–1996.
Donna Taylor Wingfield	Classmate of Bill's (Hope, Arkansas). PrCtr.
Solomon Wisenberg	Attorney in Whitewater Office of Independent Counsel (appointed by Kenneth Starr), 1997–1999.
Harris Wofford	U.S. senator (D-PA), 1991–1995; CEO, Corporation for National and Community Service, which runs AmeriCorps and other service programs, 1995–2001.
Phil Wogaman	Methodist minister, Washington, DC.
Jim Woolsey	Director of central intelligence, 1993–1994.
George Wright Jr.	Classmate of Bill's (Hope, Arkansas). PrCtr.
Janet Yellen	Chairwoman, Council of Economic Advisers, 1997–1999.

Notes

Note: Except for those interviews attributed to the Pryor Center or the Butler Center, quotations from all speakers come from interviews conducted by the author.

1. Small Town Boy

1. 1940 census.

2. David Maraniss, *First in His Class: The Biography of Bill Clinton* (New York: Simon and Schuster, 1995), 24.

3. Marie Russell Baker, interview by Michael Pierce, February 22, 2002, William Jefferson Clinton History Project: Phase One—The Hope and Hot Springs Years, Pryor Center for Arkansas Oral and Visual History, Special Collections, University of Arkansas Libraries, Fayetteville. http://libinfo.uark.edu/specialcollections/pryorcen ter/ (accessed December 1, 2006). All subsequent quotations from this speaker come from this source.

4. Maraniss, *First in His Class,* 28–29.

5. Margaret Polk, interview by Michael Pierce, February 22, 2002, William Jefferson Clinton History Project: Phase One—The Hope and Hot Springs Years, Pryor Center for Arkansas Oral and Visual History, Special Collections, University of Arkansas Libraries, Fayetteville. http://libinfo.uark.edu/specialcollections/pryorcenter/ (accessed December 1, 2006). All subsequent quotations from this speaker come from this source.

6. Maraniss, *First in His Class,* 30.

7. George Wright Jr., interview by Andrew Dowdle, September 15, 2004, William Jefferson Clinton History Project: Phase One—The Hope and Hot Springs Years, Pryor Center for Arkansas Oral and Visual History, Special Collections, University of Arkansas Libraries, Fayetteville. http://libinfo.uark.edu/specialcollections/pryorcen ter/ (accessed December 1, 2006). All subsequent quotations from this speaker come from this source.

8. Maraniss, *First in His Class,* 22.

9. Tom Purvis, interview by Michael Pierce, August 16, 2002, William Jefferson Clinton History Project: Phase One—The Hope and Hot Springs Years, Pryor Center for Arkansas Oral and Visual History, Special Collections, University of Arkansas Libraries, Fayetteville. http://libinfo.uark.edu/specialcollections/pryorcenter/ (accessed December 1, 2006).

10. MacDowell "Mac" and Mary Nell Turner, interview by Michael Pierce, August 15, 2002, William Jefferson Clinton History Project: Phase One—The Hope and Hot Springs Years, Pryor Center for Arkansas Oral and Visual History, Special Collections, University of Arkansas Libraries, Fayetteville. http://libinfo.uark.edu/special collections/pryorcenter/ (accessed December 1, 2006).

11. Virginia Kelley with James Morgan, *Leading with My Heart* (New York: Simon and Schuster, 1994), 50.

12. Baker interview.

13. Bill Clinton, *My Life* (New York: Knopf, 2004), 11.

14. Maraniss, *First in His Class,* 22.

15. Clinton, *My Life,* 18.

16. Donna Taylor Wingfield, interview by Andrew Dowdle, March 20, 2005, William Jefferson Clinton History Project: Phase One—The Hope and Hot Springs Years, Pryor Center for Arkansas Oral and Visual History, Special Collections, University of Arkansas Libraries, Fayetteville. http://libinfo.uark.edu/specialcollections/pryorcenter/ (accessed December 1, 2006). All subsequent quotations from this speaker come from this source.

17. Maraniss, *First in His Class,* 31.

18. Ibid., 32.

19. Kelley, *Leading with My Heart,* 89, 94.

20. Maraniss, *First in His Class,* 32; Kelley, *Leading with My Heart,* 91–92.

21. Clinton, *My Life,* 20; Kelley, *Leading with My Heart,* 91–92.

2. A Big City (pop. 29,307)

1. Population of Hot Springs: 1950 census.

2. Clinton, *My Life,* 22–23; Maraniss, *First in His Class,* 33; Kelley, *Leading with My Heart,* 93, 102–103.

3. Patty Howe Criner, interview by Jujuan Johnson, June 1, 2006, Butler Center for Arkansas Studies, Arkansas Studies Institute, Little Rock.

4. Roy Clinton Jr., interview by Andrew Dowdle, August 24, 2004, William Jefferson Clinton History Project: Phase One—The Hope and Hot Springs Years, Pryor Center for Arkansas Oral and Visual History, Special Collections, University of Arkansas Libraries, Fayetteville. http://libinfo.uark.edu/specialcollections/pryorcenter/ (accessed December 1, 2006). All subsequent quotations from this speaker come from this source.

5. Criner Butler Center interview.

6. Clay and Kathy Farrar, interview by Andrew Dowdle, June 24, 2005, William Jefferson Clinton History Project: Phase One—The Hope and Hot Springs Years, Pryor Center for Arkansas Oral and Visual History, Special Collections, University of Arkansas Libraries, Fayetteville. http://libinfo.uark.edu/specialcollections/pryorcenter/ (accessed December 1, 2006). All subsequent quotations from this speaker come from this source.

7. Criner, Butler Center interview.

8. Patty Howe Criner, interview by Andrew Dowdle, July 20, 2005, William Jefferson Clinton History Project: Phase One—The Hope and Hot Springs Years, Pryor Center for Arkansas Oral and Visual History, Special Collections, University of Arkansas Libraries, Fayetteville. http://libinfo.uark.edu/specialcollections/pryorcenter/ (accessed December 1, 2006).

9. Lonnie Luebben, interview by Andrew Dowdle, February 2, 2005, William Jefferson Clinton History Project: Phase One—The Hope and Hot Springs Years, Pryor Center for Arkansas Oral and Visual History, Special Collections, University of Arkansas Libraries, Fayetteville. http://libinfo.uark.edu/specialcollections/pryorcenter/ (accessed December 1, 2006). All subsequent quotations from this speaker come from this source.

10. Maraniss, *First in His Class,* 33.

11. Rose Crane, interview by Andrew Dowdle, June 25, 2005, William Jefferson Clinton History Project: Phase One—The Hope and Hot Springs Years, Pryor Center for Arkansas Oral and Visual History, Special Collections, University of Arkansas Libraries, Fayetteville. http://libinfo.uark.edu/specialcollections/pryorcenter/ (accessed December 1, 2006).

12. Ibid.

13. Criner, Pryor Center interview.

14. Kelley, *Leading with My Heart,* 109, 123.

15. Rose Crane, interview by Jujuan Johnson, May 24, 2006, Butler Center for Arkansas Studies, Arkansas Studies Institute, Little Rock.

16. Liz Clinton-Little, interview by Andrew Dowdle, March 15, 2004, William Jefferson Clinton History Project: Phase One—The Hope and Hot Springs Years, Pryor Center for Arkansas Oral and Visual History, Special Collections, University of Arkansas Libraries, Fayetteville. http://libinfo.uark.edu/specialcollections/pryorcenter/ (accessed December 1, 2006). All subsequent quotations from this speaker come from this source.

17. Dan Clinton, interview by Andrew Dowdle, March 14, 2004, William Jefferson Clinton History Project: Phase One—The Hope and Hot Springs Years, Pryor Center for Arkansas Oral and Visual History, Special Collections, University of Arkansas Libraries, Fayetteville. http://libinfo.uark.edu/specialcollections/pryorcenter/ (accessed December 1, 2006). All subsequent quotations from this speaker come from this source.

18. Clinton, *My Life,* 29.

19. Ibid., 50; Kelley, *Leading with My Heart*, 145.

20. Kelley, *Leading with My Heart*, 149; Maraniss, *First in His Class*, 41–42.

21. Clinton, *My Life*, 52.

22. Criner, Pryor Center interview.

23. Clinton, *My Life*, 79; Kelley, *Leading with My Heart*, 160–161.

24. Kelley, *Leading with My Heart*, 134. Bill's account of the incident: Clinton, *My Life*, 45–46.

25. Clinton, *My Life*, 105, 112–113.

26. Maraniss, *First in His Class*, 100.

27. Clinton, *My Life*, 55.

28. Maraniss, *First in His Class*, 45.

29. Robert Haness, interview by Andrew Dowdle, May 15, 2004, William Jefferson Clinton History Project: Phase One—The Hope and Hot Springs Years, Pryor Center for Arkansas Oral and Visual History, Special Collections, University of Arkansas Libraries, Fayetteville. http://libinfo.uark.edu/specialcollections/pryorcenter/ (accessed December 1, 2006).

30. Clinton, *My Life*, 55–56.

31. Crane, Butler Center interview.

32. Crane, Pryor Center interview.

33. Clinton, *My Life*, 60–62.

3. Positive, Positive, Positive, Positive

1. Maraniss, *First in His Class*, 50.

2. Ibid., 55–56.

3. Clinton, *My Life*, 84.

4. Ibid., 90.

4. Man of the World

1. Maraniss, *First in His Class*, 93, 102–103; Clinton, *My Life*, 114. On the history of women's eligibility for the Rhodes Scholarship, see rhodestrust.org.

2. Spencer C. Tucker, ed., *The Encyclopedia of the Vietnam War: A Political, Social, and Military History* (New York: Oxford University Press, 2000), s.v. "Draft"; "Texts of 3 Documents on Deferment from Draft," *New York Times*, February 17, 1968.

3. Maraniss, *First in His Class*, 165, 169; Clinton, *My Life*, 152.

4. Maraniss, *First in His Class*, 172.

5. Clinton, *My Life*, 154.

6. Maraniss, *First in His Class*, 173–174, 177–178.

7. Ibid., 174, 180.

8. Ibid., 192–193. For the full range of contemporary draft classifications, see "Here All 18 Statuses for Draft," *Pittsburgh Post-Gazette*, January 31, 1966.

9. David E. Rosenbaum, "Drawing Tonight Will Determine Who Is Drafted," *New York Times,* December 1, 1969; "Order of the Draft Drawing, *New York Times,* December 2, 1969.

10. Selective Service Web site, http://selectiveservice.us/military-draft/8-induction.shtml.

11. David E. Rosenbaum, "Thousands Given Draft Loophole," *New York Times,* October 1, 1970.

12. Clinton, *My Life,* 175–177; Maraniss, *First in His Class,* 230.

13. Clinton, *My Life,* 194–198.

5. On the Move

1. Nigel Hamilton, *Bill Clinton, An American Journey: Great Expectations* (New York: Random House, 2003), 274–275.

2. Criner, Butler Center interview.

3. Maraniss, *First in His Class,* 317.

4. Hillary Rodham Clinton, *Living History* (New York: Simon and Schuster, 2003), 74.

5. Clinton, *My Life,* 227.

6. Ibid., 241–242, Clinton, *Living History,* 76–77.

7. Julie Baldridge, interview by Jujuan Johnson, August 10, 2006, Butler Center for Arkansas Studies, Arkansas Studies Institute, Little Rock. All subsequent quotations from this speaker come from this source.

8. Steve Smith, interview by Jujuan Johnson, March 15, 2006, Butler Center for Arkansas Studies, Arkansas Studies Institute, Little Rock. All subsequent quotations from this speaker come from this source.

6. Too Much, Too Soon, Too Bad

1. Clinton, *My Life,* 255–258.

2. Rudy Moore Jr., interview by Jujuan Johnson, March 14, 2006, Butler Center for Arkansas Studies, Arkansas Studies Institute, Little Rock. All subsequent quotations from this speaker come from this source.

3. Criner, Butler Center interview.

4. Jack Moseley, interview by Jujuan Johnson, March 17, 2006, Butler Center for Arkansas Studies, Arkansas Studies Institute, Little Rock. All subsequent quotations from this speaker come from this source.

5. Clinton, *My Life,* 265; Maraniss, *First in His Class,* 361.

6. "Flight from Cuba: Exodus Is Very Different from '80 Boatlift," *New York Times,* August 24, 1994. "Mariel Boatlift," GlobalSecurity.org, http://www.globalsecurity.org/military/ops/mariel-boatlift.htm.

7. Clinton, *My Life,* 275.

8. "Two Decades Later, "Mariel Boat Lift Refugees Still Feel Effects of Riot," *Los Angeles Times* (Associated Press), May 5, 2001; "Cubans Riot at Fort Chaffee Center," *Pittsburgh Post-Gazette* (Associated Press), June 2, 1980; Dave Hughes, "Former POW Camp Goes up in Flames," *Arkansas Democrat-Gazette,* February 3, 2008.

9. Clinton, *My Life,* 275–276.

10. Ibid., 277.

11. Maraniss, *First in His Class,* 378.

12. Clinton, *My Life,* 279.

13. Criner, Butler Center interview.

14. Clinton, *My Life,* 282.

15. Ibid., 276.

16. Ibid., 283.

7. Out of the Woodshed

1. Clinton, *My Life,* 295.

2. Ibid., 301–302.

3. Ibid., 303.

8. Busy, Busy, Busy

1. Clinton, *My Life,* 309–310.

2. Kathy Van Laningham, interview by Jujuan Johnson, March 14, 2006, Butler Center for Arkansas Studies, Arkansas Studies Institute, Little Rock. All subsequent quotations from this speaker come from this source.

3. Bob Nash, interview by Jujuan Johnson, September 8, 2006, Butler Center for Arkansas Studies, Arkansas Studies Institute, Little Rock. All subsequent quotations from this speaker come from this source.

4. Judy Gaddy, interview by Jujuan Johnson, April 13, 2006, Butler Center for Arkansas Studies, Arkansas Studies Institute, Little Rock. All subsequent quotations from this speaker come from this source.

9. Comfort Level

1. The Encyclopedia of Arkansas History and Culture, "Desegregation of Central High School," Butler Center for Arkansas Studies, Arkansas Studies Institute, Little Rock, http://www.encyclopediaofarkansas.net/encyclopedia/entry-detail.aspx?ent ryID=718; Anthony Lewis, "President Sends Troops to Little Rock, Federalizes Arkansas National Guard; Tells Nation He Acted to Avoid an Anarchy," *New York Times,* September 25, 1957; "School Desegregation in Little Rock, Arkansas: A Staff Report of the United States Commission on Civil Rights, June 1977," http://www.law.umary land.edu/marshall/usccr/documents/cr12d4514.pdf.

11. National Democrat

1. Constitution of the State of Arkansas of 1874, Amendment 63, Four Year Terms for State Constitutional Officers. See the Web site of the Arkansas secretary of state: http://www.arkleg.state.ar.us/assembly/Summary/ArkansasConstitution1874.pdf, 134.

2. Clinton, *My Life,* 341.

3. Maraniss, *First in His Class: The Biography of Bill Clinton,* 446–447; Clinton, *My Life,* 342–343. Video at "The Tonight Show Experience," NBC.com, http://www .nbc.com/the-tonight-show-experience/video/clips/july-28-1988-bill-clinton/ 1014881/.

4. "His Side of the Story," *Time,* June 28, 2004.

5. Patrick Healy, "Bill Clinton Flatly Asserts He Opposed War at Start," *New York Times,* November 28, 2007.

6. "Remarks: 'The Road Ahead': Hon. Bill Clinton, Governor, State of Arkansas; Incoming Chairman, Democratic Leadership Council." Transcript provided to the author by the DLC.

12. Going for It

1. "The New Covenant: Responsibility and Rebuilding the American Community: Remarks to Students at Georgetown University," October 23, 1991. DLC Web site, http://www.dlc.org/ndol_ci.cfm?contentid=2783&kaid=128&subid=174.

2. "A New Covenant for American Security: Remarks to Students at Georgetown University," December 12, 1991, DLC Web site, http://www.dlc.org/ndol_ci.cfm? contentid=250537&kaid=128&subid=174.

13. Near-Death Experience

1. "In 1992, Clinton Conceded Marital 'Wrongdoing,'" Special Report: Clinton Accused, *Washington Post,* 1998. Subsequent citations of this interview are from this transcript.

2. "Testing of a President; Excerpts from the Clinton Deposition in Jones Sexual Misconduct Suit," *New York Times,* March 16, 1998.

3. "Text of 1969 Letter," *Arkansas Democrat-Gazette,* February 13, 1992. Emphasis added. Subsequent quotations of this letter are from this source.

4. "Colonel Says Clinton Deceived Him to Join ROTC," *Arkansas Democrat-Gazette,* September 17, 1992.

5. Gwen Ifill, "The 1992 Campaign: New Hampshire: Clinton Thanked Colonel in '69 For 'Saving Me from the Draft,'" *New York Times,* February 13, 1992.

6. Gwen Ifill, "The 1992 Campaign: Democrats: Vietnam War Draft Status Becomes Issue for Clinton," *New York Times,* February 7, 1992.

7. Maraniss, *First in His Class,* 190–194; Clinton, *My Life,* 159.

8. Clinton, *My Life,* 391.

9. John King, "Clinton Returns to New Hampshire," *CNN,* February 18, 1999, http://www.cnn.com/ALLPOLITICS/stories/1999/02/18/clinton.nh/index .html.

10. "1992 Presidential Primary, February 18, 1992, Democratic, Summary by Counties," Office of the Secretary of State, State of New Hampshire, http://www.sos.nh .gov/presprim1992/dem%20summary.htm.

14. All Roads Lead to Madison Square Garden

1. Richard L. Berke, "The 1992 Campaign: Political Memo: Tsongas Runs Hard on a Tightrope as He Reluctantly Goes on Offensive," *New York Times,* March 9, 1992.

2. Gwenn Ifill, "The 1992 Campaign: Clinton; Players in Familiar Roles as Vote Nears Clinton Faces Questions About His Past and Spars with Rival," *New York Times,* April 6, 1992.

3. "The 1992 Campaign: Verbatim; Heckler Stirs Clinton Anger: Excerpts from the Exchange," *New York Times,* March 28, 1992.

4. Gwen Ifill, "The 1992 Campaign: New York; Clinton Admits Experiment with Marijuana in 1960's," *New York Times,* March 30, 1992.

5. Robin Toner, "The 1992 Campaign: Primaries; Clinton Is Victor in New York with 41% of Democratic Vote; Tsongas Edges Brown for 2d," *New York Times,* April 8, 1992.

6. B. Drummond Ayres Jr., "The 1992 Campaign: On the Sidelines; Tsongas Declares He Won't Re-enter Democratic Race," *New York Times,* April 10, 1992.

7. "Statement of Vote, Primary Election, June 2, 1992," Office of the Secretary of State, State of California, http://www.sos.ca.gov/elections/sov/1992-primary/1992 -primary-sov.pdf.

8. "The 1992 Campaign: On The Trail; Poll Gives Perot a Clear Lead," *New York Times,* June 11, 1992.

9. Sheila Rule, "The 1992 Campaign: Racial Issues; Rapper, Chided by Clinton, Calls Him a Hypocrite," *New York Times,* June 17, 1992.

10. Clinton, *My Life,* 411.

15. A Bubba, Not a Bozo

1. Andrew Rosenthal, "Bush Encounters the Supermarket, Amazed," *New York Times,* February 5, 1992.

2. Andrew Rosenthal, "The 1992 Campaign: The Republicans; Bush Questions Clinton's Account of Vietnam-Era Protests and Trip," *New York Times,* October 8, 1992.

3. Nicholas D. Kristof, "Crackdown in Beijing: Troops Attack and Crush Beijing

Protest; Thousands Fight Back, Scores Are Killed," *New York Times,* June 4, 1989; "1989: Massacre in Tiananmen Square," On This Day, June 4, Web site of BBC, http://news.bbc.co.uk/onthisday/hi/dates/stories/june/4/newsid_2496000/2496277.stm.

4. Robert Pear, "Crackdown in Beijing: President Assails Shootings in China," *New York Times,* June 4, 1989; "Excerpts from the President's News Conference," *New York Times,* November 8, 1989.

5. Laurence I. Barrett, Ann Blackman, Ratu Kamlani, and Richard Woodbury, "Perot Takes a Walk," *Time,* July 27, 1992; Richard L. Berke, "The 1992 Campaign: The Overview; Perot Says He Quit in July to Thwart G.O.P. 'Dirty Tricks,' " *New York Times,* October 26, 1992.

6. "October 15, 1992 Second Half Debate Transcript," Web site of Commission on Presidential Debates, http://www.debates.org/index.php?page=october-15-1992-second-half-debate-transcript.

17. Bedlam at Birth

1. Richard L. Berke, "The New Presidency: His Long Goodbye; Clinton Wraps Up a Fond Farewell to Little Rock," *New York Times,* January 17, 1993.

2. Clinton, *My Life,* 468.

3. Ibid., 471.

18. Bill Asks, Colin Tells

1. Eric Schmitt, "The Transition: News Analysis—Challenging the Military; In Promising to End Ban on Homosexuals, Clinton Is Confronting a Wall of Tradition," *New York Times,* November 12, 1992.

2. "Powell Praises Gay Ban, but Says Clinton Is Boss: Conform or Quit, He Warns Officers," *Atlanta Journal and Constitution,* January 12, 1993, originally from *Baltimore Sun.*

3. "President Meets with Leaders of Congress," *All Things Considered,* National Public Radio, January 26, 1993.

4. Adam Clymer, "Lawmakers Revolt on Lifting Gay Ban in Military Service," *New York Times,* January 27, 1993.

5. Gwen Ifill, "The Gay Troop Issue: Clinton Accepts Delay in Lifting Military Gay Ban," *New York Times,* January 30, 1993.

6. "About 'Don't Ask, Don't Tell': Servicemembers Legal Defense Network, http://www.sldn.org/pages/about-dadt; "Military Personnel: Financial Costs and Loss of Critical Skills Due to DOD's Homosexual Conduct Policy Cannot Be Completely Estimated," Report to Congress, United States Government Accountability Office, February 2005.

7. Anne Hull, "How 'Don't Tell' Translates: The Military Needs Linguists, but It Doesn't Want This One," *Washington Post,* June 18, 2004.

8. Richard L. Berke, "Unaccustomed Role for Clinton at Sea," *New York Times,* March 13, 1993.

19. New Kid in Town

1. Sally Quinn, "Making Capital Gains: Welcome to Washington, But Play by Our Rules," *Washington Post,* November 15, 1992.

2. Michael Putzel, "Clinton Seeks Control After Rocky Beginning," *Boston Globe,* January 31, 1993.

3. Art Buchwald, "Eight Days in January," *Washington Post,* February 2, 1993.

4. Ruth Marcus, "Clinton's Astroturf Answer: No That Wasn't It," *Washington Post,* February 18, 1994.

5. Thomas L. Friedman, "White House Retreats on Ouster at Travel Office, Reinstating 5," *New York Times,* May 26, 1993; Thomas L. Friedman, "White House Rebukes 4 in Travel Office Shake-Up," *New York Times,* July 3, 1993; "House Votes to Repay 7 Workers," *New York Times* (Associated Press), March 20, 1996.

6. Margaret Carlson and Michael Duffy, "Shear Dismay," *Time,* May 31, 1993.

7. David Johnston, "Reno Completes Most of Lineup at Justice Dept.," *New York Times,* April 30, 1993.

8. Clint Bolick is credited with coining the phrase "Quota Queen" in an op-ed piece: Clint Bolick, "Clinton's Quota Queens," *Wall Street Journal,* April 30, 1993.

9. Taylor Branch, *The Clinton Tapes: Wrestling History with the President* (New York: Simon and Schuster, 2009), 70.

10. Clinton, *My Life,* 524.

11. "For the Record," *Washington Post,* November 6, 1992.

20. Debt on Arrival

1. Robert Pear, "Clinton Backs Off His Pledge to Cut the Deficit in Half," *New York Times,* January 7, 1993.

2. Clinton, *My Life,* 458.

21. A Casino for Jesus

1. Robert Pear, "Clinton's Economic Plan: Health Care; Putting Limits on Growth of Medicare," *New York Times,* February 18, 1993; R. W. Apple Jr., "Clinton's Economic Plan: The Overview; Clinton Plan to Remake the Economy Seeks to Tax Energy and Big Incomes," *New York Times,* February 18, 1993; William J. Clinton, "Address Before a Joint Session of Congress on Administration Goals," February 17, 1993, American Presidency Project, http://www.presidency.ucsb.edu/ws/index.php?pid=47232; "Earned Income Tax Credit," Web site of DLC, http://www.dlcppi.org/ndol_ci.cfm?kaid=139&subid=277&contentid=3607.

2. Bob Woodward, *The Agenda: Inside the Clinton White House* (New York: Simon and Schuster, 1994), 150, 170–173.

3. David E. Rosenbaum, "The Budget Struggle; Clinton Wins Approval of His Budget Plan as Gore Votes to Break Senate Deadlock," *New York Times*, August 7, 1993.

22. The Yanks Are Coming

1. R. W. Apple Jr., "The 1992 Elections: President-Elect, the Overview; Clinton, Savoring Victory, Starts Sizing Up Job Ahead," *New York Times*, November 5, 1992.

2. "Milosevic's Yugoslavia," BBC News http://news.bbc.co.uk/hi/english/static/in_depth/europe/2000/milosevic_yugoslavia/rise.stm.

3. Background on Bosnia used in this section found in Samantha Power, *"A Problem from Hell": America and the Age of Genocide* (New York: Basic, 2002), 247–249.

4. Adam Tanner, "Biden Seeks New U.S. Start in Balkans," Reuters, May 18, 2009.

5. Frank J. Prial, "Conflict in the Balkans: U.N.; Resolution Establishes Safe Areas but Lacks Enforcement Provision," *New York Times*, May 7, 1993.

6. Power, *"A Problem from Hell,"* 303.

24. Heroic Measures

1. "In Their Own Words: Transcript of Speech by Clinton Accepting Democratic Nomination," *New York Times*, July 17, 1992.

2. William J. Clinton, "Remarks and an Exchange with Reporters on Health Care Reform," January 25, 1993, American Presidency Project, http://www.presidency.ucsb.edu/ws/index.php?pid=46378.

3. Ronald Smothers, "Tobacco Country Is Quaking over Cigarette Tax Proposal," *New York Times*, March 22, 1993.

4. John Pekkanen, "Thank You for Smoking," *Washingtonian*, December 1, 2007.

5. William J. Clinton, "Address Before a Joint Session of the Congress on the State of the Union," January 25, 1994, American Presidency Project, http://www.presidency.ucsb.edu/ws/index.php?pid=50409&st=&st1=.

6. " 'Harry and Louise' Health Care Advertisements," posted by C-SPAN on YouTube, http://www.youtube.com/watch?v=CwOX2P4s-Iw.

7. "The Past Is Prologue: Reviewing the Opposition to the Last Major Push for Health Care Reform," Center for American Progress, December 10, 2008, http://www.americanprogressaction.org/issues/2008/1994health.html.

25. Stand-Up Guys

1. Susan Page and Jack Kelley, "Bill & Boris: Buddies Both Have Voters Watching as Summit Opens; Cozy Ties Mask Tough Issues, Critics Say," *USA Today*, April 18, 1996.

2. Todd S. Purdum, "Virginia Clinton Kelley, 70, President's Mother, Is Dead," *New York Times,* January 7, 1994; Clinton, *My Life,* 567.

3. Erik Eckholm with David E. Sanger, "The Trade Deal: The Overview; U.S. Reaches an Accord to Open China Economy as Worldwide Market," *New York Times,* November 16, 1999.

26. Action, Inaction

1. Richard W. Stewart, *The United States Army in Somalia, 1992–1994,* U.S. Army Center of Military History, http://www.history.army.mil/brochures/Somalia/Somalia.htm, 8.

2. David Binder, "Bush Ready to Send Troops to Protect Somalia Food," *New York Times,* November 26, 1992; Michael R. Gordon, "Mission to Somalia: U.N. Backs a Somalia Force as Bush Vows a Swift Exit; Pentagon Sees Longer Stay," *New York Times,* December 4, 1992; "United Nations Operations in Somalia I," Department of Public Information, United Nations, http://www.un.org/Depts/DPKO/Missions/unosomi.htm.

3. Paul Lewis, "U.N. Will Increase Troops in Somalia," *New York Times,* March 27, 1993.

4. Douglas Jehl, "An Elusive Clan Father Is Peacekeepers' Nemesis," *New York Times,* October 7, 1993; Stewart, *The United States Army in Somalia,* 10.

5. Stewart, *The United States Army in Somalia,* 16. A U.N. account gives the totals as twenty-five killed, ten reported missing, and fifty-four wounded: "Somalia—UNOSOM II: United Nations Operations in Somalia," Department of Public Information, United Nations, http://www.un.org/en/peacekeeping/missions/past/unosom2backgr1.html.

6. Stewart, *The United States Army in Somalia,* 16.

7. Ibid., 23.

8. Ibid., 19–21.

9. Ibid., 24–25.

10. Background information on Rwanda from Power, *"A Problem from Hell,"* 329–345; "Rwanda: How the Genocide Happened," BBC, http://news.bbc.co.uk/2/hi/africa/1288230.stm; William E. Schmidt, "Troops Rampage in Rwanda: Dead Said to Include Premier," *New York Times,* April 8, 1994.

11. Paul Lewis, "U.N. Backs Troops for Rwanda but Terms Bar Any Action Soon," *New York Times,* May 17, 1994.

12. Julia Preston, "Death Toll in Rwanda Is Said to Top 100,000; U.N. Votes to Pull Out Most Peacekeepers," *Washington Post,* April 22, 1994; Julia Preston, "250,000 Flee Rwanda for Tanzania; Ethnic Warfare May Have Killed 200,000, U.N. Says," *Washington Post,* April 30, 1994; Lawrence Van Gelder, "The Toll in Rwanda: Estimates at Best," *New York Times,* May 17, 1994; Keith B. Richburg, "Rebels Take Key Parts of Rwandan City," *Washington Post,* May 23, 1994.

27. No Way to Run a Railroad

1. Michael Kelly, "Man in the News; A Master of the Image: David Richmond Gergen," *New York Times*, May 30, 1993; Gwen Ifill, "White House Tries Out a Cheerful Face," *New York Times*, June 8, 1993; Gwen Ifill, "Washington Talk; White House Offices: Matter of Inches," *New York Times*, June 9, 1993; Dan Balz and Ann Devroy, "White House Staff Starting to Shift into Drive: Engine of the Administration, Designed to Purr with Efficiency, Had Stalled Frequently," *Washington Post*, June 27, 1993; Ann Devroy, "Latest White House Reorganization Plan Leaves Some Insiders Skeptical," *Washington Post*, December 12, 1993; Michael Kranish, "Ickes Fights Two-Front War for Clinton: A Key Player on Health Care, Deputy Chief of Staff also Embroiled in Whitewater," *Boston Globe*, March 19, 1994.

2. Jack Anderson and Michael Binste, "Clinton's Chief of Staff Finally Up and Running," *Oregonian*, May 16, 1994.

28. From Humiliation to Celebration

1. Gwen Ifill, "Haitian Is Offered Clinton's Support on an End to Exile," *New York Times*, March 17, 1993; Howard W. French, "Months of Terror Bring Rising Toll of Deaths in Haiti," *New York Times*, April 2, 1994; Larry Rohter, "Haiti Attacks Critics and Restricts Civil Rights," *New York Times*, August 3, 1994; "The United Nations: Mission to Haiti: Chronology; A Recent History of Haiti," *New York Times*, October 16, 1994.

2. Howard W. French, "Haiti Army Celebrates U.S. Withdrawal," *New York Times*, October 13, 1993; "Resolution 867 (1993) Adopted by the Security Council at its 3282nd meeting, on 23 September 1993," Web site of United Nations High Commissioner for Refugees, http://www.unhcr.org/refworld/publisher,UNSC,,HTI,3b00f16510,0.html.

3. French, "Haiti Army Celebrates."

4. Paul Lewis, "U.N. Council Votes Tougher Embargo on Haitian Trade," *New York Times*, May 7, 1994; Steven Greenhouse, "U.S. Bars Flights and Money Deals with the Haitians," *New York Times*, June 11, 1994; Richard D. Lyons, "U.N. Authorizes Invasion of Haiti to Be Led by U.S.," *New York Times*, August 1, 1994; Branch, *Clinton Tapes*, 199.

5. Clinton, *My Life*, 616–618; "Mission to Haiti: Diplomacy; On the Brink of War, a Tense Battle of Wills," *New York Times*, September 20, 1994.

29. Picturing Peace

1. Thomas L. Friedman, "Mideast Accord: The Overview; Rabin and Arafat Seal Their Accord as Clinton Applauds 'Brave Gamble,'" *New York Times*, September 14, 1993; Dennis Ross, *The Missing Peace: The Inside Story of the Fight for Middle East Peace* (New York: Farrar, Straus and Giroux, 2004), 116.

2. "Remarks at the Signing Ceremony for the Israeli-Palestinian Declaration of

Principles," September 13, 1993, American Presidency Project, http://www.preside
ncy.ucsb.edu/ws/index.php?pid=47063.

30. Something Is Rotten in the State of Arkansas

1. Jeff Gerth, "The 1992 Campaign: Personal Finances; Clintons Joined S. & L. Operator in an Ozark Real-Estate Venture," *New York Times*, March 8, 1992.

2. Joe Conason and Gene Lyons, *The Hunting of the President: The Ten-Year Campaign to Destroy Bill and Hillary Clinton* (New York: St. Martin's, 2000), 30.

3. Roger Morris, *Partners in Power: The Clintons and Their America* (New York: Henry Holt, 1996), 360; Gene Lyons, "Fool for Scandal: How the *Times* Got Whitewater Wrong," *Harper's Magazine*, October 1994, reprinted on Frontline Online, http://www.pbs.org/wgbh/pages/frontline/shows/arkansas/whitewater/lyonsarticle.html.

4. R. W. Apple Jr., "Note Left by White House Aide: Accusation, Anger and Despair," *New York Times*, August 11, 1993; Ken Gormley, *The Death of American Virtue: Clinton vs. Starr* (New York: Crown, 2010), 75.

5. Stephen Labaton, "Clinton Aide Removed Files About Legal Work on S. & L.," *New York Times*, December 12, 1995.

6. William Safire, "Foster's Ghost," *New York Times*, January 6, 1994.

7. "Problems That Can't Be Managed," *Washington Post*, January 11, 1994.

8. Gwen Ifill, "The Whitewater Inquiry; Clinton Asks Reno to Name a Counsel on His Land Deals," *New York Times*, January 13, 1994. Bill himself recalls (*My Life*, 572–574) that he made the decision during a conference call with aides after he'd arrived in Moscow. His travel schedule makes it more likely, however, that the call took place while he was in the Czech Republic, as the *Times* reports. "Presidential Visits Abroad, William J. Clinton, from January 20, 1993," U.S. State Department, http://www.state.gov/www/about_state/history/prestravels/ptravel6.html.

9. Clinton, *My Life*, 574.

10. Russell Watson, "Vince Foster's Suicide: The Rumor Mill Churns," *Newsweek*, March 21, 1994.

11. Clinton, *My Life*, 606.

12. Conason and Lyons, *Hunting*, 127. See also "Judge to Consider Immunity for Clinton," *New York Times*, July 24, 1994.

31. Golfing with Willie Mays

1. Branch, *Clinton Tapes*, 232.

32. Rebuke

1. "Republican Contract with America," http://www.house.gov/house/Contra
ct/CONTRACT.html.

2. William J. Clinton, "The President's News Conference," November 9, 1994, American Presidency Project, http://www.presidency.ucsb.edu/ws/index.php?pid=49468&st.

33. Picking up the Pieces

1. Francis X. Clines, "The Powell Decision: The Announcement; Powell Rules out '96 Race; Cites Concerns for Family and His Lack of 'A Calling,'" *New York Times*, November 9, 1995.

34. Relevant

1. William J. Clinton, "The President's News Conference," April 18, 1995, American Presidency Project, http://www.presidency.ucsb.edu/ws/index.php?pid=51237.

35. Pastor to the Nation

1. Tim Weiner, "Terror in Oklahoma: The Overview; F.B.I. Hunts 2d Bombing Suspect and Seeks Links to Far Right; Rain Stalls Search of Rubble," *New York Times*, April 23, 1995; John Kifner, "McVeigh's Mind: A Special Report; Oklahoma Bombing Suspect: Unraveling of a Frayed Life," *New York Times*, December 31, 1995; Jo Thomas, "Terry Nichols Gets Life Term in Bombing Plot," *New York Times*, June 5, 1998; Jo Thomas, "'No Sympathy' for Dead Children, McVeigh Says," *New York Times*, March 29, 2001; Rick Bragg, "The McVeigh Execution: The Overview; McVeigh Dies for Oklahoma City Blast," *New York Times*, June 12, 2001; "McVeigh Chronology," Chronology prepared by McVeigh's defense team, *Frontline*, http://www.pbs.org/wgbh/pages/frontline/documents/mcveigh/index.html#anchor1; Lou Michel and Dan Herbeck, *American Terrorist: Timothy McVeigh and the Oklahoma City Bombing* (New York: ReganBooks, 2001), 234.

2. William J. Clinton, "Remarks at a Memorial Service for the Bombing Victims in Oklahoma City, Oklahoma," April 23, 1995, American Presidency Project, http://www.presidency.ucsb.edu/ws/index.php?pid=51265&st=&st1=.

3. William J. Clinton, "Remarks at the Michigan State University Commencement Ceremony in East Lansing, Michigan," May 5, 1995, American Presidency Project, http://www.presidency.ucsb.edu/ws/index.php?pid=51317&st=&st1=.

4. William J. Clinton, "The President's News Conference with Prime Minister Jean Chretien of Canada in Ottawa," February 24, 1995, American Presidency Project, http://www.presidency.ucsb.edu/ws/index.php?pid=51022&st=&st1=; Alison Mitchell, "Clinton Calls G.O.P. Plan on Budget 'Too Extreme,'" *New York Times*, June 24, 1995; "Excerpts from President's News Conference at White House," *New York Times*, August 2, 1995; Todd S. Purdum, "President Hints at Budget Compromise," *New York Times*, October 20, 1995.

36. End of an Era

1. Eric Pooley, "Convention '96: Who Is Dick Morris?" *Time*, September 2, 1996.

2. William J. Clinton, "State of the Union Address," January 23, 1996, version 2, White House Web sites, William J. Clinton Presidential Library and Museum, http://clinton2.nara.gov/WH/New/other/sotu.html.

37. This Town Ain't Big Enough

1. William J. Clinton, "Address to the Nation on the Plan to Balance the Budget," June 13, 1995, American Presidency Project, http://www.presidency.ucsb.edu/ws/index.php?pid=51491.

2. Adam Clymer, "As Demonstrators Gather, Gingrich Delays a Speech," *New York Times*, August 8, 1995.

3. William J. Clinton, "Remarks on the 30th Anniversary of the Passage of Medicare," July 25, 1995, American Presidency Project, http://www.presidency.ucsb.edu/ws/index.php?pid=51650&st=&st1=.

4. Jerry Gray, "Battle over the Budget: The Overview; Feuding Goes on as G.O.P. Presents Its Budget Plan," *New York Times*, November 17, 1995.

5. "Politics: Gingrich on Medicare," *New York Times*, July 20, 1996; William J. Clinton, "The President's Radio Address," October 28, 1995, American Presidency Project, http://www.presidency.ucsb.edu/ws/index.php?pid=50712&st=&st1=.

6. Bob Woodward, *The Choice* (New York: Simon and Schuster, 1996), 327; Clinton, *My Life*, 683; George Stephanopoulos, *All Too Human: A Political Education* (New York: Little, Brown, 1999), 405.

7. Robert D. Hershey Jr., "Federal Government Starts Another Shutdown," *New York Times*, December 16, 1995; Adam Clymer, "Congress Votes to Return 760,000 to Federal Payroll and Resume Some Services; Step Is Temporary," *New York Times*, January 6, 1996; Brian Knowlton, "But They Threaten Another Shutdown if Talks Stall Again: Republicans Welcome Budget Step By Clinton," *New York Times*, January 8, 1996.

38. Shalom, Chaver

1. Serge Schmemann, "Assassination in Israel: The Overview; Rabin Slain after Peace Rally in Tel Aviv; Israeli Gunman Held; Says He Acted Alone," *New York Times*, November 5, 1995; Serge Schmemann, "Assassination in Israel: The Overview; A Stunned Israel Mourns and Honors Its Fallen Leader," *New York Times*, November 6, 1995.

2. " 'Soldier for Peace' Rabin Buried: World, Family Pay Tribute to Assassinated Leader," CNN, November 6, 1995, http://www.cnn.com/WORLD/9511/rabin/funeral/wrap/index.html.

3. William J. Clinton, "Remarks on the Death of Prime Minister Rabin," November

NOTES TO PAGES 266–276

4, 1995, American Presidency Project, http://www.presidency.ucsb.edu/ws/index .php?pid=50738&st=&st1=.

4. Serge Schmemann, "Peres Proposes Inclusive Peace to Syrian Chief," *New York Times,* November 23, 1995.

5. William J. Clinton, "Remarks at the Funeral of Prime Minister Rabin in Jerusalem, Israel," November 6, 1995, American Presidency Project, http://www.preside ncy.ucsb.edu/ws/index.php?pid=50742&st=&st1=.

6. Ross, *Making Peace,* 149.

39. I'll Show You Mine If . . .

1. Referral to the United States House of Representatives pursuant to Title 28, United States Code, § 595(c), Submitted by the Office of the Independent Counsel, September 9, 1998 (Starr Report), narrative, part II; Andrew Morton, *Monica's Story* (New York: St. Martin's, 1999), 71–72.

2. Morton, *Monica's Story,* 72–75.

3. Starr Report, table of contents and narrative, part VI.

40. A Commander in Chief (Finally) Commands

1. Power, *"A Problem from Hell,"* 324; Bernard E. Trainor, "Gorazde Cease-Fire Is Irrelevant," *New York Times,* April 27, 1994; Power, *"A Problem from Hell,"* 324.

2. Ivo H. Daalder, *Getting to Dayton: The Making of America's Bosnia Policy* (Washington: Brookings, 2000), 67, 68; Chris Hedges, "Conflict in the Balkans: The Overview; Bosnian Serbs Overrun Town Protected by U.N.," *New York Times,* July 12, 1995; Power, *"A Problem from Hell,"* 400.

3. Power, *"A Problem from Hell,"* 439; Richard C. Holbrooke, *To End a War* (New York: Random House, 1998), 3–13.

4. Daalder, *Getting to Dayton,* 131–134.

5. "Bosnia War Dead Figure Announced," BBC NEWS, June 21, 2007, http:// news.bbc.co.uk/2/hi/europe/6228152.stm.

6. William J. Clinton, "Address to the Nation on Implementation of the Peace Agreement in Bosnia-Herzegovina," November 27, 1995, American Presidency Project, http://www.presidency.ucsb.edu/ws/index.php?pid=50808&st=&st1=.

41. Ballot-Box Missionary

1. Debbie McGoldrick, "Huge Support Greets New Lobby Group," *Irish Voice,* undated online version, http://www.irishabroad.com/news/irishinamerica/news/ huge-support-dec1405.asp; *State Department: 1991 Immigrant Visa Lottery,* Report to the Honorable Brian Donnelly, House of Representatives, May 1992, United States General Accounting Office.

2. "1969: British Troops Sent into Northern Ireland," *On This Day,* August 14, BBC,

http://news.bbc.co.uk/onthisday/hi/dates/stories/august/14/newsid_4075000/4075437.stm.

3. Steven Greenhouse, "U.S. to Give I.R.A. Political Chief Visa to Attend Talks in New York," *New York Times*, January 31, 1994.

4. John Darnton, "Militant Protestants in Truce, Lifting Peace Hopes in Ulster," *New York Times*, October 14, 1994.

5. Douglas Jehl, "Clinton Lifts Ban on Contacts with Sinn Fein," *New York Times*, October 4, 1994; Douglas Jehl, "Clinton to Permit Fund-Raising in the U.S. by Top I.R.A. Figure," *New York Times*, March 10, 1995; Steven Greenhouse, "Gerry Adams Shakes Hands with Clinton," *New York Times*, March 17, 1995.

6. "Presidential Visits Abroad."

7. Barry Hillenbrand, "A Celebration of Hope," *Time*, December 11, 1995; Richard W. Stevenson, "British and Irish Break Ulster Jam," *New York Times*, November 29, 1995.

8. Hillenbrand, "Celebration of Hope."

9. "Timeline: Northern Ireland's Road to Peace," *BBC News*, http://news.bbc.co.uk/2/hi/uk_news/northern_ireland/4072261.stm.

42. A Deal. With the Devil?

1. Douglas Jehl, "President Offers Delayed Proposal to Redo Welfare," *New York Times*, June 15, 1994.

2. Robert Pear, "Clinton Objects to Key Elements of Welfare Bill, *New York Times*, March 26, 1995.

3. Robert Pear, "Clinton to Sign Welfare Bill That Ends U.S. Aid Guarantee and Gives States Broad Power," *New York Times*, August 1, 1996; Monica Borkowski, "The Welfare Bill: Points of Agreement, and Disagreement, on the Welfare Bill," *New York Times*, August 1, 1996.

4. William J. Clinton, "Remarks on Signing the Personal Responsibility and Work Opportunity Reconciliation Act of 1996 and an Exchange with Reporters," August 22, 1996, American Presidency Project, http://www.presidency.ucsb.edu/ws/index.php?pid=53218&st=&st1=.

5. Pear, "Clinton to Sign."

43. Slippery or Steadfast?

1. Marvine Howe, "U.S. Agrees to Provide Portugal a $300 Million Emergency Loan, *New York Times*, January 1, 1977; Steven R. Weisman, "President Pledges to Give Brazilians a $1.2 Billion Loan," *New York Times*, December 2, 1982.

2. David E. Sanger, "Mexico Repays Bailout by U.S. Ahead of Time," *New York Times*, January 16, 1997.

44. Piece of Cake

1. James Bennet, "Democratic Air War Hits Michigan," *New York Times,* April 23, 1996.

2. Will Snell and Stephen Goetz, "Overview of Kentucky's Tobacco Economy," University of Kentucky College of Agriculture, http://www.ca.uky.edu/agc/pubs/aec/aec83/aec83.htm; "Clinton Assails Dole on Tobacco and Liquor Company on TV Ads," *New York Times* (Associated Press), June 16, 1996.

3. "Clinton Assails Dole."

4. William J. Clinton, "The President's Radio Address," June 15, 1996, American Presidency Project, http://www.presidency.ucsb.edu/ws/index.php?pid=52952&st=&st1=.

5. "Dole's Speech Accepting the G.O.P. Nomination for President," *New York Times,* August 16, 1996.

6. William J. Clinton, "Remarks Accepting the Presidential Nomination at the Democratic National Convention in Chicago," August 29, 1996, American Presidency Project, http://www.presidency.ucsb.edu/ws/index.php?pid=53253&st=&st1=.

7. Richard W. Stevenson, "Clinton Signs a Bill Raising Minimum Wage by 90 Cents," *New York Times,* August 21, 1996; Todd S. Purdum, "Clinton Signs Bill to Give Portability in Insurance," *New York Times,* August 22, 1996.

8. Francis X. Clines, "Clinton Signs Bill Cutting Welfare; States in New Role," *New York Times,* August 23, 1996.

9. "1996 Popular Vote Summary for All Candidates Listed on at Least One State Ballot," Federal Election Commission, http://www.fec.gov/pubrec/fe1996/summ.htm.

10. William J. Clinton, "Remarks at a Victory Celebration in Little Rock, Arkansas," November 5, 1996, American Presidency Project, http://www.presidency.ucsb.edu/ws/index.php?pid=52218&st=&st1=.

11. Alison Mitchell, "President Clinton Makes a Celebratory Return to His Starting Point in Arkansas," *New York Times,* November 6, 1996.

45. Reckless, Stupid, Human

1. William J. Clinton, "Inaugural Address," January 20, 1997, American Presidency Project, http://www.presidency.ucsb.edu/ws/index.php?pid=54183&st=&st1=.

2. Address by Bill to presidential conference William Jefferson Clinton: The "New Democrat" From Hope at Hofstra University, Hempstead, New York, November 10, 2005. Transcript provided to the author by Hofstra Cultural Center.

46. Big Bucks Bedroom

1. John F. Harris, *The Survivor: Bill Clinton in the White House* (New York: Random House, 2005), 268–270.

2. "The File on President Clinton," *New York Times,* February 27, 1997.

48. Pants on Fire

1. Jeffrey Toobin, *A Vast Conspiracy: The Real Story of the Sex Scandal That Nearly Brought Down a President* (New York: Random House, 1999), 10, 28, 36.

2. David Brock, "Living with the Clintons: Bill's Arkansas Bodyguards Tell the Story the Press Missed," *American Spectator,* January 1994.

3. Conason and Lyons, *Hunting,* 120.

4. Neil A. Lewis, "Clinton's Lawyer Asks for Delay on Sex Harassment Lawsuit," *New York Times,* June 28, 1994.

5. Nina Totenberg, "Court Allows Jones Lawsuit to Proceed Against Clinton," *All Things Considered,* National Public Radio, May 27, 1997.

6. "Excerpts from Supreme Court Ruling on a Lawsuit Against the President," *New York Times,* May 28, 1997.

7. Totenberg, "Court Allows."

8. Toobin, *A Vast Conspiracy,* 149, 163–165.

9. Ibid., 166–167.

10. Ibid., 177–179; Starr Report, grounds, part VI.

11. Toobin, *A Vast Conspiracy,* 195.

12. Ibid., 187–188.

13. Ibid., 180; Gormley, *Death of American Virtue,* 347.

14. Gormley, *Death of American Virtue,* 347–349; Toobin, *A Vast Conspiracy,* 201.

15. Toobin, *A Vast Conspiracy,* 119–121, 125–128; Gormley, *Death of American Virtue,* 258–259.

16. Morton, *Monica's Story,* 231.

17. Toobin, *A Vast Conspiracy,* 218–219.

18. "Transcript of President's Civil Deposition," in the Factual Record presented by House Impeachment Managers, "In the Senate of the United States, Sitting as a Court of Impeachment," http://frwebgate.access.gpo.gov/cgi-bin/getdoc.cgi?dbname=10 6_cong_documents&docid=f:sd3v14p2.106.pdf.

19. Starr Report, narrative, part I.

49. The Bombshell Wears a Beret

1. Toobin, *A Vast Conspiracy,* 230.

2. Ibid., 231, 238.

3. William J. Clinton, "Interview with Jim Lehrer of the PBS 'News Hour,'" January 21, 1998, American Presidency Project, http://www.presidency.ucsb.edu/ws/index.php?pid=56080&st=&st1=.

4. William J. Clinton, "Remarks on the After-School Child Care Initiative," January 26, 1998, American Presidency Project, http://www.presidency.ucsb.edu/ws/index.php?pid=56257&st=&st1=.

5. Richard L. Berke, "The President Under Fire: The Overview; White House Acts

to Contain Furor as Concern Grows," *New York Times*, January 26, 1998; Richard L. Berke, "The President Under Fire: The Public View; Clinton Job Rating Remains High Despite Doubts on Moral Values," *New York Times*, January 27, 1998.

6. Robert Pear, "The Clinton Budget: The Projected Surplus; Clinton Sees $1.1 Trillion in Excess Revenue in Decade," *New York Times*, February 3, 1998.

51. The Puritan and the Pol

1. Don Van Natta Jr., "Testing of a President: The Investigation; Starr Won't Be Swayed from the Criminal Inquiry," *New York Times*, April 3, 1998.

2. "Testing of a President: Federal Judge's Order Dismissing Jones Lawsuit Against the President," *New York Times*, April 2, 1998.

3. Van Natta, "Testing of a President."

4. Ibid.

52. Respite

1. "Testing of a President: Jordan's Statement After Testifying," *New York Times*, March 6, 1998; "Testing of a President: Excerpts from Clinton Testimony for Deposition in Jones Lawsuit," *New York Times*, March 14, 1998; John M. Broder, "Testing of a President: The Overview; White House Volunteer, on TV, Details Encounter with President," *New York Times*, March 16, 1998; James Bennet, "Clinton Packs up His Care and Woe to Trot the Globe," *New York Times*, March 23, 1998.

2. "Press Briefing by Mike McCurry," March 23, 1998, American Presidency Project, http://www.presidency.ucsb.edu/ws/index.php?pid=48283&st=&st1=.

3. William J. Clinton, "Remarks to the People of Ghana in Accra," March 23, 1998, American Presidency Project, http://www.presidency.ucsb.edu/ws/index.php?pid=55666&st=&st1=.

4. William J. Clinton, "Remarks to Genocide Survivors in Kigali, Rwanda," March 25, 1998, American Presidency Project, http://www.presidency.ucsb.edu/ws/index.php?pid=55677&st=&st1=.

5. William J. Clinton, "Remarks at Goree Island, Senegal," April 2, 1998, American Presidency Project, http://www.presidency.ucsb.edu/ws/index.php?pid=55729&st=&st1=.

6. R. W. Apple Jr., "Clinton in Africa: The Overview; From Mandela, a Gentle Admonishment," *New York Times*, March 28, 1998; Biography of Nelson Mandela, African National Congress, http://www.anc.org.za/people/mandela.html.

53. Today's Word Is *Is*

1. Toobin, *A Vast Conspiracy*, 304.

2. John M. Broder and Don Van Natta Jr., "The Testing of a President: The Oppo-

nents; Clinton and Starr, a Mutual Admonition Society," *New York Times,* September 20; Gormley, *Death of American Virtue,* 525.

3. Clinton, *My Life,* 800, 803, 811, 846; Hillary Rodham Clinton, *Living History,* 465–466.

4. "Testimony of William Jefferson Clinton," August 17, 1998, Office of the Independent Counsel, House Document 105-311: Appendices to the Starr Report, vol. 3, Document Supplement, part A, William J. Clinton Statements, http://icreport.access.gpo.gov / hd105-311 / vol3.html.

5. "Deposition of Monica S. Lewinsky," August 26, 1998, House Document 105-311: Appendices to the Starr Report, vol. 4, Document Supplement, part B, Monica S. Lewinsky Statements, http://icreport.access.gpo.gov / hd105-311 / vol4.html.

6. John M. Broder with Neil A. Lewis, "Clinton Is Found to Be in Contempt on Jones Lawsuit," *New York Times,* April 13, 1999.

7. "Excerpts from the Judge's Ruling," *New York Times,* April 13, 1999.

54. Speech Defect

1. William J. Clinton, "Address to the Nation on Testimony Before the Independent Counsel's Grand Jury," August 17, 1998, American Presidency Project, http://www.presidency.ucsb.edu / ws / index.php?pid=54794&st=&st1=.

2. William J. Clinton, "Remarks at a Breakfast with Religious Leaders," September 11, 1998, American Presidency Project, http://www.presidency.ucsb.edu / ws / index.php?pid=54886&st=&st1=.

55. Sine Qua Non

1. "The Good Friday Agreement in Full," BBC, http://news.bbc.co.uk / 2 / hi / uk_news / northern_ireland / 4079267.stm.

2. Eamon Quinn and Alan Cowell, "Ulster Factions Agree to a Plan for Joint Rule," *New York Times,* March 27, 2007.

56. Softcore

1. Chronology and details of encounters: Starr Report, narrative.

57. For Mature Audiences Only

1. "The Testing of a President; Vote on Investigation," *New York Times,* October 6, 1998.

2. Lawrie Mifflin, "The Testing of a President: The Networks; Hesitantly, TV Executives Decide Show Must Go On," *New York Times,* September 22, 1998; Lawrie Mifflin, "The Testing of a President: The Videotape; 22.5 Million Saw Broadcast of

Testimony," *New York Times*, September 23, 1998; Edmund L. Andrews, "The Testing of a President: The Chancellor; Tape's Release Disgusts Kohl, but German TV Will Show It," *New York Times*, September 22, 1998.

58. DeLayed Reaction

1. "Bucking History, Dems Hold Off GOP Gains," Power in the Balance: Election '98, Time.com, http://www.time.com/time/reports/election98/.

2. Eric Schmitt, "Judiciary Chairman Asks Clinton to Admit or Deny 81 Findings," *New York Times*, November 6, 1998; "Testing of a President: Clinton's Responses to Questions from the House Judiciary Committee," *New York Times*, November 28, 1998.

3. Richard W. Stevenson with Michael R. Kagay, "Impeachment: The Poll; Republicans' Image Eroding Fast, Poll Shows," *New York Times*, December 19, 1998.

4. Sylvia Nasar, "Jump in November Sent Work Force to a Record High," *New York Times*, December 5, 1998; "Consumer Prices Show Slight Rise," *New York Times*, December 16, 1998; "A Turbulent but Profitable Year," *New York Times*, January 1, 1999.

59. Impeach the Rapist!

1. Conason and Lyons, *Hunting*, 346; Toobin, *A Vast Conspiracy*, 141, 363; Howard Kurtz, "Clinton Accuser's Story Aired," *Washington Post*, February 25, 1999.

2. Richard A. Serrano and Marc Lacey, "Tapes of Clinton's Testimony Used in Closing Arguments," *Los Angeles Times*, December 11, 1998.

3. Alison Mitchell, "Testing of a President: The Vote; Panel, on Party Lines, Votes Impeachment; Clinton Voices Remorse, Invites Censure," *New York Times*, December 12, 1998; R. W. Apple Jr., "Testing of a President: The Overview; Panel Completes Impeachment Votes and Defeats Democrats' Censure Bid," *New York Times*, December 13, 1998; "Testing of a President: Text of the Articles of Impeachment," *New York Times*, December 13, 1998.

60. Amazing

1. Steven Erlanger, "Mideast Accord: The Overview; Arafat and Netanyahu in Pact on Next Steps Toward Peace; Modest Deal to 'Rebuild Trust,'" *New York Times*, October 24, 1998; Ethan Bronner, "The World: Blueprint; Filling in Peace's Details Is the Painful Part," *New York Times*, October 25, 1998; Text of the Wye River Memorandum, U.S. State Department, http://www.state.gov/www/regions/nea/981023_interim_agmt.html.

2. Alison Mitchell and James Dao, "Impeachment: The Overview; Polls Aside, G.O.P. Stance on Impeachment Hardens," *New York Times*, December 15, 1998.

3. Ross, *Missing Peace,* 486.

4. William J. Clinton, "Remarks to the Palestine National Council and Other Palestinian Organizations in Gaza City," December 14, 1998, American Presidency Project, http://www.presidency.ucsb.edu/ws/index.php?pid=55410&st=&st1=.

5. James Bennet, "Clinton in the Mideast: A Controversy; Children of Killers, Children of Victims: Clinton Shares Their Pain," *New York Times,* December 16, 1998; Ross, *Missing Peace,* 485.

61. Bad Guys

1. James C. McKinley Jr., "Bombings in East Africa: The Overview; Bombs Rip Apart 2 U.S. Embassies in Africa; Scores Killed; No Firm Motive or Suspects," *New York Times,* August 8, 1998; "Report of the Accountability Review Boards: Bombings of the US Embassies in Nairobi, Kenya and Dar es Salaam, Tanzania," U.S. State Department, http://www.state.gov/www/regions/africa/board_overview.html.

2. Clinton, *My Life,* 798.

3. Marc Lacey, "Look at the Place! Sudan Says, 'Say Sorry,' but U.S. Won't," *New York Times,* October 20, 2005; Steven Lee Myers, "After the Attacks: The Overview; U.S. Says Iraq Aided Production of Chemical Weapons in Sudan," *New York Times,* August 25, 1998; Steven Lee Myers, "U.S. Fury on 2 Continents: The Weapons; Dozens of Ship-Launched Cruise Missiles Strike at Same Moment, 2,500 Miles Apart," *New York Times,* August 21, 1998.

4. Risen, "Question of Evidence."

5. Todd S. Purdum, "U.S. Fury on 2 Continents: Congress; Critics of Clinton Support Attacks," *New York Times,* August 21, 1998.

6. Madeleine Albright with Bill Woodward, *Madame Secretary: A Memoir* (New York: Miramax, 2003), 275.

7. Ibid., 276–280; Barbara Crossette, "Iraq Issues Order Barring Americans from U.N. Inquiry," *New York Times,* October 30, 1997; Francis X. Clines, "The Deal on Iraq: The Overview; Clinton Says U.S. Will Wait and See as Iraqis Back Off," *New York Times,* November 21, 1997.

8. Albright, *Madame Secretary,* 276–284; Barbara Crossette, "Iraq Bars Arms Inspectors Again, Saying American in Charge Is Spy," *New York Times,* January 14, 1998; James Bennet, "Standoff with Iraq: The Overview; Clinton Describes Goals for a Strike on Iraqi Arsenals," *New York Times,* February 18, 1998; Barbara Crossette, "U.N. Report Sees No Iraqi Progress on Weapons Issue," *New York Times,* April 17, 1998; Barbara Crossette, "In New Challenge to the U.N., Iraq Halts Arms Monitoring," *New York Times,* November 1, 1998.

9. Steven Lee Myers and Barbara Crossette, "Iraq Is Accused of New Rebuffs to U.N. Team," *New York Times,* December 16, 1998.

10. Steven Lee Myers, "Attack on Iraq: The Overview; U.S. and Britain End Raids on Iraq, Calling Mission a Success," *New York Times,* December 20, 1998; William J.

Clinton, "Address to the Nation on Completion of Military Strikes in Iraq," December 19, 1998, American Presidency Project, http://www.presidency.ucsb.edu/ws/index.php?pid=55436&st=&st1=.

11. Clinton, "Address to the Nation on Completion of Military Strikes in Iraq."

12. Eric Schmitt, "Attack on Iraq: Capitol Hill; G.O.P. Splits Bitterly over Timing of Assault," *New York Times*, December 17, 1998.

13. "Transcript: William Jefferson Clinton on 'FOX News Sunday,'" *Fox News*, September 26, 2006, http://www.foxnews.com/story/0,2933,215397,00.html.

14. Judith Miller, "Dissecting a Terror Plot from Boston to Amman," *New York Times*, January 15, 2001; David Johnston, "Few Answers About Man Being Held in Bomb Case," *New York Times*, December 21, 1999; Laura Mansnerus and Judith Miller, "Bomb Plot Insider Details Training," *New York Times*, July 4, 2001.

15. Ron Suskind, *The One Percent Doctrine: Deep Inside America's Pursuit of Its Enemies Since 9/11* (New York: Simon and Schuster, 2006), 2.

62. The Hypocrisy Police

1. Katharine Q. Seelye, "The Speaker Steps Down: The Overview; Facing a Revolt, Gingrich Won't Run for Speaker and Will Quit Congress," *New York Times*, November 7, 1998.

2. Francis X. Clines and Katharine Q. Seelye, "On Two Fronts: The Leadership; Speaker-Elect Informs Caucus of Past Affairs," *New York Times*, December 18, 1998.

3. Katharine Q. Seelye, "Impeachment: The Fallout; Livingston Urges Clinton to Follow Suit," *New York Times*, December 20, 1998.

4. "Publisher Larry Flynt Levels Accusations at Rep. Bob Barr," CNN.com, January 12, 1999, http://www.cnn.com/ALLPOLITICS/stories/1999/01/12/flynt.01/.

63. It's Official

1. Alison Mitchell, "Impeachment: The Overview; Clinton Impeached; He Faces a Senate Trial, 2d in History; Vows to Do Job till Term's 'Last Hour,'" *New York Times*, December 20, 1998.

2. Francis X. Clines, "Impeachment: The Scene; After the Vote, a Pause, Then Back-Pats and Glumness," *New York Times*, December 20, 1998.

3. Richard L. Berke, "Impeachment: The Motivations; Democrats Stand by Clinton, But It Isn't Personal," *New York Times*, December 21, 1998.

64. It's About Sex

1. Alison Mitchell and Eric Schmitt, "The Trial of the President: The Overview; Clinton Trial Opens, but Process Talks Go On," *New York Times*, January 8, 1999.

2. "The President's Trial; From Monica Lewinsky: 'I Feel Very Uncomfortable Making Judgments,'" *New York Times*, February 6, 1999.

3. "Trial of William Jefferson Clinton, President of the United States," *Congressional Record*, January 21, 1999, S844–S845.

4. "Clinton's Acquittal; The Senate and Rehnquist, Strangers No More," *New York Times*, February 13, 1999.

65. Seventy-Eight Days

1. Power, *"A Problem from Hell,"* 443–445; Laura Rozen, "Beginner's Guide to the Balkans," *Salon*, March 31, 1999, http://www.salon.com/news/1999/03/31newsa.html; Chris Hedges, "Rebels in Kosovo Striking Back Against Yugoslav Forces," *New York Times*, June 19, 1998.

2. Rozen, "Beginner's Guide"; Power, *"A Problem from Hell,"* 445.

3. "Mutilated Kosovo Bodies Found After Serb Attack," *New York Times*, January 17, 1999; Power, *"A Problem from Hell,"* 446, 447–448.

4. "Kosovo Crisis; Balkan Flashpoint: Air attacks—Day One," *BBC News*, March 25, 1999; "Francis X. Clines, Conflict in the Balkans: The Overview; Nato Opens Broad Barrage Against Serbs as Clinton Denounces Yugoslav President," *New York Times*, March 25, 1999; "Conflict in the Balkans; On a U.S. Ship, Click and Shoot," *New York Times*, March 25, 1999; Francis X. Clines, "Conflict in the Balkans: The Overview; NATO Strikes Go On as Serbs Step Up Campaign," *New York Times*, March 26, 1999; "Press Conference by Secretary General, Dr. Javier Solana and SACEUR, Gen. Wesley Clark," March 25, 1999, NATO, http://www.nato.int/Kosovo/press/p990325a.htm.

5. William J. Clinton, "Address to the Nation on Airstrikes Against Serbian Targets in the Federal Republic of Yugoslavia (Serbia and Montenegro)," March 24, 1999, American Presidency Project, http://www.presidency.ucsb.edu/ws/index.php?pid=57305&st=&st1=.

6. Jane Perlez, "Delayed by Serbian Maneuvering, Kosovo Talks Begin," *New York Times*, February 7, 1999; Elizabeth Becker, "Pentagon Sees Risk in Going into Kosovo," *New York Times*, February 11, 1999.

7. Power, *"A Problem from Hell,"* 449–450; David E. Rosenbaum, "Crisis in the Balkans: Kosovo; Expulsion of Kosovars to Be Total, U.S. Says," *New York Times*, April 22, 1999.

8. Power, *"A Problem from Hell,"* 458–459.

9. Ibid., 472; "Milosevic Suffered Heart Attack," *BBC News*, March 13, 2006; "Q&A: Milosevic Trial," *BBC News*, March 11, 2006.

10. William J. Clinton, "Remarks at Ganimet Terbeshi Elementary School in Ferizaj, Kosovo," American President Project, http://www.presidency.ucsb.edu/ws/?pid=56986.

66. Down to the Wire

1. Ross, *Missing Peace*, 494.

2. Ibid., 549–590.

3. Ibid., 591–649.

4. Ibid., 654–655, 752–753.

5. Ibid., 696.

6. Ibid., 650–711.

7. Ibid., 694.

8. William J. Clinton, "Remarks on the Middle East Peace Summit and an Exchange with Reporters," July 25, 2000, American Presidency Project, http://www.presidency.ucsb.edu/ws/index.php?pid=1558&st=&st1=.

9. Joel Greenberg, "Sharon Touches a Nerve, and Jerusalem Explodes," *New York Times*, September 29, 2000; William A. Orme Jr., "Mideast Violence Continues to Rage; Death Toll Rises," *New York Times*, October 1, 2000.

10. Ross, *Missing Peace*, 730.

11. Ibid., 743–744.

12. Ibid., 751–755; Clinton, *My Life*, 936–938. Ross (751) gives five days as the length of time within which the parties had to respond; Bill (936) puts it at four.

13. Ross, *Missing Peace*, 11–13; Clinton, *My Life*, 944.

67. In Denial

1. David Fleshler with C. Ron Allen, "Bush Assures Seniors He Has the Right Rx: Candidate in South Florida to Raise Funds Hits Hot-Button Issues of Concern to Elderly," *South Florida Sun-Sentinel*, September 12, 2000, http://articles.sun-sentinel.com/2009-09-12/news/0009120082_1_prescription-drugs-social-security-bush-plans.

2. Kevin Sack, "The 2000 Campaign: The Vice President; For Limited Government? That's Me, Gore Says," *New York Times*, October 25, 2000.

3. "Democrats: In His Own Words; Gore to Delegates and Nation: 'My Focus Will Be on Working Families,'" *New York Times*, August 18, 2000.

4. Harris, *The Survivor*, 426.

68. Parting Shots

1. Branch, *Clinton Tapes*, 630, 638.

2. "Nearing a Forest Legacy," *New York Times*, January 8, 2001.

3. Neil A. Lewis, "Transition in Washington: The President; Exiting Job, Clinton Accepts Immunity Deal," *New York Times*, January 20, 2001; "Transition in Washington; Correspondence and Agreed Order in the Settlement of Clinton's Case," *New York Times*, January 20, 2001.

4. Frank Bruni and David E. Sanger, "The Inauguration: The President; Bush, Taking Office, Calls for Civility, Compassion and 'Nation of Character,'" *New York Times*, January 21, 2001.

5. Eric N. Berg, "Marc Rich Indicted in Vast Tax Evasion Case," *New York Times*, September 20, 1983; Patrick McGeehan, "The New Administration: The Pardon; Prosecutors Not Consulted by Clinton on a Pardon," *New York Times*, January 23,

2001; Milt Freudenheim, "The Fugitive Commodities Trader Who Can Go Home Again," *New York Times*, January 22, 2001.

6. Alison Leigh Cowan and Raymond Bonner, "Lawyer Tells of His Pursuit of Pardon for His Client, and Conversation with Clinton," *New York Times*, January 25, 2001; McGeehan, "The New Administration"; Jack Quinn, "Bill Clinton and Marc Rich," Letter to the Editor, *New York Times*, January 25, 2001; Raymond Bonner and Alison Leigh Cowan, "Notes Show Justice Official Knew of Pardon Application," *New York Times*, February 2, 2001.

7. Alison Leigh Cowan, "Ex-Wife of Pardoned Financier Pledged Money to Clinton Library," *New York Times*, February 9, 2001 (correction appended February 10, 2001); Alison Leigh Cowan, "Plotting a Pardon; Rich Cashed In a World of Chits to Win Pardon," *New York Times*, April 11, 2001.

8. Alison Leigh Cowan, "Documents Show a Complex Campaign to Win a Pardon," *New York Times*, February 10, 2001; Cowan, "Plotting a Pardon"; Neil A. Lewis, "Clinton and Barak Discuss Rich Pardon in a Transcript," *New York Times*, August 21, 2001.

9. Joseph Kahn, "Clinton's Defense of Pardons Brings Even More Questions," *New York Times*, February 19, 2001.

10. Cowan, "Ex-Wife of Pardoned Financier"; Neil A. Lewis, "Pardon Investigators to Issue Subpoenas," *New York Times*, February 13, 2001; David Johnston and Marc Lacey, "Aides Say Clinton Ignored Pardon Advice," *New York Times*, March 2, 2001.

11. David Johnston and Don Van Natta Jr., "Prospect of Pardon Inquiry Sets Off Sparks, but Little Zeal," *New York Times*, February 14, 2001; David Johnston, "U.S. Is Beginning Criminal Inquiry in Pardon of Rich," *New York Times*, February 15, 2001.

12. William Jefferson Clinton, "My Reasons for the Pardons," *New York Times*, February 18, 2001.

13. Frank Bruni, "The New Administration: Settling In; New White House Staff Faces a Few Mysteries," *New York Times*, January 24, 2001; Marc Lacey, "January 21–27: A Transition Tradition," *New York Times*, January 28, 2001; Kerry Lauerman and Alicia Montgomery, "The White House Vandal Scandal That Wasn't," *Salon*, May 23, 2001, http://www.salon.com/news/politics/feature/2001/05/23/vandals. (*Salon* incorrectly reported the heading on the fake magazine cover.)

14. Christopher Marquis, "White House Vandalism Caper Was Overblown, a Report Finds," *New York Times*, May 19, 2001; Lauerman and Montgomery, "White House Vandal Scandal."

15. "Irresistible Lies: Fox News on White House 'Vandalism,'" FAIR: Fairness and Accuracy in Reporting, May 21, 2001, http://www.fair.org/index.php?page=1689.

16. Lauerman and Montgomery, "White House Vandal Scandal."

17. "Irresistible Lies."

18. Marquis, "White House Vandalism Caper."

69. Convening Power

1. "Fighting Childhood Obesity: Alliance for a Healthier Generation: Why Tackle Childhood Obesity?" The Clinton Foundation, http://www.clintonfoundation.org/what-we-do/alliance-for-a-healthier-generation/why-childhood-obesity-; "Fighting Childhood Obesity: Alliance for a Healthier Generation: President Clinton's Call to Action," The Clinton Foundation, http://www.clintonfoundation.org/what-we-do/alliance-for-a-healthier-generation/why-childhood-obesity-/we-must-act-now-by-bill-clinton.

2. Michael Crowley, "Bill Clinton, Messiah," *New Republic,* October 3, 2005; "About Us," Clinton Global Initiative, http://www.clintonglobalinitiative.org/aboutus/defa ult.asp?Section=AboutUs&PageTitle=About%20Us; "Browse/Search Commitments," Clinton Global Initiative, http://www.clintonglobalinitiative.org/commitme nts/commitments_search.asp?Section=Commitments&PageTitle=Browse%20and %20Search%20Commitments.

3. "CGI Annual Meeting 2009: Featured Attendees," Clinton Global Initiative, http://www.clintonglobalinitiative.org/ourmeetings/meeting_2009_annual_fea turedattendees.asp?Section=OurMeetings&PageTitle=Featured%20Attendees.

4. "Fighting Childhood Obesity . . . President Clinton's Call to Action."

70. Chasing a Buck

1. Greg Anrig Jr. and Elizabeth M. Macdonald, "How Hillary Manages the Clintons' Money," *Money,* July 1, 1992, http://money.cnn.com/magazines/moneymag/moneymag_archive/1992/07/01/87389/index.htm.

2. Richard A. Oppel Jr., "Mrs. Clinton Reports That Her Husband Made $9.2 Million from Speeches Last Year," *New York Times,* June 15, 2002; Don Van Natta Jr., "Clintons Ask for Millions from U.S. in Whitewater Legal Fees," *New York Times,* July 27, 2002.

3. Mike McIntire, "Clintons Made $109 Million in Last 8 Years," *New York Times,* April 5, 2008; Don Van Natta Jr. and Jo Becker, "Many Dealings of Bill Clinton Are Under Review," *New York Times,* November 17, 2008.

4. Jo Becker and Don Van Natta Jr., "After Mining Deal, Financier Donated to Clinton," *New York Times,* January 31, 2008.

5. Philip P. Pan, "Clinton Adviser Intervened to Help with Uranium Deal, Ex-Kazakh Official Says," *Washington Post,* February 24, 2010.

6. "National News Briefs: $3.9 Million in Legal Fees Still Owed by the Clintons," *New York Times,* March 15, 2001.

7. Oppel, "Mrs. Clinton Reports"; Van Natta, "Clintons Ask for Millions."

8. Peter Baker, "The Mellowing of William Jefferson Clinton," *New York Times Magazine,* May 26, 2009; John M. Broder and Patrick Healy, "How a Billionaire Friend of Bill Helps Him Do Good, and Well," *New York Times,* April 23, 2006.

71. Bill in a China Shop

1. Video at "Bill on Obama: Big Fairy Tale," abcnews.go.com, January 8, 2008, http://abcnews.go.com/video/playerIndex?id=4102345.

2. "The Situation Room: Bill Clinton on Obama: 'Fairy Tale'; Interview with Mike Huckabee," broadcast transcript, CNN, January 8, 2008, http://transcripts.cnn.com/TRANSCRIPTS/0801/08/sitroom.01.html.

3. Josh Marshall, "Try to Explain This: Bill Clinton on Barack Obama, Jan. 26th, 2008," video posted by Talking Points Memo, January 26, 2008, http://www.talkingpointsmemo.com/archives/163036.php.

4. Jake Tapper, "Bubba: Obama Is Just Like Jesse Jackson," Political Punch, blog at ABC News, January 26, 2008, http://blogs.abcnews.com/politicalpunch/2008/01/bubba-obama-is.html.

5. "Bill Clinton's Selfish Myopia," The Anonymous Liberal, January 26, 2008, http://www.anonymousliberal.com/2008/01/bill-clintons-selfish-myopia.html.

6. Mark Murray, "Bill: 'My Message' 99.9% Positive," First Read, MSNBC, January 26, 2008, http://firstread.msnbc.msn.com/archive/2008/01/26/611927.aspx.

7. "Obama: Reagan Changed Direction of Country; Bill Clinton Didn't, January 14, 2008," video posted by Talking Points Memo, http://www.youtube.com/watch?v=HFLuOBsNMZA.

8. "Exclusive: Obama Rips Bill Clinton Slams as 'Troubling' and Inaccurate," Political Radar blog, ABC News, January 20, 2008, http://blogs.abcnews.com/politicalradar/2008/01/exclusive-obama/comments/page/2/.

9. "Bill Clinton: Obama 'Played the Race Card on Me' . . . Listen to Audio," Huffington Post, April 22, 2008, http://www.huffingtonpost.com/2008/04/22/bill-clinton-obama-played_n_97927.html.

10. "Bill: 'I'm Not Going to Play Your Games,'" First Read, MSNBC, April 22, 2008, http://firstread.msnbc.msn.com/archive/2008/04/22/931095.aspx.

72. Unintended Consequences

1. Stephen Labaton, "A New Financial Era: The Overview; Accord Reached on Lifting of Depression-era Barriers Among Financial Industries," New York Times, October 23, 1999; Joseph Kahn, "A New Financial Era: The Impact; Financial Services Industry Faces a New World," New York Times, October 23, 1999; "The Financial Services Modernization Act of 1999: A Brief Summary of Gramm-Leach-Bliley," Federal Reserve Bank of Minneapolis, March 2000, http://www.minneapolisfed.org/publications_papers/pub_display.cfm?id=3534.

2. Peter Baker, "The Mellowing of William Jefferson Clinton," New York Times Magazine, May 26, 2009.

3. Maria Bartiromo, "Bill Clinton on the Banking Crisis, McCain, and Hillary," BusinessWeek, September 24, 2008.

73. Envoy

1. Laura Ling and Euna Lee, "Hostages of the Hermit Kingdom," *Los Angeles Times*, September 1, 2009; Choe Sang-hun, "2 U.S. Journalists on Trial in N. Korea," *New York Times*, June 4, 2009; Choe Sang-hun, "N. Korea Sentences 2 U.S. Journalists to 12 Years of Hard Labor," *New York Times*, June 8, 2009.

2. Choe Sang-hun, "North Korea Claims to Conduct 2nd Nuclear Test," *New York Times*, May 24, 2009; Choe Sang-hun, "North Korea Is Said to Test-Fire 3 More Missiles," *New York Times*, May 26, 2009.

3. Mark Landler and Peter Baker, "In Release of Journalists, Both Clintons Had Key Roles," *New York Times*, August 4, 2009.

4. Alice Gomstyn, "Steve Bing to Pay $200K for Clinton Korea Trip," ABC News, August. 5, 2009, http://abcnews.go.com/Business/story?id=8260264&page=1; Landler and Baker, "In Release of Journalists."

5. Mark Landler and Peter Baker, "Bill Clinton and Journalists in Emotional Return to U.S.," *New York Times*, August 5, 2009.

74. And Now?

1. Peter Baker and Charlie Savage, "In Clinton List, a Veil Is Lifted on Foundation," *New York Times*, December 18, 2008; Baker, "Mellowing."

2. Peter Baker, "Bill Clinton to Name Donors as Part of Obama Deal," *New York Times*, November 29, 2008.

Acknowledgments

Thanks first to my longtime agent and friend, Craig Kayser, for his industry and imagination in getting this project started and for his unflagging support over the years it took to bring it to print. I am glad that he has teamed with the resourceful Jason Allen Ashlock to form a new literary agency, Moveable Type Literary Group.

I owe a great debt to everyone at Yale University Press, beginning with my editor, Christopher Rogers. Writers complain that editors no longer edit; Chris is the exception, spending entire days staring with me at my computer screen. I credit him with the vision to see from the beginning what this book could be and the skill to guide that vision to fulfillment. Chris's superb assistant, Laura Davulis, never failed to provide timely answers to my questions. The book's manuscript editor, the incomparable Dan Heaton, made sure everything fit together and looked right.

I am also grateful for the generous support of the Newman's Own Foundation and for the gracious assistance of David Stricklin and Jujuan Johnson of the Butler Center for Arkansas Studies in Little Rock. The American Presidency Project at the University of California, Santa Barbara, was a vital resource—my thanks go to John Woolley and Gerhard Peters, who created it. I also appreciate the time taken by Geoffrey Stark of the Pryor Center for Arkansas Oral and Visual History in Fayetteville, Rosie Dixon of the *Arkansas Democrat-Gazette*, Irena Briganti of Fox News, and, especially, everyone I interviewed on the subject of our forty-second president.

Five researchers proved invaluable to this enterprise. Aileen Torres and Barbara Weber-Floyd, both supremely competent, did yeoman duty to contact some six hundred people I thought to interview, to secure the consent of nearly a third of them—some after a dozen or more phone calls—and to schedule the conversations. John Hamill and Erin Markman did conscientious, intelligent work in assembling background material for each interview. Niklaus Wasmoen provided a meticulous, dogged check of the facts once the book was written.

Thanks also to Natalie Giboney, of FreelancePermissions.com, for her expertise and effort in securing the numerous permissions needed before this book could be published.

These people have only improved the book. All shortcomings are my doing.

On a day when I was far from home, Myra Reese fed me a home-cooked country lunch; her husband, Hugh, took the time to show me his hometown, Hope, Arkansas. My sister, Deborah Takiff Smith, as fine a person as I have ever known, provided shelter and sustenance on my countless trips to Washington, D.C.

In the acknowledgments to my last book I noted that my four-year-old son had spent far too many Sunday afternoons without his father. He's eleven now, and still does. I have tried to make up for that absence during the rest of the week. I will keep trying.

And I am grateful above all for Amy. Devoted, smart, decent, beautiful. It was a lucky day when I first met her; it's a lucky day every day I am married to her.

Photo Credits

Clinton Family Historical Series: figures 1–4, 6, 7.

University of Arkansas Fayetteville Library: figure 5.

William J. Clinton Presidential Library: figures 8–25.

Index

Note: Page numbers in boldface refer to an individual's spoken text.